AF574862

POOLS

Mommsenstraße 43, D-10629 Berlin

Idea and Concept: Peter Feierabend
Photography: © Pere Planells
Translations: *Books Factory Translations*
Wendy Griswold, Matthey Clarke, Harry Paul (English)
Sven Mettner (German)
Christelle Roche (French)
Graphic design and layout: David Maynar, Mar Nieto
Prining and binding: Cayfosa-Quebecor. Spain

Printed in Spain

DL: B-37.170-2003
ISBN:3-89985-320-2
40-02035-1

POOLS

Feierabend

Contents

Introduction

Few constructions illustrate better the culture of leisure than the swimming pool. Although on some occasions it can play a religious, landscapist or sporting role, the image of a swimming pool is almost always associated with lazy hours enjoyed in a bathing suit in the warm sun.

Adding a swimming pool to a private house certainly increases the quality of life, not only because of its intrinsic advantages, but also because it suggests a benign climate and an idyllic life in the open air.

A swimming pool is obviously a privilege that depends on geography. With the exceptions of a few brave enthusiasts who have built a pool in Germany, Illinois or Scotland, in general a swimming pool is associated with Mediterranean countries, with California or Australia, that is, regions that enjoy a mild climate, typically with a variety of holiday resorts nearby. Swimming pools located next to the sea are common, and this book illustrates several examples. In some, the surfaces of the two waters are even visually superimposed.

In the following pages we have set out to show the extraordinary richness and diversity of an architectural element that has deep historical roots. In every case the construction of the pool was decided with a clear goal in mind based on a singular composition that recreates the designer's own particular aesthetic universe, that is a transformation of the setting or that is the skillful coalescence of the manmade landscape with the natural.

The book has been divided into four chapters, with each covering a particular theme: Nature, The Historical Inheritance, Water In Architecture and Pure Geometry. These chapters do not try to back up any thesis or doctrine, nor do they aim to favor any particular style compared to another. They simply group together different types of pools according to their design approach.

Introducción

Existen pocas construcciones que ilustren mejor la cultura del ocio. Aunque en algunas ocasiones su función pueda tener un carácter religioso, paisajístico o deportivo, resulta difícil desvincular la imagen de una piscina de las horas indolentes transcurridas al calor de un sol generoso.

Ciertamente, la incorporación de la piscina a la vivienda privada supone un aumento incuestionable de la calidad de vida no sólo por sus ventajas intrínsecas sino también porque implica la existencia de un jardín, un clima benigno y la posibilidad desarrollar vida al aire libre.

Aunque existen aficionados que son capaces de construirse una piscina en Alemania, Illinois o Escocia, se trata de un elemento más propio del Mediterráneo, California, Florida, el Pacífico, Australia o Centroamérica: zonas de clima templado o cálido y destinos vacacionales típicos. Resulta habitual, y en este libro hay varios ejemplos, ver piscinas situadas junto al mar e, incluso, con una conexión visual directa entre sendas superficies de agua.

En la páginas siguientes, hemos querido mostrar la extraordinaria riqueza y diversidad de un elemento con profundas raíces históricas.

En todos los casos, la construcción de la piscina está determinada por una estrategia singular que nace de una especial apuesta compositiva, de la recreación de un universo estético particular, de la sorprendente transformación del entorno inmediato o bien de la cuidadosa integración entre el paisaje privado y el paisaje natural. Hemos propuesto una clasificación temática resumida en cuatro capítulos:

En la naturaleza, La herencia de la Historia, El agua en la arquitectura y Pura Geometría. Estos temas no resumen ninguna tesis ni ninguna doctrina, tampoco pretenden criticar una tipología y elogiar otra, sino simplemente agrupar los distintos ejemplos de acuerdo a una afinidad de actitudes.

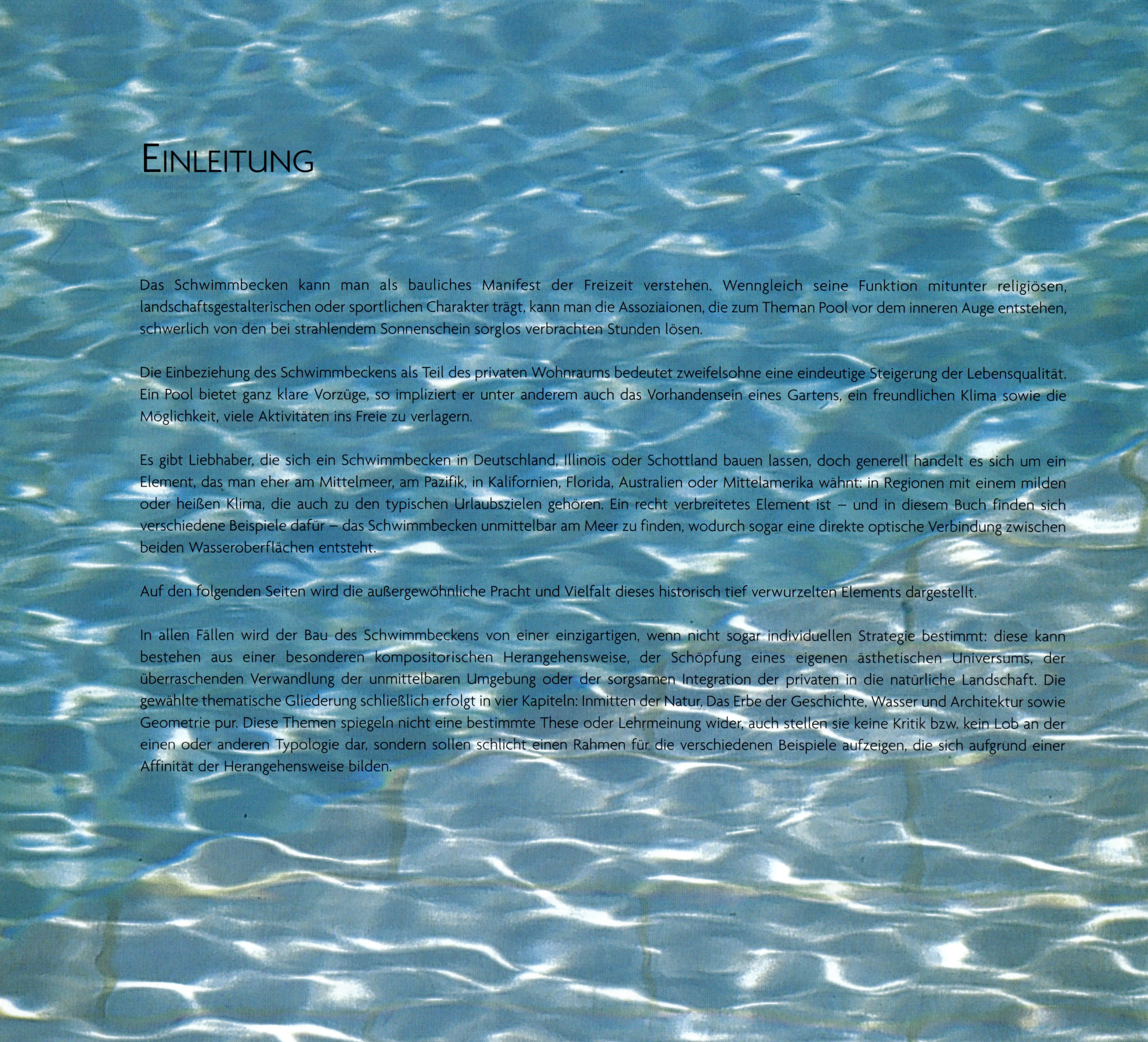

Einleitung

Das Schwimmbecken kann man als bauliches Manifest der Freizeit verstehen. Wenngleich seine Funktion mitunter religiösen, landschaftsgestalterischen oder sportlichen Charakter trägt, kann man die Assoziaionen, die zum Theman Pool vor dem inneren Auge entstehen, schwerlich von den bei strahlendem Sonnenschein sorglos verbrachten Stunden lösen.

Die Einbeziehung des Schwimmbeckens als Teil des privaten Wohnraums bedeutet zweifelsohne eine eindeutige Steigerung der Lebensqualität. Ein Pool bietet ganz klare Vorzüge, so impliziert er unter anderem auch das Vorhandensein eines Gartens, ein freundlichen Klima sowie die Möglichkeit, viele Aktivitäten ins Freie zu verlagern.

Es gibt Liebhaber, die sich ein Schwimmbecken in Deutschland, Illinois oder Schottland bauen lassen, doch generell handelt es sich um ein Element, das man eher am Mittelmeer, am Pazifik, in Kalifornien, Florida, Australien oder Mittelamerika wähnt: in Regionen mit einem milden oder heißen Klima, die auch zu den typischen Urlaubszielen gehören. Ein recht verbreitetes Element ist – und in diesem Buch finden sich verschiedene Beispiele dafür – das Schwimmbecken unmittelbar am Meer zu finden, wodurch sogar eine direkte optische Verbindung zwischen beiden Wasseroberflächen entsteht.

Auf den folgenden Seiten wird die außergewöhnliche Pracht und Vielfalt dieses historisch tief verwurzelten Elements dargestellt.

In allen Fällen wird der Bau des Schwimmbeckens von einer einzigartigen, wenn nicht sogar individuellen Strategie bestimmt: diese kann bestehen aus einer besonderen kompositorischen Herangehensweise, der Schöpfung eines eigenen ästhetischen Universums, der überraschenden Verwandlung der unmittelbaren Umgebung oder der sorgsamen Integration der privaten in die natürliche Landschaft. Die gewählte thematische Gliederung schließlich erfolgt in vier Kapiteln: Inmitten der Natur, Das Erbe der Geschichte, Wasser und Architektur sowie Geometrie pur. Diese Themen spiegeln nicht eine bestimmte These oder Lehrmeinung wider, auch stellen sie keine Kritik bzw. kein Lob an der einen oder anderen Typologie dar, sondern sollen schlicht einen Rahmen für die verschiedenen Beispiele aufzeigen, die sich aufgrund einer Affinität der Herangehensweise bilden.

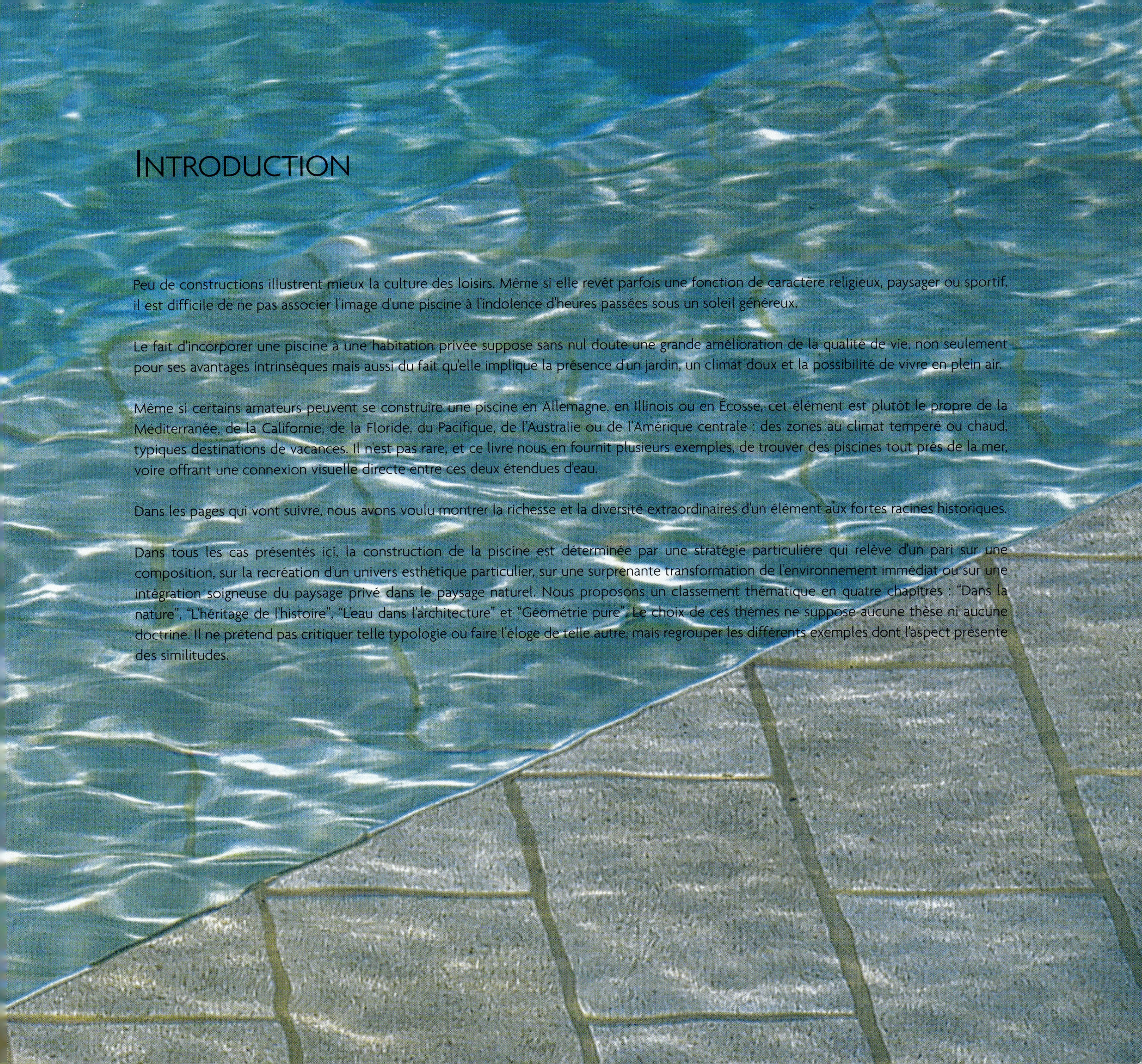

Introduction

Peu de constructions illustrent mieux la culture des loisirs. Même si elle revêt parfois une fonction de caractère religieux, paysager ou sportif, il est difficile de ne pas associer l'image d'une piscine à l'indolence d'heures passées sous un soleil généreux.

Le fait d'incorporer une piscine à une habitation privée suppose sans nul doute une grande amélioration de la qualité de vie, non seulement pour ses avantages intrinsèques mais aussi du fait qu'elle implique la présence d'un jardin, un climat doux et la possibilité de vivre en plein air.

Même si certains amateurs peuvent se construire une piscine en Allemagne, en Illinois ou en Écosse, cet élément est plutôt le propre de la Méditerranée, de la Californie, de la Floride, du Pacifique, de l'Australie ou de l'Amérique centrale : des zones au climat tempéré ou chaud, typiques destinations de vacances. Il n'est pas rare, et ce livre nous en fournit plusieurs exemples, de trouver des piscines tout près de la mer, voire offrant une connexion visuelle directe entre ces deux étendues d'eau.

Dans les pages qui vont suivre, nous avons voulu montrer la richesse et la diversité extraordinaires d'un élément aux fortes racines historiques.

Dans tous les cas présentés ici, la construction de la piscine est déterminée par une stratégie particulière qui relève d'un pari sur une composition, sur la recréation d'un univers esthétique particulier, sur une surprenante transformation de l'environnement immédiat ou sur une intégration soigneuse du paysage privé dans le paysage naturel. Nous proposons un classement thématique en quatre chapitres : “Dans la nature”, “L'héritage de l'histoire”, “L'eau dans l'architecture” et “Géométrie pure”. Le choix de ces thèmes ne suppose aucune thèse ni aucune doctrine. Il ne prétend pas critiquer telle typologie ou faire l'éloge de telle autre, mais regrouper les différents exemples dont l'aspect présente des similitudes.

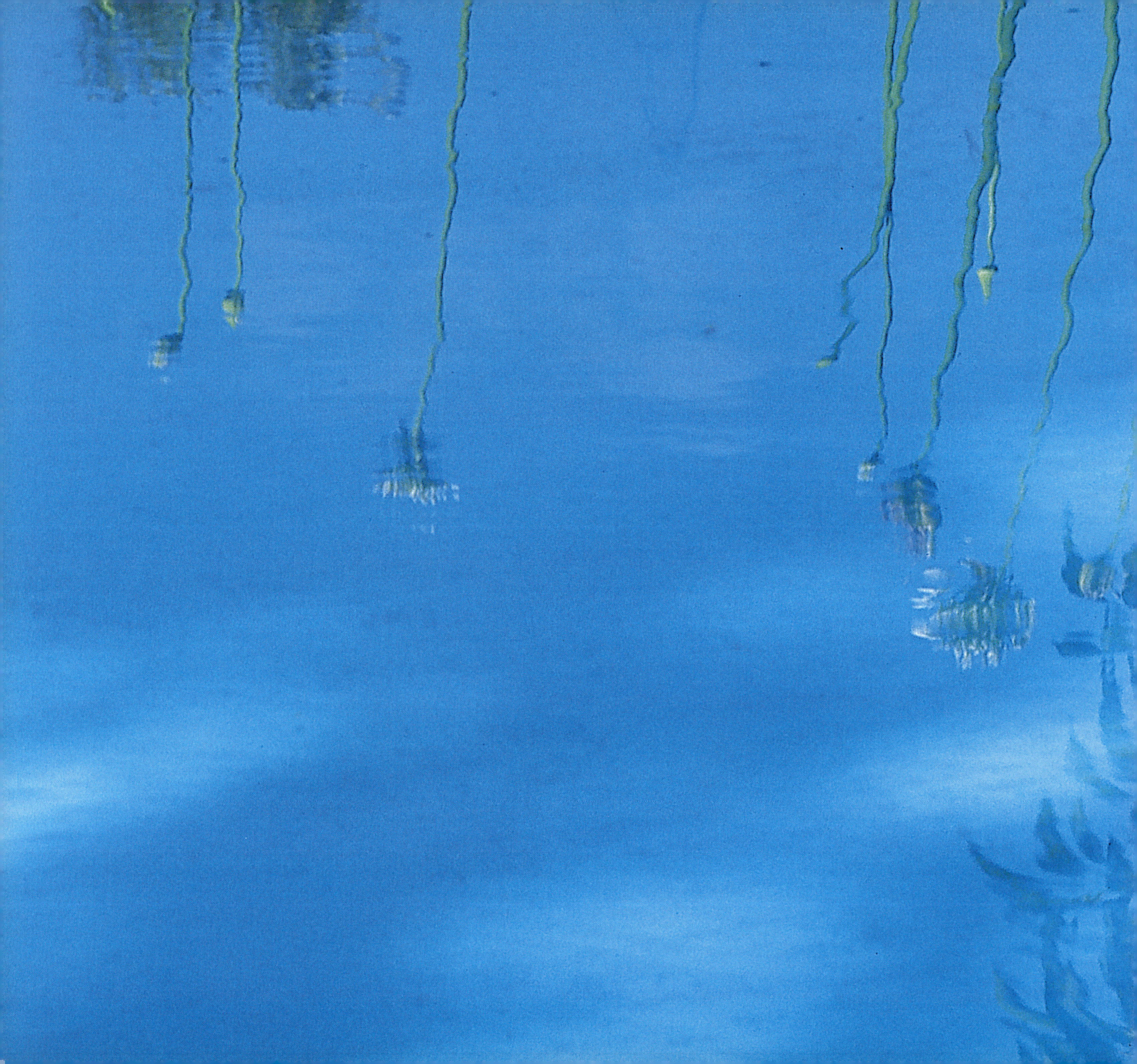

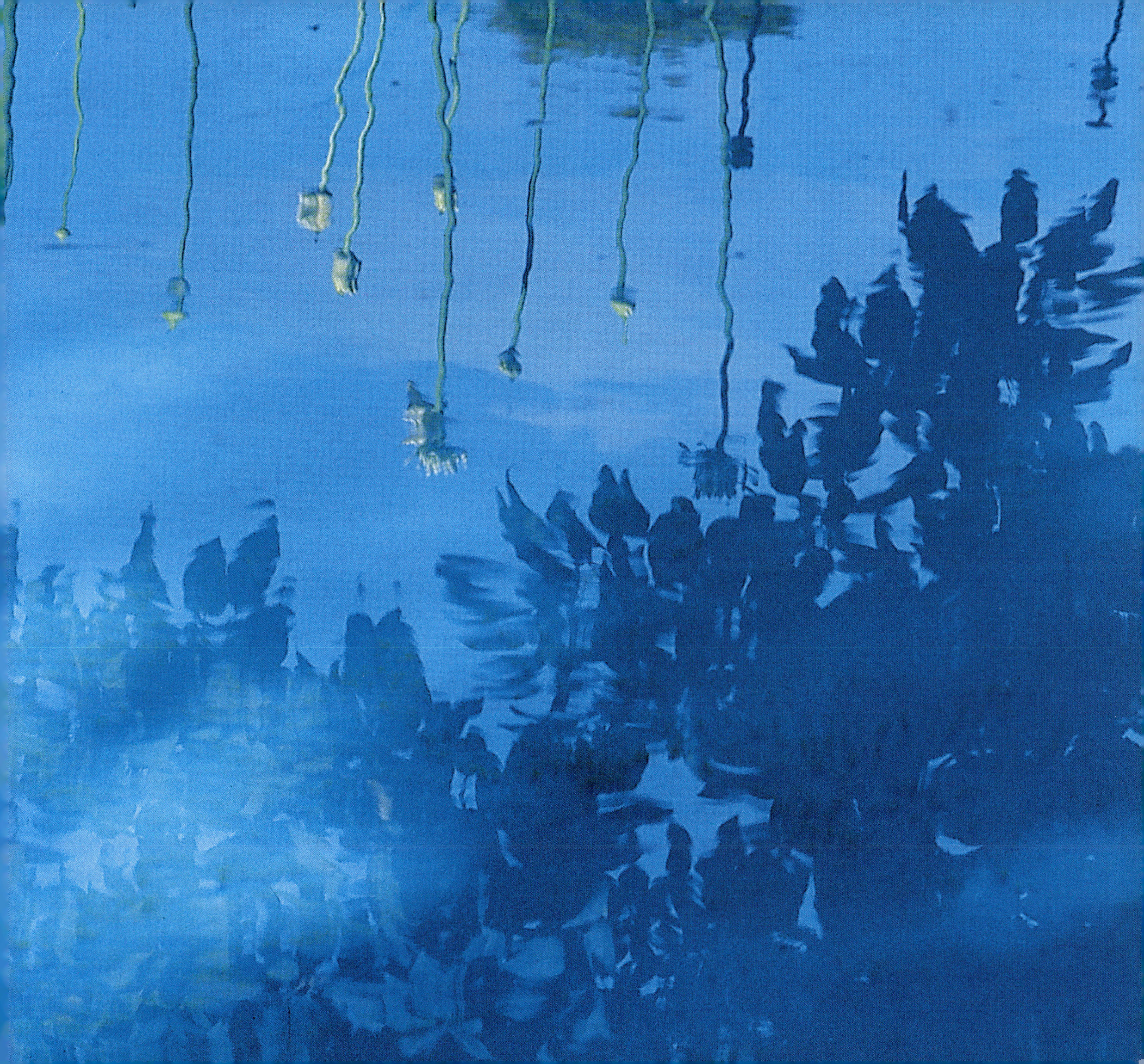

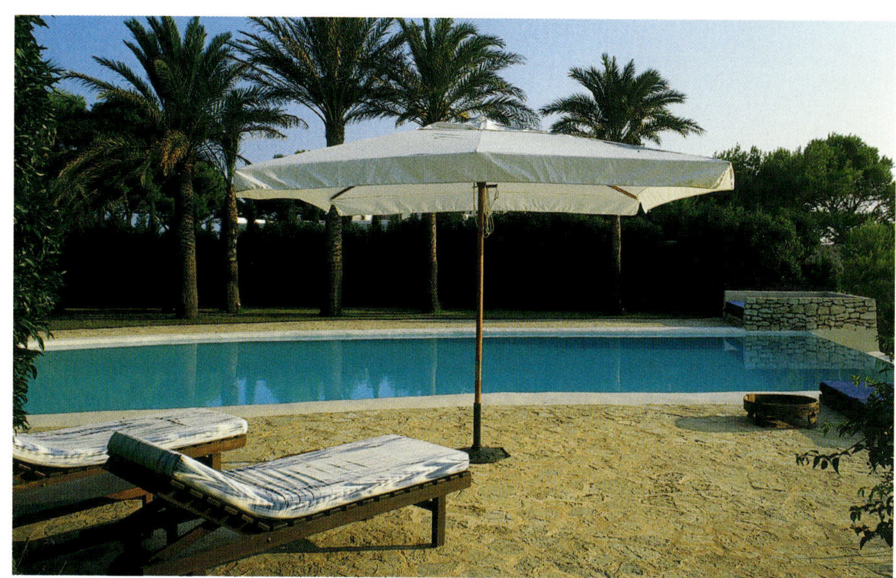

In the bay

En la bahía | In der Bucht | Dans la baie

Rolph Blakstad allowed the idyllic location to inspire his design of this pool, which is sited on a small meseta that ends abruptly on the edge of cliffs that drop down into the sea. Its irregular shape has a small area of sand and a cascade, which provides a charming visual link to the sea. A simple rectangular marquee-like construction made with wooden beams sits at the edge of the cliff. It consists of four sets of Doric columns placed at right angles to each other.

Según Rolph Blakstad, su diseñador, la forma de esta piscina se inspira en su emplazamiento. La piscina se encuentra situada en una pequeña meseta que se corta súbitamente por un acantilado que desciende hacia el mar. Presenta un perímetro irregular que incluye una playa y una cascada, que se ha construido aprovechando el precipicio. El agua de la cascada une visualmente la piscina y el mar. En el borde del precipicio se ha construido un pabellón de estilo clásico. Se trata de una sencilla marquesina rectangular construida con vigas de madera que está soportada por cuatro conjuntos de columnas dóricas dispuestas en ángulo recto.

Laut Rolph Blakstad, der dieses Schwimmbecken entwarf, diente dessen Standort als Inspiration für seine Form. Das Schwimmbecken liegt auf einem kleinen Plateau, das jäh an eine Küste stößt, die wiederum steil zum Meer hin abfällt.
Die unregelmäßigen Konturen binden einen Strand und einen Wasserfall ein, der unter Ausnutzung des Abhangs angelegt wurde. Das herabfallende Wasser stellt die optische Verbindung zwischen Schwimmbecken und Meer her.
Am Rande des Abhangs wurde ein Pavillon im klassischen Stil errichtet. Ein schlichtes rechteckiges Sonnendach aus Holzbalken wird von vier Gruppen rechtwinklig aufgestellter dorischer Säulen getragen.

Selon Rolph Blakstad, son concepteur, la forme de cette piscine s'inspire de son emplacement. La piscine se situe sur un petit plateau subitement rompu par une falaise qui se jette dans la mer.
Elle présente un périmètre irrégulier qui inclut une plage ainsi qu'une cascade construite en utilisant le précipice. L'eau de la cascade unit visuellement la piscine et la mer.
Au bord du précipice a été construit un pavillon de style classique : une marquise rectangulaire toute simple, construite avec des poutres en bois et soutenue par quatre ensembles de colonnes doriques disposées en angle droit.

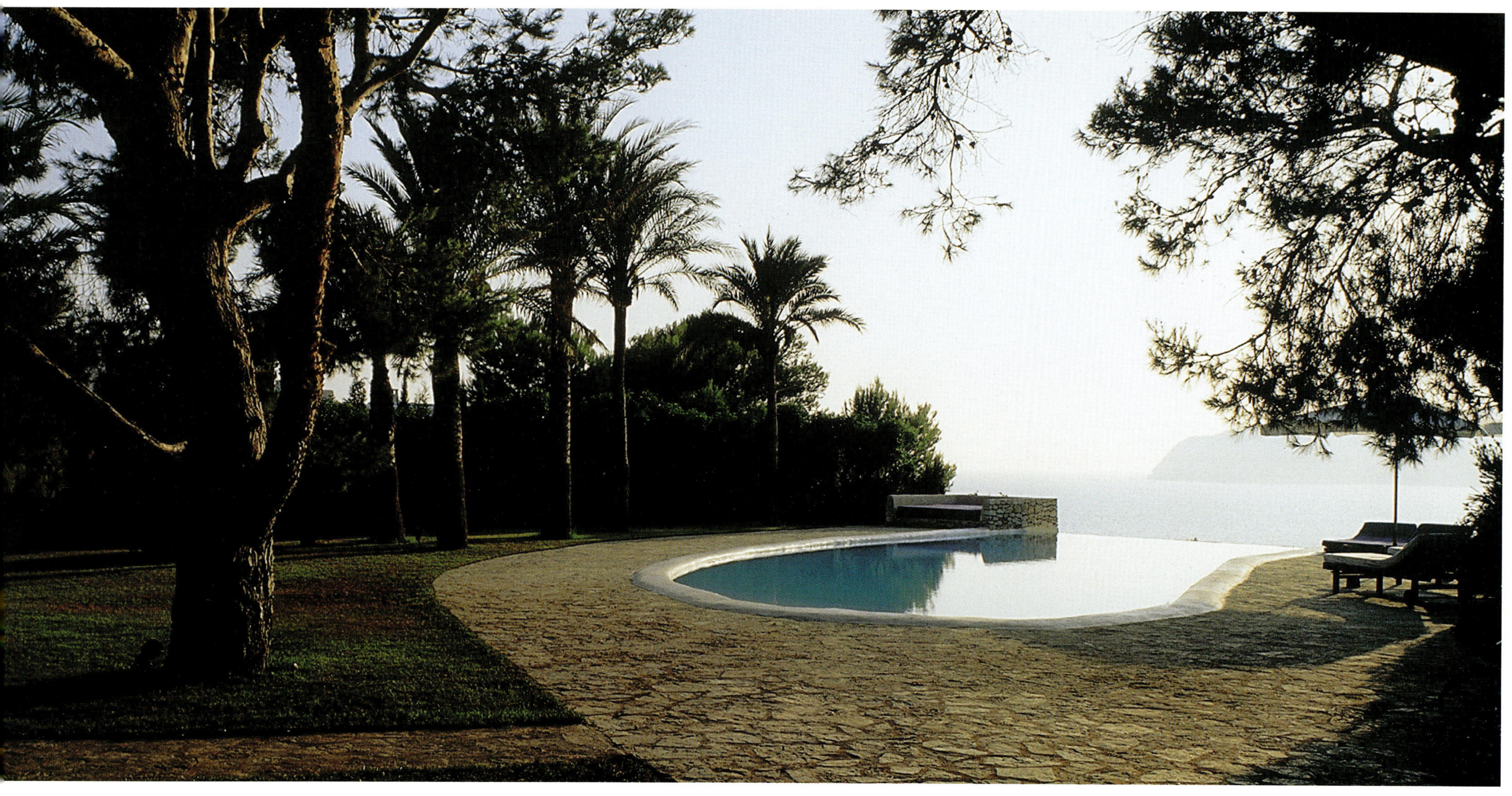

One of the main attractions of this pool is its orientation and its integration with the landscape. Its perimeter forms a type of bay that culminates in a cascade connecting the pool visually with the sea.

Una de las principales cualidades de esta piscina es su orientación y su integración en el paisaje. El perímetro forma una bahía que acaba en una cascada donde la piscina conecta visualmente con el mar.

Zu den Vorzügen dieses Schwimmbeckens zählen seine Ausrichtung und die Integration in die Landschaft. Der buchtförmiger Umriss mündet in einen Wasserfall, über den das Schwimmbecken optisch mit dem Meer verbunden wird.

Les principaux atouts de cette piscine sont son orientation et son intégration dans le paysage. Son périmètre forme une baie se terminant en une cascade, où la piscine offre une connexion visuelle avec la mer.

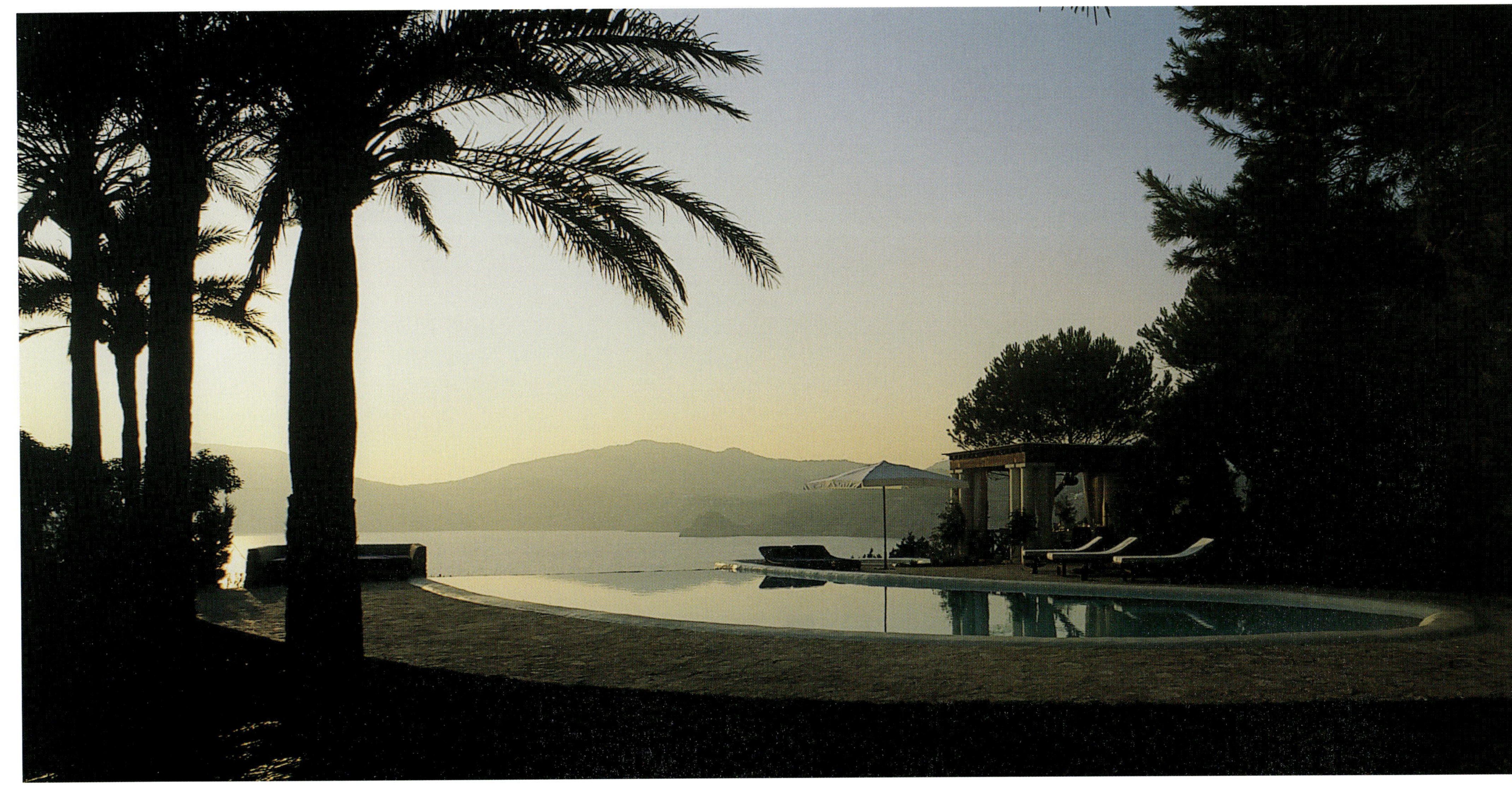

The pool is surrounded by a ring of flagstones, which gives way to a large expanse of grass. The cascade is framed by two asymmetrical constructions; a long bench and a wooden gazebo.

Un anillo formado por un pavimento de piedra natural rodea la piscina, más allá se extiende una superficie de césped. La cascada queda enmarcada por dos construcciones asimétricas: un banco y una glorieta.

Ein Belag aus Naturstein bildet einen Ring um das Becken und grenzt dieses von der Rasenfläche ab. Der Wasserfall wird von zwei asymmetrischen Strukturen eingerahmt: einer Bank und einem Pavillon.

Un anneau formé par un pavement de pierre naturelle entoure la piscine, qui ouvre sur une étendue de pelouse. La cascade est encadrée par deux constructions asymétriques : un banc et une gloriette.

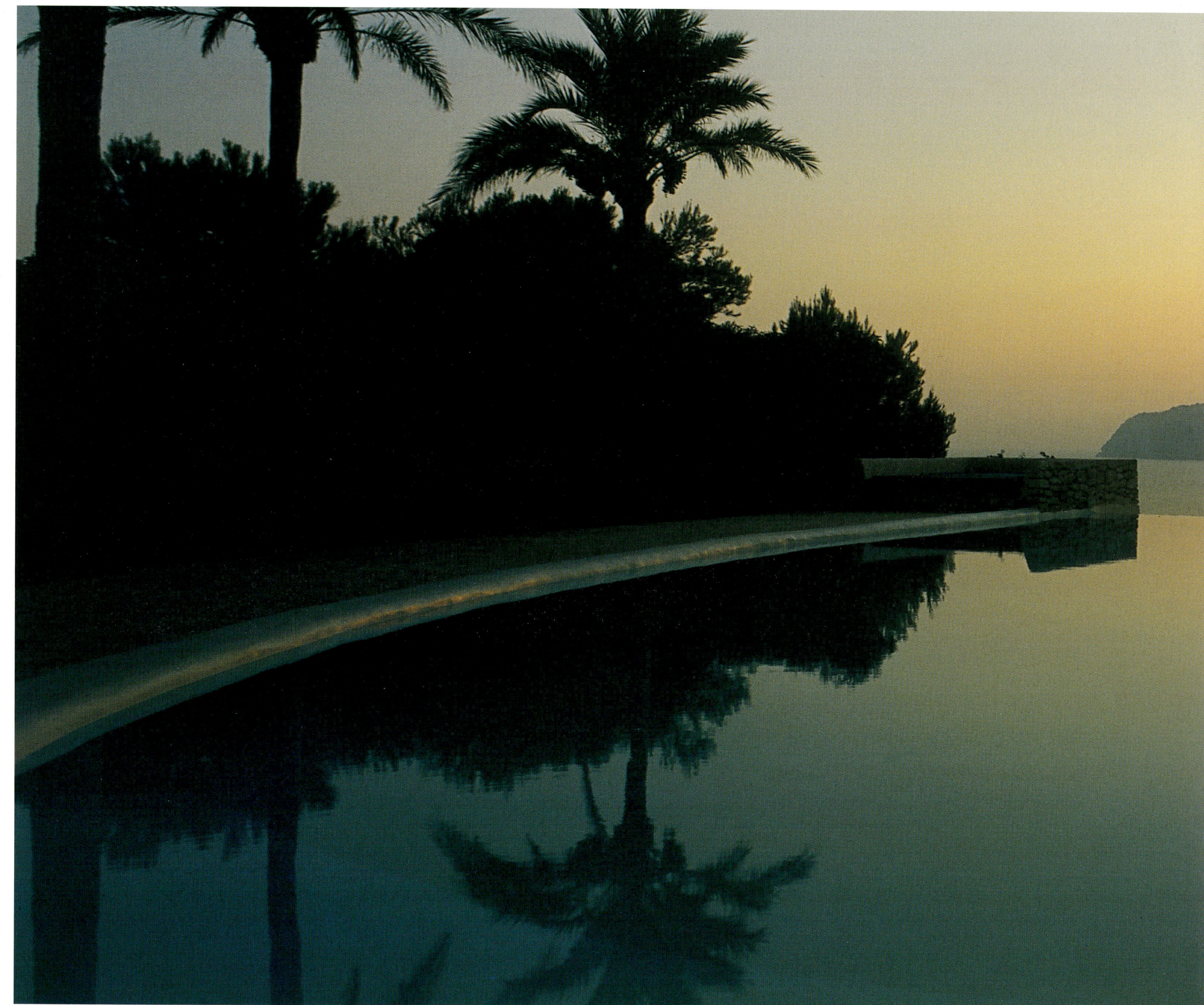

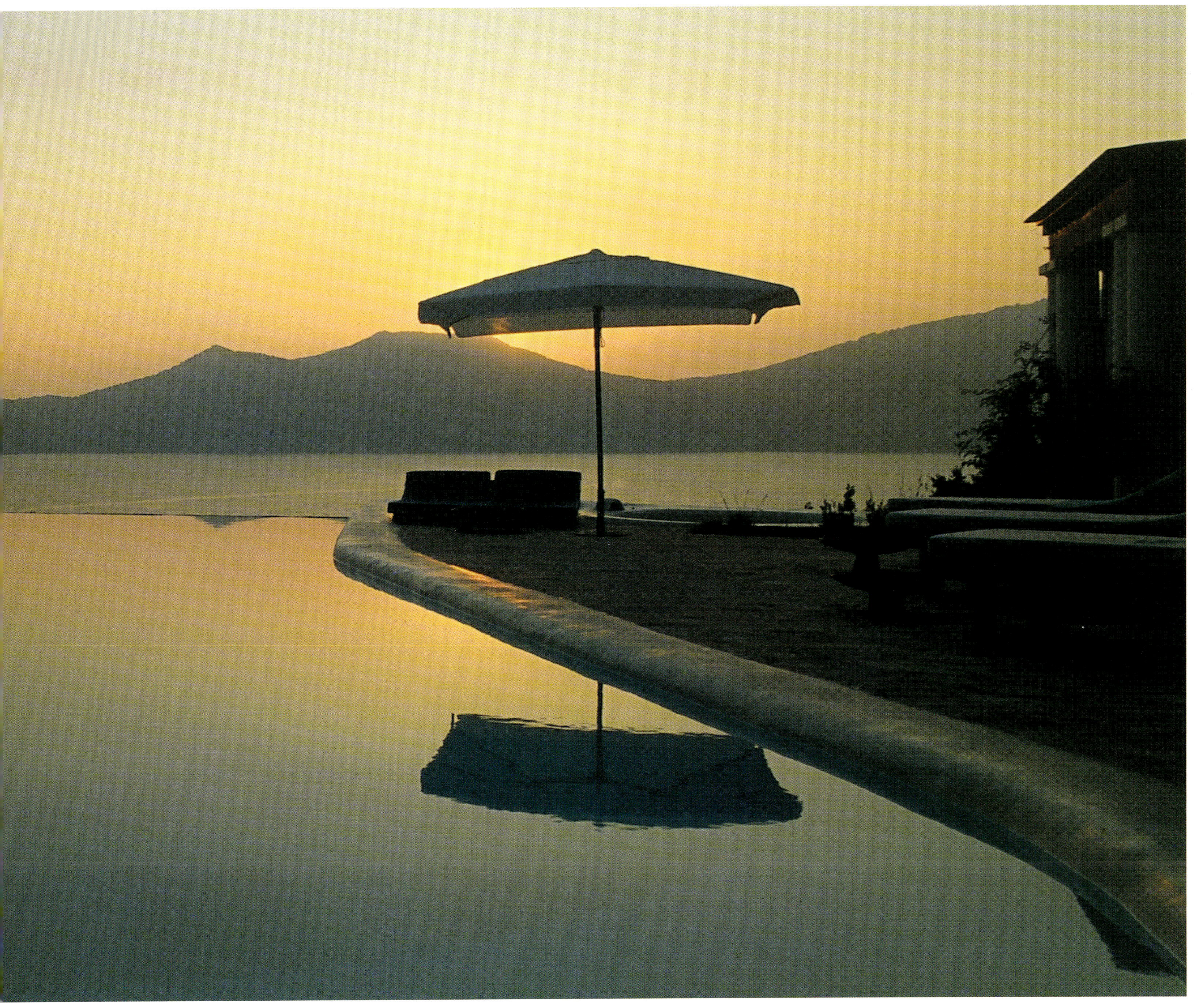

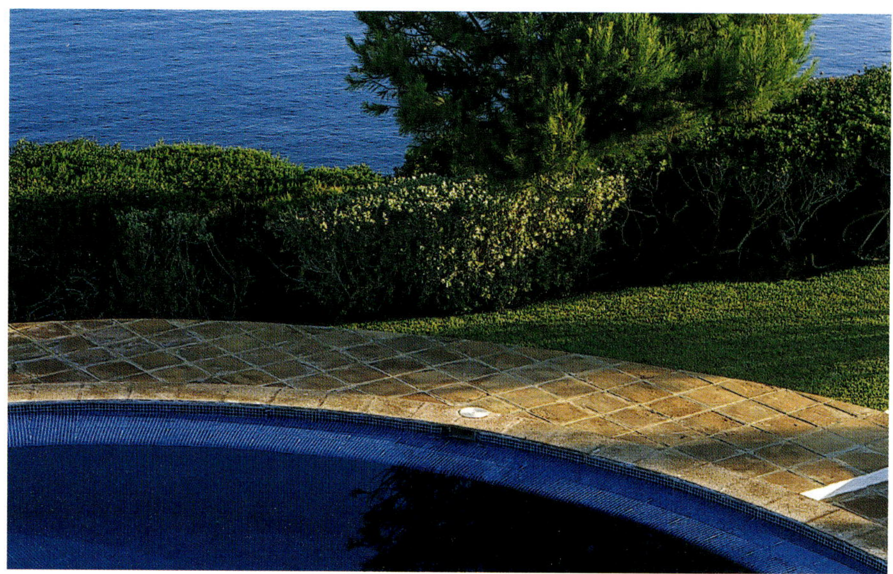

No Limits

Sin límite | Grenzenlos | Sans limites

Inhabitants of warm climes spend a great deal of time outdoors. Not surprisingly, hot climates strongly influence architecture and design. Coastal areas make use of roofs with eaves and cantilevered balconies that form terraces and porches, which create shade. Often, the swimming pool is the hub of activities and social relations, so its ideal placement must be carefully studied. Here, the spectacular views of the sea are given priority. Its curved shape fits the contour of the terrain. It is placed in a treeless area delimited by a low wall of shrubs and is outlined by porous, anti-slip, rustic quarry stones.

Los habitantes de climas cálidos pasan una gran parte de su tiempo al aire libre. La arquitectura de estas zonas costeras presenta una serie de elementos comunes que responden a las características del clima. Los aleros en las cubiertas o los voladizos de forjados que forman terrazas y porches son elementos que crean sombra. En este ambiente, la piscina sería el lugar aglutinador de las actividades y relaciones humanas. Por ello el emplazamiento debe ser cuidadosamente estudiado según las preferencias del usuario. En este caso la piscina se sitúa dando prioridad a las vistas sobre el mar en una zona despejada de árboles y únicamente delimitada por un muro vegetal bajo. Para adaptarse al perfil del terreno se escoge una forma curva remarcada por un bordillo revestido de toba cerámica rústica bastante porosa y antideslizante.

Menschen in warmen Klimazonen verbringen einen Großteil ihrer Zeit im Freien. Die Architektur solcher Küstengebiete weist eine Reihe gemeinsamer Merkmale auf, die eine Antwort auf die klimatischen Verhältnisse darstellen. Dachvorsprünge oder Auskragungen des Fachwerks von Terrassen und Vorbauten sind Schatten spendende Elemente. In einem derartigen Ambiente wird das Schwimmbecken Mittelpunkt der menschlichen Aktivitäten und Beziehungen. Sein Standort will daher gemäß den Wünschen der Benutzer wohl überlegt sein. Im vorliegenden Fall wird durch die Lage des Schwimmbeckens die Sicht auf das Meer in einem baumlosen Gebiet priorisiert, der Blick lediglich durch eine niedrige Pflanzenwand begrenzt. Zur Anpassung an das Geländeprofil wurde für das Becken eine gewölbte Form gewählt, unterstrichen durch einen Rand, der mit porösem und rutschsicherem rustikalen Tuffgestein verkleidet ist.

Les habitants des zones à climat chaud passent une grande partie de leur temps à l'air libre. L'architecture de ces zones côtières présente une série d'éléments communs qui répondent aux caractéristiques du climat. Les auvents des toits ou les saillies des forgeages qui composent les terrasses et les porches deviennent autant de possibilités de créer de l'ombre. Dans cette atmosphère, la piscine devient lieu de rassemblement pour les activités et les relations humaines. Son emplacement doit donc être choisi avec soin en fonction des préférences de l'usager. Ici, pour situer la piscine, priorité a été donnée aux vues sur la mer dans une zone sans arbres et uniquement délimitée par un mur végétal peu élevé. Pour s'adapter au profil du terrain, une forme courbe a été choisie, rehaussée par une bordure recouverte de tuffeau de céramique poreux et antidérapant, d'allure rustique.

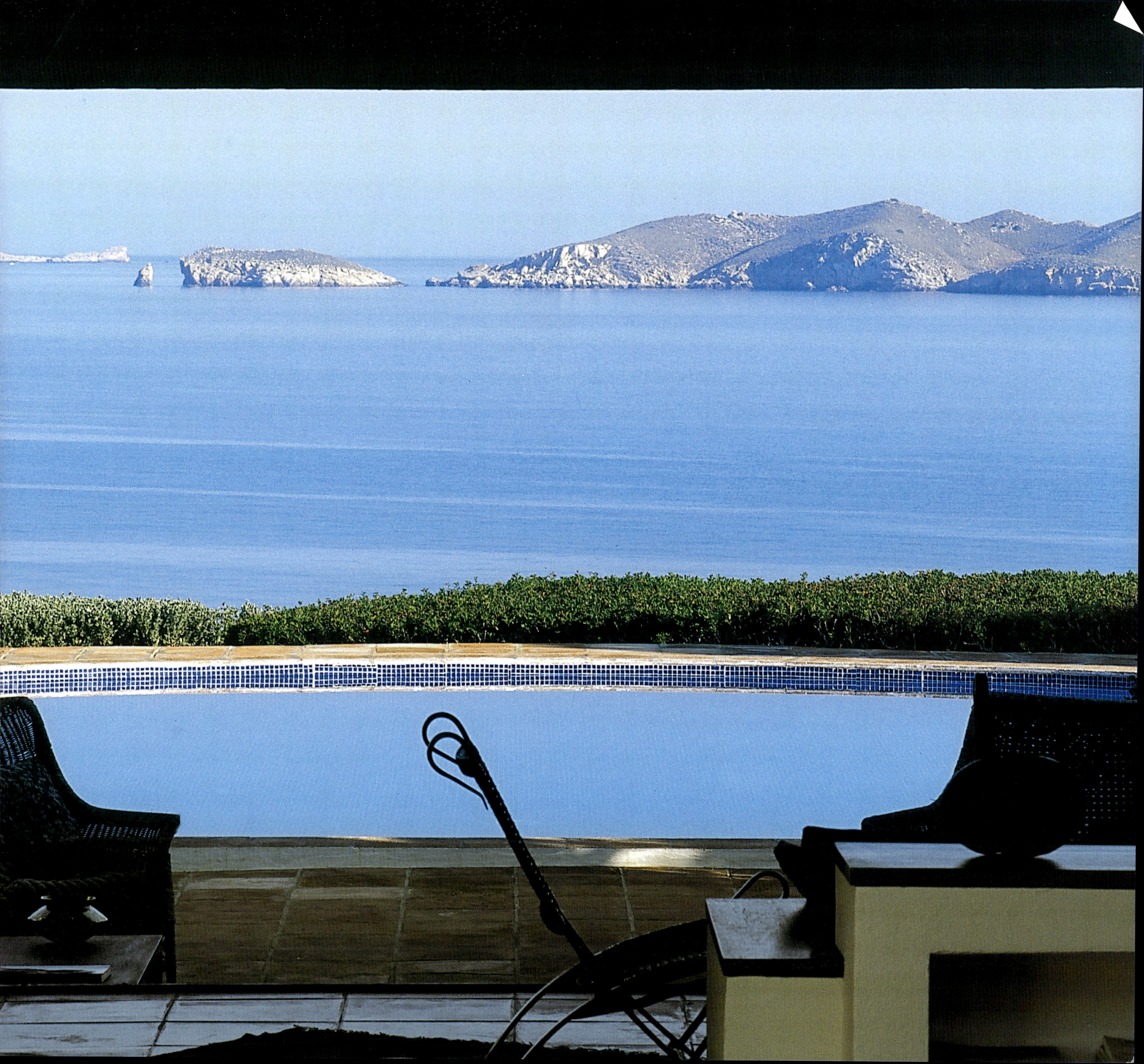

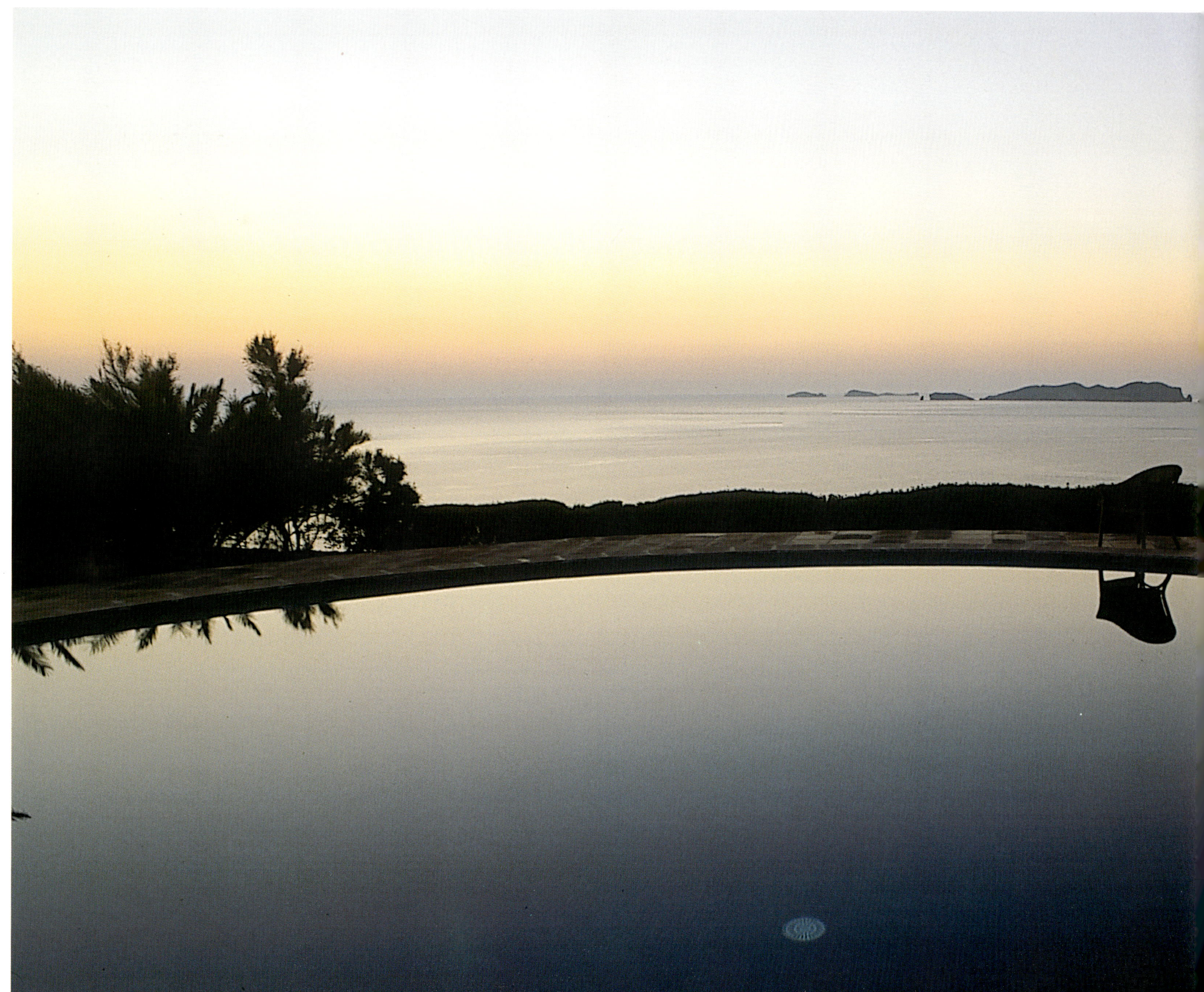

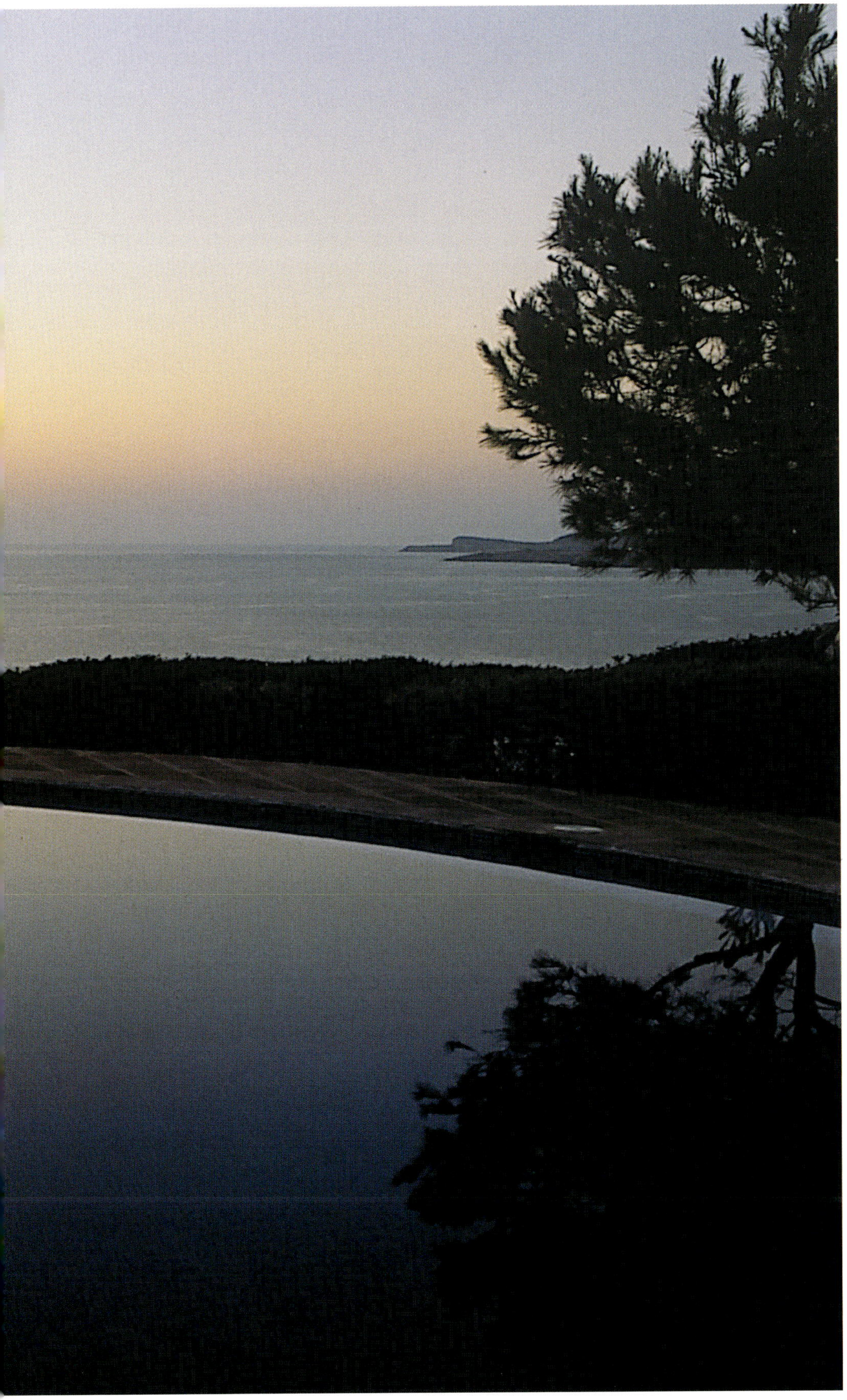

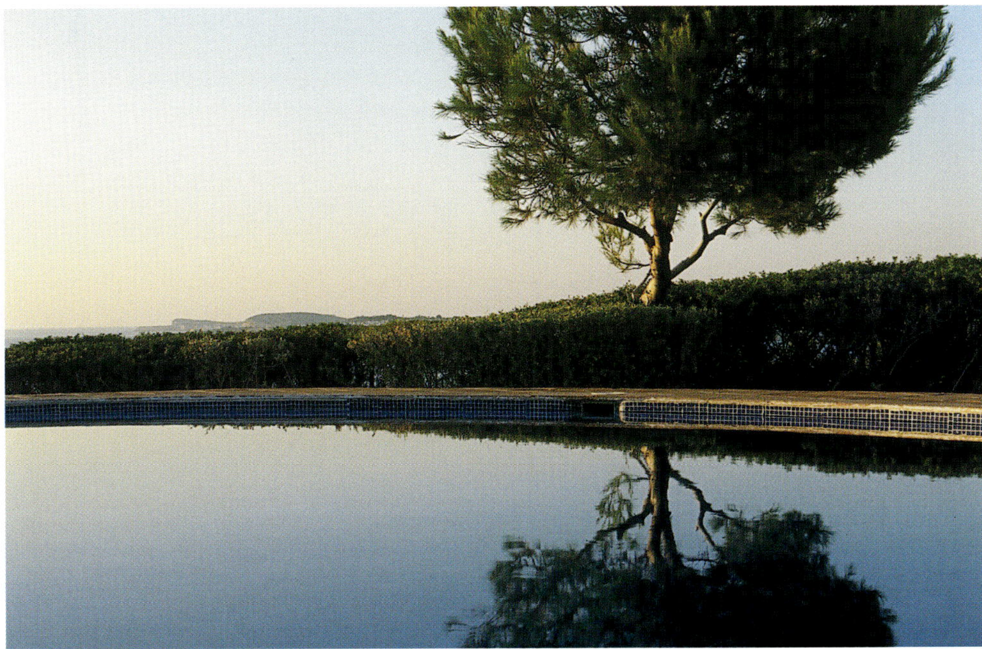

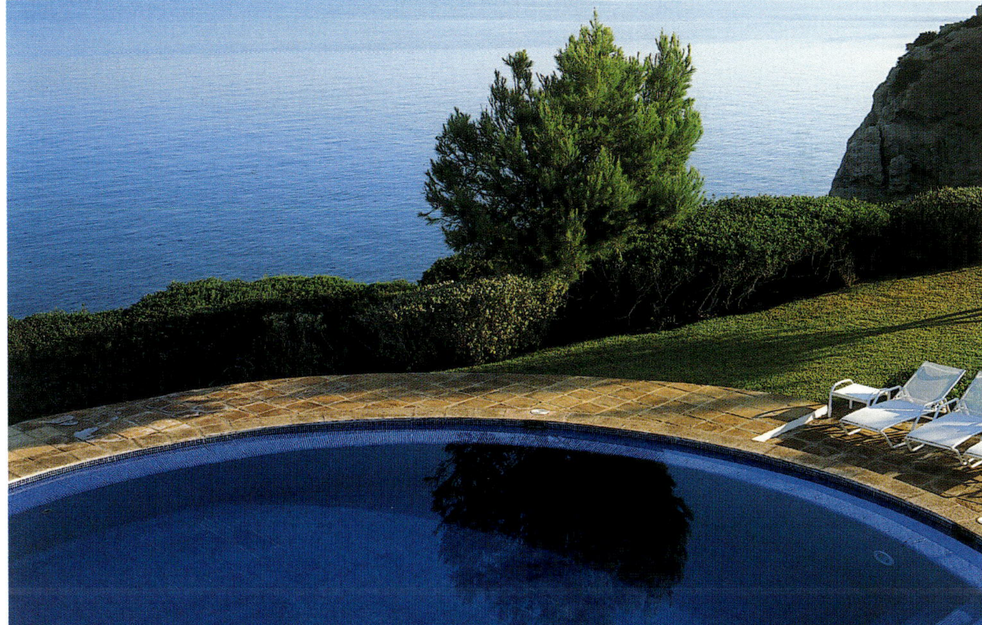

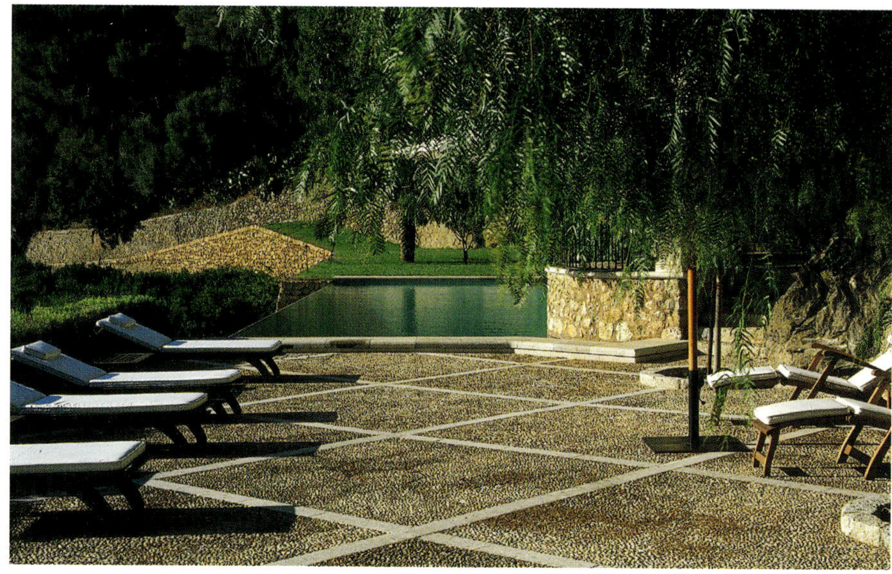

Constructing a Slope

La pendiente construida | Am Abhang gebaut | Construire sur une pente

This multi-level rural house takes advantage of the slope of the terrain, and the pool is placed on one of the terraces. The lines, surfaces and volumes of the house take in and integrate the garden into its overall architectural design. There is not only one vantage point from which to capture the beauty of the spaces. The vegetation complements the architecture and creates areas of shade that afford respite from the strong summer sun.
The water of the pool touches one of the containment walls of the ground and the house. Consequently, it is perfectly integrated into the ensemble of volumes afforded by the house.
The diverse colors form a varied palette where each element is a brushstoke that changes textures.

Esta es una casa rural organizada en diferentes niveles aprovechando la pendiente de la montaña. En una de estas terrazas se sitúa la piscina. La arquitectura no se detiene en las paredes exteriores sino que con sus líneas, superficies y volúmenes, va incorporando el jardín para la vivienda. No podemos captar la belleza de los espacios desde un único punto de vista. La vegetación aparece completando la arquitectura, creando unas zonas de sombra que nos protegen de la fuerte insolación del verano.
En esta piscina el agua está en contacto con uno de los muros de contención del terreno y de la casa, de esta manera se integra perfectamente con los diferentes volúmenes que forman esta vivienda. Los colores de los materiales componen una paleta muy rica en la que cada elemento es una pincelada que cambia la textura.

Die Sruktur dieses Landhauses erfolgt auf verschiedenen Ebenen unter Ausnutzung des Bergabhangs. Auf einer dieser Terrassen liegt das Schwimmbecken. Die Architektur macht nicht an den Außenwänden halt, sondern bezieht mit ihren Linien, Flächen und Volumina den Garten in den Wohnraum ein. Die Schönheit der Räume ist nicht von einem einzelnen Blickpunkt aus zu begreifen. Die Vegetation scheint die Architektur zu ergänzen und schafft schattige Plätze zum Schutz vor der starken Sommersonne. Das Wasser des Schwimmbeckens berührt eine der Stützmauern für Gelände und Haus und wird so perfekt in die verschiedenen Baukörper dieses Wohnhauses integriert. Die Farben der Materialien fügen sich zu einer reichen Farbpalette, die mit jedem Pinselstrich neue Oberflächenstrukturen schafft.

Voici une maison rurale qui a été organisée sur différents niveaux en utilisant le versant de la montagne. La piscine se situe sur l'une de ces terrasses. L'architecture, loin de se limiter aux murs extérieurs, insère le jardin dans l'habitation à l'aide de ses lignes, de ses superficies et de ses volumes. La beauté de ces espaces ne peut être conçue d'un point de vue unique. La végétation vient compléter l'architecture en créant des zones ombragées qui protègent des zones fortement ensoleillées l'été. Dans cette piscine, l'eau est en contact avec un des murs de soutènement du terrain et de la maison. Ainsi, elle s'intègre parfaitement aux différentes unités qui composent cette habitation. Les couleurs des matériaux composent une palette très riche dans laquelle chaque élément est un coup de pinceau qui modifie la texture.

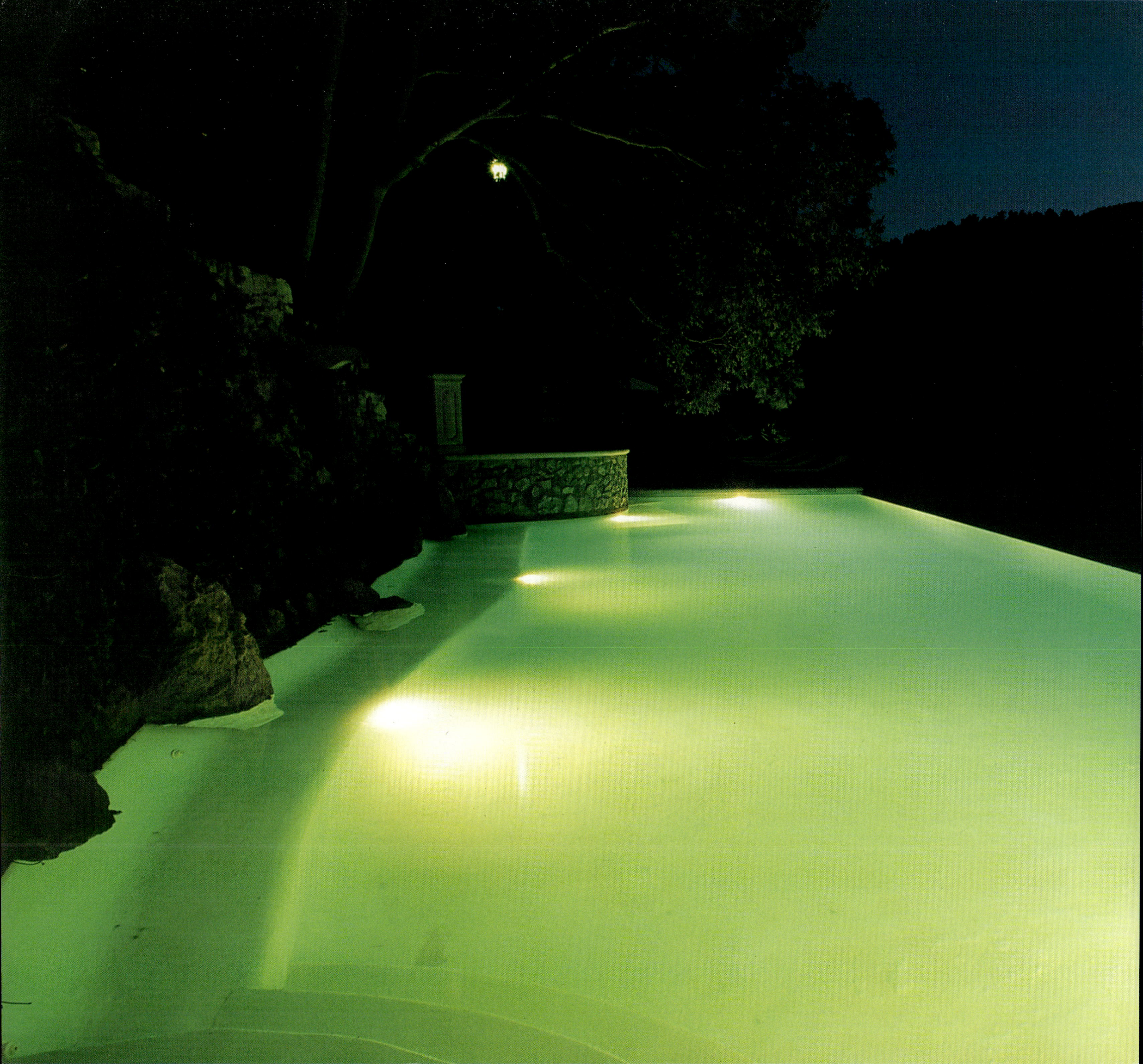

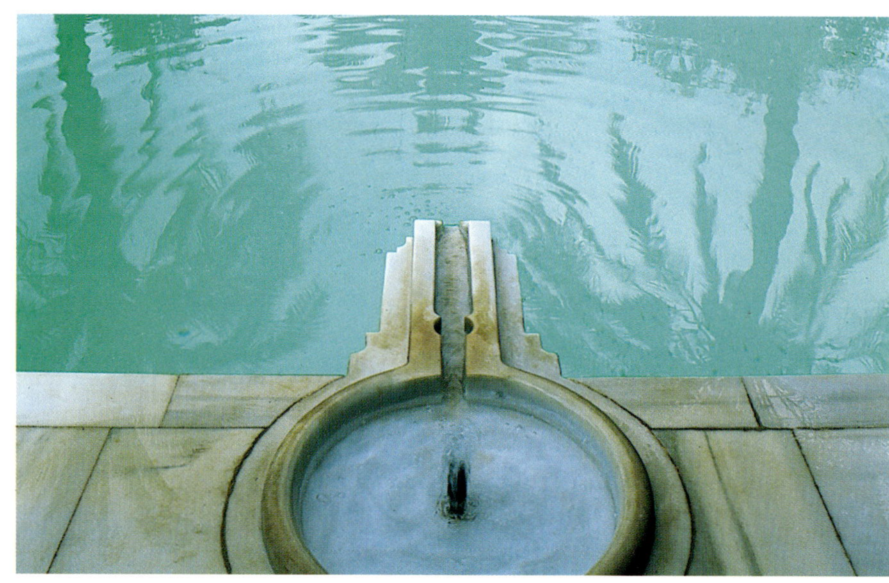

Space and Proportion

Espacio y proporción | Raum und Proportion | Espace et proportion

The attempt of this project was to organize an open space with the swimming pool at the hub. Furthermore, it is an orientalized formal style, as evoked by the small marquee-like structure to one side with thin marble columns and elaborately-carved wooden arches.
In this Islamic-style garden, the water zones are the centerpiece and convey great sensitivity. The theme evoked is the intersection of the four rivers of paradise. This cosmic cross is formed by the placement of two small lotus pools. Functionality and aesthetics are combined to create a geometric tapestry of different textures. Thus, the ground becomes a palette of colors running the range of greens and blues, and is framed by the ochre tone of the stone.

En este proyecto se ha intentado organizar el espacio abierto en torno a la piscina, reproduciendo incluso un estilo formal orientalizante, como el del pequeño pabellón situado en un lateral, con arquerías de madera trabajada y finas columnas de mármol.
Las zonas de agua están pensadas con una gran dosis de sensibilidad y como foco de un jardín de estilo islámico. El tema evocado es el cruce de los cuatro ríos del Paraíso. Esta cruz cósmica se consigue colocando dos pequeños estanques cuadrados llenos de lotos. La parte funcional y la estética se combinan creando un tapiz geométrico de diferentes texturas. Así, el suelo se convierte en una paleta de diferentes colores que recorre la gama de los azules y verdes, enmarcados por el tono ocre de la piedra.

Ziel dieses Bauprojekts war es, den offenen Raum um das Schwimmbecken herum zu gestalten, wobei teilweise ein orientalisch anmutender Stil gewählt wurde, wie z. B. an einer der Längsseiten bei dem kleinen Pavillon mit Bögen aus bearbeitetem Holz und zierlichen Marmorsäulen gearbeitet wurde. Die Wasserzonen wurden mit großer Sensibilität und als Mittelpunkt eines Gartens im islamischen Stil geplant. Thematischer Hintergrund ist hierbei der Zusammenfluss der vier Flüsse des Paradieses. Das kosmische Kreuz wird durch die Anlage zweier kleiner, quadratischer Teiche voller Seerosen geschaffen. Funktionalität und Ästhetik vereinen sich zu einem geometrischen Geflecht verschiedener Oberflächenstrukturen. Der Boden wird gleichsam zur reichen Farbpalette, die das Spektrum der vom Ocker der Steine eingerahmten Blau- und Grüntöne abdeckt.

Ce projet a cherché à organiser l'espace ouvert figurant autour de la piscine en s'inspirant d'un orientalisme formel, comme l'évoque le petit pavillon situé sur un côté avec ses arcatures de bois travaillé et ses fines colonnes de marbre.
Les zones d'eau, dont la conception traduit une grande sensibilité, sont le foyer d'un jardin de style islamique. Le thème évoqué est la traversée des quatre fleuves du paradis. Cette croix cosmique a été obtenue en aménageant deux petits bassins carrés envahis de lotus. La partie fonctionnelle et la partie esthétique se combinent, créant ainsi un tapis géométrique de différentes textures. Le sol devient ainsi une palette de couleurs déclinant la gamme des bleus et des verts, rehaussés par le ton ocre de la pierre.

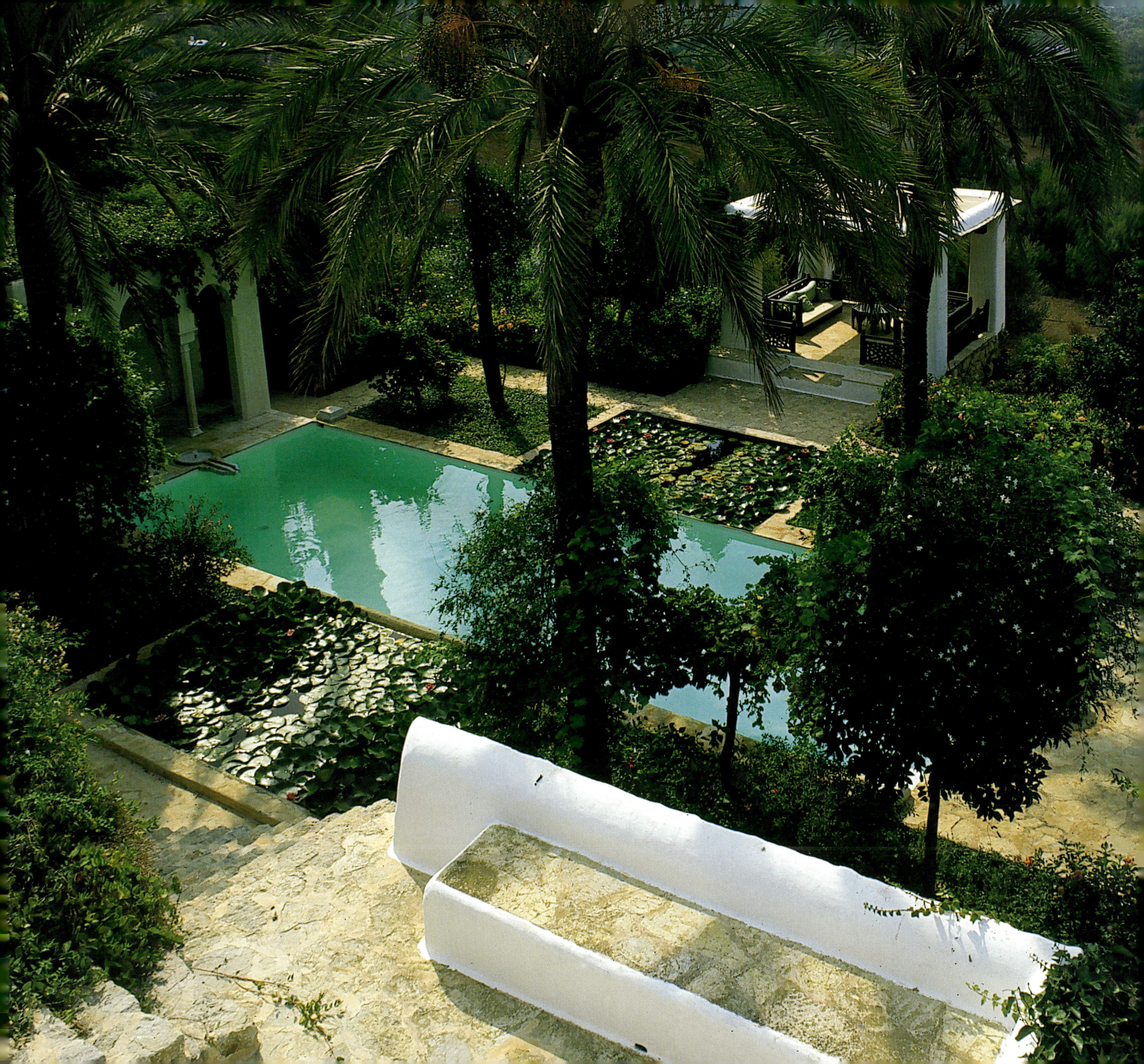

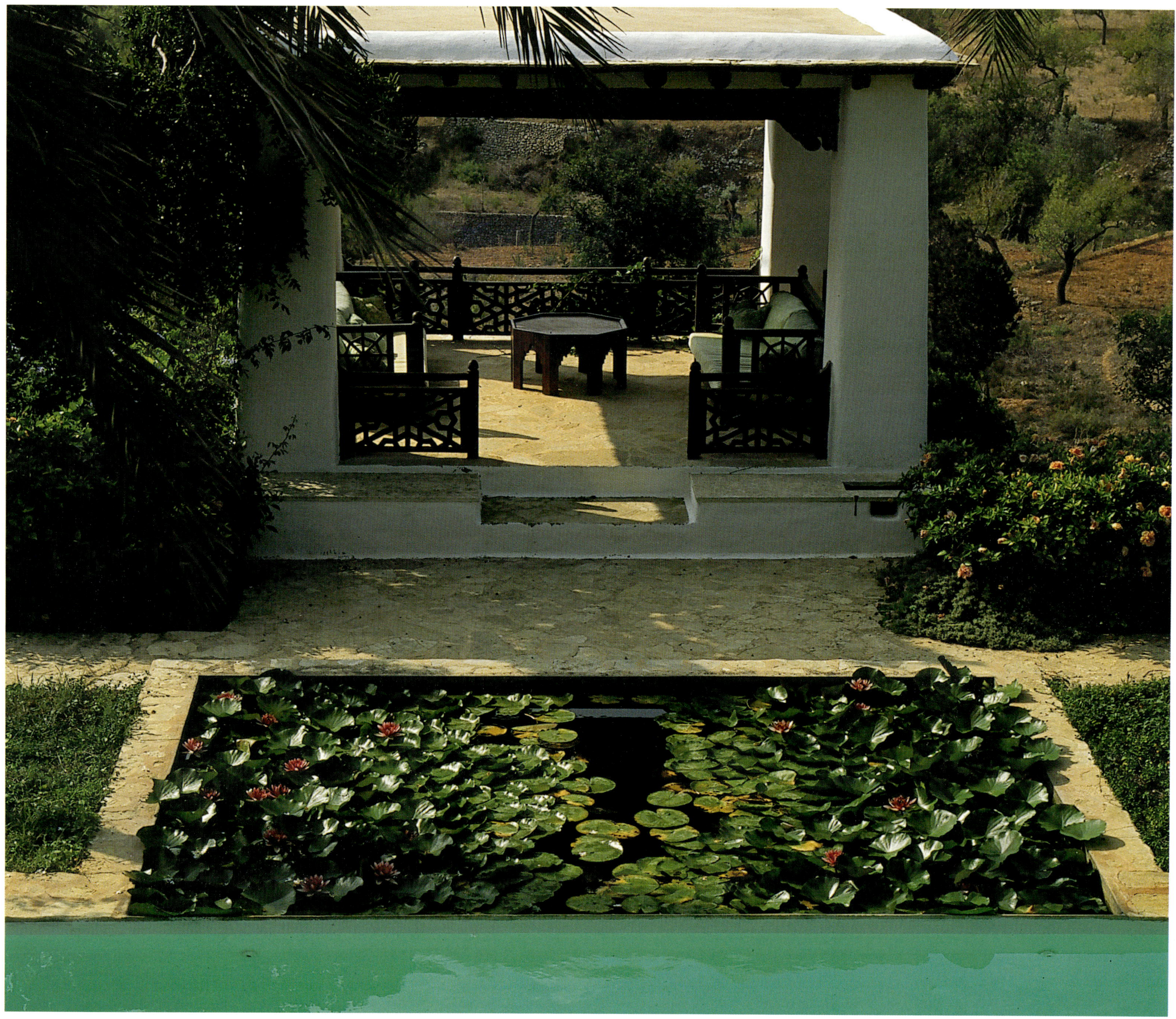

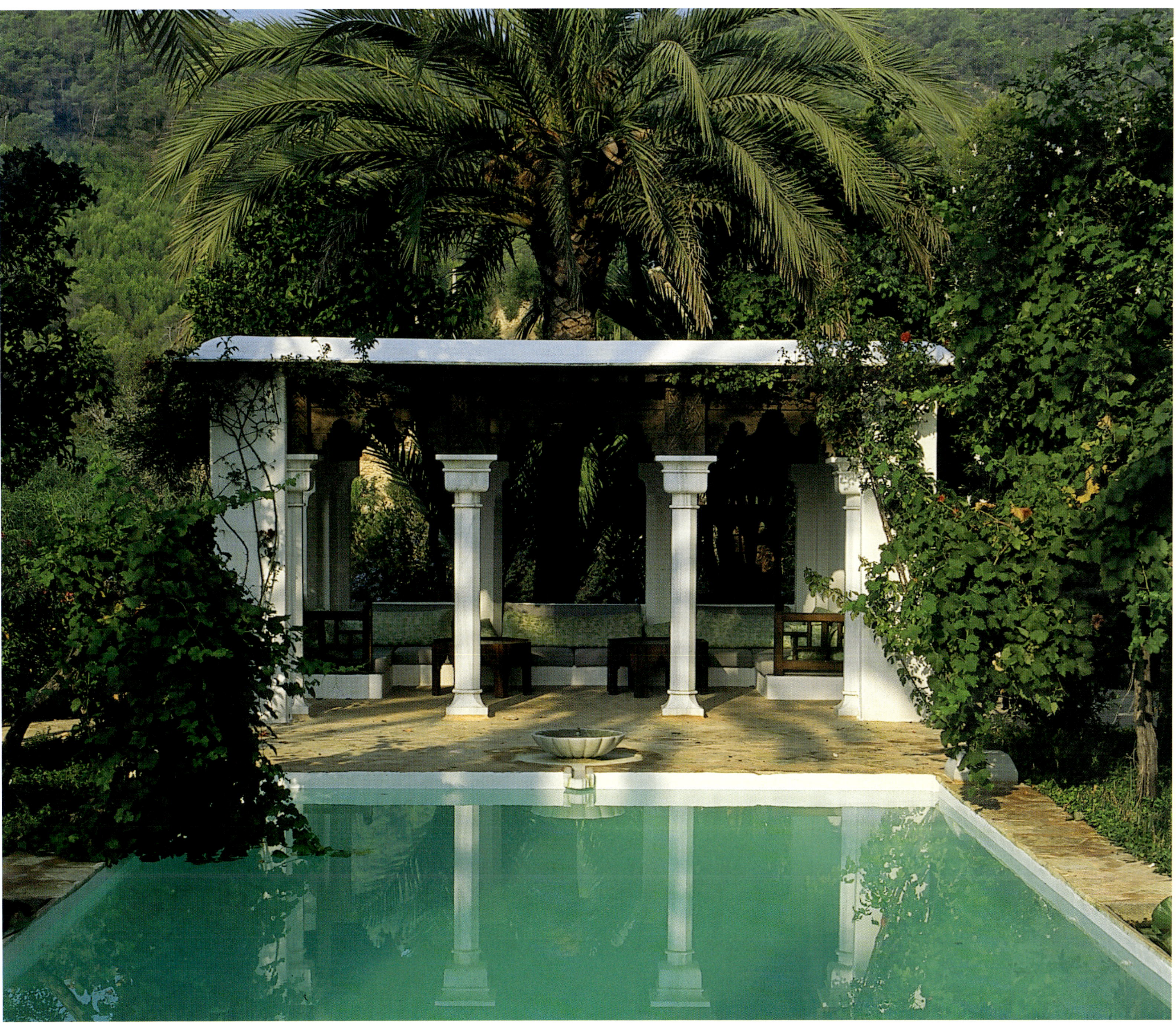

Classical Atmosphere

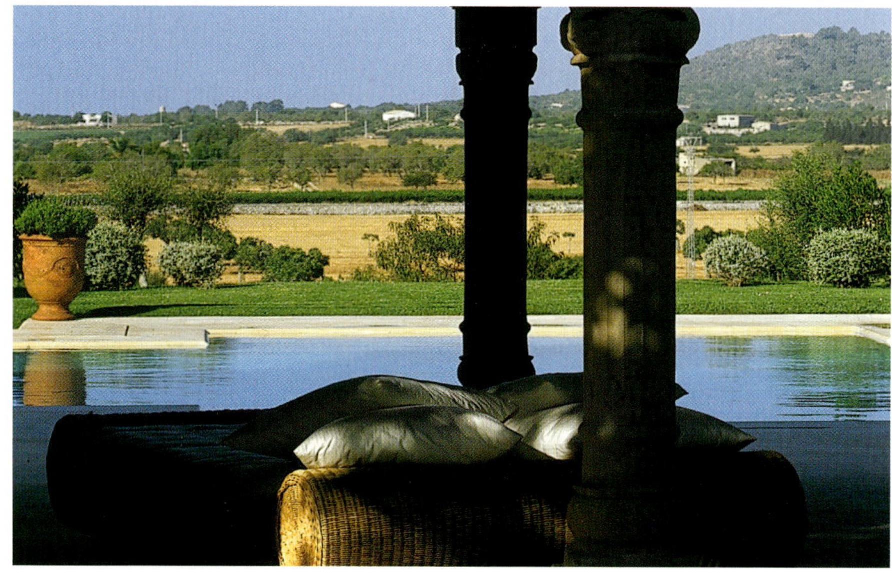

Atmósfera clásica | Klassische Atmosphäre | Une atmosphère classique

Normally it is the Cretans who are attributed with having imported from the Orient the first explanations about gardening. Other versions believe that it was in Tartessus, which now corresponds to the region of Cadiz, where the first Mediterranean gardens were created.
A path flanked by low stone walls and a fence leads up to this house of traditional architectural style. The house takes center stage in this peaceful garden traced with paths. The main volume of the house is diluted by smaller annexes, which in turn give way to other leisure areas. The delightful garden combines trees, stone walls and banked plant beds, which lead to a lodge that presides over the swimming pool. Despite the Classical overtones, including a gallery of arches, the sensation is not that of a rigid architectural ensemble.

Gemeinhin wird den Kretern zugeschrieben, aus dem Orient die ersten Anleitungen zum Gartenbau importiert zu haben, wenngleich andere Versionen die Anlage der ersten mediterranen Gärten in Tartessos ansiedeln, der heutigen Region von Cádiz. Über einen von niedrigen Steinmauern und einem Zaun geschützten Weg gelangt man zu dem im traditionellen Architekturstil erbauten Haus. Der große Hauptbaukörper des Gebäudes löst sich in kleine Anbauten auf, welche die Türen zu neuen Räumen öffnen, die der Ruhe und Erholung dienen. Das durch eher niedrige Bepflanzung in Kombination mit Bäumen, Beeten und Steinmauern gestaltete Gelände erstreckt sich bis hin zu einer Loggia, die dem Schwimmbecken vorsteht. Dieser Bereich zeigt Beispiele klassischen Reminiszenzen und entfaltet sich in einer Bogengalerie mit absoluter Freiheit und bar jeder architektonischen Ordnung.

Suele atribuirse a los cretenses el hecho de haber importado de Oriente las primeras explicaciones de jardinería; aunque otras versiones consideran que fue en Tartessos donde se crearon los primeros jardines mediterráneos, lugar que coincide con la región de Cádiz. A través de un camino protegido por muros bajos de piedra y por una verja, llegamos a la casa construida según la arquitectura tradicional. El gran volumen principal de la casa se va disgregando en pequeñas construcciones anexas que abren las puertas a nuevos espacios de recreo y descanso. Organizado a base de jardinería baja combinada con árboles, bancales y muros de piedra, el terreno se extiende hasta llegar a una loggia que preside la piscina. Esta zona de reminiscencia clásica se desarrolla con total libertad, prescindiendo de órdenes arquitectónicos pero con galería de arcos.

On attribue aux Crétois l'introduction, depuis l'Orient, des premiers rudiments de jardinerie, bien que d'autre versions avancent que c'est à Tartessos - l'actuelle région de Cadix - qu'ont été créés les premiers jardins méditerranéens. En suivant un chemin protégé par des murs de pierre peu élevés et par une grille, nous arrivons à la maison, construite selon l'architecture traditionnelle. L'importante unité principale de la maison se désagrège en petites constructions annexes qui débouchent sur de nouveaux espaces de loisirs et de repos.
Basé sur un jardinage simple associant arbres, cultures en paliers et murs de pierre, le terrain s'étend jusqu'à une loggia qui préside la piscine. Cette zone d'évocation classique évolue dans une liberté totale, se passant d'impératifs architectoniques non sans offrir une galerie d'arcs.

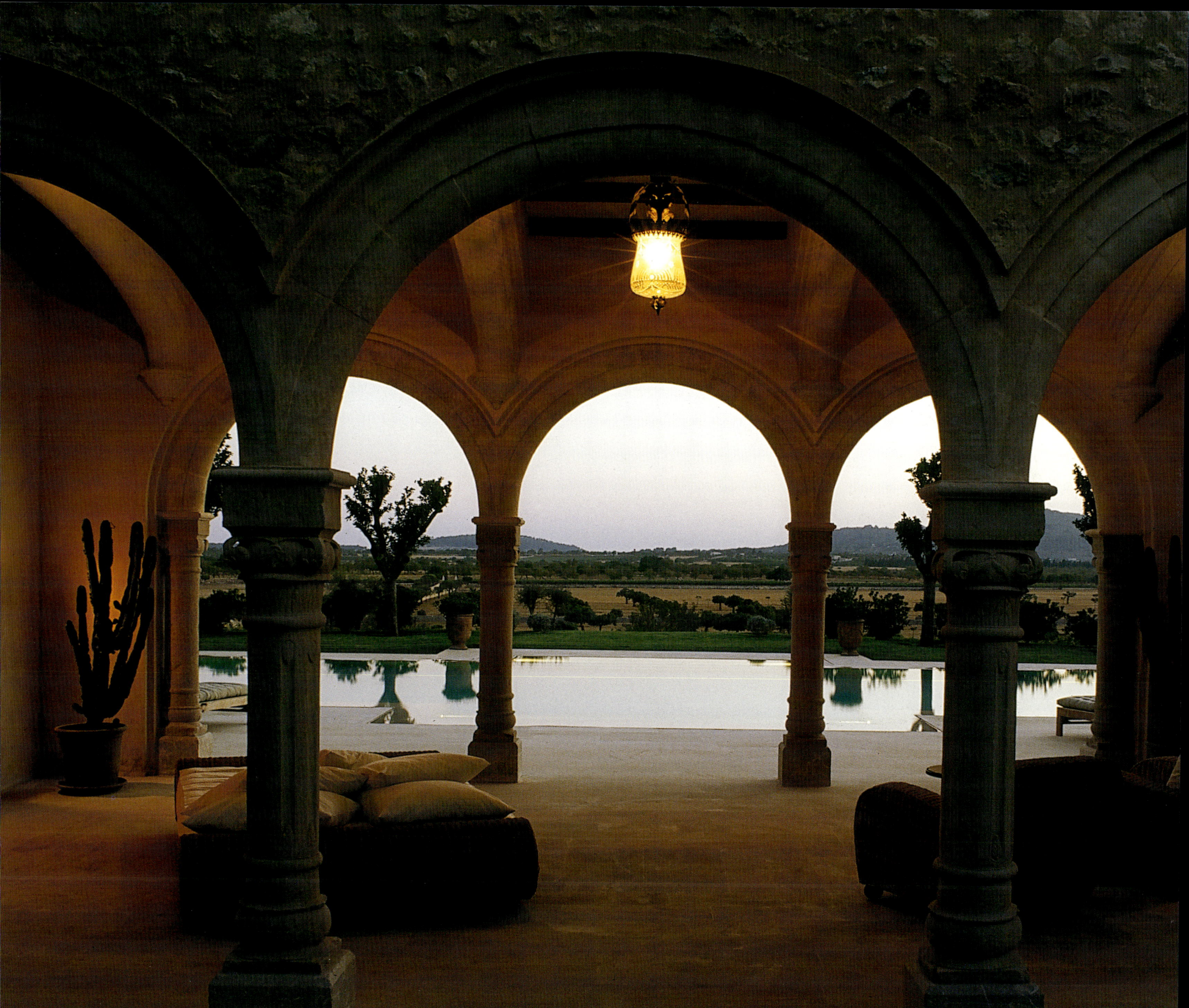

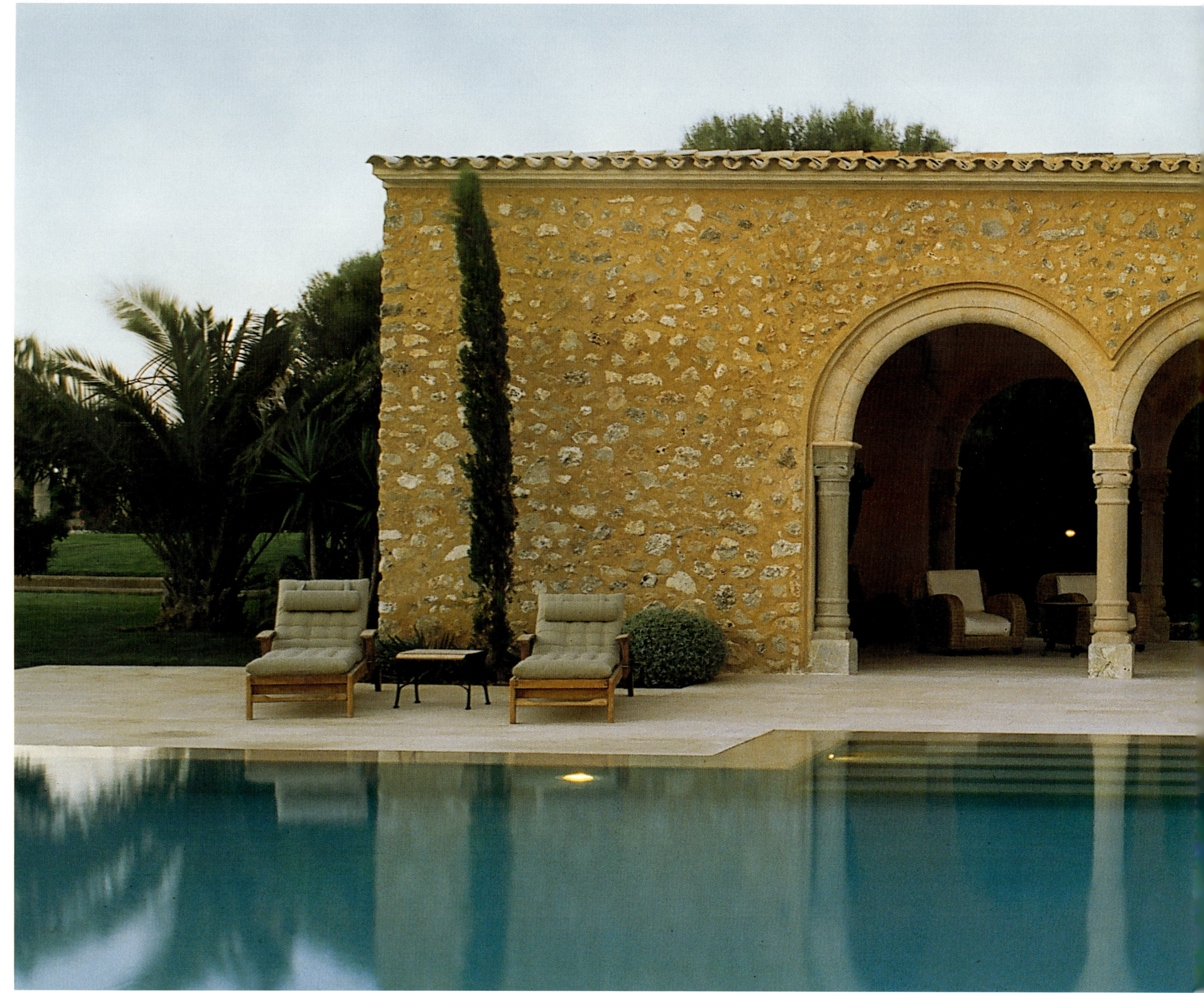

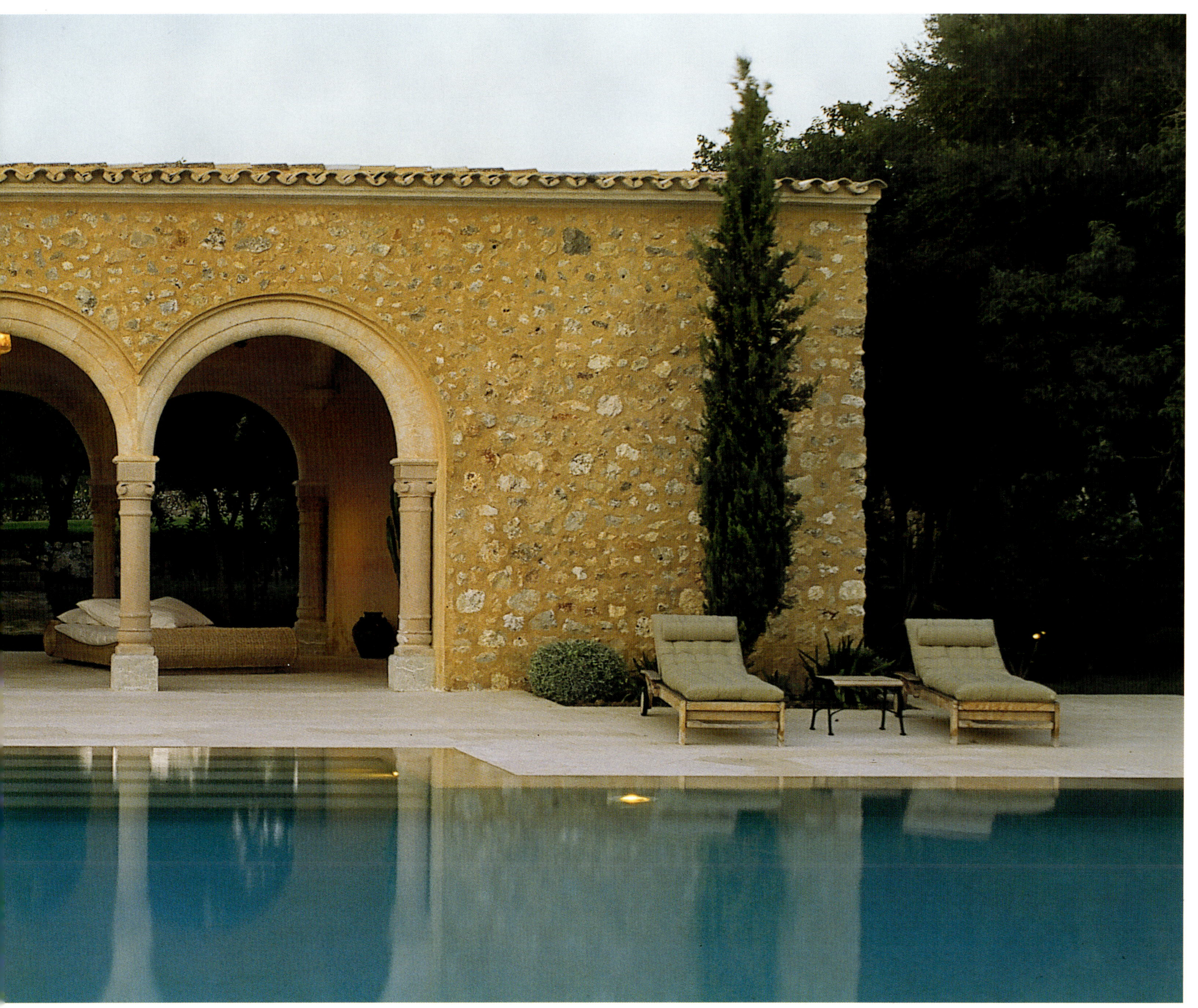

Framing The Landscape

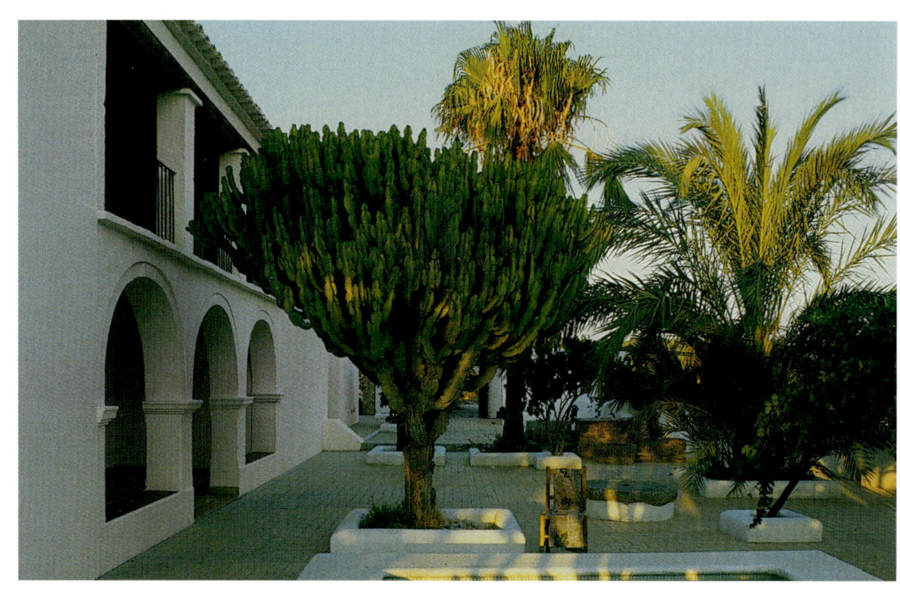

Paisaje enmascarado | Gerahmte Landschaft | Un paysage dissimulé

In this architectural garden the elements are delimited with white rims that isolate them and grant them a sculpturesque quality. In this solid, sturdy, static atmosphere the right angles of the swimming pool accentuate the hard geometry of the architecture and the wall. The arcade-style porch affords shadows that are in stark contrast with the white façade. A wall pergola goes around the patio and frames views of the palm tree-dotted slope.
This style of landscape art is inspired from the art of land art artists, those solitary sculptures placed on untouched high plateaus in the American Southwest, which evoke the distinctivess of the scenario.

Estamos frente a un jardín arquitectónico. Los elementos que aparecen están remarcados por un bordillo blanco que los aísla y les otorga una calidad casi escultórica. La forma estricta de la piscina de ángulos rectos, refuerza la geometría dura de la arquitectura y el muro. Predomina un aire de fijeza, de solidez y estatismo. La casa se desdobla en la zona de entrada dando paso a un porche de arcadas. Éste actúa como un profundo corte de oscuridad en la superficie blanca de la fachada. Rodeando esta plaza privada, un muro-pérgola nos enmarca las vistas sobre la ladera arbolada. Esta forma de paisajismo nos pone en contacto con las esculturas realizadas por los artistas del land art. Estas esculturas solitarias situadas en los páramos vírgenes del suroeste americano, evocaban la especificidad del lugar.

Dieses Beispiel zeigt einen architektonisch gestalteten Garten. Die Elemente, die einem sofort ins Auge fallen, werden durch eine weiße Umrandung betont, die sie isoliert und ihnen einen nahezu skulpturenhaften Anschein gibt. Die rigorose Form des rechteckigen Schwimmbeckens verstärkt die strenge Geometrie von Architektur und Mauer. Die Stimmung wird geprägt von Bestimmtheit, Solidität und Unbeweglichkeit. Das Haus entfaltet sich im Eingangsbereich und gibt den Weg auf einen Arkadengang frei. Dieser wirkt wie ein tiefer Einschnitt von Dunkelheit in die weiße Oberfläche der Fassade. Der private Platz ist von einer berankten Mauer umgeben, die den Blick auf den baumbestandenen Hang einrahmt. Diese Form des Landschaftsbildes stellt den Kontakt zu den Skulpturen von Landart-Künstlern her. Diese einzeln stehenden Skulpturen in den unberührten Einöden des amerikanischen Südwestens sind Ausdruck der Besonderheit des Ortes.

Nous nous trouvons en face d'un jardin architectonique. Ses éléments sont rehaussés d'une bordure blanche qui les isole et leur confère quasiment une allure de sculptures. La forme stricte de la piscine, avec ses angles droits, renforce la dureté géométrique de l'architecture et du mur. La dominante est à la fixité, à la solidité et au statisme. Dans la zone d'entrée, la maison se dédouble, s'ouvrant sur un porche à arcades. L'obscurité ainsi produite crée une forte rupture sur la blancheur de la superficie de la façade. Cette place privée est entourée d'un mur-pergola qui encadre les vues sur le coteau boisé. Ce type de paysagisme nous évoque les sculptures réalisées par les artistes du land-art. Ces sculptures solitaires situées sur les étendues désertiques du sud-ouest américain soulignaient la spécificité de l'endroit.

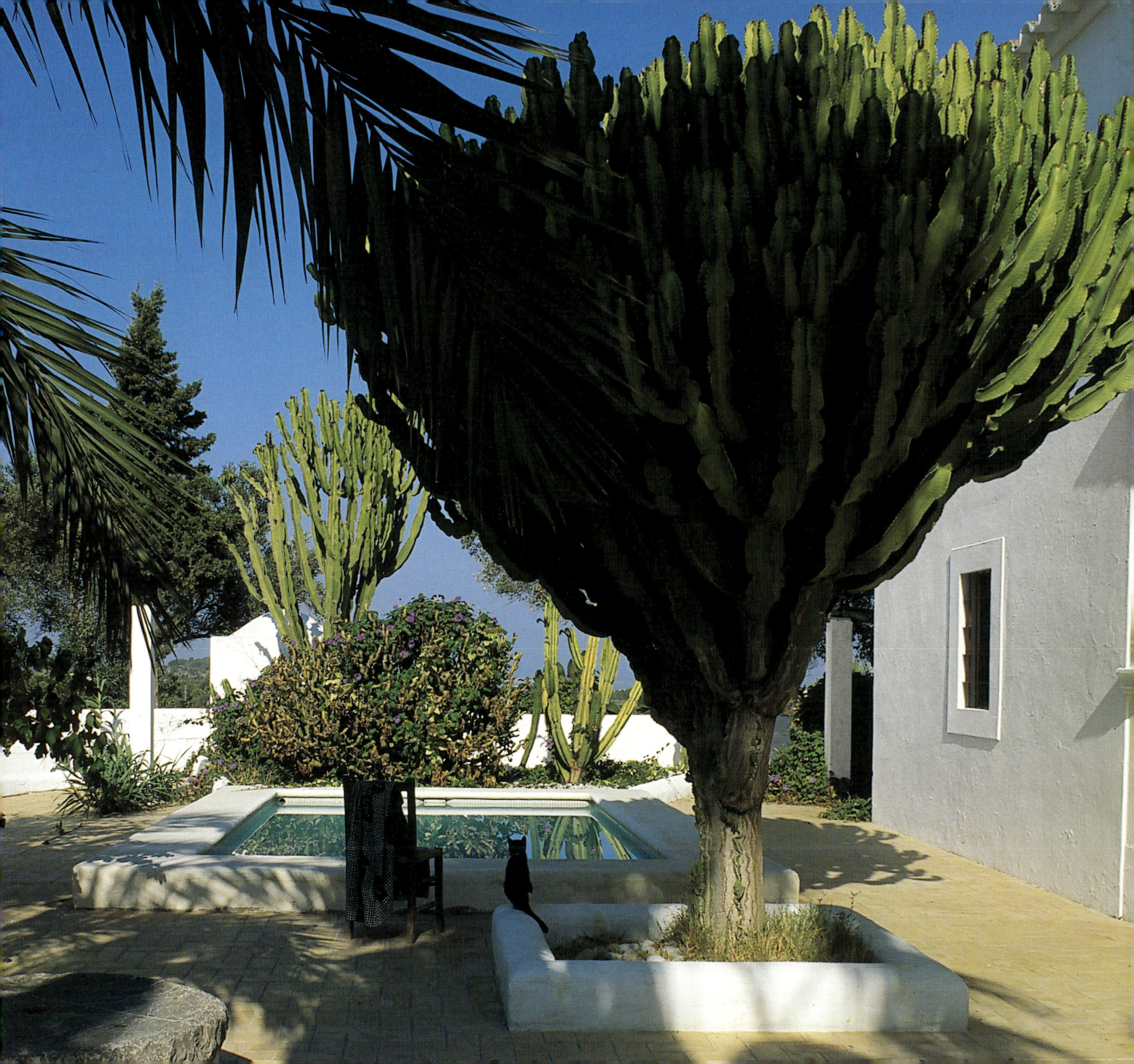

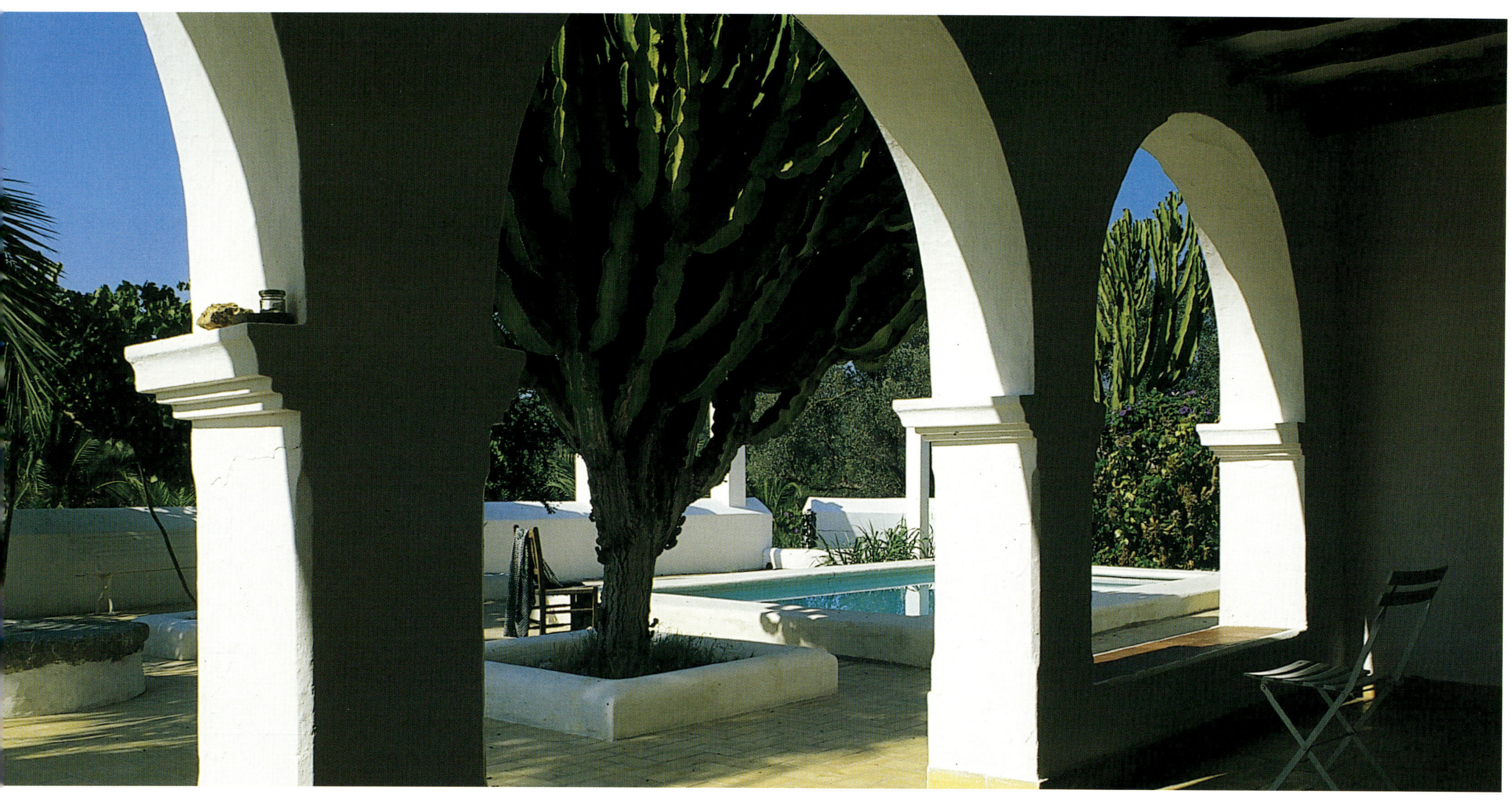

The entrance is a shady zone that acts as a transition space between the soft light inside and the blinding sun in the garden.

El ámbito de entrada es una zona de sombra que actúa de espacio de transición entre la penumbra interior y la luz deslumbrante del jardín.

Der Eingangsbereich ist im Schatten und bildet den Übergang zwischen dem Halbdunkel im Inneren und dem gleißenden Licht des Gartens.

L'entrée est une zone ombragée qui sert d'espace de transition entre la pénombre intérieure et l'éblouissante lumière du jardin.

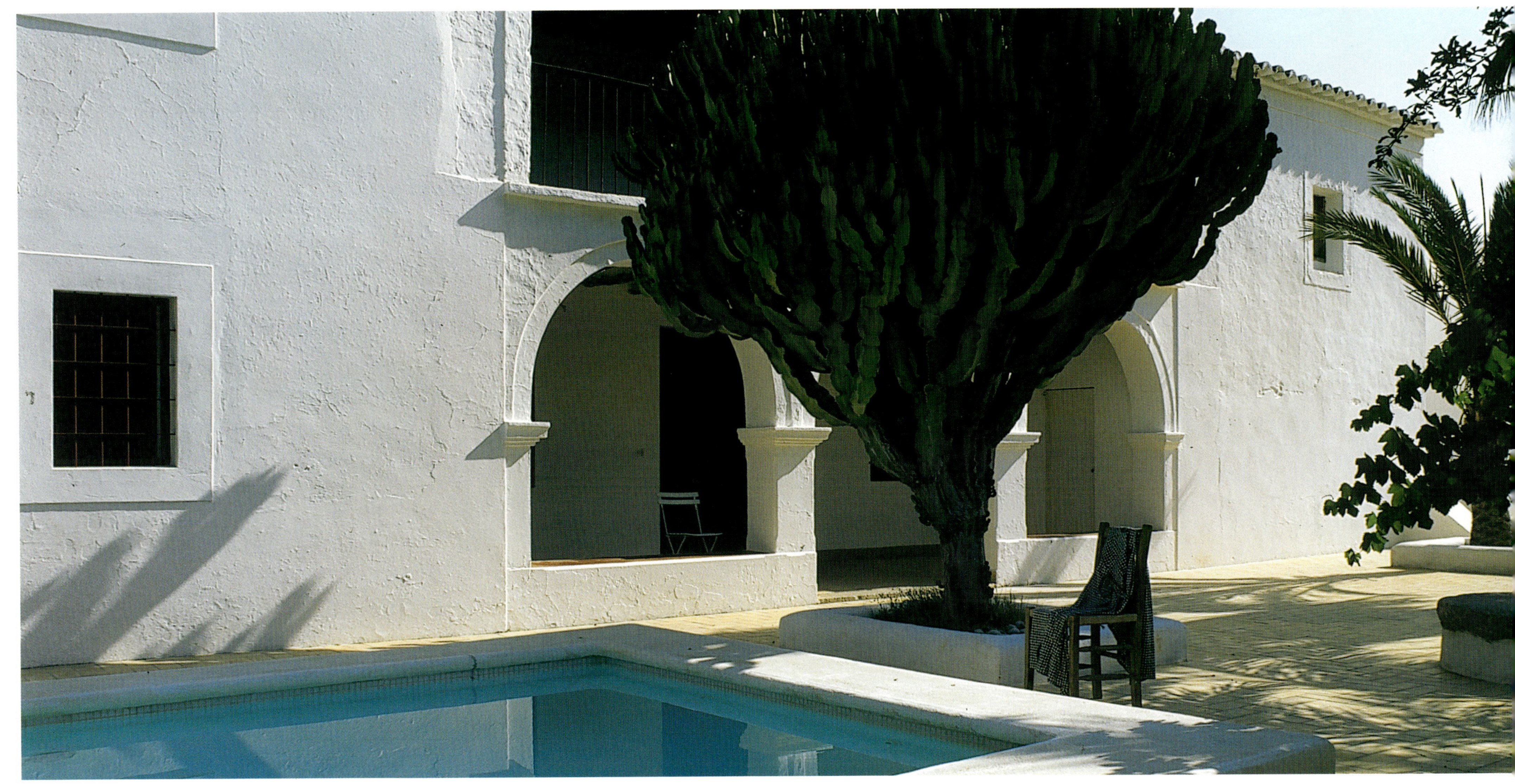

The swimming pool container juts out of the ground slightly,
making a very useful rim.

El contenedor de agua que forma la piscina sobresale ligeramente del nivel del pavimento creándose un bordillo muy útil.

Der Beckenrand des Bassins ragt leicht über den Bodenbelag hinaus und bildet so einen nützlichen Rand.

Le bassin qui constitue la piscine est légèrement plus haut que le niveau du sol, créant ainsi un rebord bien utile.

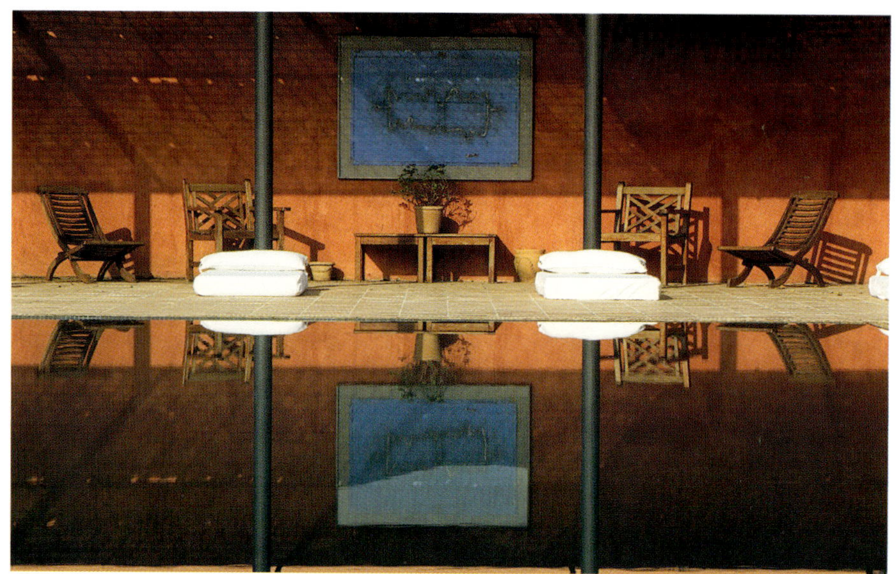

Red House

Una casa roja | Rotes Haus | Une maison rouge

It is situated between two small bodies of water; a pond and a swimming pool. It is a one-storey structure with a gabled roof that is formed by several parallel modules, where the red colored façades evoke a surrealistic image. Like the pavilion of a Moorish garden, it orders the landscape and establishes symmetries, axes and visual interplays.
The collaboration of Fernando Caruncho as the landscape artist was of primary importance. Around the house the well-balanced ensemble is organized into a succession of small, ordered, closed-in spaces that are interconnected. The garden, where the pool is situated, is surrounded by a continuous line of vegetation, which closes it off and converts it into a private reserve.

La casa se encuentra entre dos superficies de agua: un estanque y una piscina. De una sola planta y formada por varios módulos paralelos cubiertos con un tejado a dos aguas, sus fachadas de color rojo le transmiten una imagen surrealista. Parecido a los pequeños templetes de los jardines árabes, el edificio funciona como una pauta que ordena el paisaje estableciendo simetrías, ejes y juegos visuales.
La colaboración de Fernando Caruncho como paisajista ha sido fundamental. Alrededor de la casa, se habilitan una serie de espacios exteriores cerrados sobre sí mismos y a su vez interconectados, que dibujan una sucesión de planos ordenados. El jardín en el que se encuentra la piscina está rodeado por una línea continua de vegetación que lo cierra convirtiéndolo en un espacio acotado.

Das Haus liegt zwischen zwei Wasserflächen: einem Teich und einem Schwimmbecken. Es verfügt über nur eine Etage und besteht aus mehreren parallelen Modulen mit Satteldach, die durch die roten Fassaden ein surrealistisches Aussehen erhalten. Das den Pavillons in arabischen Gärten ähnelnde Gebäude hat eine richtungsweisende Rolle: es soll die Landschaft ordnen und stellt Symmetrien, Achsen und optische Wechselspiele her. Die Mitwirkung von Fernando Caruncho als Landschaftsgärtner war von grundlegender Bedeutung. Um das Haus herum wurde eine Reihe von in sich geschlossenen und zugleich miteinander verbundenen Außenräumen eingerichtet, die eine Abfolge geordneter Ebenen bilden. Der das Schwimmbecken umgebende Garten wird von einer durchgehenden Vegetationslinie eingefass, die diesen abschließt und in einen eingefriedeten Raum verwandelt.

La maison se situe entre deux étendues d'eau : un étang et une piscine. Composée d'un seul étage et de plusieurs modules parallèles recouverts d'un toit pointu, ses façades de couleur rouge lui prêtent une allure surréaliste.
Rappelant les petits temples des jardins arabes, l'édifice constitue une ligne qui ordonne le paysage en établissant des symétries, des axes et des jeux visuels. La collaboration de Fernando Caruncho en tant que paysagiste a été fondamentale. Autour de la maison s'organisent une série d'espaces extérieurs fermés et interconnectés, qui dessinent une suite de plans ordonnés.
Le jardin qui héberge la piscine est entouré d'une ligne continue de végétation qui le clôture, le convertissant ainsi en un espace gardé.

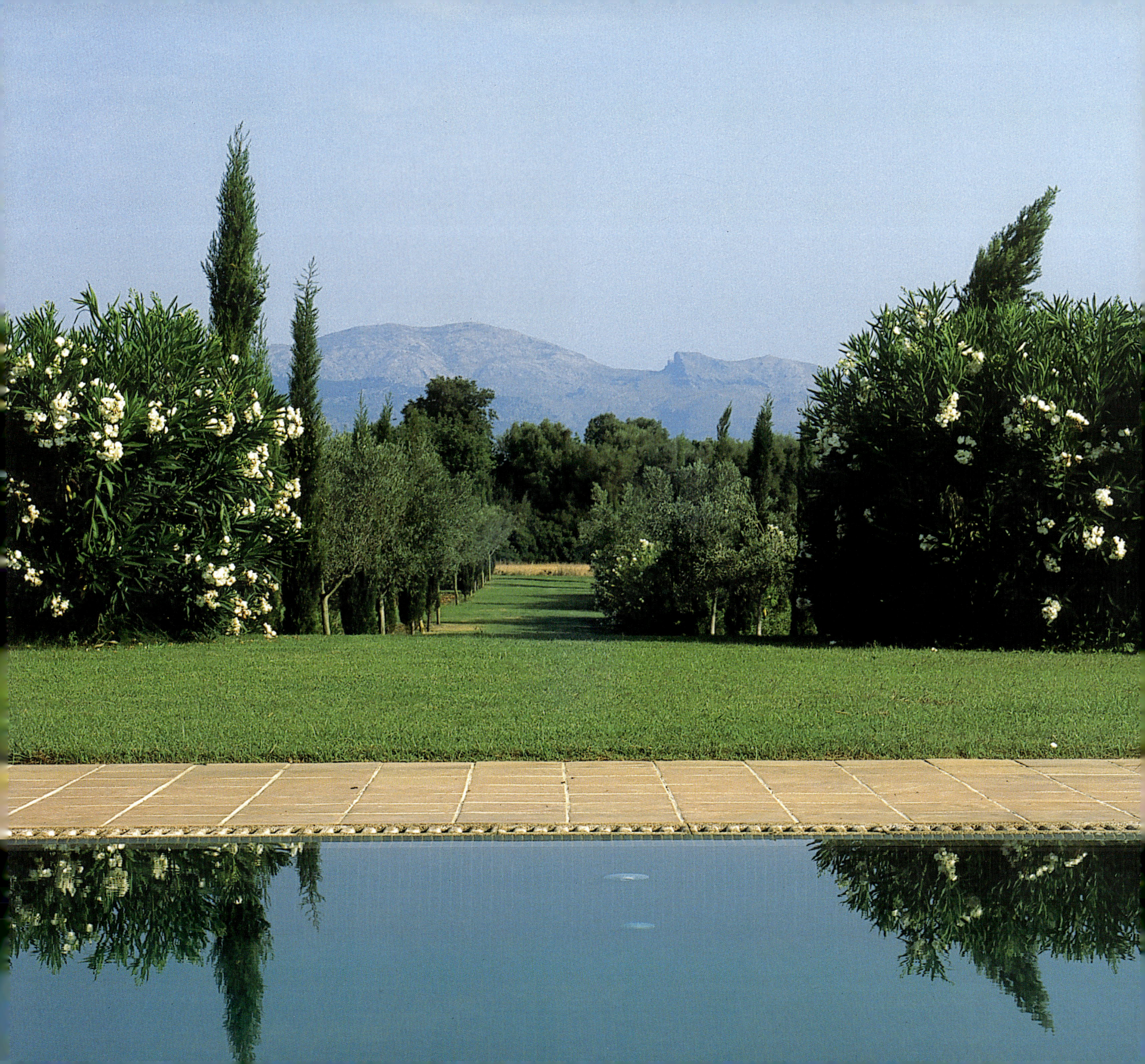

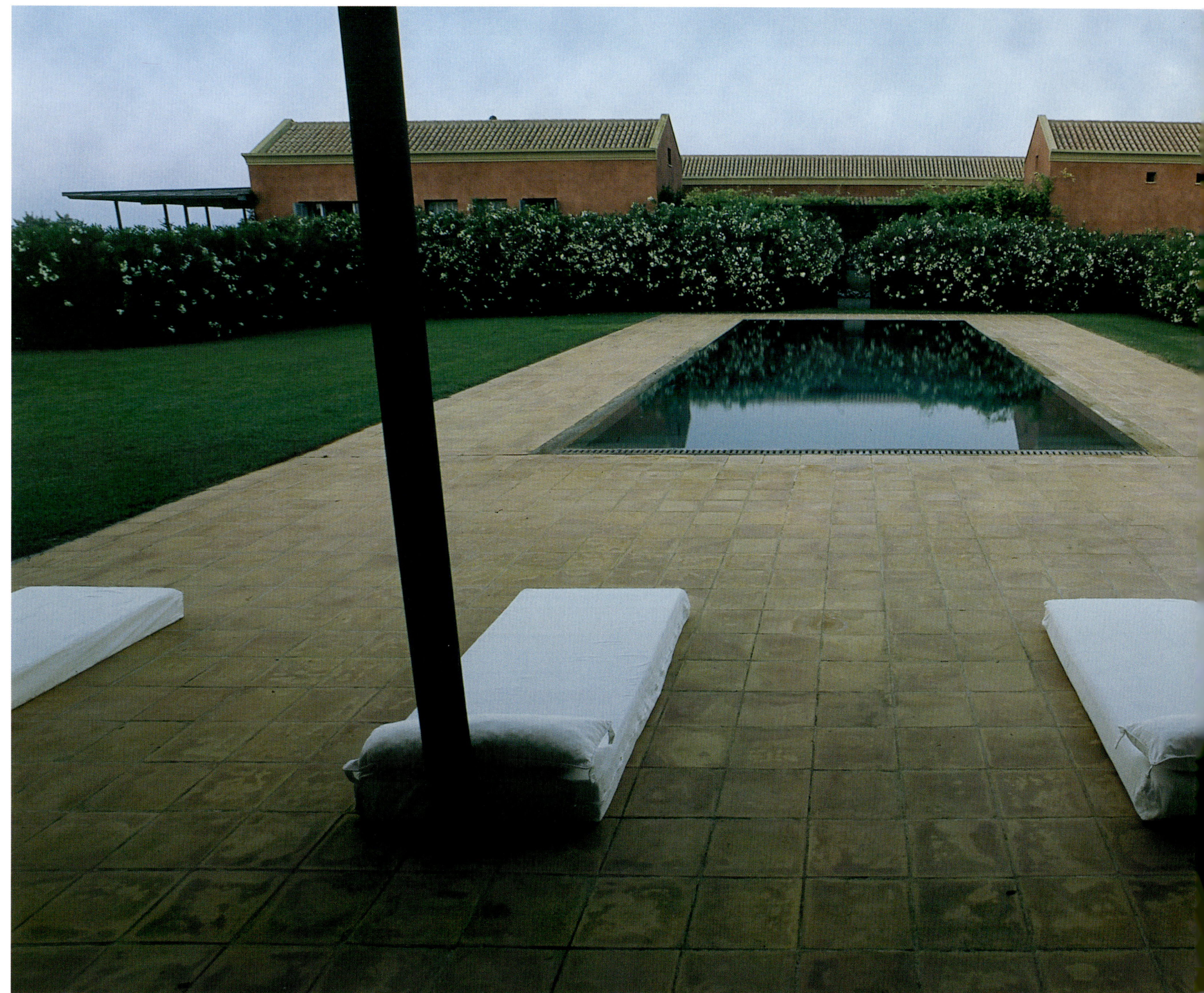

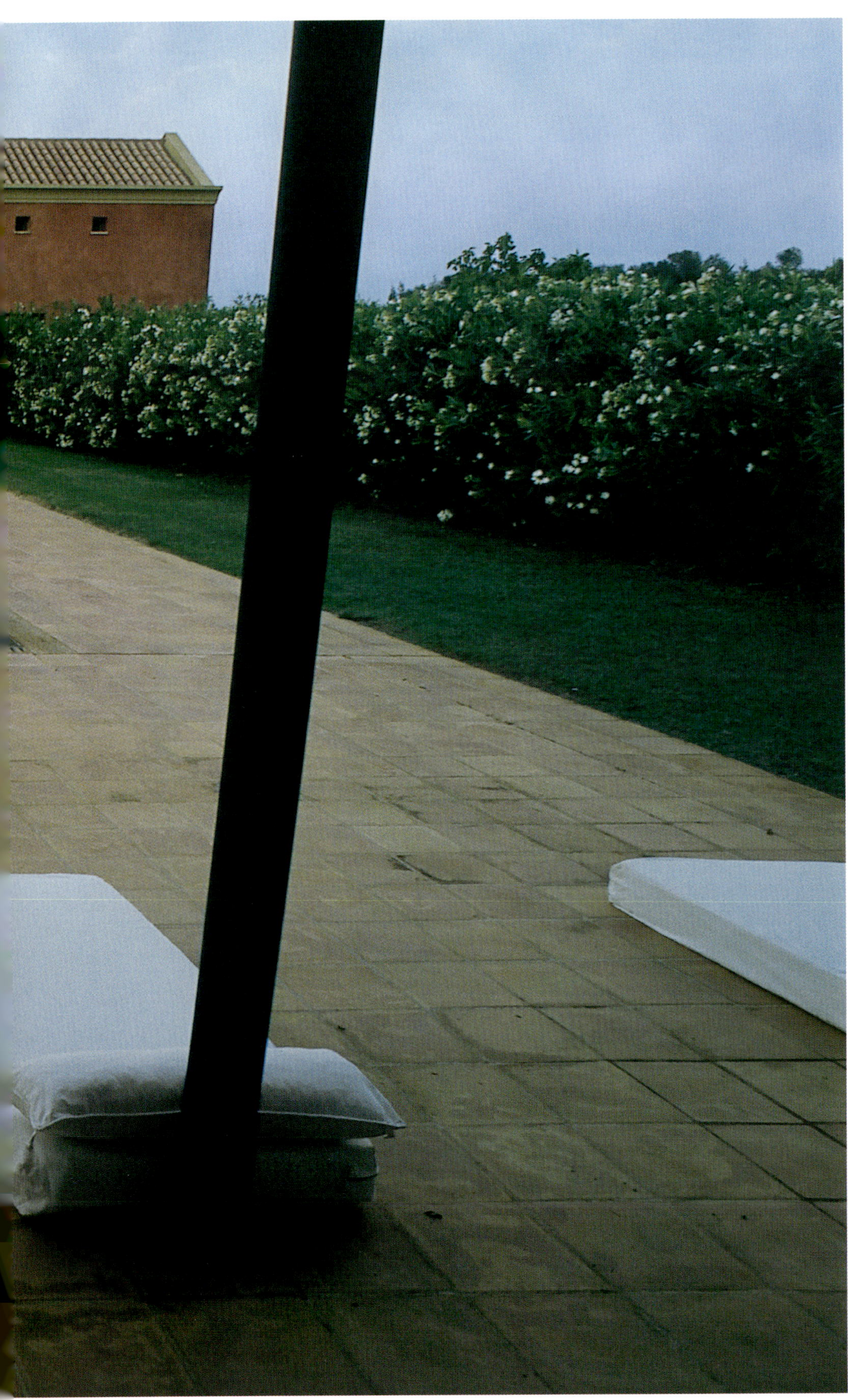

As if it were one sole surface, the water extends out at the same level as the pavement, thanks to a draining system that affords the perception that it is practically on a continuum at the same ground level.
Four hammocks, placed in front of the porch, are awaiting to be used, either, in the shade of the porch, or for resting after a dip in the pool.

Como una sola superficie, el agua se extiende al mismo nivel que el pavimento gracias a un sistema de drenaje que permite una percepción casi continua del suelo.
Cuatro hamacas en blanco se han situado delante del porche de la entrada para protegerse del sol o, si se prefiere, para descansar después del baño cerca del agua de la piscina.

Als einheitliche Oberfläche erstreckt sich das Wasser auf einer Höhe und eben mit dem Bodenbelag. Möglich macht dies ein Abflusssystem, das eine nahezu ununterbrochene Betrachtung des Bodens möglich macht.
Vier weiße Liegen wurden vor dem Vorbau des Eingangsbereichs aufgestellt, wo man Schutz vor der Sonne findet oder, je nach Wunsch, nach dem Baden in der Nähe des Schwimmbeckens ruhen kann.

Comme s'il s'agissait d'une même superficie, l'eau s'étend au même niveau que le sol. Cette continuité entre les deux éléments est assurée par un système de drainage.
Quatre hamacs blancs ont été placés devant le porche de l'entrée pour se protéger du soleil ou se reposer tout près de l'eau de la piscine après une baignade.

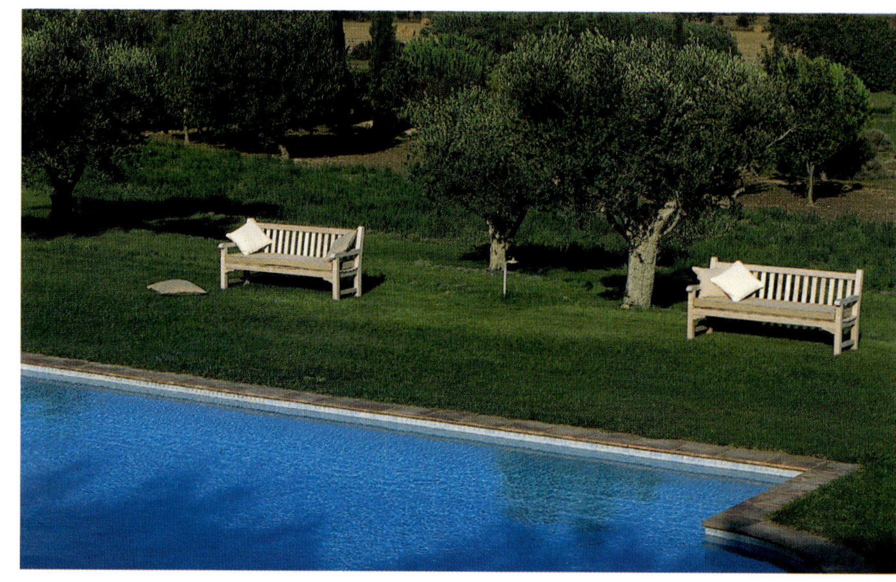

Between The Olives

A través de los olivos | Zwischen Olivenbäumen | Au milieu des oliviers

The swimming pool is situated in an olive grove that has been converted into a private garden. The olive trees and the succession of flat terraces with masonry walls were maintained. However, grass was planted and so the old dry fields were converted into irrigated gardens. A rectangular pool aligned with the retaining wall occupies the middle of a terrace. At one end the pool extends out in a semicircle and is finished with steps that allow one to descend into it. At one end of the terrace, a pergola was built. On one side, camouflaged by the retaining wall, there is a small service room. The rhythmic placement of the pillars evokes a classical construction and the climbing plants climbing the columns and creeping along the beams bring to mind romantic images such as in Piranesi engravings.

Dieses Schwimmbecken liegt in einem Olivenhain, der in einen Privatgarten umgestaltet wurde. Die Olivenbäume blieben ebenso erhalten wie die Abfolge ebener, von halbhohen Bruchsteinmauern gesäumter Terassenflächen. Es wurde jedoch Rasen gepflanzt, wodurch die einst unbewässerten Felder heute zu bewässerten Gärten wurden. In der Mitte einer der Terassen befindet sich das Schwimmbecken, das sich zu den Trennmauern der Terassen ausrichtet. Sein eines Ende formt einen Halbkreis, von dem einige Stufen in das Becken hinab führen. An einem Ausläufer der Terasse wurde ein Laubengang errichtet. An seiner Seite liegt versteckt in einer Stützmauer ein kleiner Serviceraum. Der Rhythmus der Säulen ist eine Reminiszenz an die klassische Bauweise, und die sich an den Säulen emporwindende und zwischen die Balken schlängelnde Kletterpflanze scheint eine Anspielung auf die romantischen Bilder der Stiche von Piranesi.

Esta piscina se encuentra en un olivar reconvertido en jardín privado. Se han conservado los olivos y la sucesión de plataformas planas acabadas con muretes de mampostería. Pero se ha plantado césped, por lo que los antiguos campos de secano son ahora jardines de regadío. En el centro de una plataforma se halla la piscina casi alineada en la dirección de lo muretes divisorios de las plataformas y en uno de sus extremos se dibuja un semicírculo que contiene unas escaleras que permiten descender a ella. En un extremo de la plataforma se ha construido una pérgola. A un lado, camuflada en un muro de contención, se encuentra una pequeña habitación de servicio. El ritmo de los pilares evoca las construcciones clásicas y la planta enredadera que asciende por las columnas y se enrosca en las vigas alude a las imágenes románticas de los grabados de Piranesi.

Cette piscine se trouve dans une oliveraie devenue jardin privé. Les oliviers ont été conservés ainsi que la suite de plates-formes que limitent des murets de ciment. Du gazon a été planté, transformant les anciens champs de culture sèche en jardins irrigués. Au centre d'une plate-forme figure la piscine, presque alignée dans la même direction que les murets qui divisent les plates-formes. À l'une de ses extrémités, un demi-cercle se dessine, offrant des escaliers qui permettent d'y descendre. Une pergola a été construite à une extrémité de la plate-forme. Sur un côté, camouflée par un mur de soutènement, se trouve une petite chambre de service. Le rythme des piliers évoque les constructions classiques et la plante grimpante qui escalade les colonnes pour s'enrouler autour des poutres évoque les images de Piranesi.

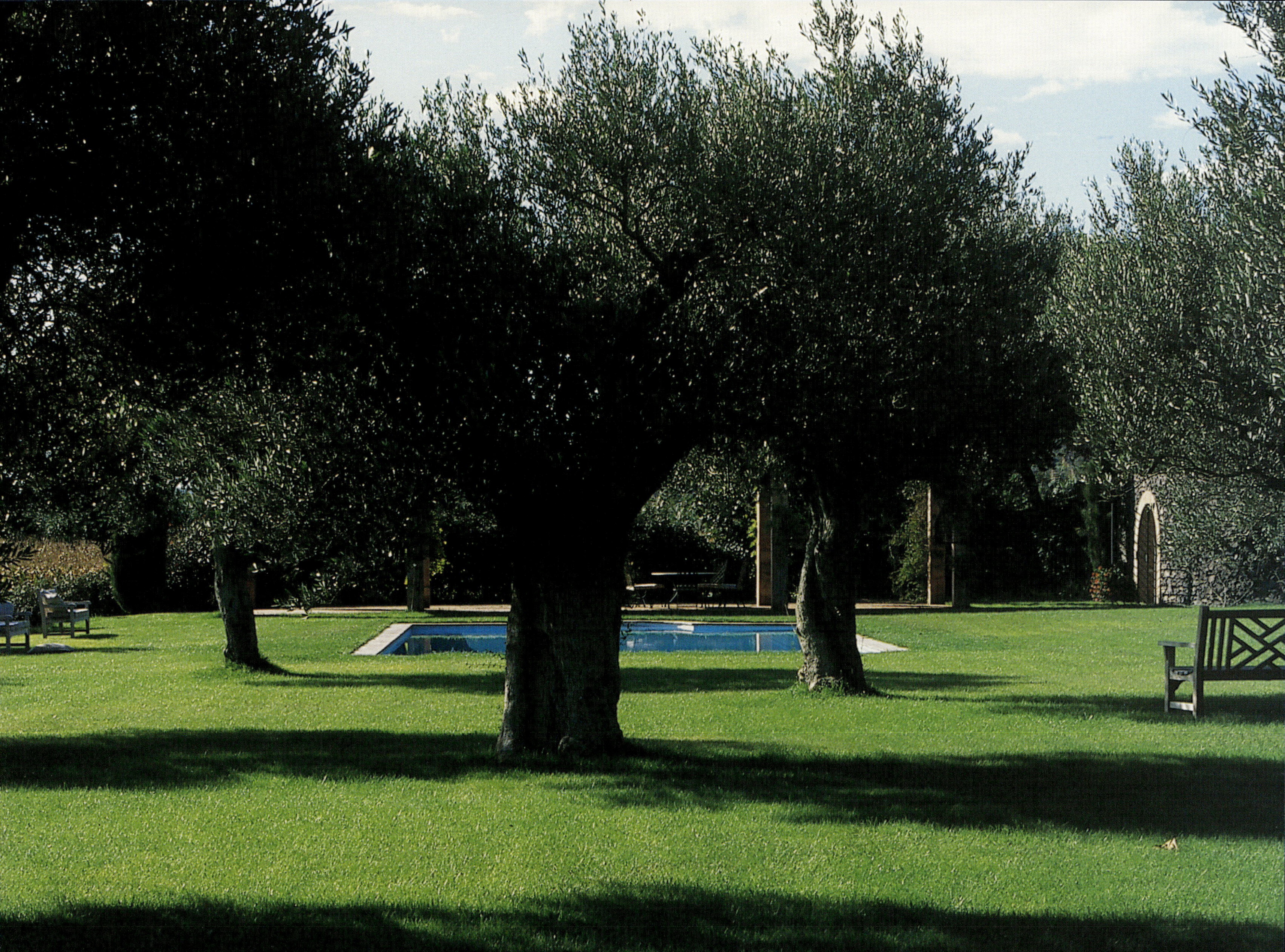

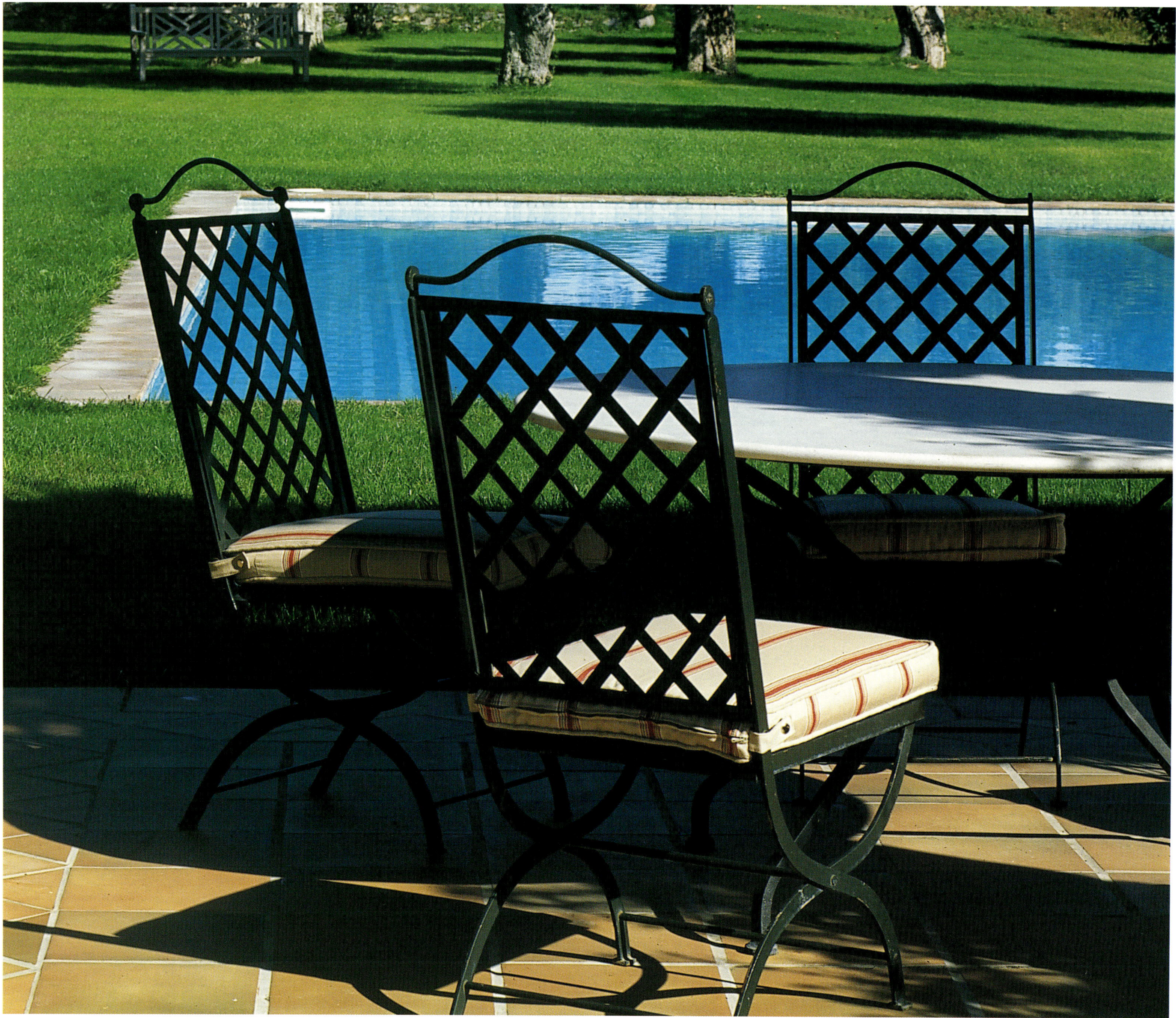

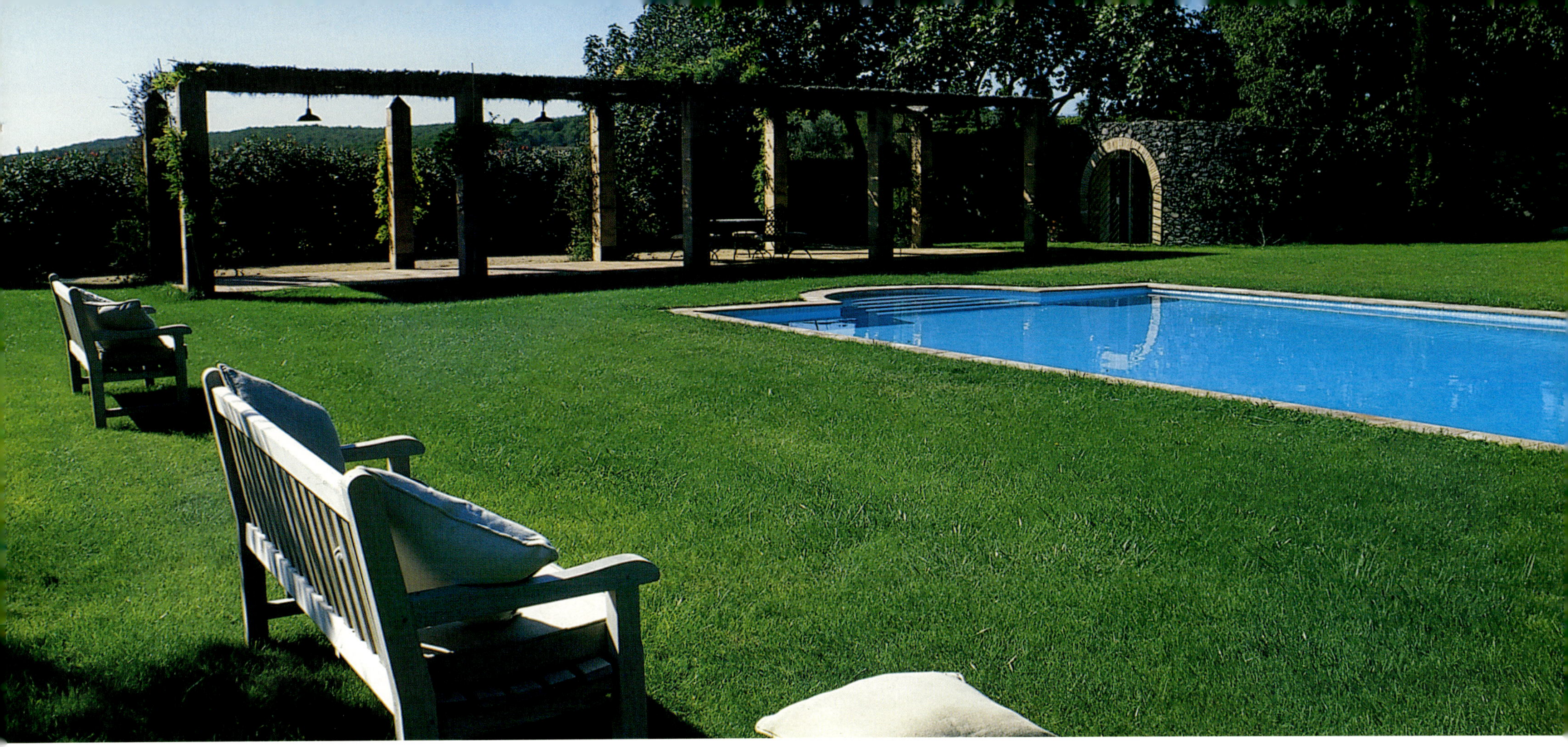

The pool is covered with white mosaic tiles, and a narrow strip of surrounding terracotta tiles separates it from the grass.

La piscina se ha revestido con mosaico blanco. Alrededor de la misma, una estrecha franja construida con baldosas de terracota separa el agua del césped.

Das Schwimmbecken wurde mit weißen Mosaikfliesen verkleidet. Ein schmaler Streifen aus Terrakottafliesen trennt das Wasser vom Rasen.

La piscine a été revêtue de mosaïque blanche. Tout autour, une frise étroite composée de carreaux en terre cuite sépare l'eau de la pelouse.

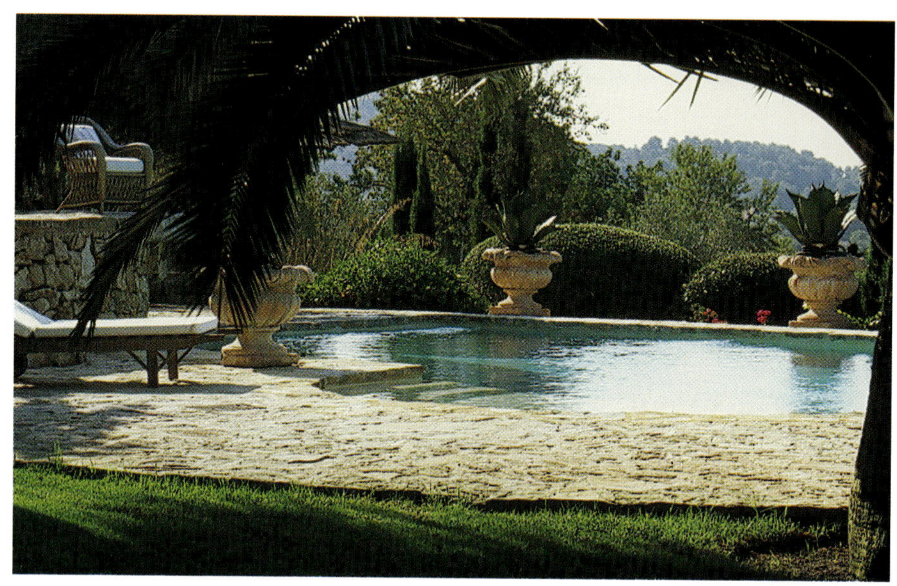

The Privilege of a Secluded Hideaway

El privilegio de la intimidad | Das Privileg der Intimität | Le privilège de l'intimité

In this space a microclimate, which is ideally suited for enjoying life in the country, was created. When the landscape artist fashions a landscape he makes use of the topographic elements there, the plant species and the vistas, to fashion the finished work as he so desires.
In creating a landscape it also means including real time as one of the variables, given that, the materials used change with the seasons, vary according to the temperature and vary depending on whether it is night or day. This temporal dimension with cyclical variations is basic to landscape architecture and involves the spectator in the experiential process of the project. Nothing remains the same for very long and it is the spectator who is charged with the responsibility of witnessing the variations that are unfolding all around.

Auf dieser Fläche wurde ein sehr günstiges Mikroklima geschaffen, um das Leben auf dem Land zu genießen. Wer eine Landschaft gestaltet, greift auf die vorhandenen topografischen Elemente, die dort anzutreffenden Pflanzenarten oder die sich dem Auge darbietenden Ausblicke zurück und verarbeitet all diese Parameter so, wie er es für angebracht hält. Ein Eingriff in die Landschaft bedeutet zugleich, die zeitliche Wirklichkeit als Projektkoordinate mit einzubeziehen, denn das verwendete Material verändert sich mit den Jahreszeiten, den Temperaturschwankungen, mit dem Wechsel zwischen Tag und Nacht. Diese zeitliche Dimension zyklischer Veränderung ist eine Eigenheit der Landschaftsarchitektur und bindet den Betrachter in den Erlebensprozess der Umgebung ein. Alles ist in Bewegung, und es liegt beim Betrachter, die sich vollziehenden Veränderungen wahr zu nehmen.

En este espacio se crea un microclima muy propicio para disfrutar de la vida en el campo. Quien construye un paisaje utiliza los elementos topográficos que tiene a su disposición, las especies vegetales que allí encuentra o las vistas de las que puede disfrutar, manipulando todos estos parámetros en la medida que cree conveniente.
Intervenir en el paisaje significa también incluir el tiempo real como coordenada de proyecto, dado que el material con el que trabaja cambia con las estaciones, con las variaciones de temperatura, con el día y la noche. Esta dimensión temporal de variación cíclica es propia de la arquitectura del paisaje e implica al espectador en el proceso de experiencia del proyecto. Nada es idéntico a sí mismo durante mucho tiempo y es el espectador el encargado de registrar las variaciones que se sucederán.

Cet espace dispose d'un microclimat tout à fait propice aux plaisirs de la vie à la campagne. Un constructeur de paysage utilise les éléments topographiques qu'il a sa disposition, les espèces végétales qu'il trouve sur place ou les vues qui s'offrent à lui, et manipule tous ces paramètres dans la mesure qui lui semble convenable. Intervenir dans le paysage signifie aussi considérer le temps réel comme une des coordonnées du projet, étant donné que le matériel sur lequel il travaille change avec les saisons, les variations de température, le jour et la nuit. Cette dimension temporelle de variation cyclique, propre de l'architecture de paysages, implique le spectateur dans le processus du projet en tant qu'expérience. Rien ne reste longtemps identique et c'est le spectateur qui est chargé de constater les variations qui se succéderont.

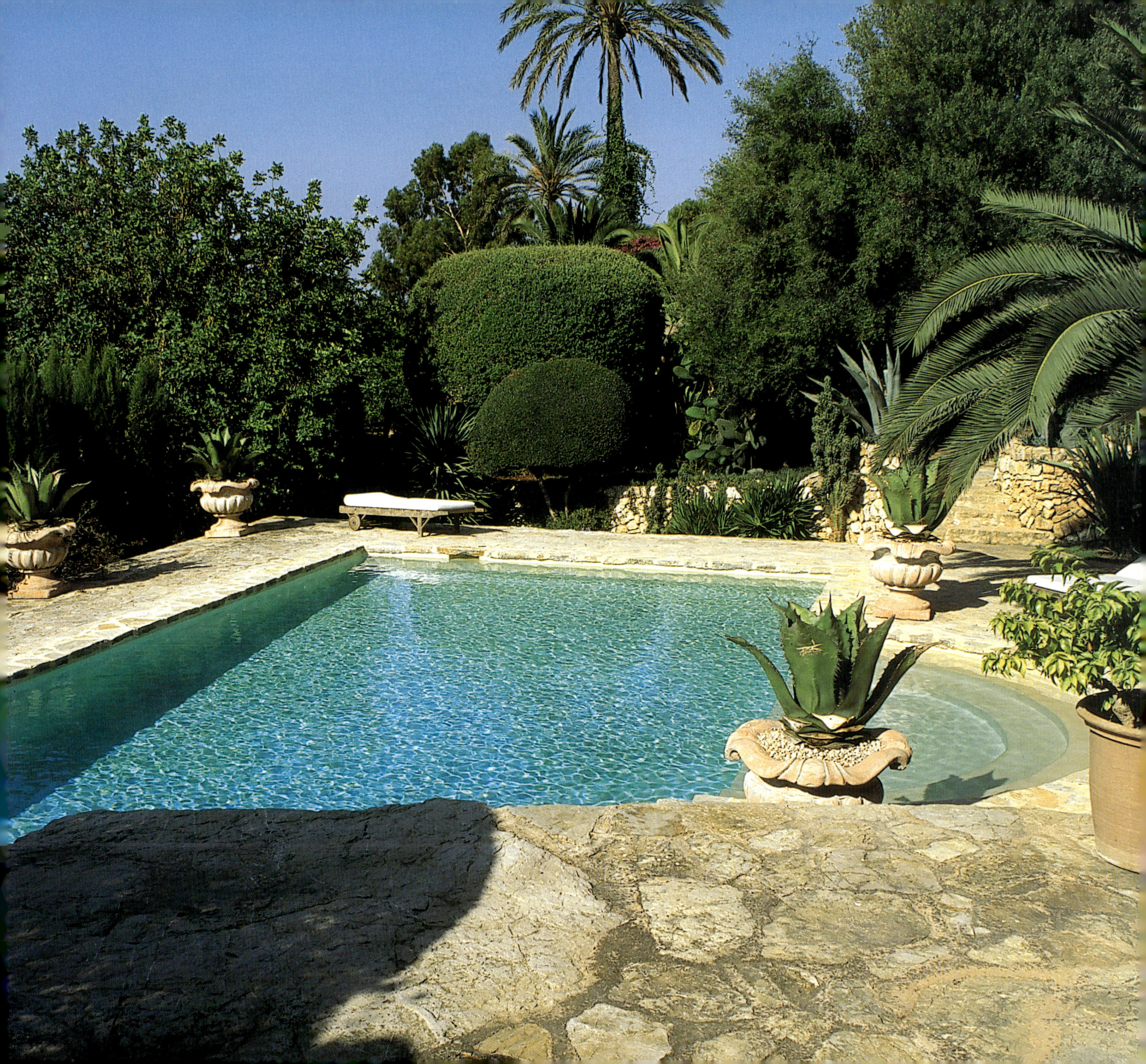

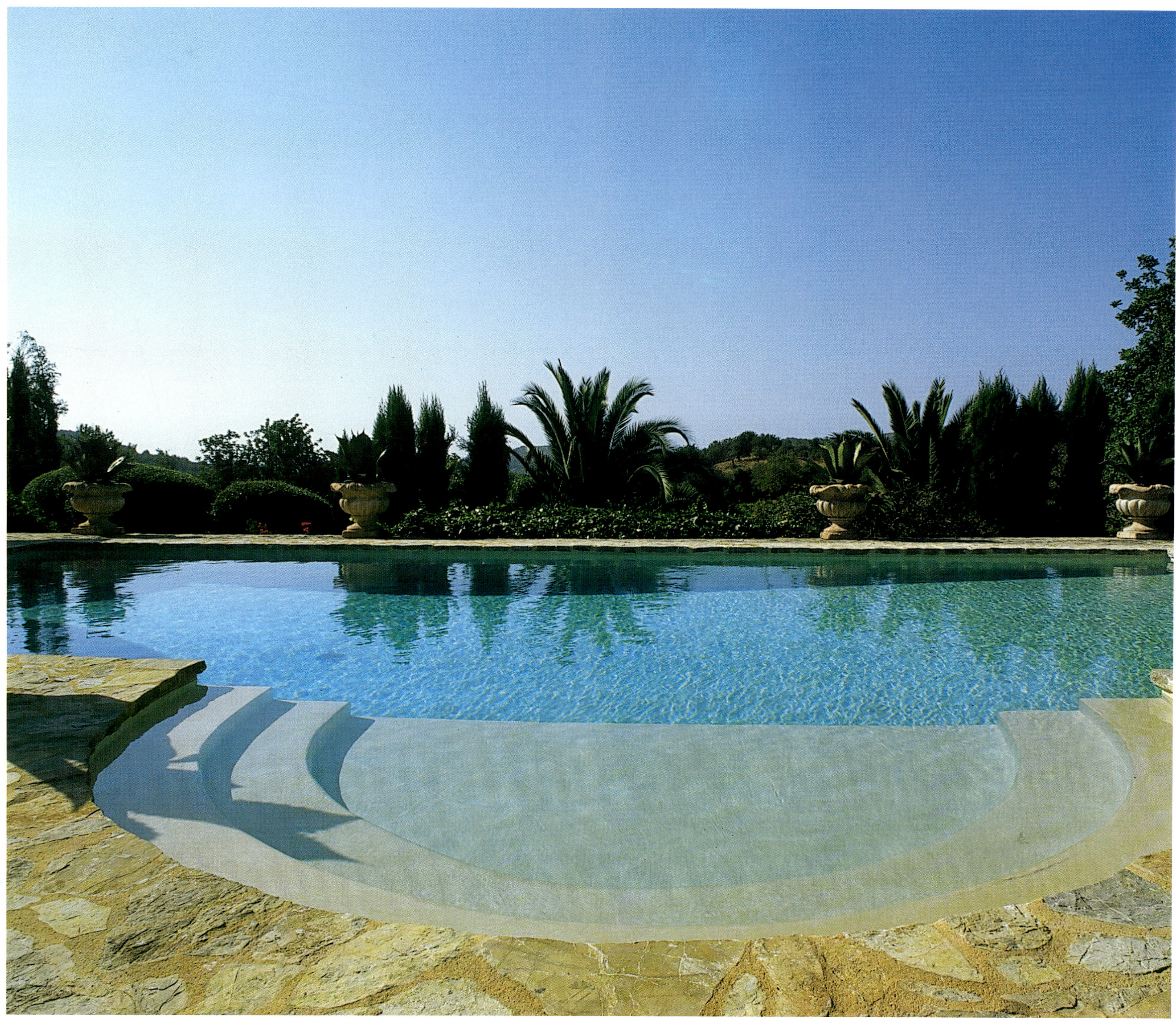

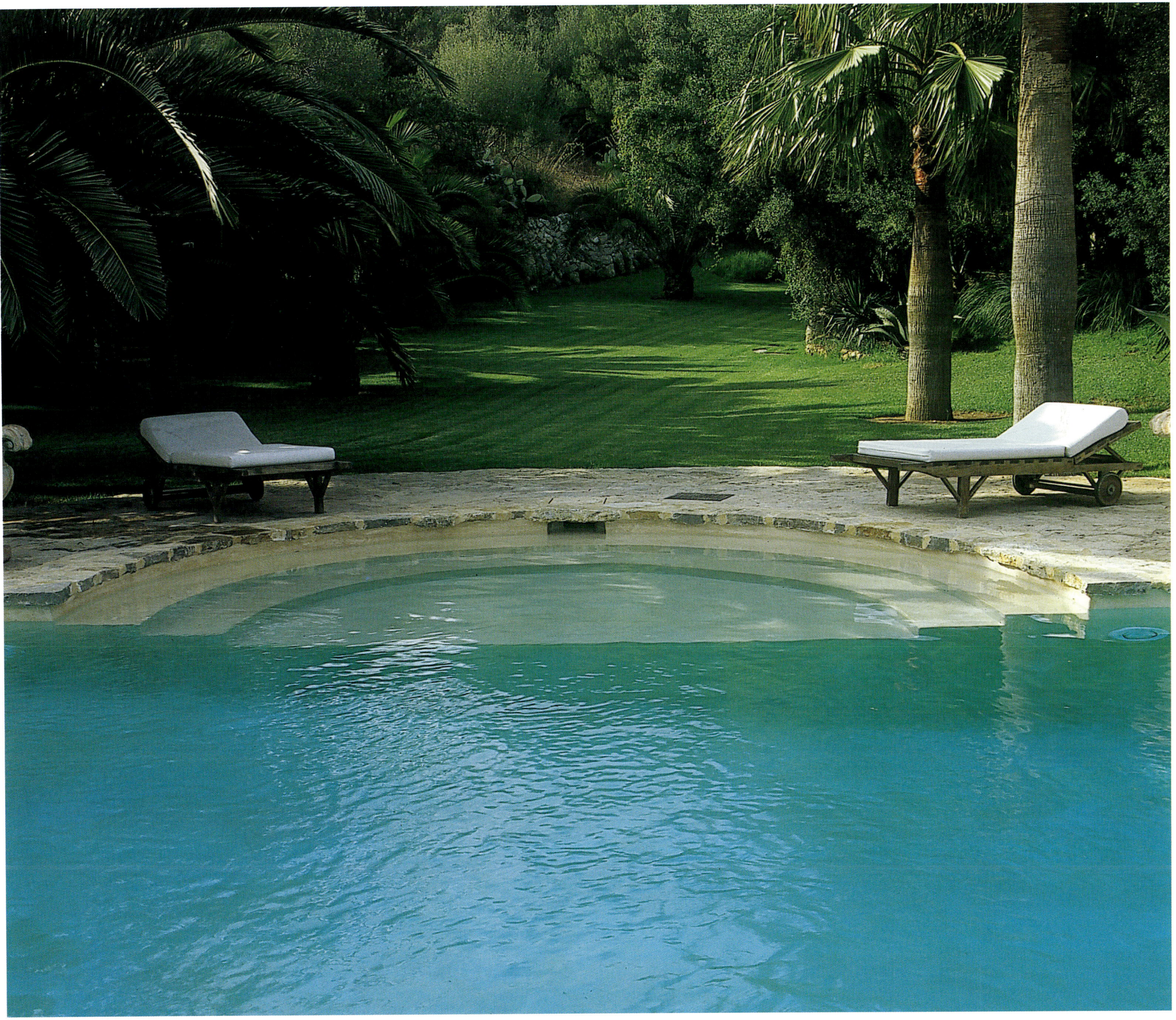

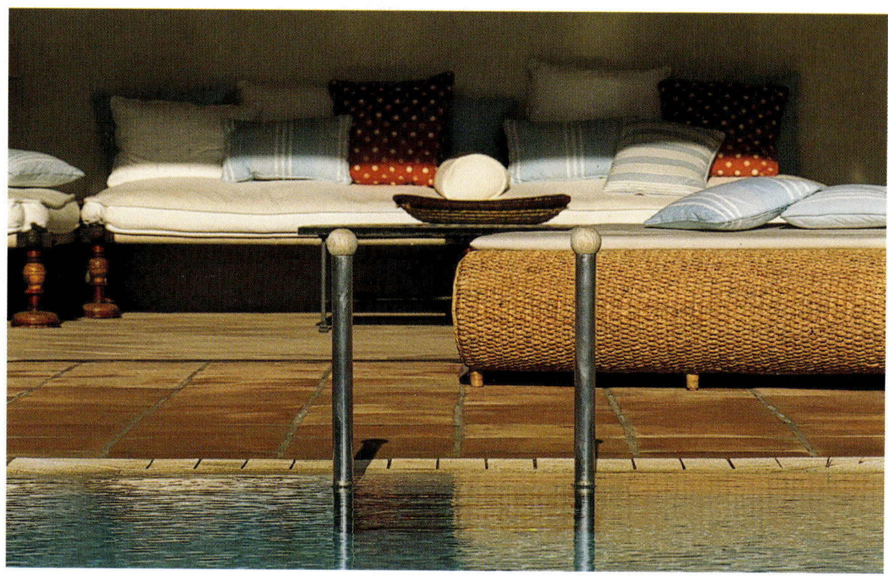

Sophisticated Geometry

Geometria Sofisticada | Ausgeklügelte Geometrie | Une géométrie sophistiquée

Terra-cotta flagstones delimit the geometric shape of the pool. Another strip, made of embossed marble stones made with lime and pigments, leads into the carpet of blue which is the swimming pool, thanks to the light blue mosaic tiles lining it. Underwater steps run the length of the narrowest part of the pool. Opposite these are narrower steps made of stainless steel that are framed by austere parallel poles topped by round wooden handrests. After a refreshing dip, one may retire to the porch, crowned with a dome, which is attached to the house.

Un perfil de losas de terracota dibuja la geométrica forma de la piscina. Otra franja, esta vez de mármol repujado –material obtenido a partir de mármol mezclado con cal y pigmentos-, da paso a una alfombra de agua de una tonalidad azul intenso que se consigue al revestir el fondo y el interior de la piscina con gresite azul claro. La parte más estrecha de la piscina, se aprovecha para situar unas escaleras sumergidas que recorren todo el espacio disponible. Justo encarada a ellas se ha instalado otra escalera más estrecha de acero inoxidable. Esta se materializa en dos austeras barras paralelas rematadas con una pieza redonda de madera. Una vez se ha disfrutado del agua, uno se puede abandonar en el porche, coronado por una cúpula y anexo a la casa principal.

Ein Band von Terrakottafliesen beschreibt die geometrische Form des Schwimmbeckens. Ein anderer Streifen aus getriebenem Marmor – einem durch Mischen von Marmor mit Kalk und Farbstoffen gewonnenen Material – bildet den Übergang zu einem Wasserteppich in intensivem Blau, das durch die Verkleidung des Bodens und des Beckeninneren mit hellblauer Glaskeramik hervorgerufen wird.
Die eine Seite des Schwimmbeckens wurde für eine bis ins Wasser reichende Treppe genutzt, die den gesamten zur Verfügung stehenden Raum einnimmt. Ihr genau gegenüber findet sich eine schmale Leiter aus Edelstahl. Diese besteht aus zwei schlichten parallelen Stangen mit einem runden Holzstück als Abschluss. Nach dem erfrischenden Bad lädt ein zum Hauptgebäude gehörender und von einer Kuppel gekrönter Vorbau zur Entspannung ein.

Un contour de dalles en terre cuite dessine la forme géométrique de la piscine. Une autre bordure, cette fois en stuc à base de marbre – matériel obtenu en mélangeant du marbre avec de la chaux et des pigments – encadre un tapis d'eau d'un bleu intense, obtenu grâce à un revêtement en Gresite bleu clair appliqué au fond et aux parois de la piscine.
La partie la plus étroite de la piscine est pourvue d'échelles immergées qui occupent tout l'espace disponible. En face, on trouve une autre échelle plus étroite, en acier inoxydable : deux barres parallèles austères avec une finition constituée d'une pièce ronde en bois. En sortant de l'eau, le baigneur peut se reposer sous le porche, couronné d'une coupole et annexe à la maison principale.

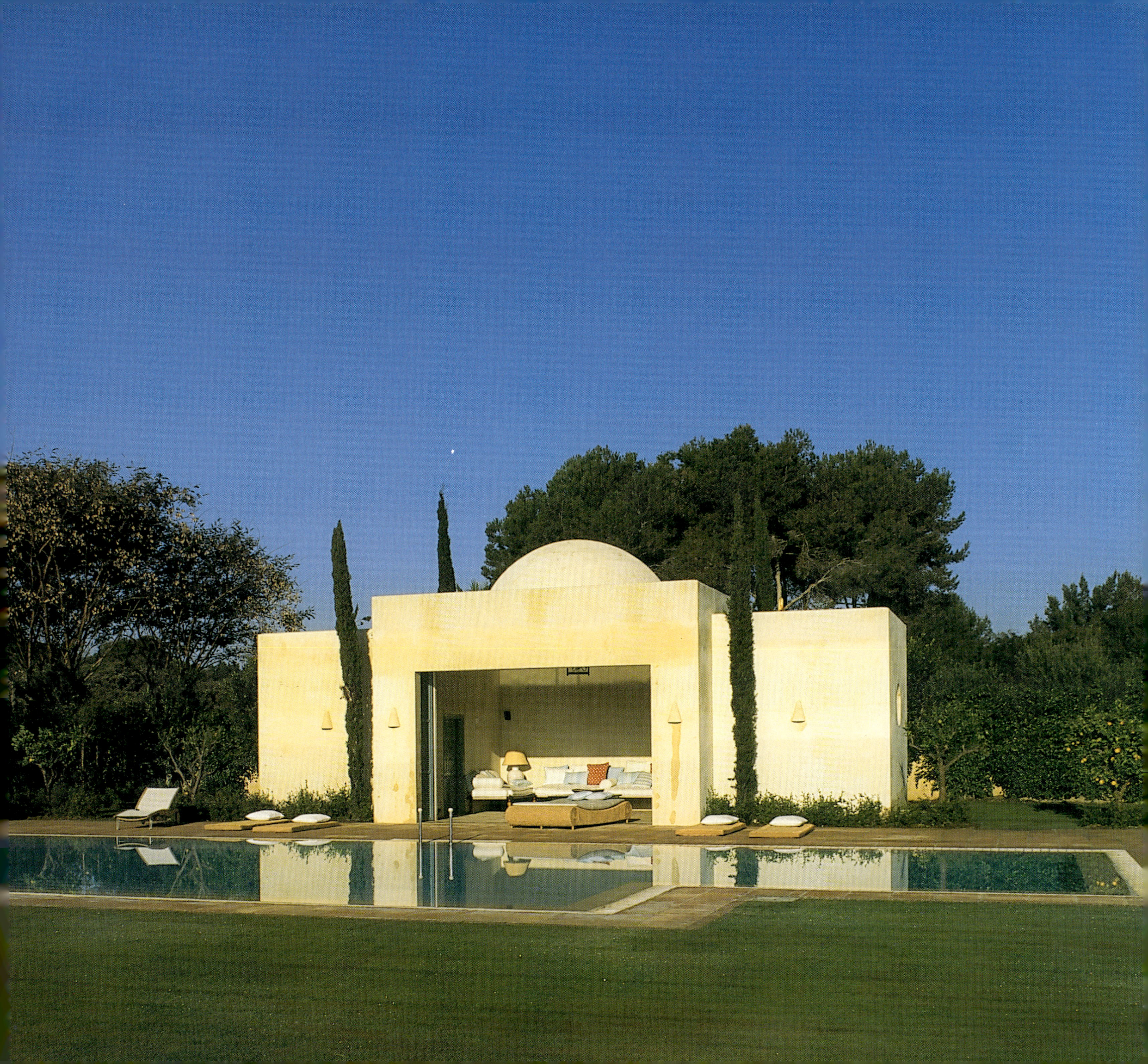

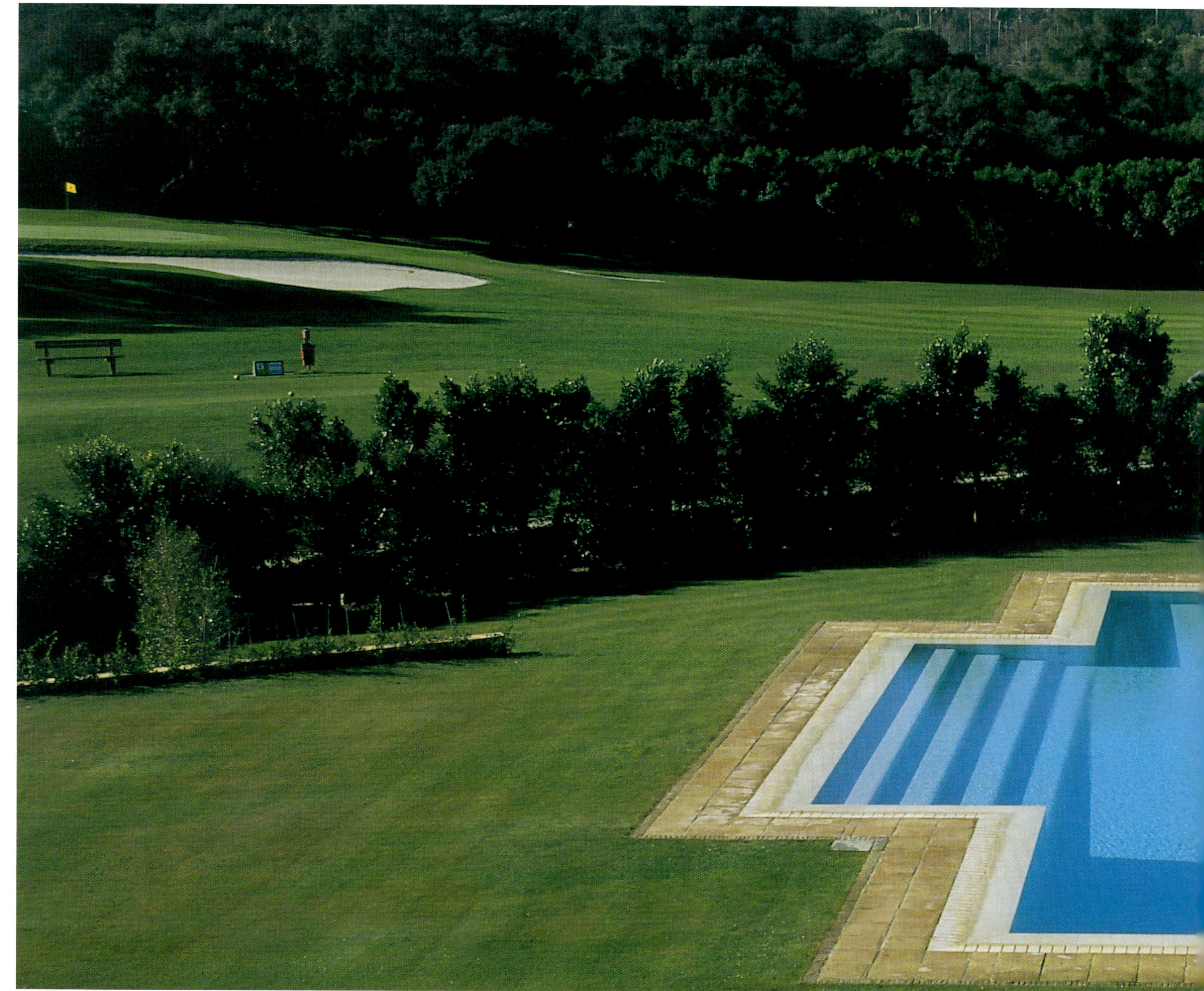

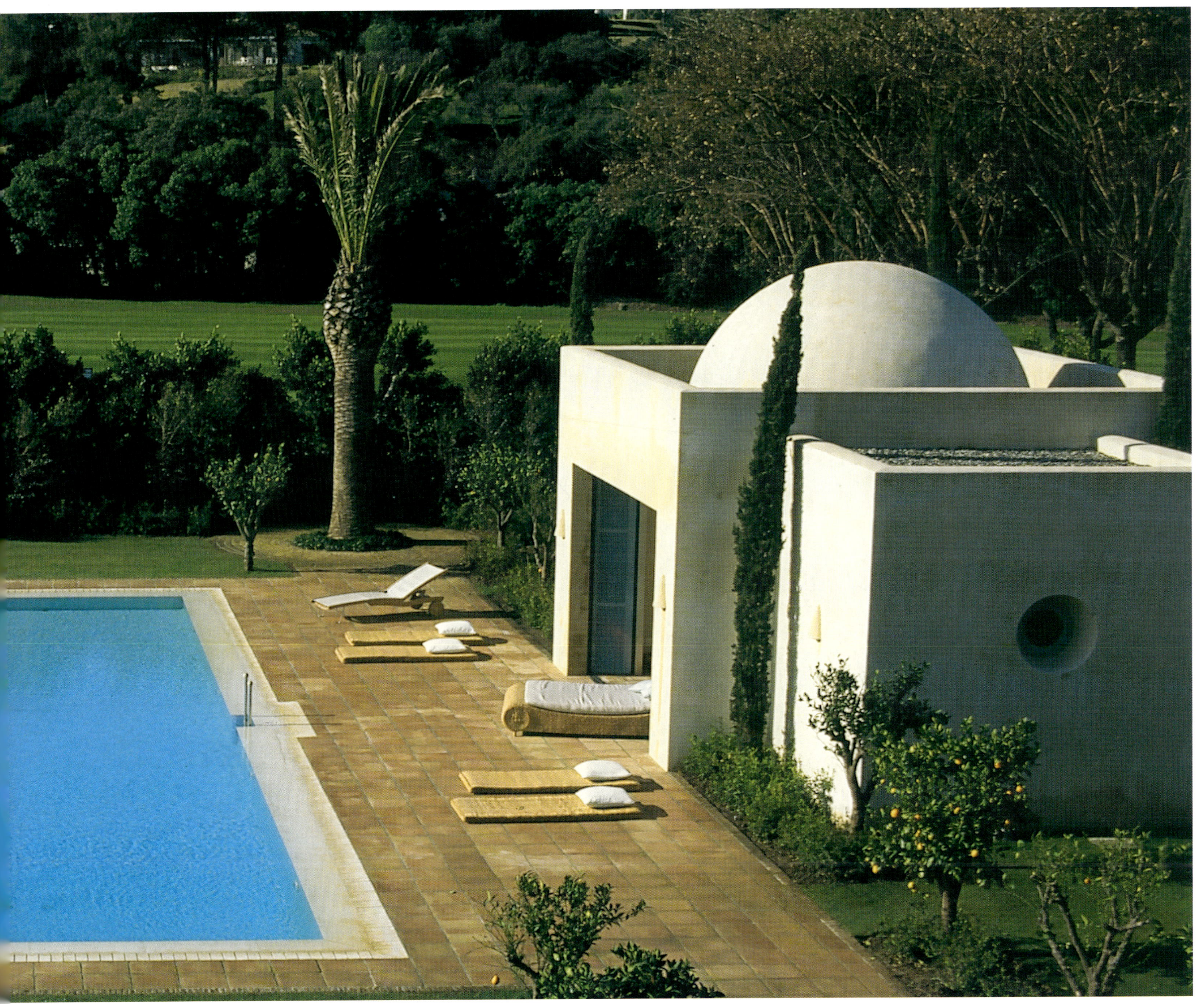

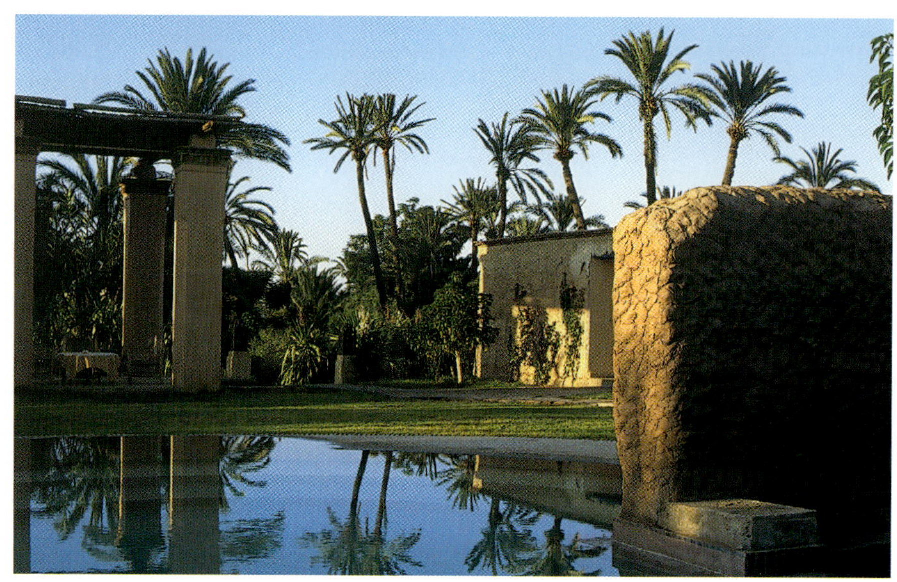

THE VALUE OF THE PAST

EL VALOR DEL PASADO | WERTVOLLE VERGANGENHEIT | LA VALEUR DU PASSÉ

This project is located in one of the natural paradises of Morocco, El Palmeral De Marrakech. Some old ruins were transformed into an evocative sculpture that is perfectly integrated with the landscape and the volume of the swimming pool.

The walls were restored with adobe brick, then covered by hand with unbaked adobe, and then coated with plant oils for preservation. A pavilion of sober design presides over the pool. It is united chromatically with the grouping by means of an intense ochre color, the color of the earth, which is also used on the dividing walls. Because adobe is ecological and insulates well in a totally natural way -it keeps the structure cool in the summer and warm in the winter- as of late it is enjoying a strong resurgence.

En este proyecto, ubicado en uno de los paraísos naturales de Marruecos –el palmeral de Marrakech–, se han transformado unas antiguas ruinas en una evocadora escultura perfectamente integrada en el paisaje y en el volumen de la piscina. Las paredes han sido restauradas con ladrillos de adobe, revestidas a mano con tierra sin cocer y finalmente embadurnadas con aceites vegetales como medida de protección y mantenimiento. Un pabellón de estilo sobrio preside la piscina, cromáticamente unida al conjunto por un intenso tono ocre, el color de la tierra, presente también en forma de revestimiento en las paredes divisorias. La recuperación de la técnica del adobe resurge ahora con fuerza por su carácter ecológico y su capacidad como regulador térmico, ya que permite disfrutar de un ambiente fresco en verano y cálido en invierno de una forma totalmente natural.

Für dieses Projekt in einem der Naturparadiese von Marokko – dem Palmenhain von Marrakesch – wurden Teile der alten Ruinen in eine interaktive Skulptur verwandelt, die vollkommen mit der Landschaft und dem Schwimmbecken harmoniert. Die Wände wurden mit Lehmziegeln restauriert, per Hand mit ungebranntem Ton verkleidet und schließlich als Schutz und Konservierung mit Pflanzenölen eingestrichen. Ein schlichter Pavillon steht am Schwimmbecken, das sich farblich durch einen intensiven Ockerton – den Farbton der Erde, der auch in den Verkleidungen der Trennmauern präsent ist – in das Ensemble einfügt. Die Wiederbelebung der Lehmziegeltechnik hat wegen ihes ökologischen Charakters und der wärmeregulierenden Eigenschaften einen neuen Impuls erhalten – sie sorgt auf ganz natürliche Weise für Frische im Sommer und Wärme im Winter.

Dans ce projet situé dans un des paradis naturels du Maroc - la palmeraie de Marrakech - d'anciennes ruines ont été transformées en une sculpture évocatrice qui s'intègre parfaitement dans le paysage et dans l'unité de la piscine. Les murs ont été restaurés en utilisant de la brique crue : chaque brique a été recouverte manuellement de terre non cuite, puis badigeonnée d'huiles végétales dans un souci de protection et d'entretien. Un pavillon au style sobre préside la piscine, unie chromatiquement à l'ensemble par un ton ocre intense, la couleur de la terre, présente également dans le revêtement des murs de division. La réutilisation de la technique de la brique crue ressurgit aujourd'hui avec force en raison de son caractère écologique et de sa fonction de régulateur thermique : en effet, elle offre fraîcheur en été et chaleur en hiver de façon entièrement naturelle.

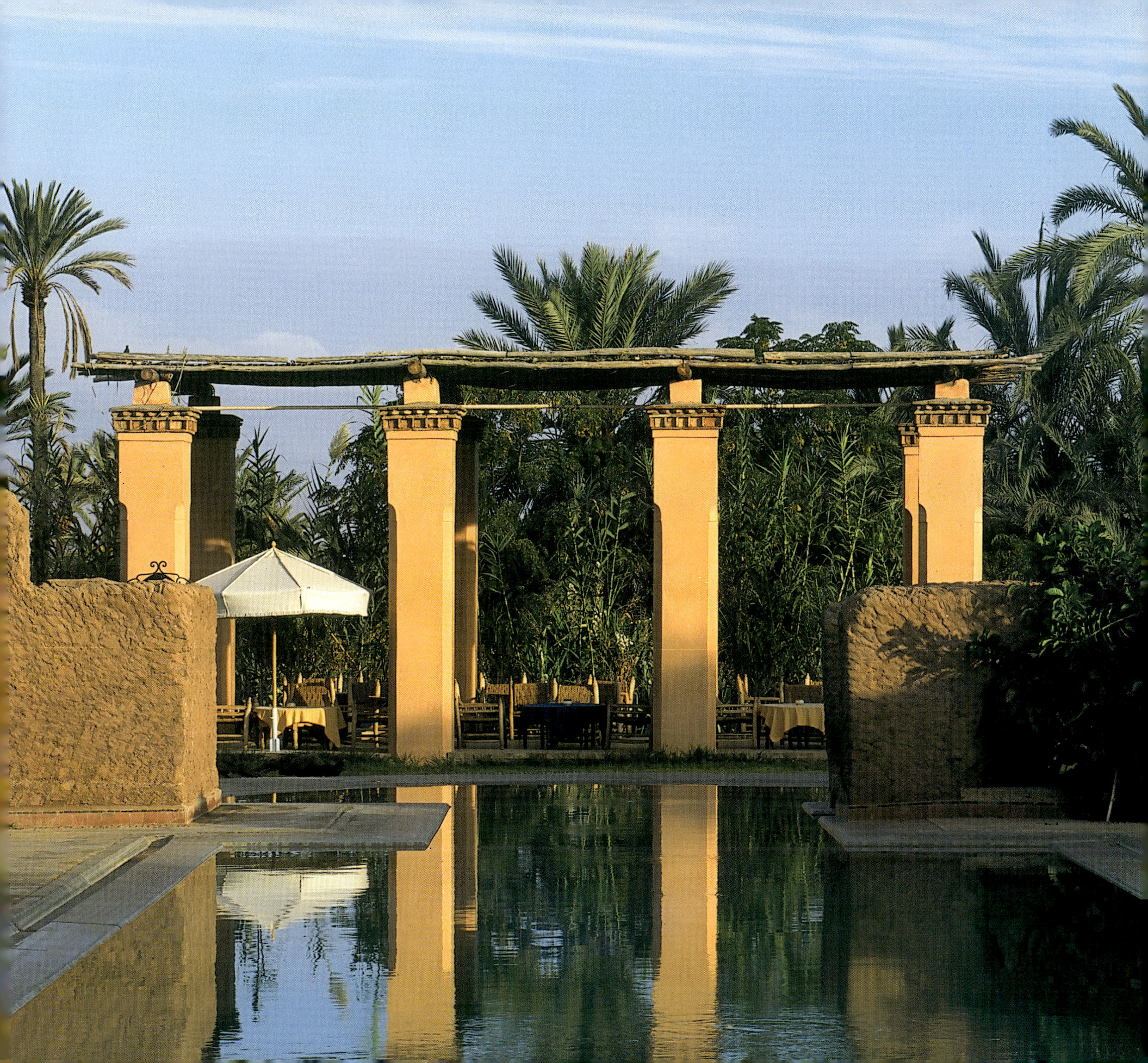

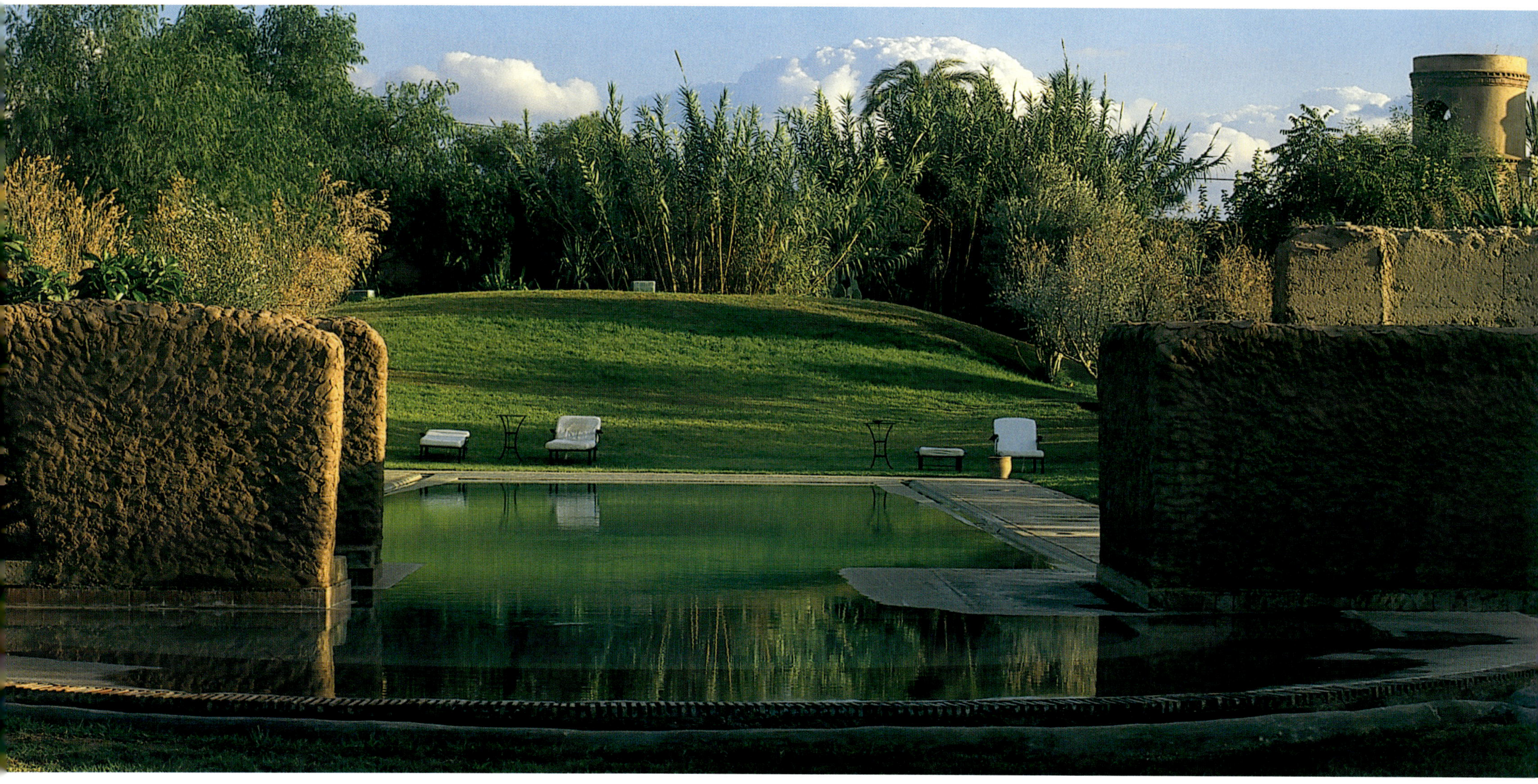

This overview of the pool allows you to appreciate the original stunning effect. The basis of the design of the pool is a series of discontinuous planes, whose central axis is made up of some old ruins that have now been restored and integrated into the project.

Vista general de la piscina, desde donde se puede apreciar el original efecto desbordante. Esta piscina se desarrolla a partir de una sucesión de planos discontinuos cuyo eje central lo constituyen unas antiguas ruinas ahora restauradas e integradas en el proyecto.

Der Blick auf das Schwimmbecken, wodurch der originelle, überquellende Effekt deutlich wird. Das Becken ist eingebettet in eine Abfolge diskontinuierlicher Ebenen, in deren Mittelpunkt alte Ruinen stehen, die nunmehr restauriert und in das Projekt integriert sind.

Vue générale de la piscine montrant l'effet de débordement original. Cette piscine se développe à partir d'une série de plans discontinus dont l'axe central est constitué d'anciennes ruines restaurées et intégrées au projet.

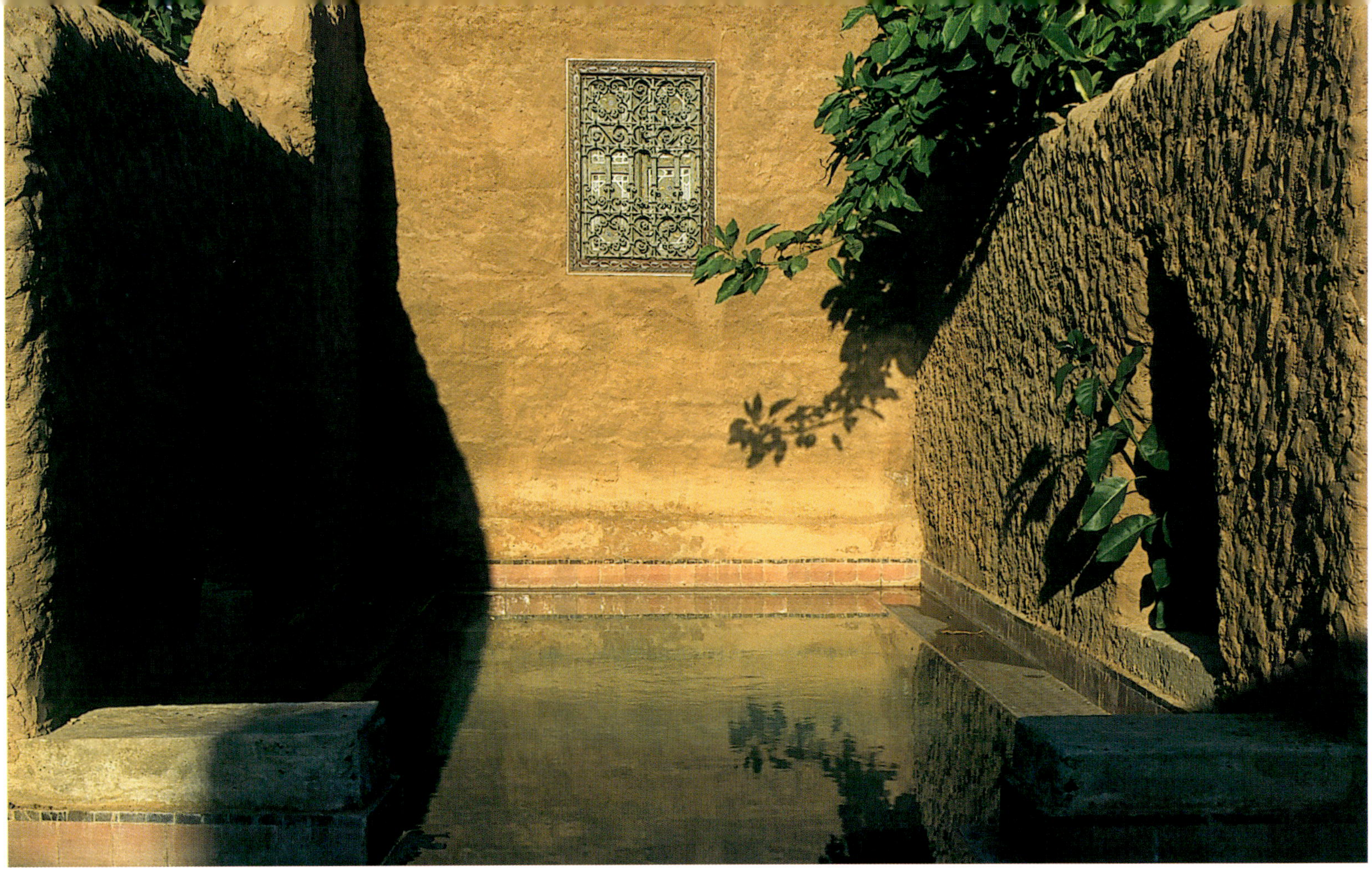

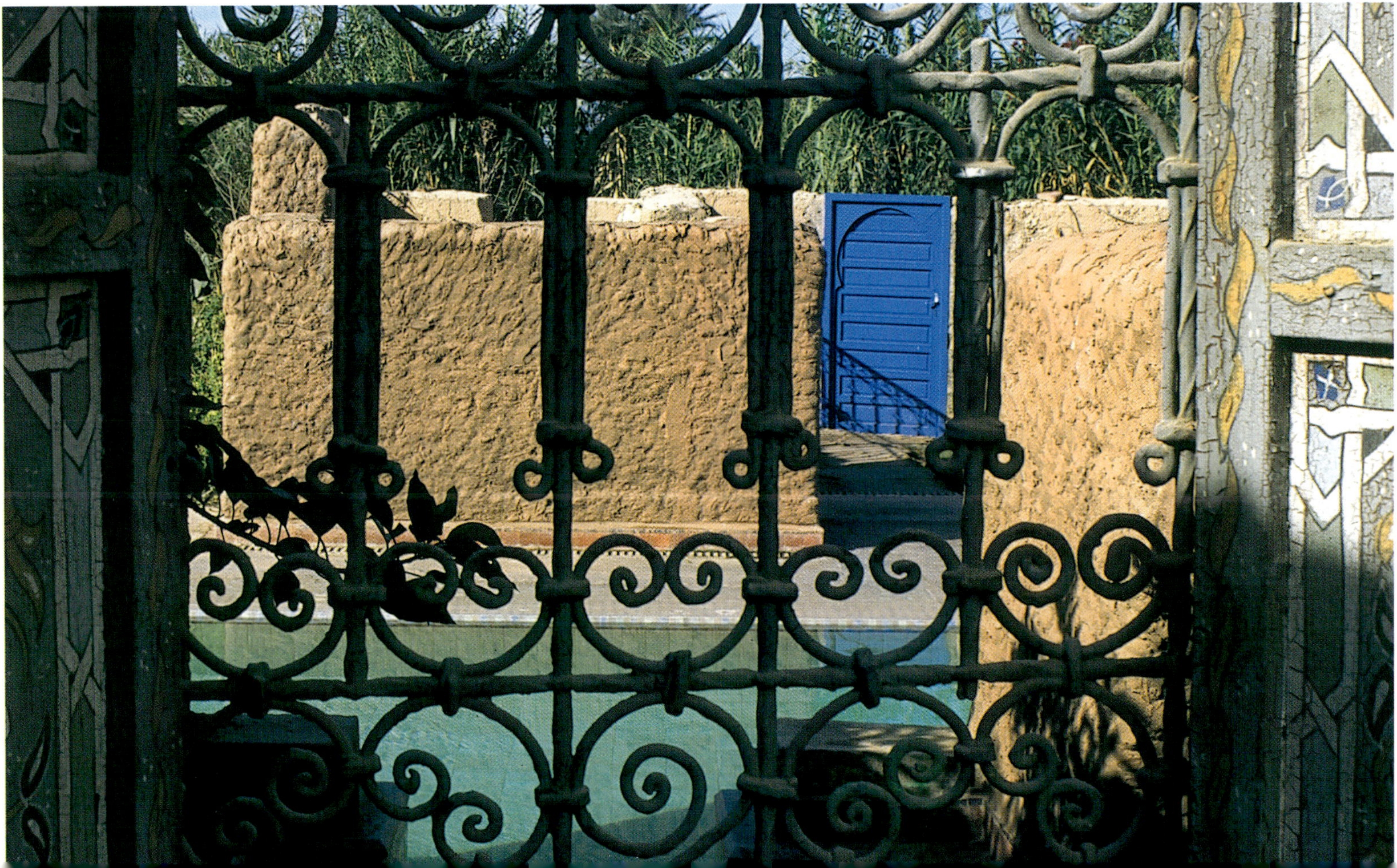

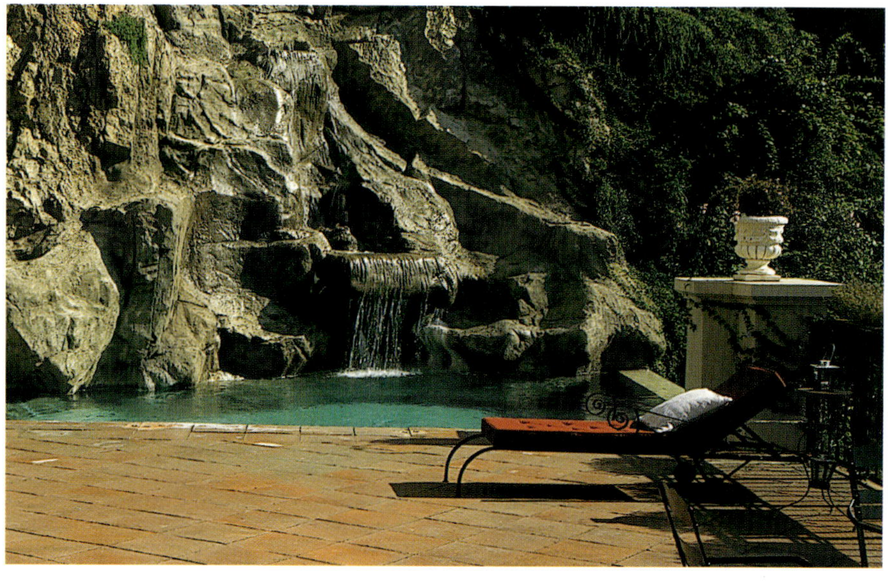

In the Heart of a Quarry

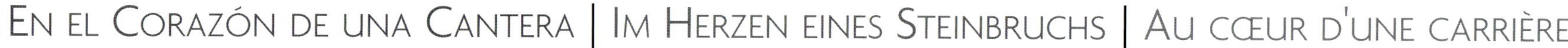

En el Corazón de una Cantera | Im Herzen eines Steinbruchs | Au cœur d'une carrière

This unique pool is tucked away in the rocky wall of an old quarry high on a hill. To attain the perfect harmony of the construction project with the setting, they made use of a recess in the rocky wall. It is an imposing wall that is eroded on one side by water from an artificial waterfall, and covered on the other side by blanket of plant life.
The natural rocky ponds in the high Alps are the source of inspiration for this pool. In keeping with this approach, the rocky wall was left practically intact, even the underwater part. Levels and gradients structure the placement of two extensive terraces paved with fired clay flagstones, whose red color provides a warm note while at the same time accentuating the contrast with the light color of the rock.

En la pared rocosa de una antigua cantera se esconde esta original piscina. Para lograr la perfecta fusión de la obra constructiva con el entorno paisajístico, se aprovechó un hueco natural de la pared rocosa. El resultado es una pared de roca imponente, por un lado erosionada por el agua de una cascada artificial y por otro tapizada por un manto vegetal que mitiga la aspereza de la piedra. Hay que buscar el origen de esta piscina en los estanques naturales de piedra que se encuentran en las latitudes alpinas. A partir de este planteamiento, se ha mantenido prácticamente intacta la pared rocosa, incluso la zona sumergida.
Niveles y desniveles estructuran la ubicación de dos terrazas amplias y pavimentadas con losas de barro cocido cuyo color rojizo aporta una nota de calidez a la vez que potencia el contraste con el tono claro de la roca.

In der Felswand eines ehemaligen Steinbruchs versteckt liegt dieses originelle Schwimmbecken. Zur perfekten Verschmelzung von Pool und umgebender Landschaft wurde eine natürliche Lücke in der felsigen Wand genutzt. So wurde diese mächtige Felsenwand eingebunden, die auf der einen Seite durch das Wasser eines künstlichen Wasserfalls erodiert und auf der anderen durch einen Pflanzenteppich bedeckt wird, der die Rauheit des Gesteins kaschiert. Die Ursprünge dieses Schwimmbeckens gehen zurück auf die natürlichen Wasserbecken aus Stein, wie sie in den Alpen zu finden sind. Auf dieser Basis blieb die Felswand selbst unter der Wasseroberfläche praktisch unberührt. Ebenen und Gefälle prägen den Standort zweier weitläufiger Terrassen, deren Belag aus rötlichen Terrakottafliesen Wärme ausstrahlt und zugleich den Kontrast zu dem hellen Felsen verstärkt.

Dans la paroi rocheuse d'une ancienne carrière se cache cette piscine originale. Pour obtenir cette fusion parfaite entre la construction et le paysage, on a tiré parti d'une cavité naturelle. Résultat : une imposante paroi rocheuse, érodée d'un côté par l'eau d'une cascade artificielle et tapissée de l'autre par une végétation foisonnante qui mitige l'aspérité de la pierre. Il faut chercher l'origine de cette piscine dans les bassins naturels en pierre caractéristiques des latitudes alpines. Grâce à ce principe, la paroi rocheuse est quasiment restée intacte, même dans la zone immergée. Nivellements et dénivellements constituent le cadre de deux vastes terrasses pavées de dalles de glaise cuite dont la couleur rougeâtre apporte une note de chaleur et accentue le contraste avec le ton clair de la roche.

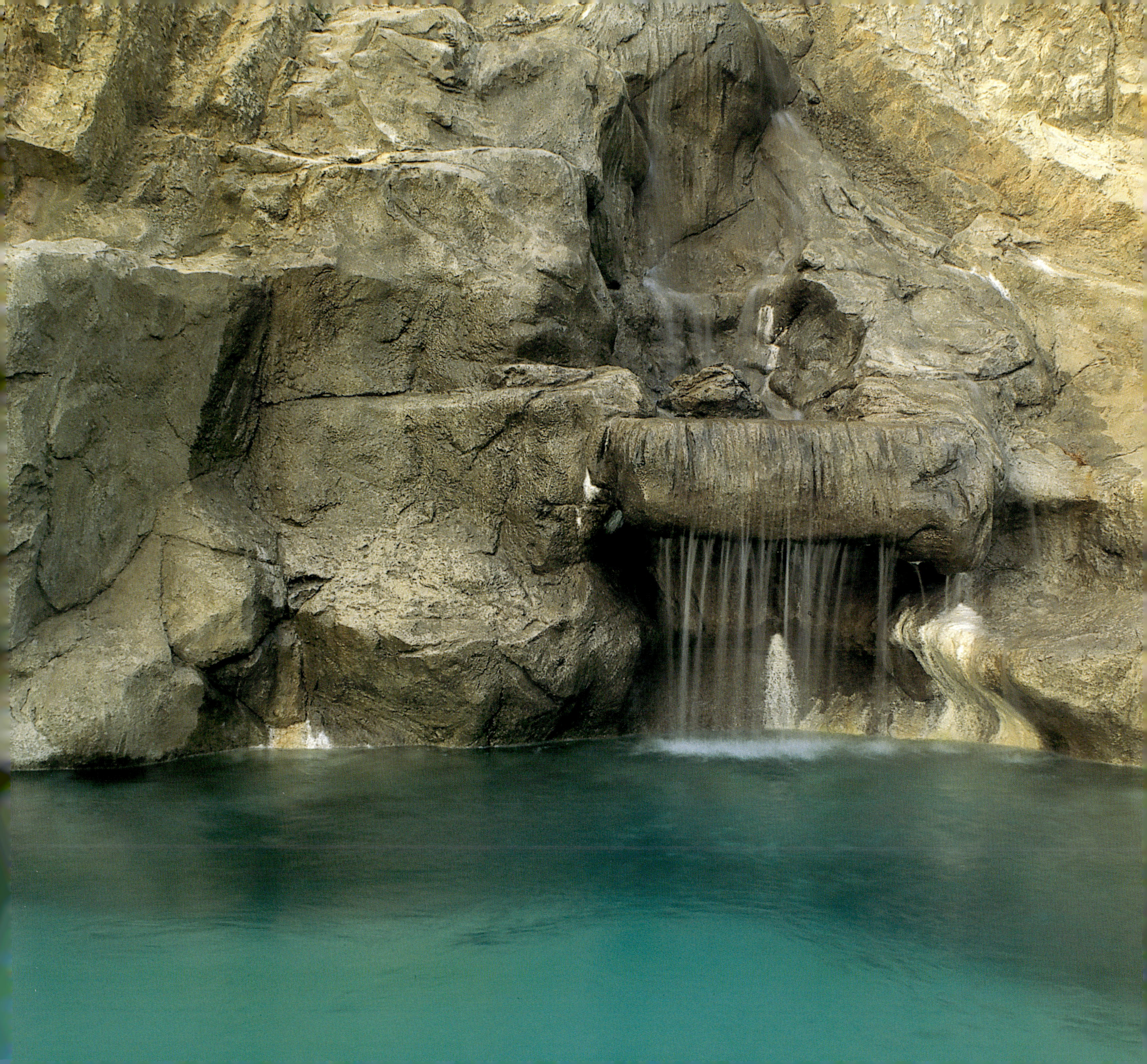

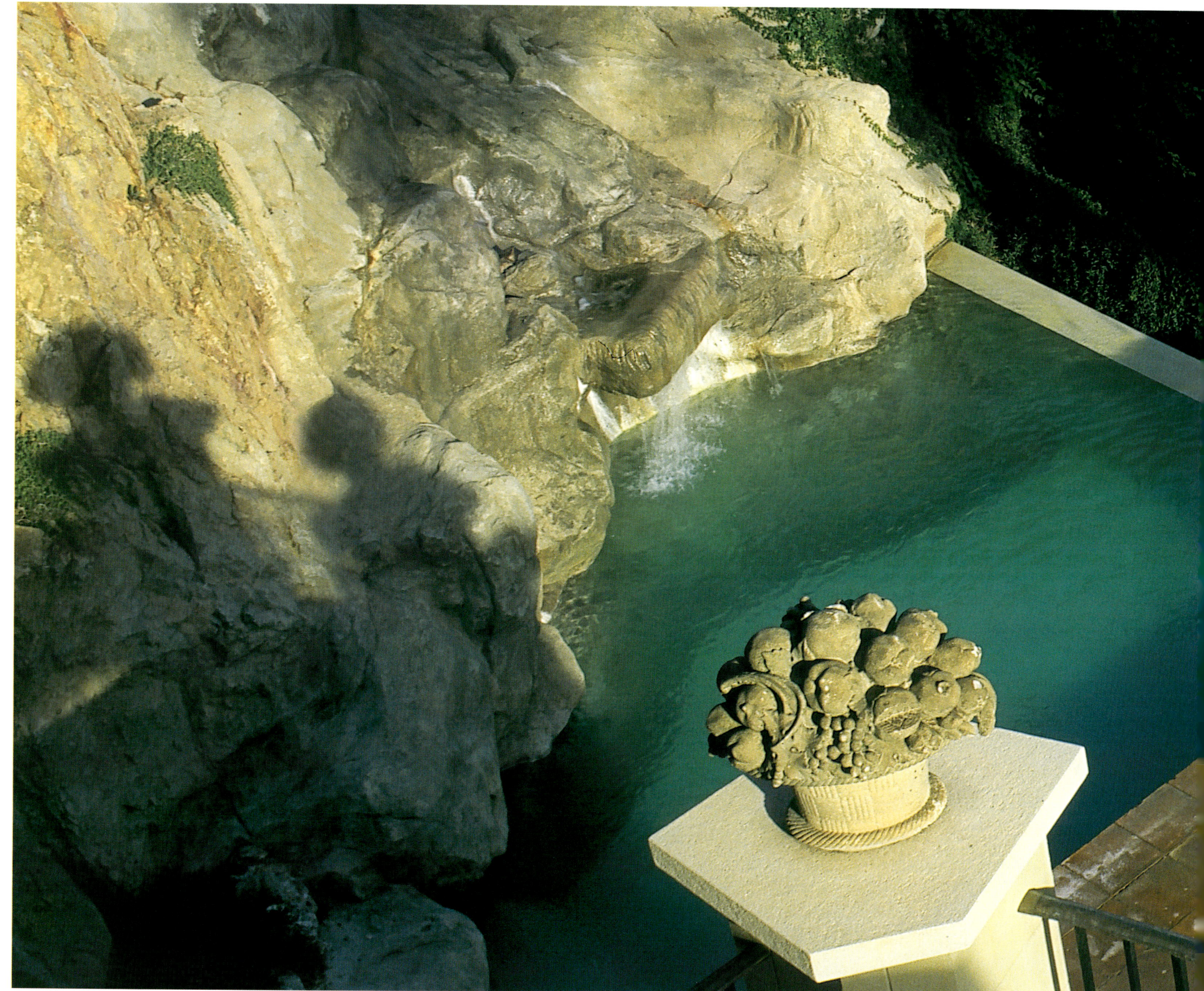

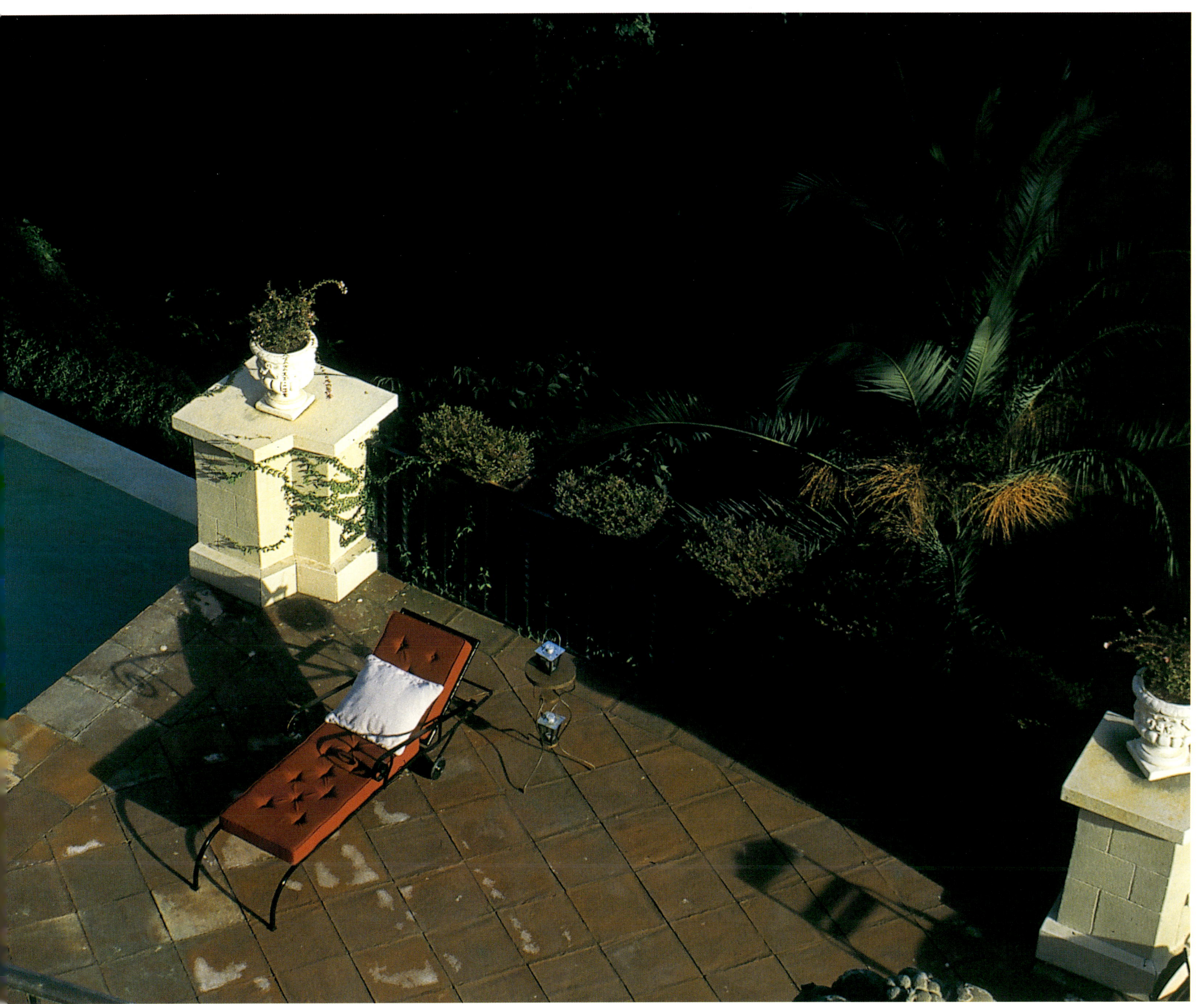

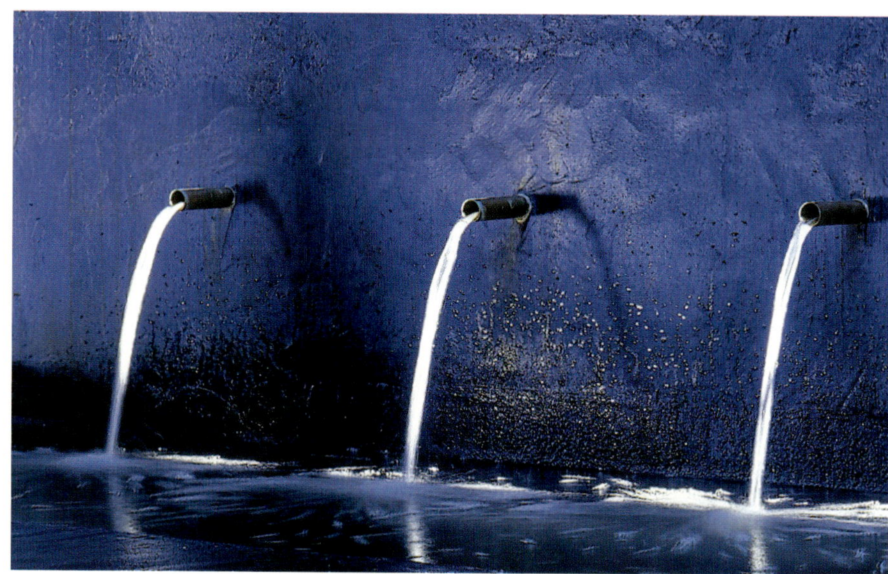

Chromatic Personality

Personalidad Cromática | Persönlichkeit in Farbe | Une personnalité chromatique

Located on the house's semi-covered patio in a restored house, this pool was conceived as a small, cistern-like trough, inspired by old-fashioned washhouses. Symmetrically aligned above the pool, six spouts circulate the water. The chromatic impact of a deep blue has a dual purpose: to soften the soberness of the area and to visually lower the height of the structure. A striking earth color, almost orangish, was the choice for the floor, which grants a clear contrast. A collection of bronze statues at strategic locations around the pool, a painting subtly placed at one end, and the old swinging bench on the upper level, all take on a special prominence which once again is heightened by the presence of color.

Esta original zona de agua se ubica en una antigua hacienda restaurada. Situada en el patio descubierto de la casa, la piscina ha sido concebida como un estanque en forma de alberca inspirada en los lavaderos de antaño. Simétricamente alineados, seis surtidores se encargan de hacer circular el agua. La contundencia cromática de un profundo azul añil tiene aquí una doble función: suavizar la sobriedad de la zona y rebajar visualmente la altura de la estancia. En el suelo se ha optado por un intenso color tierra, casi anaranjado, que resalta en un claro contraste. Una colección de "lindos" –pequeñas figuras modeladas en bronce– situados estratégicamente alrededor del estanque, un cuadro sutilmente ubicado en uno de los laterales, el antiguo balancín del piso superior, adquieren en este lugar un relieve especial potenciado de nuevo por la presencia del color.

Diese originelle Wasserbassin liegt auf einer rekonstruierten alten Hacienda. Das Schwimmbecken im freien Innenhof des Hauses wurde als Wasserbecken in Form einer Zisterne angelegt, die an die Waschplätze von früher erinnert. Sechs symmetrisch verteilte Wasserstrahler sorgen für die Zirkulation des Wassers. Die Kraft der Farbe des hier gewählten tiefen Indigoblaus hat eine doppelte Funktion: die Kargheit der Zone zu lindern und das Wohnhaus weniger hoch erscheinen zu lassen. Für den Boden wählte man einen intensiven, fast ins Orange gehenden Erdton, der einen klaren Kontrast bildet. Eine Gruppe strategisch um das Becken aufgestellter „Lindos", das sind kleine Bronzefiguren, ein intelligent platziertes Bild, der alte Schaukelstuhl aus dem Obergeschoss oder auch die Gruppe von Farnen, die den einzigen pflanzlichen Akzent in dem Ensemble setzt, erlangen hier ein besonderes, durch die entsprechende Farbekombination verstärktes Gewicht.

Cette zone d'eau appartient à une ancienne maison restaurée. Située dans la cour découverte de la maison, la piscine a été conçue comme un bassin en forme de cuve s'inspirant des lavoirs d'autrefois. Six arrivées d'eau alignées symétriquement assurent la circulation de celle-ci. L'impact chromatique du bleu indigo foncé remplit ici une double fonction : adoucir la sobriété de l'endroit et abaisser visuellement la hauteur de l'élément. Dans un souci de contraste, une couleur terre intense, presque orangée, a été choisie pour le sol. Une collection de "lindos" - figurines modelées en bronze – situés de manière stratégique autour du bassin, un tableau subtilement placé sur l'un des côtés, le vieux fauteuil à bascule de l'étage et même le tapis de fougères qui constitue l'unique note végétale de l'ensemble sont autant d'éléments qui acquièrent en ce lieu un relief particulier, que renforce la présence de la couleur.

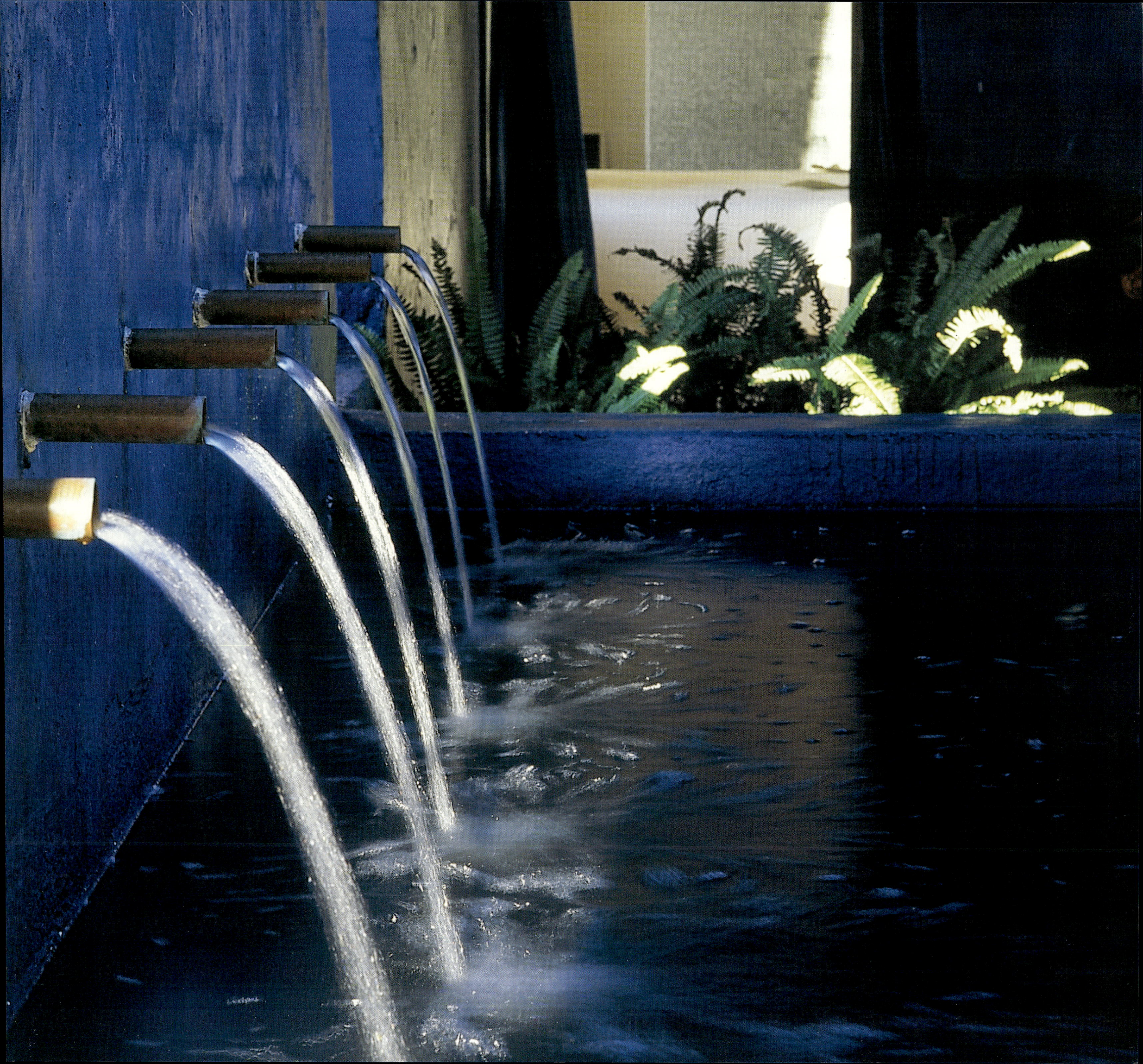

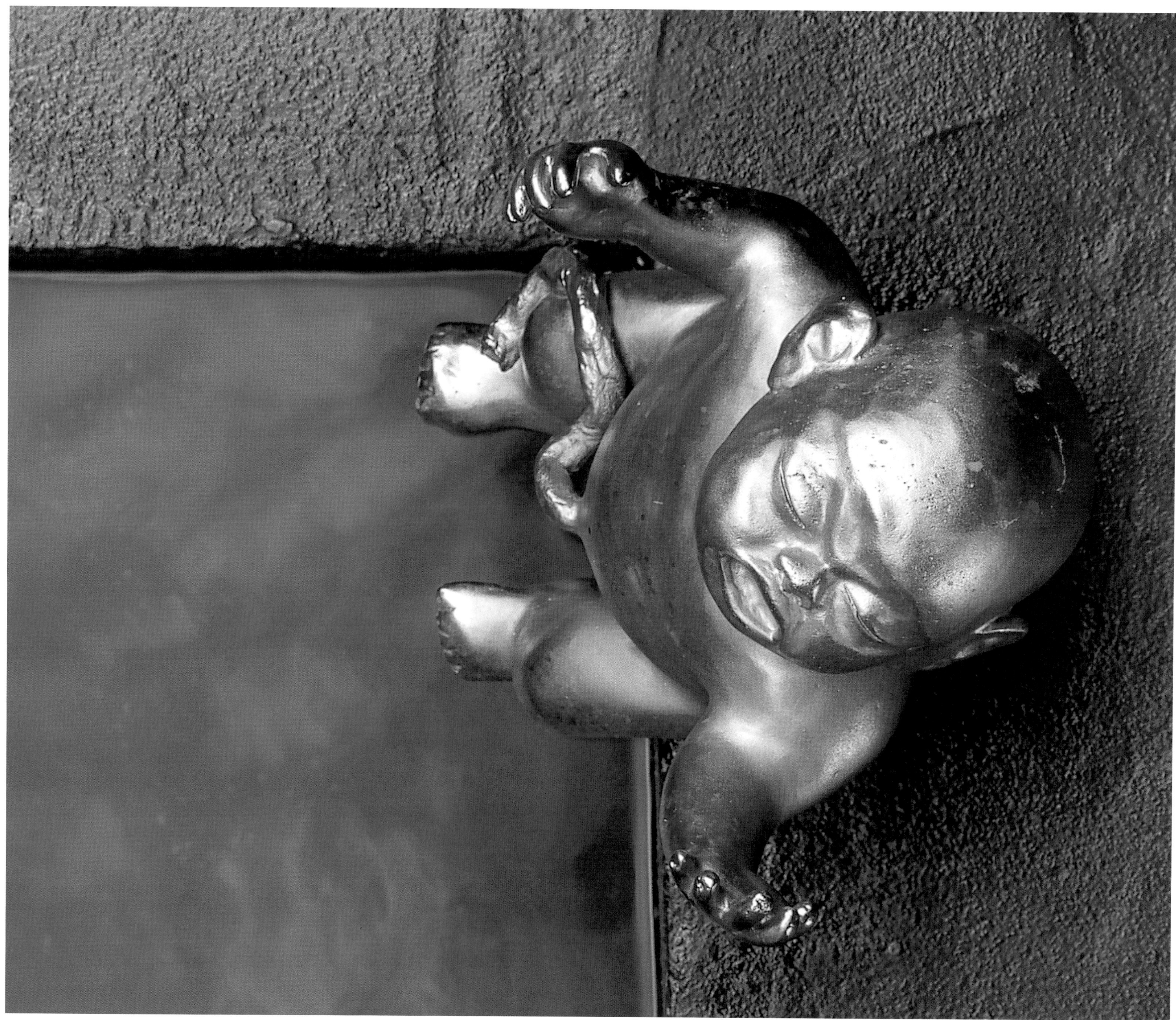

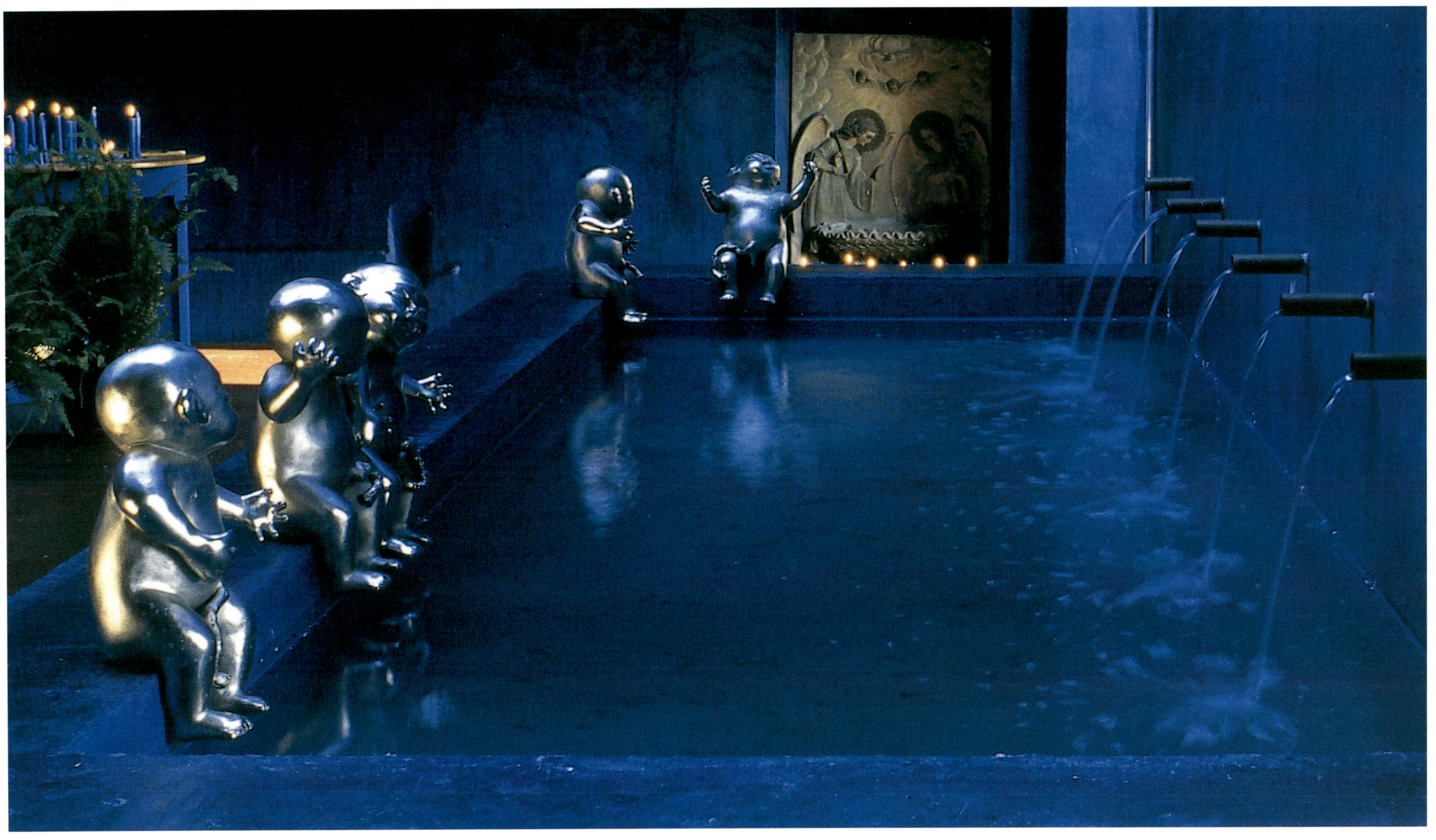

The deep blue pond is made of concrete, which is the same material used for the earth-colored ground. The advantage of this material is that it is easy to maintain and is water-resistant, which is important as this area of the patio is only partially covered.

El estanque, de un intenso color azul añil, ha sido construido en hormigón, el mismo material que reviste el suelo pintado de color tierra y que presenta la ventaja de ser fácil de mantener y es resistente al agua, ya que esta zona del patio está semidescubierta.

Das Becken in kräftigem Indigoblau ist aus Beton, das ebenfalls für den erdfarben gestrichenen Boden verwendet wurde. Letzterer ist pflegeleicht und Wasser abweisend, da dieser Bereich des Hofs nur teilweise überdacht ist.

Le bassin, d'un bleu indigo intense, a été construit en béton, matériau qui recouvre aussi le sol peint de couleur terre. Il présente l'avantage d'être facile à entretenir et résistant à l'eau, cette zone de la cour étant semi découverte.

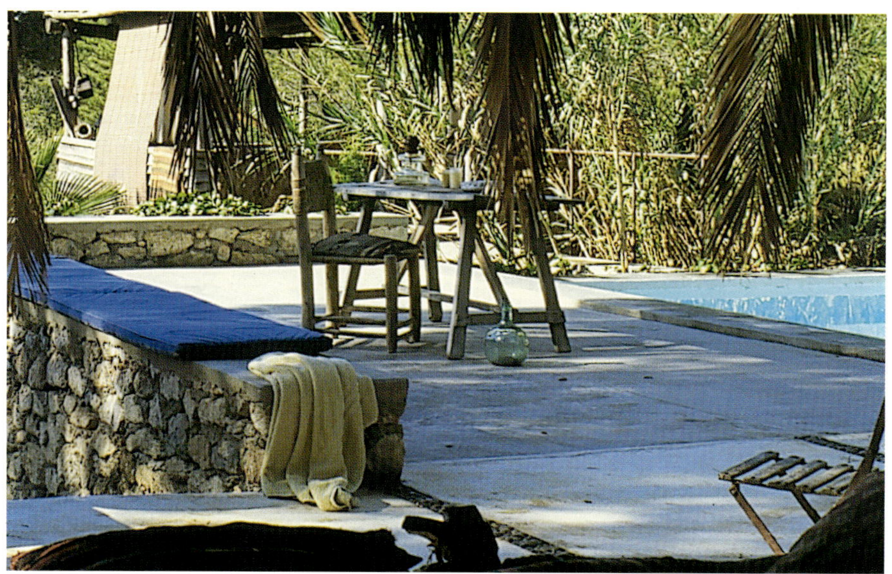

Perfect Blend

Combinación perfecta | Perfekte Mischung | Alliance parfaite

The ensemble affords an attractive place from which to relax and enjoy the surrounding natural wonders of the island of Ibiza. They took advantage of the topographical peculiarities and the swimming pool was designed as a prolongation of the two main volumes: the house and the small annex. It is an elegant rectangle housed in a polished frame whose interior is painted white. The garden surrounding it was laid out so that every element is perfectly integrated, from the shape of the pool to the colors of the furnishings. All of this affords a simple, austere design that highlights the vegetation that surrounds it.

Desde este emplazamiento es posible contemplar los espectaculares paisajes que la isla de Ibiza brinda mientras se disfruta de un baño de sol o de agua. Aprovechando las particularidades topográficas, la piscina se concibió como una prolongación de los dos volúmenes principales: la vivienda y un pequeño anexo. Así, se ha proyectado como un perímetro rectangular perfectamente enmarcado por un pulido perfil que la alberga y remata, y se ha pintado de blanco su interior. El área que envuelve la piscina se ha organizado de manera que todo quede encajado minuciosamente, desde la forma que esta adopta hasta las tonalidades del mobiliario. Con ello se consigue un estilo depurado y austero que permite realzar la vegetación que rodea la piscina.

Von dieser Stelle aus kann man die spektakulären Landschaften, welche die Insel Ibiza auszeichnen, betrachten und gleichzeitig ein Bad in der Sonne oder im Wasser genießen. Unter Ausnutzung der topografischen Besonderheiten wurde das Schwimmbecken als Verlängerung der beiden Hauptbaukörper – des Wohnhauses und eines kleinen Anbaus – entworfen. So wählte man einen rechteckigen Umriss, der durch ein glänzendes Profil perfekt eingerahmt wird, welches das Becken zugleich aufnimmt und abschließt. Das Poolinnere ist ganz in Weiß gehalten. Der das Schwimmbecken umgebenden Bereich wurde bis ins kleinste Detail aufeinander abgestimmt: von seiner Form bis hin zu den Farbtönen des Mobiliars. Das Ergebnis ist ein klarer und nüchterner Stil, der die das Schwimmbecken einfassende Vegetation betont.

Cet emplacement permet de contempler les paysages spectaculaires qu'offre l'île d'Ibiza tout en prenant un bain, qu'il soit d'eau ou de soleil. Profitant des particularités topographiques, la piscine a été conçue comme une prolongation des unités principales : la maison et une petite annexe. Ainsi, elle a été pensée comme un périmètre rectangulaire parfaitement encadré par un contour soigné, à la fois contenant et finition, et son intérieur a été peint en blanc.
L'espace qui entoure la piscine a minutieusement été organisé dans un effort d'harmonie, de la forme de la piscine aux tonalités du mobilier. Il en résulte un style épuré et austère qui met en valeur la végétation entourant la piscine.

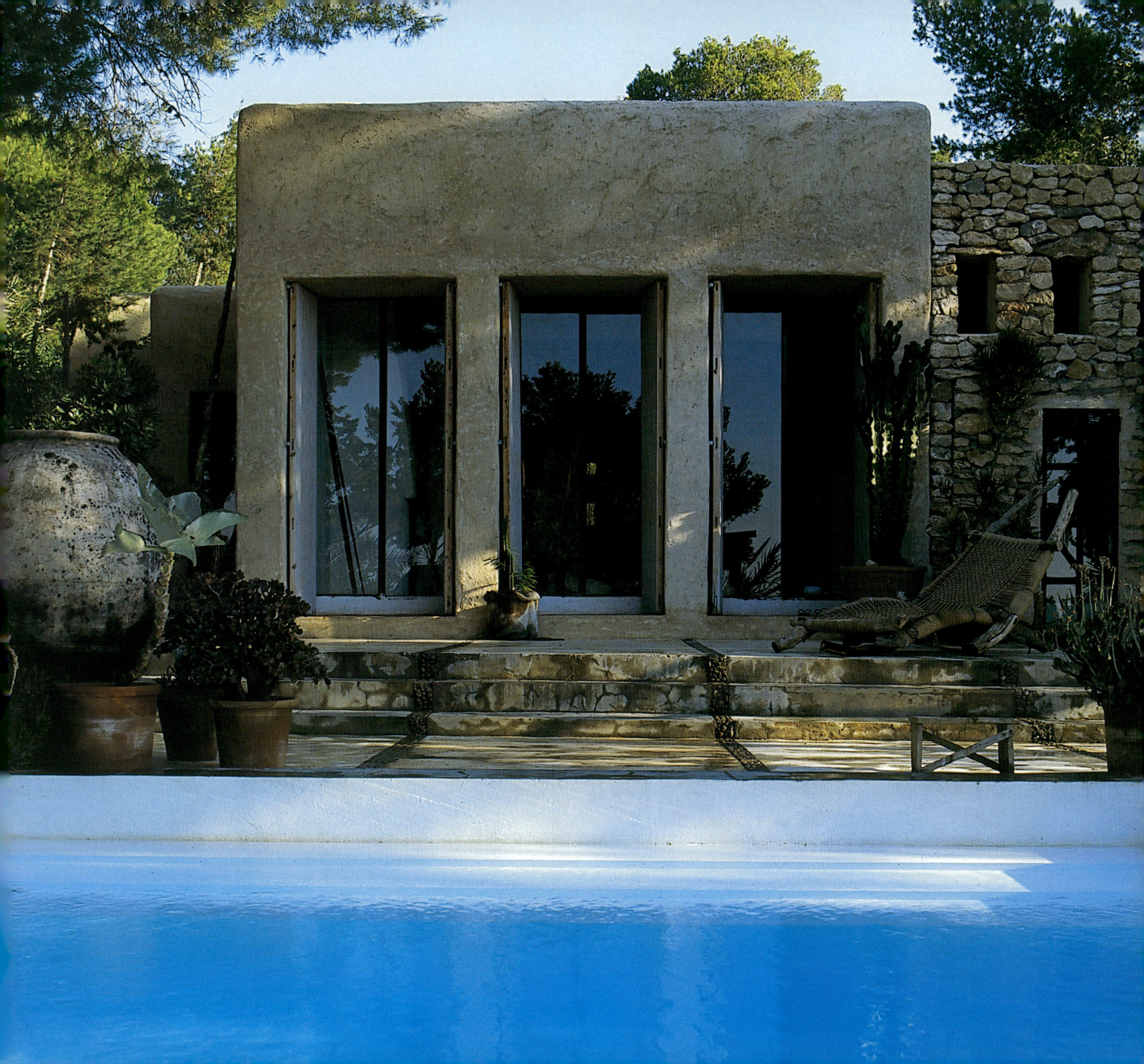

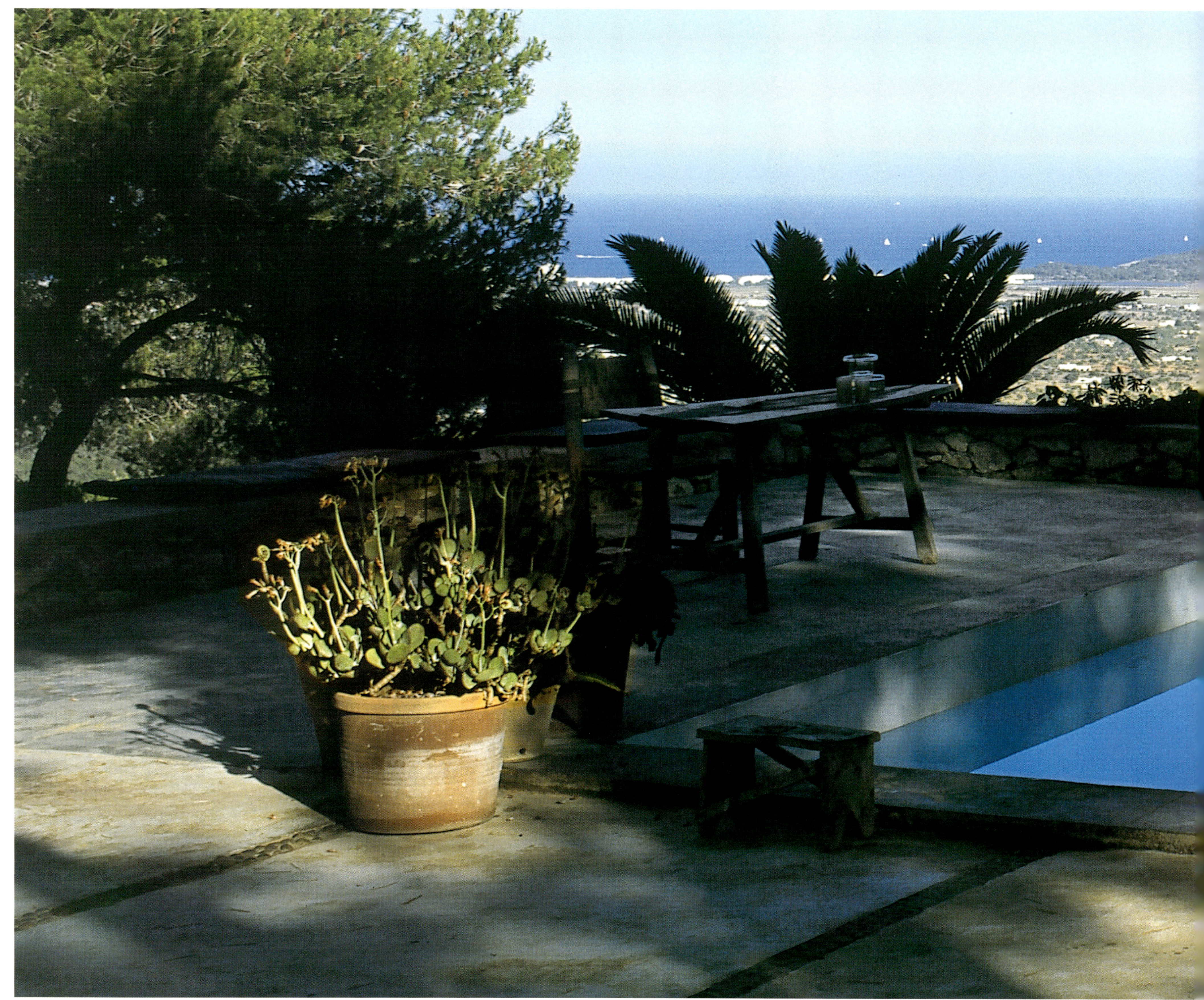

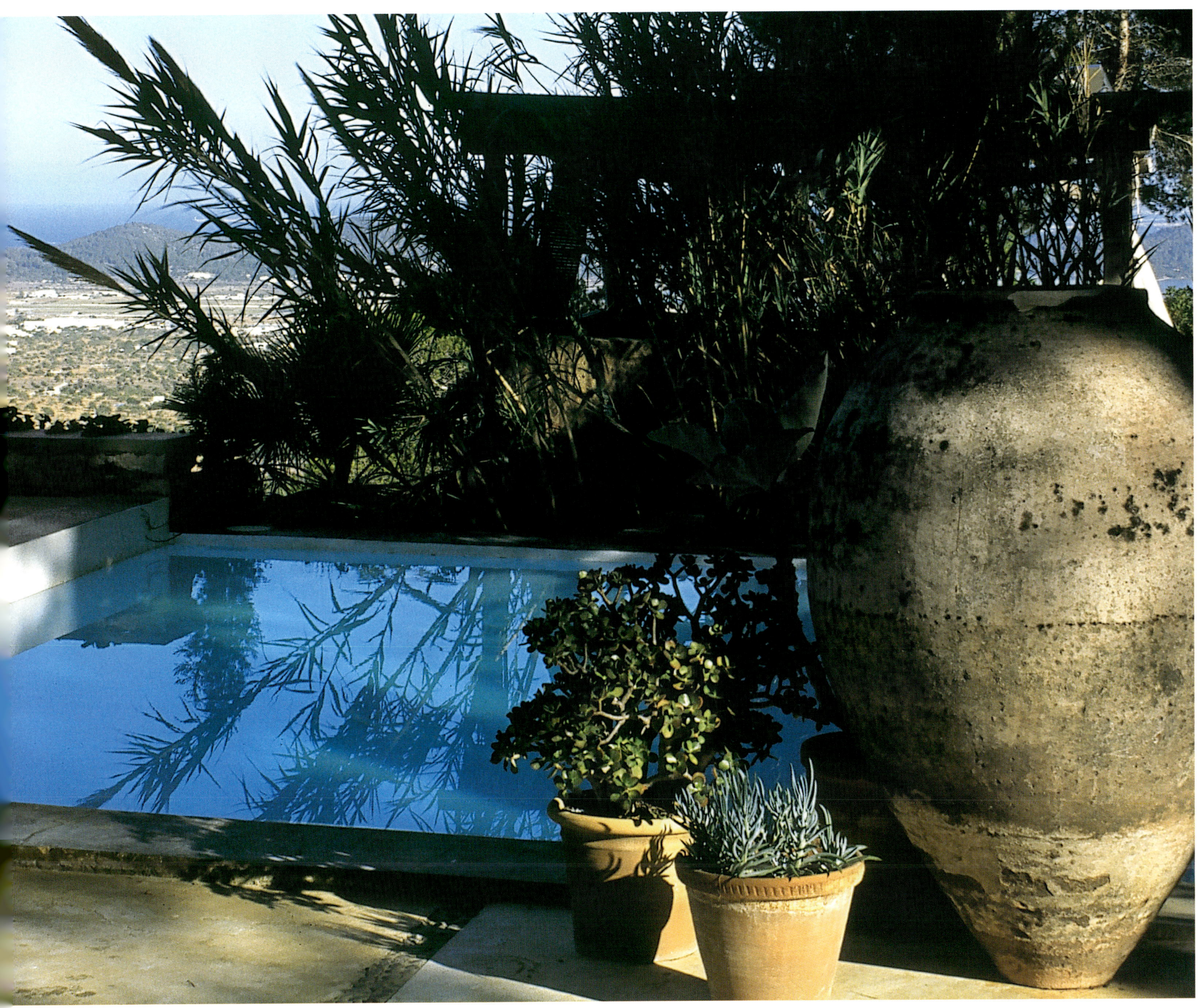

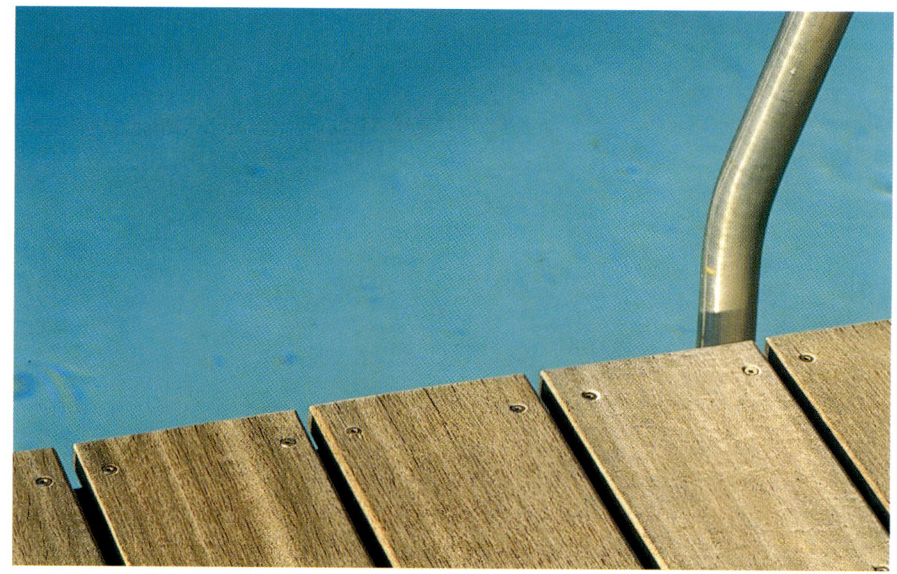

Bordering on the Theatrical

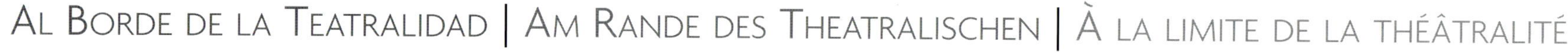

Al Borde de la Teatralidad | Am Rande des Theatralischen | À la limite de la théâtralité

This pool, situated on a wooded hill, with the sea in the background, enjoys a visual connection with the interior of the home. A glass wall extends the entire length of it, making for a fluid relationship between interior and exterior spaces. Notwithstanding, when desired, evocative and theatrical curtains can be drawn which impede visual communication between the two ambiences. The pool is placed parallel to the house. By taking advantage of the irregularities of the terrain, it overcomes the spatial limitations imposed by the location and the structure of the house.

La piscina, situada sobre una ladera cercana al bosque y el mar de fondo, guarda una atractiva comunicación visual con el interior de la vivienda.
Una pared acristalada de generosas dimensiones recorre toda la longitud de la piscina, consiguiendo que la relación entre las estancias interiores y el exterior sea fluida. Sin embargo, unas sugerentes y teatrales cortinas permiten prescindir de esta comunicación, puesto que una vez desplegadas impiden la visión entre ambos ambientes.
Construida en paralelo a la vivienda, la piscina aprovecha en su ubicación las irregularidades del terreno y permite salvar las limitaciones espaciales impuestas tanto por el lugar como por la construcción.

Das Schwimmbecken liegt an einem Abhang in der Nähe des Waldes, das Meer im Hintergrund. In diesen Kontext eingebettet kommuniziert das Becken optisch auf interessante Weise mit dem Inneren des Hauses. Eine großzügig dimensionierte Glaswand erstreckt sich über die gesamte Länge des Schwimmbeckens, wodurch eine fließende Beziehung zwischen den Innenräumen und dem Außenbereich entsteht. Durch ebenso suggestive wie theatralische Vorhänge kann man jedoch diesen Dialog unterbrechen, indem man die Vorhänge zuzieht und damit den Blick von einem Bereich in den anderen verhindert. Das parallel zum Wohnhaus errichtete Schwimmbecken nutzt die Unebenheiten des Geländes und überwindet dadurch die räumlichen Grenzen, die durch Standort und Bau gesetzt wurden.

La piscine, située sur un coteau jouxtant un bois avec la mer en toile de fond, offre une belle communication visuelle avec l'intérieur de l'habitation.
Sur toute la longueur de la piscine, une paroi vitrée aux dimensions généreuse crée une communication fluide entre l'intérieur et l'extérieur. Toutefois, des rideaux aussi théâtraux que fascinants permettent d'occulter cette communication, puisque une fois tirés, ils empêchent la vision entre un espace et l'autre.
L'emplacement de la piscine, construite parallèlement à l'habitation, a été déterminé de manière à tirer parti des irrégularités du terrain, échappant ainsi aux limites liées à l'endroit et à la construction.

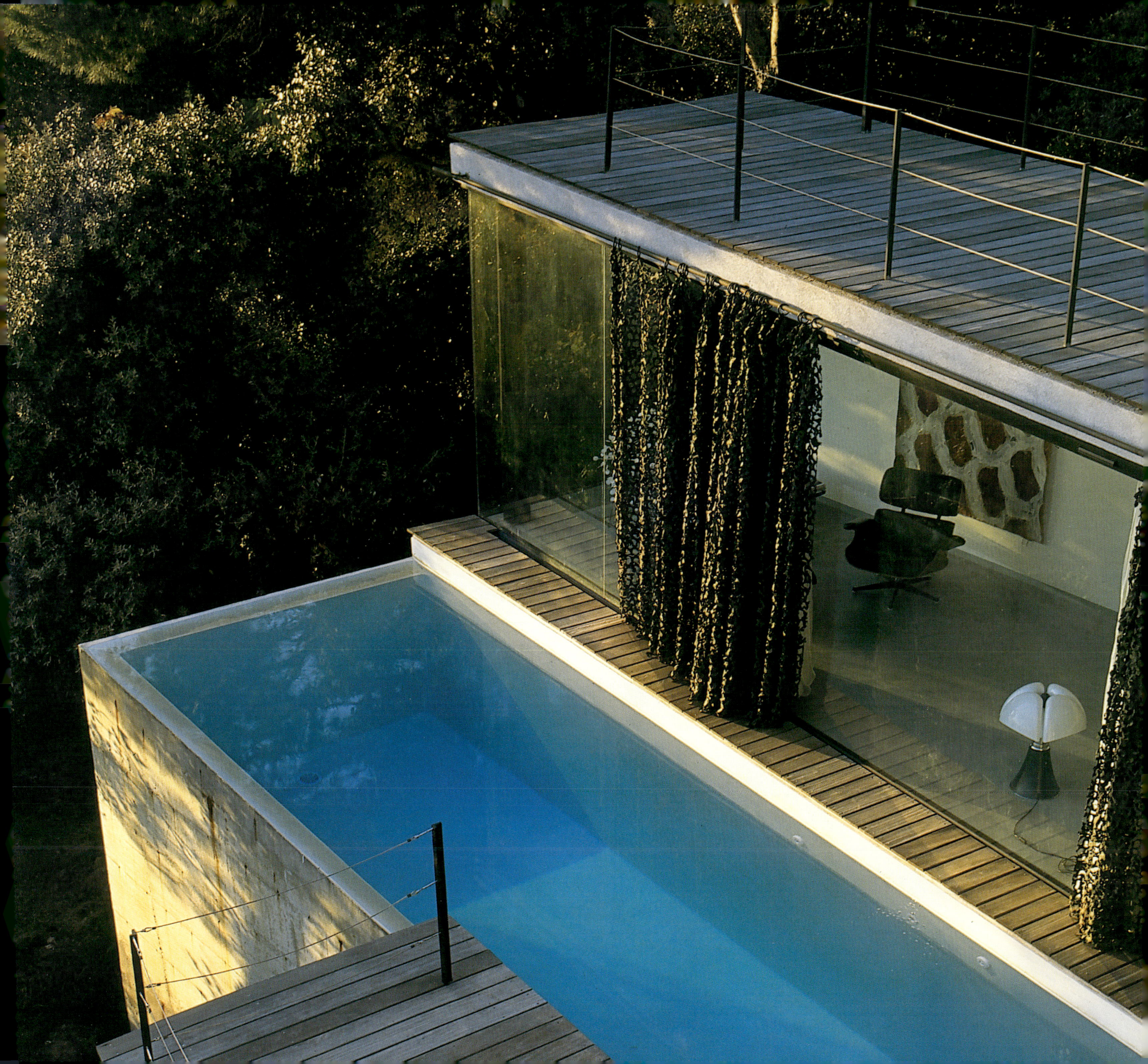

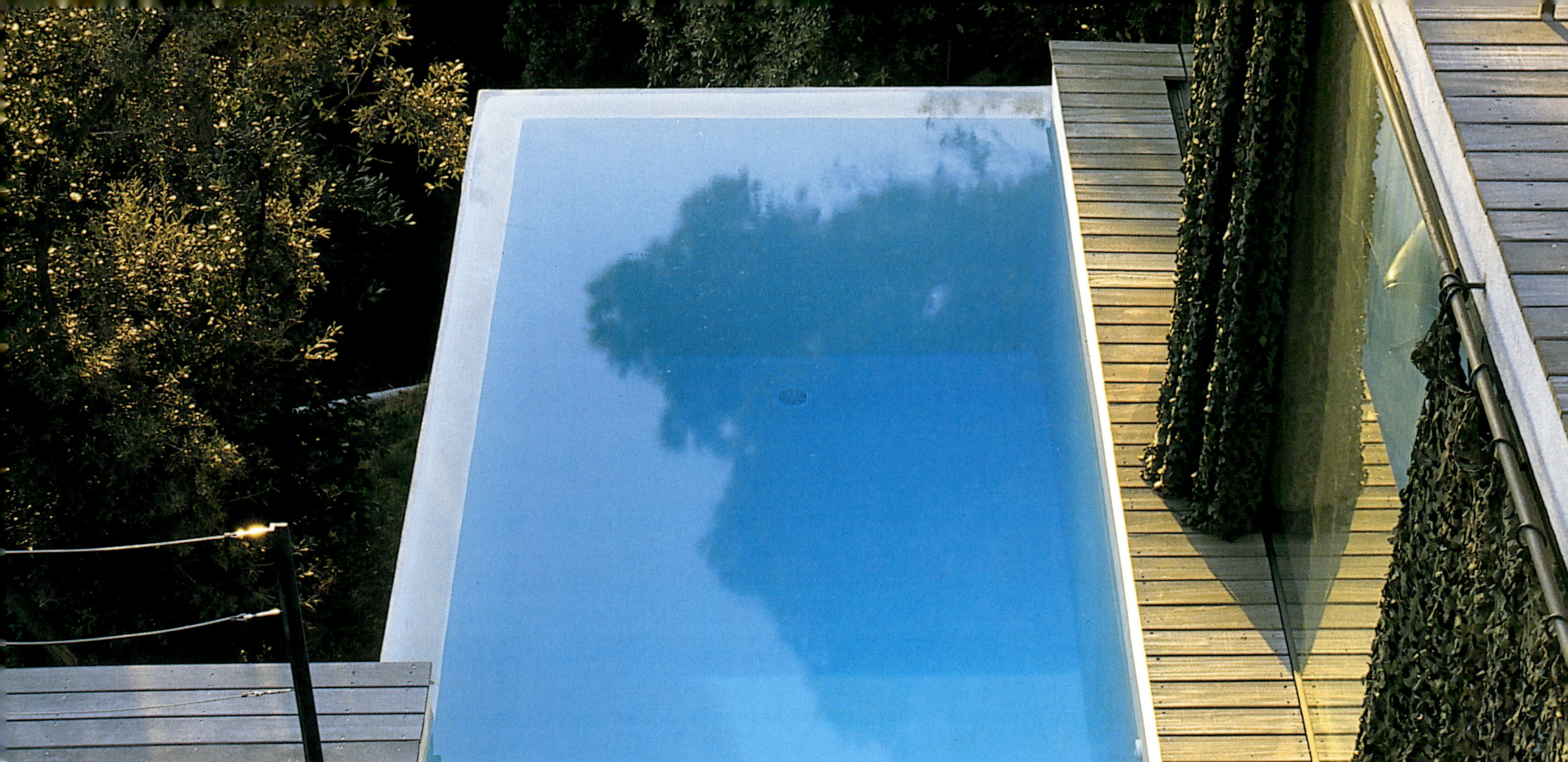

The wooden planks alongside the pool, as well as the evocative texture of the thick curtain, give the grouping an exquisite warmth, in pleasant contrast to the austere interior décor, the cold glass walls, and the plain railings.

El borde de listones de madera que rodea la piscina, así como la textura de la generosa cortina, consigue dar al conjunto una exquisita calidez que contrasta con la austera decoración interior, la frialdad de las paredes de cristal o la discreción de las escuetas barandillas.

Der Schwimmbeckenrand besteht aus Holzlatten. Das Holz wie auch die Struktur des üppigen Vorhangs verleihen dem Ensemble eine Wärme, die einen Kontrast zu der kargen Innendekoration, den kalten Glaswänden und der Unaufdringlichkeit des minimalen Geländers bildet.

La bordure de lattes de bois qui entoure la piscine ainsi que la texture du généreux rideau fournissent à l'ensemble une chaleur exquise qui contraste avec l'austérité de la décoration intérieure, la froideur des parois vitrées ou la sobre discrétion des rambardes.

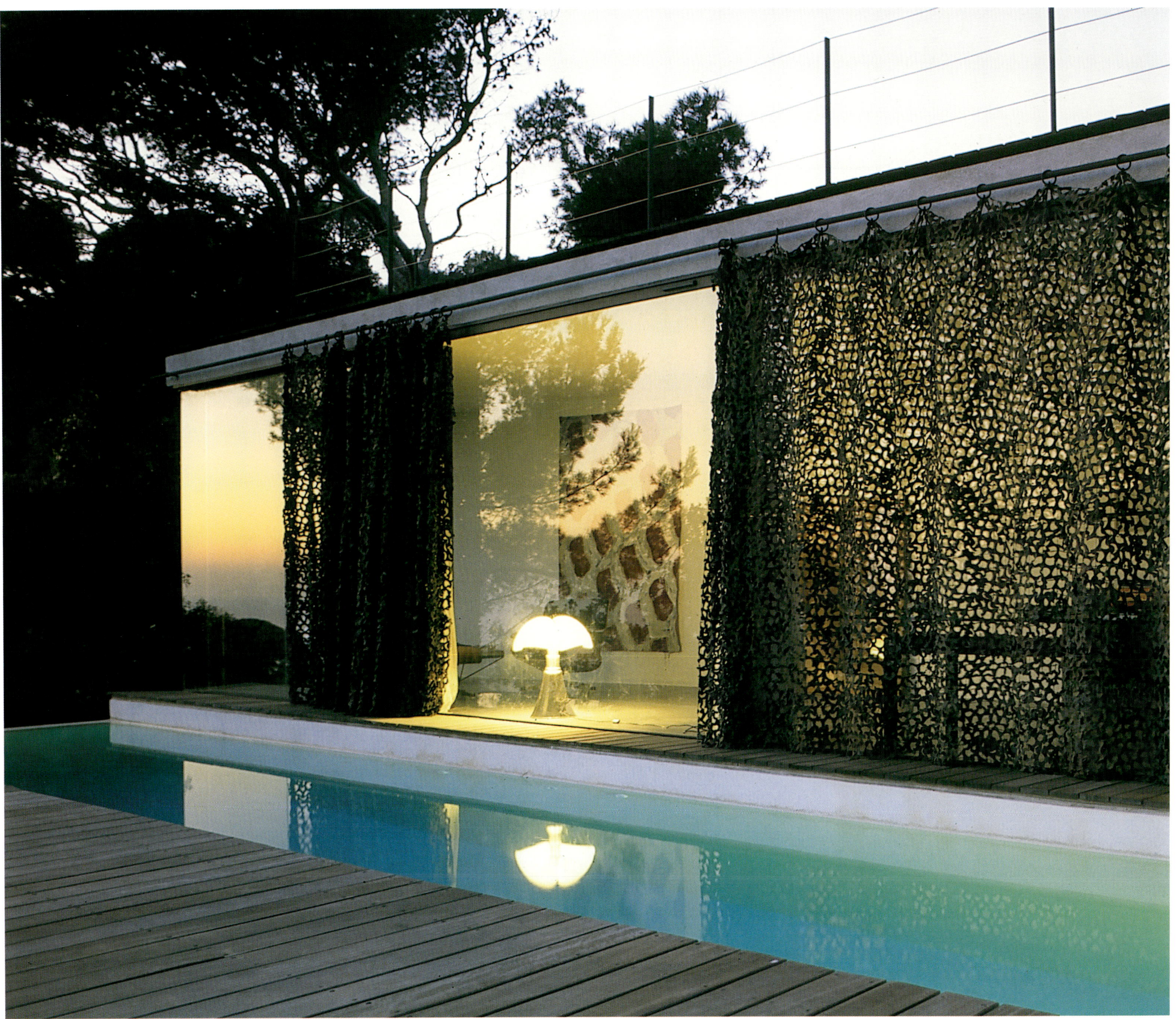

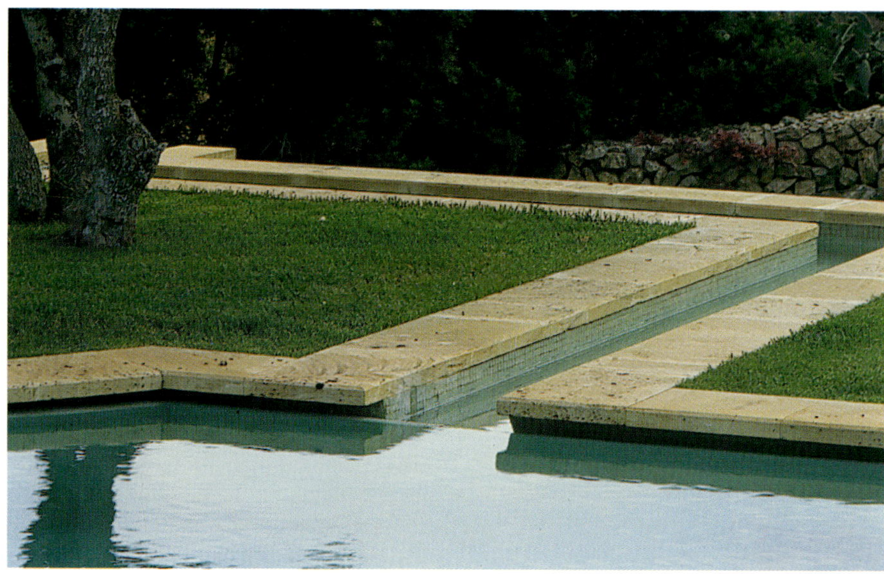

THE ETERNAL CYCLE OF WATER

EL CICLO ETERNO DEL AGUA | DER EWIGE KREISLAUF DES WASSERS | LE CYCLE ÉTERNEL DE L'EAU

This swimming pool imitates the evocative shapes of the gardens at Versailles. However, it is original in that it consists of a system of channels surrounding a small island where six symbolic olive trees grow. This keeps the pool clean and converts a retaining wall into a charming waterfall.
The pool is perfectly symmetrical, its symmetry broken only by two semicircles. The first forms the island and second, contains underwater steps. The immensity of the garden was strictly respected both on the upper and lower levels and the project integrated the entire ensemble. The refined style respects the setting and allows the central axis, created by the pool, to come to the fore.

De inspiración versallesca, esta piscina emula las sugerentes formas de los jardines del palacio real francés. Sin embargo, posee una característica propia: un ingenioso sistema de canales que rodea una pequeña isla donde se alzan seis olivos simbólicos. Esta solución permite mantener la piscina limpia y convertir un muro de contención en una cascada.
A nivel formal, la piscina presenta una perfecta simetría: solamente dos semicírculos rompen la linealidad. El primero conforma la silueta de la isla y el segundo, da paso a una escalinata que se sumerge en el agua. Se ha respetado de manera rigurosa la inmensidad del jardín, tanto en el nivel superior como en el inferior. El proyecto ha procurado integrar el conjunto respetando el entorno mediante un estilo depurado, que permite realzar el eje central constituido por la piscina.

Bei diesem Schwimmbecken wurden die suggestiven Formen und der Stil der Gärten des Versailler Königsschlosses nachempfunden. Allerdings besticht der Pool durch eine individuelle Note: ein Kanalsystem, das eine kleine Insel, auf der sehr symbolträchtig sechs Olivenbäumen stehen, umgibt. Dadurch wird das Schwimmbecken sauber gehalten, und die Stützmauer wird zum Wasserfall. In formaler Hinsicht weist das Schwimmbecken eine vollkommene Symmetrie auf: Lediglich zwei Halbkreise unterbrechen diese Linearität. Der erste gehört zum Umriss der Insel und der zweite bildet den Übergang zu einer ins Wasser hinabführenden Freiteppe. Die unermessliche Weite des Gartens wurde respektiert, was auf der oberen wie auf der unteren Ebene klar ersichtlich ist. Das Pojektziel war, durch klare Stilmittel ein Ensemble zu kreieren, das auf die Umgebung Rücksicht nimmt und diese integriert. Dadurch wird nun das Schwimmbecken als zentrale Achse hervorgehoben.

D'inspiration versaillaise, cette piscine reproduit les formes attrayantes des jardins du palais royal français. Elle possède toutefois une caractéristique qui lui est propre : un ingénieux système de canaux qu'entoure une petite île où se dressent six oliviers symboliques. Grâce à cette solution, la piscine reste propre et un mur de soutènement devient cascade. Formellement, la piscine présente une symétrie parfaite : seuls deux demi-cercles rompent la linéarité. Le premier réplique la silhouette de l'île et le second ouvre sur un perron qui s'immerge dans l'eau. L'immensité du jardin a été rigoureusement respectée, au niveau supérieur comme au niveau inférieur.
Le projet traduit un effort d'intégration de l'environnement à travers un style épuré qui rehausse l'axe central constitué par la piscine.

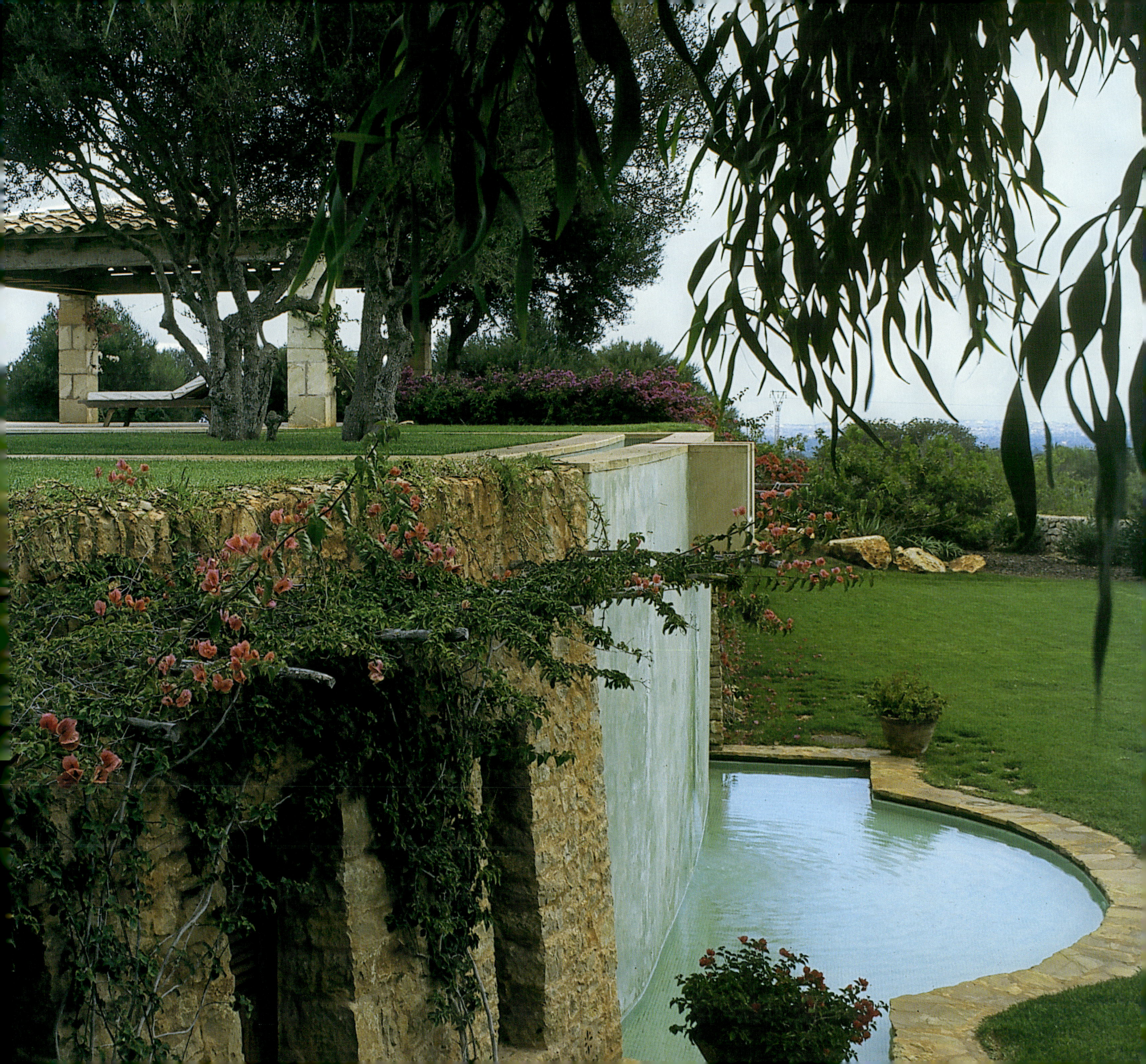

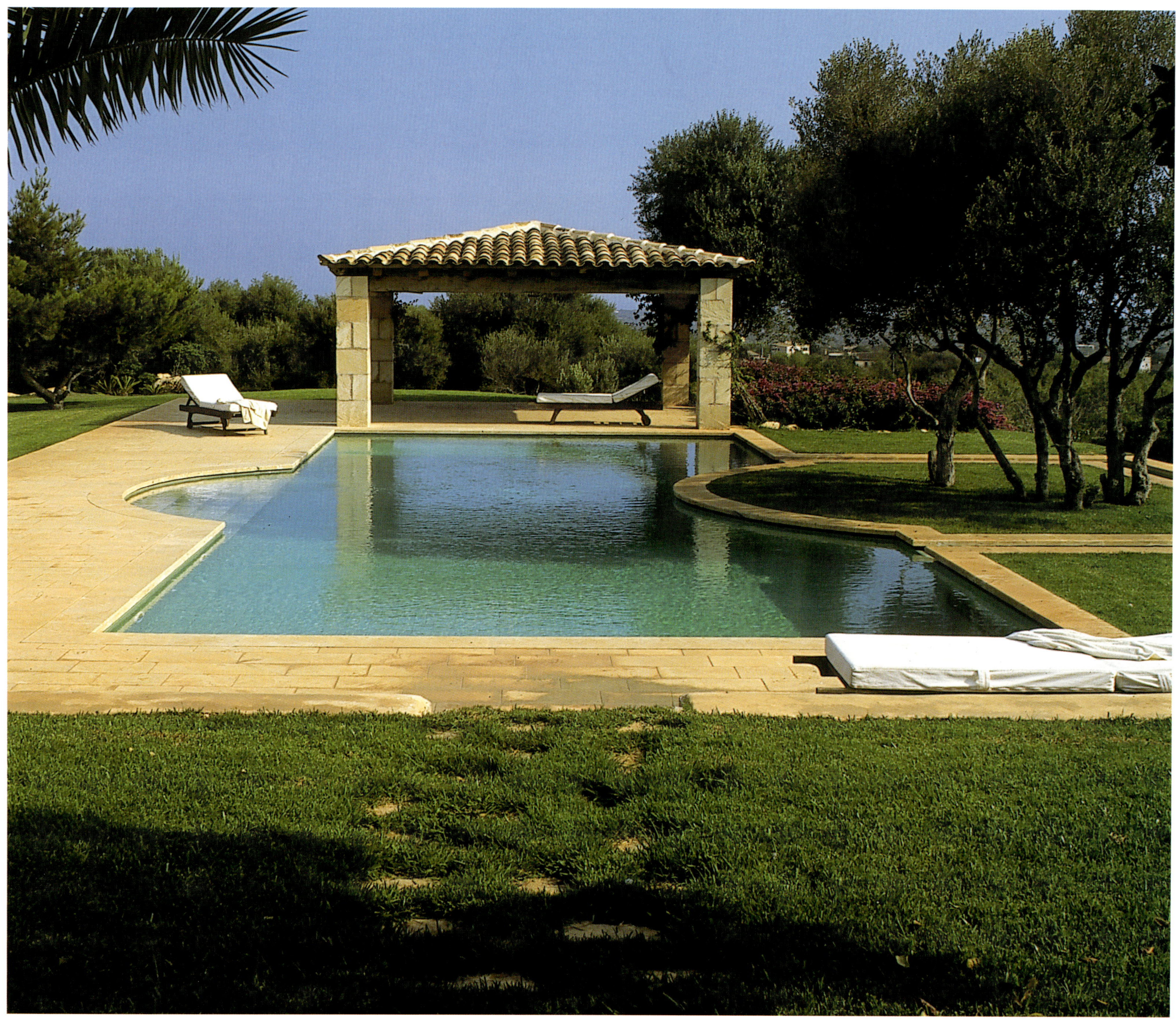

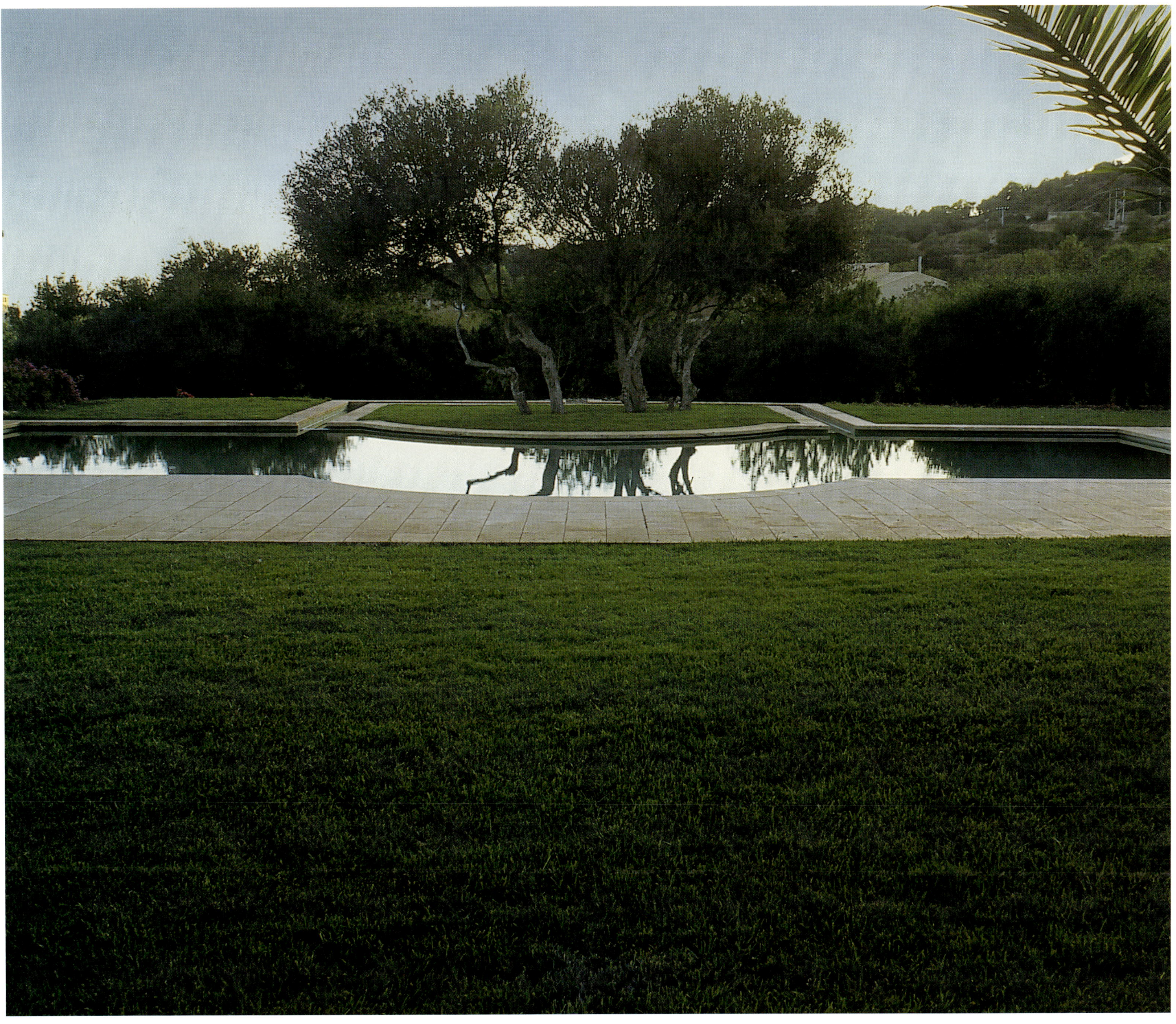

The Reinterpretation of Water

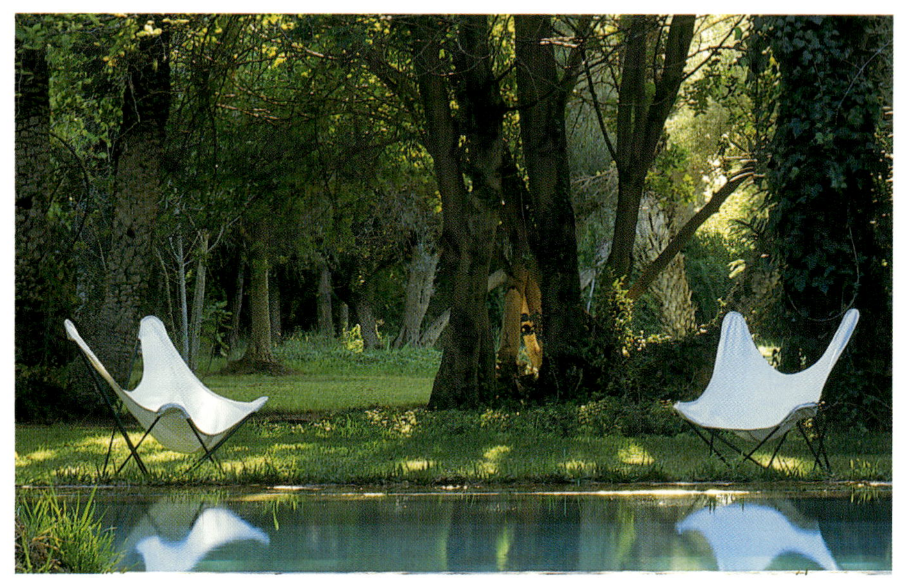

La Reinterpretación del Agua | Wasser neu entdeckt | Réinterpréter l'eau

This magnificent pool, surrounded by a dense wall of vegetation, both blends in perfectly, and at the same time, emerges from its natural setting.
The chromatic intensity in combination with the complex geometric exercise as seen in the double crown of fired clay tiles that top off the pool, is a sampling of the craftsmanship still practised today in Marrakech. This small sampling of ornamental richness is manifest in the glazed mosaic work on the central band of the small channel that divides the edging, and the various geometric finishes located both inside and outside the pool. On one of the sides six slender jets of water reach up and communicate directly with the highest part of the pool.

Rodeada por una densa muralla vegetal emerge esta magnífica piscina colorista, perfectamente integrada en su entorno natural.
La intensidad cromática de esta piscina, combinada con el complejo ejercicio de geometría plasmado en la doble corona de barro cocido que remata la piscina, representa una muestra del trabajo artesanal que todavía se lleva a cabo en Marrakech. El excelente trabajo realizado con mosaico vidriado en la cenefa central del canalillo que divide la corona y en los diferentes remates geométricos, situados tanto en el interior como en el exterior de la piscina, son una pequeña muestra de la riqueza ornamental. En uno de los laterales de la piscina se elevan seis estilizados chorros de agua que se comunican directamente con la parte más elevada de la piscina.

Dieses herrliche und farbenfreudige Schwimmbecken wird von einer dichten Pflanzenwand umgeben und fügt sich vollkommen in seine natürliche Umgebung ein. Die farbliche Intensität dieses Schwimmbeckens in Verbindung mit der komplexen Geometrie, wie sie in der den Beckenabschluss bildenden, doppelten Terrakottaeinfassung deutlich wird, stellt eine Kostprobe des handwerklichen Schaffens dar, das man heute noch in Marrakesch antreffen kann. Die hervorragende Glasmosaikarbeit im Mittelstreifen des die Einfassung trennenden Kanals sowie in den verschiedenen geometrischen Abschlüssen im Inneren und außerhalb des Schwimmbeckens sind nur ein paar Beispiel für die reiche Ornamentik. An einer Seite des Schwimmbeckens erheben sich sechs stilisierte Wasserfontänen, die im direkten Dialog mit dem höheren Teil des Beckens stehen.

Au cœur d'une muraille végétale dense, cette magnifique piscine coloriste s'intègre parfaitement au décor naturel.
L'intensité chromatique de cette piscine, combinée avec un exercice de géométrie complexe – une couronne en glaise cuite assurant la finition de la piscine – illustre bien le travail artisanal qui s'effectue encore à Marrakech. Le superbe ouvrage en mosaïque vitrée réalisé sur la lisière centrale du petit canal divisant la couronne et sur les différentes finitions géométriques, à l'intérieur comme à l'extérieur de la piscine, constitue un bon exemple de cette richesse ornementale.
Sur l'un des côtés de la piscine s'élèvent six jets d'eau très stylisés qui communiquent directement avec la partie la plus élevée de la piscine.

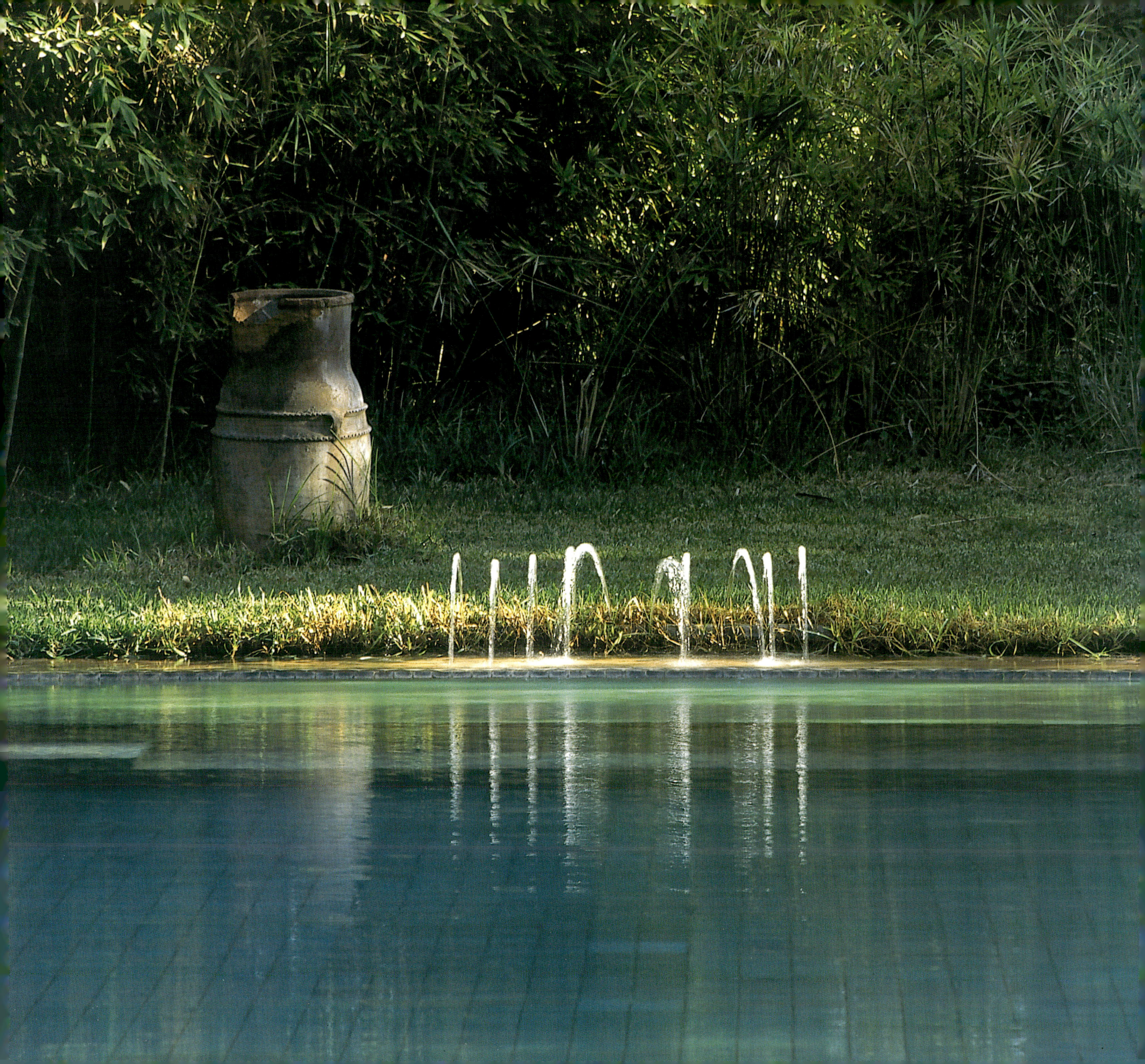

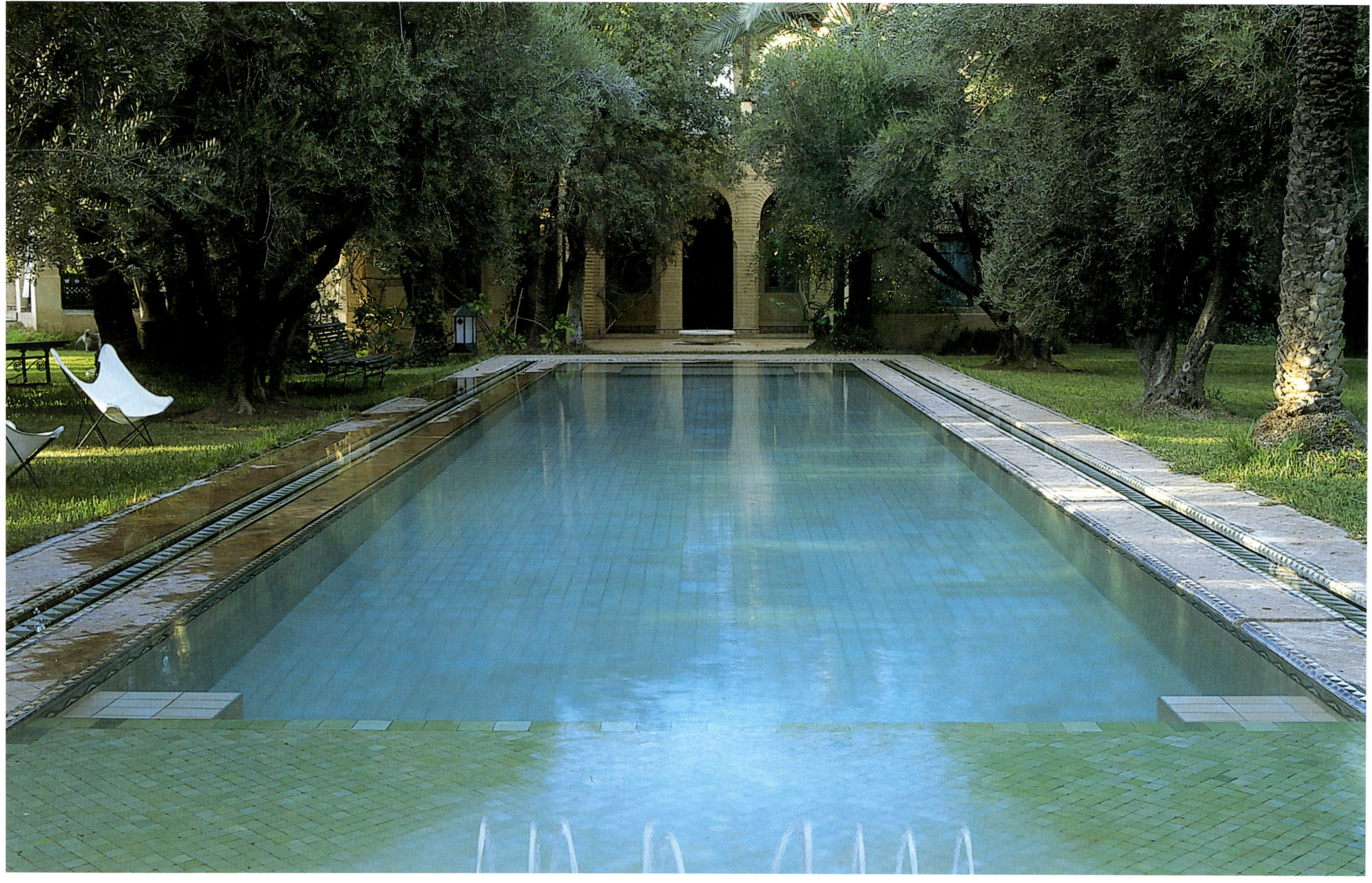

Behind the water fountain, on the carpet of grass, there is a glimpse of the past in the form of an ancient fired-clay vessel. The entire pool is surrounded by grass that comes right up to the edge.

Detrás de la fuente de agua, sobre la pradera de hierba, encontramos un destello del pasado en forma de antigua vasija de barro cocido. Toda la piscina está rodeada por una espesa alfombra de césped que llega hasta la misma corona.

Auf der Wiese hinter dem Springbrunnen befindet sich eine Reminiszenz an die Vergangenheit: antike Terrakottagefäße. Das Becken ist völlig von einem dichten Rasenteppich eingeschlossen, der bis an die Einfassung heranreicht.

Derrière la fontaine, dans la prairie, une ancienne pièce de vaisselle en terre cuite incarne un éclair du passé. Toute la piscine est entourée d'un épais tapis de gazon qui s'étend jusqu'à la couronne.

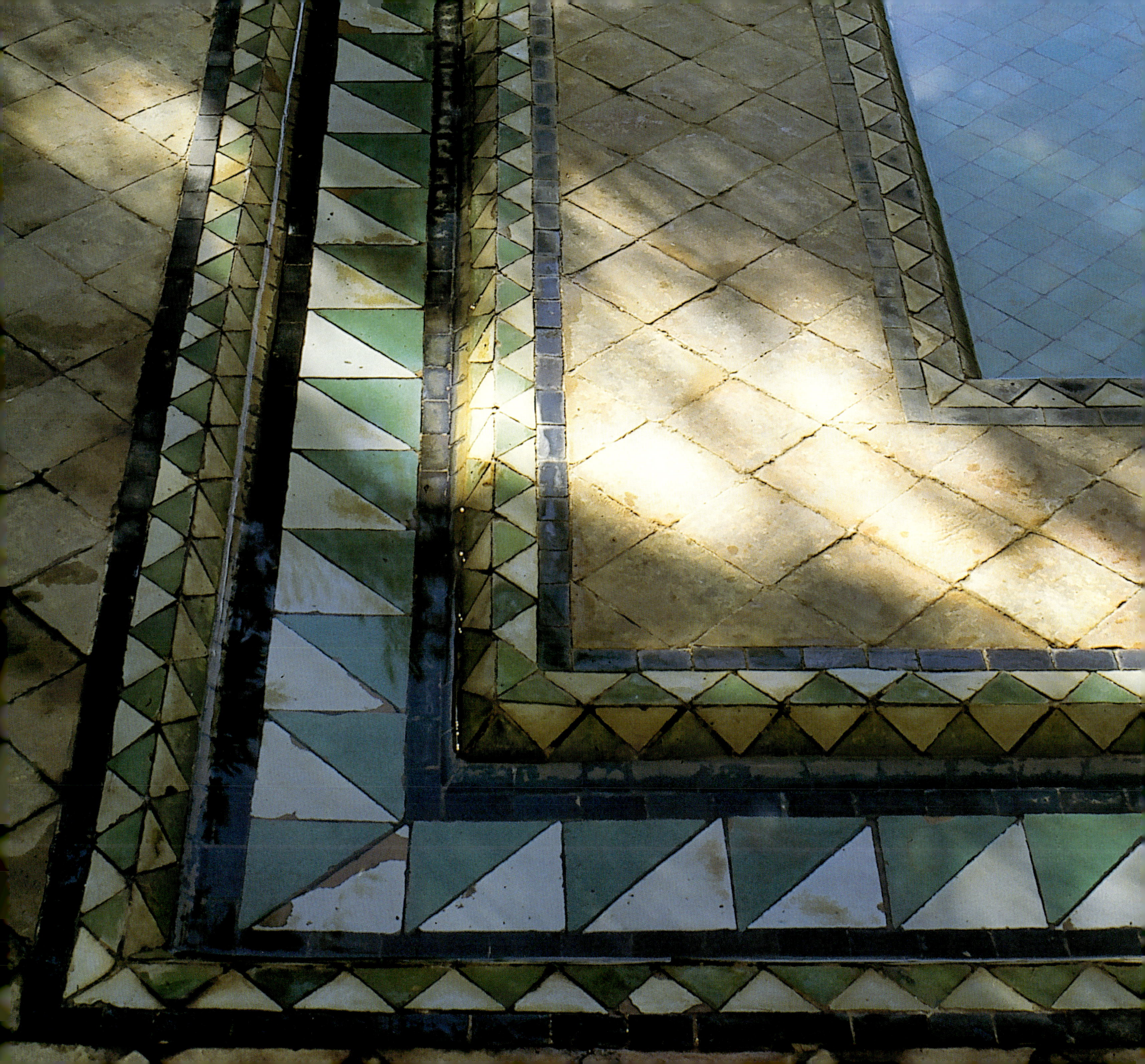

In the Garden of the Imaginary

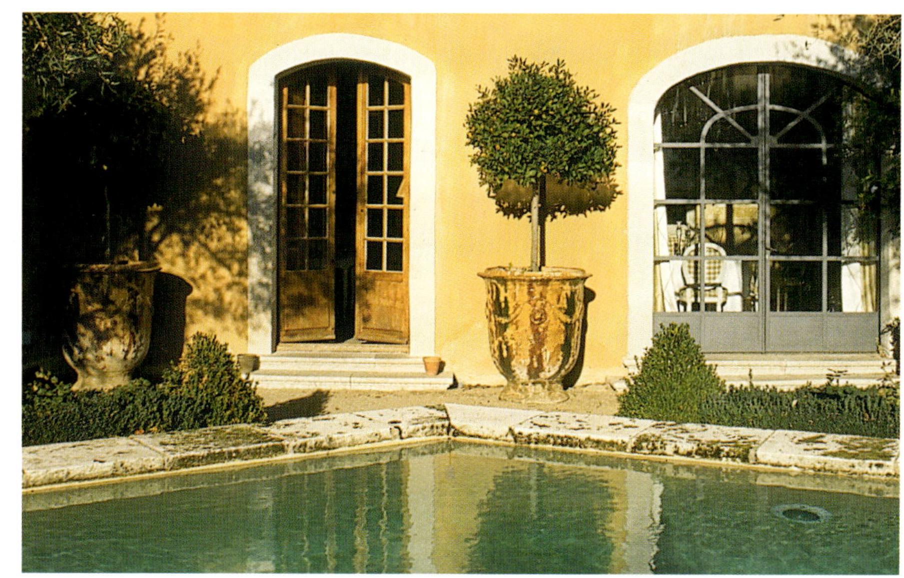

En el Jardín de lo Imaginario | Im Garten der Fantasie | Dans le jardin de l'imaginaire

This restored rustic house was originally equipped with an irrigation pond. Now, thanks to the installation of a motor that circulates the water, it was transformed into a small pool. Simple austere lines of thick rough stone outline the house where chromatic harmony and harmony of textures and materials achieve surprising results. The white color, echoed in the façade's window and doorframes, stands out against the green, overwhelming scenery drawn by nature, and contrasts with the stone. A dirt path marks the pool's entire perimeter and leads to other hideaways of the evocative garden.

La vivienda, una construcción restaurada de aire rústico, contaba originariamente con un estanque cuya agua se utilizaba para el regadío de los terrenos de la finca. Hoy, aquel estanque se ha metamorfoseado en una pequeña piscina gracias a la instalación de un motor que renueva el agua. Un austero contorno de líneas simples trazado por un marco de piedra gruesa sin pulir define la casa, en la que tanto la armonía cromática como las texturas y los materiales logran unos sorprendentes resultados. El color albero rematado por el perfil blanco de las puertas y ventanas que salpican la fachada resalta sobre la escenografía que la naturaleza dibuja. Un camino de tierra recorre todo el perímetro de la piscina a la vez que conduce a otros escondrijos del sugerente jardín.

Zu dem Haus, einem rustikal wirkenden, restaurierten Gebäude, gehörte ursprünglich ein Wasserbecken, das zur Bodenewässerung verwendet wurde. Inzwischen wurde ein Motor zur Wassererneuerung eingebaut und aus dem Becken ist heute ein kleines Schwimmbecken geworden. Die nüchternen Konturen einfacher Linien, die durch grobe, unpolierte Steine vorgegebenen sind, definieren das Haus. Im Haus entstehen durch die Harmonie der Farben wie auch durch Strukturen und Materialien so macher überraschende Moment. Die weiße Farbe, die sich auch an den Fenster und Türen der Hausfassade wiederholt, hebt sich kontrastreich von der fast in Szene gesetzt wirkenden Natur ab. Ein schmaler Weg führt um das Schwimmbecken herum und verliert sich in den Schlupfwinkeln des inspirierenden Gartens.

L'habitation, une construction restaurée d'allure rustique, disposait à l'origine d'un bassin dont l'eau servait à arroser les terrains de la propriété. Ce bassin est devenu une petite piscine grâce à l'installation d'un moteur qui renouvelle l'eau.
Un contour austère aux lignes simples tracé par un cadre de pierre épaisse non poli définit la maison, où l'harmonie des couleurs, des textures et des matériaux aboutit à un résultat surprenant. La couleur blanche, que l'on retrouve dans le contour des portes et des fenêtres qui éclabousse la façade, ressort sur cette scénographie dessinée par la nature.
Un chemin de terre longe tout le périmètre de la piscine et conduit à d'autres recoins de ce fascinant jardin.

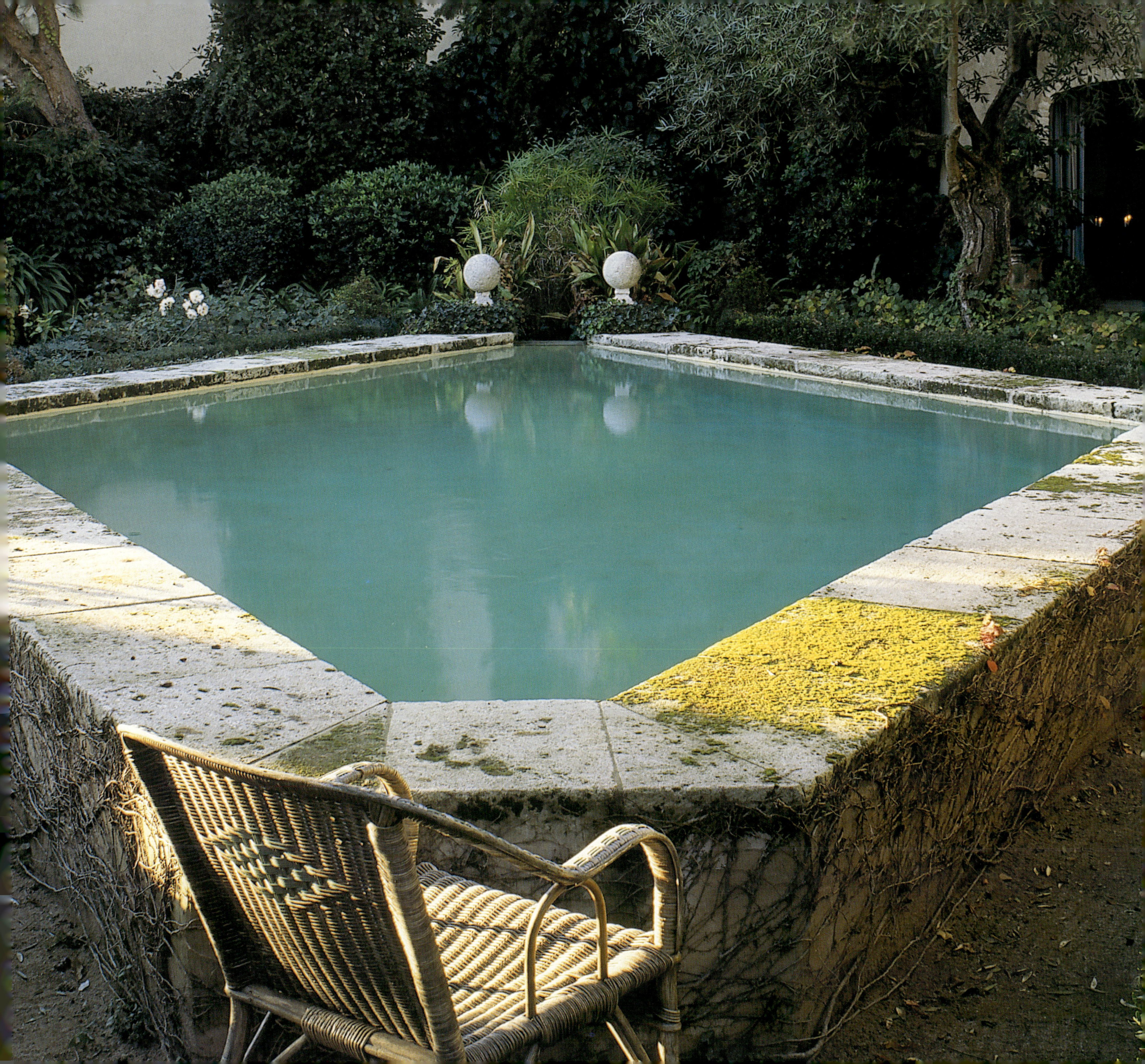

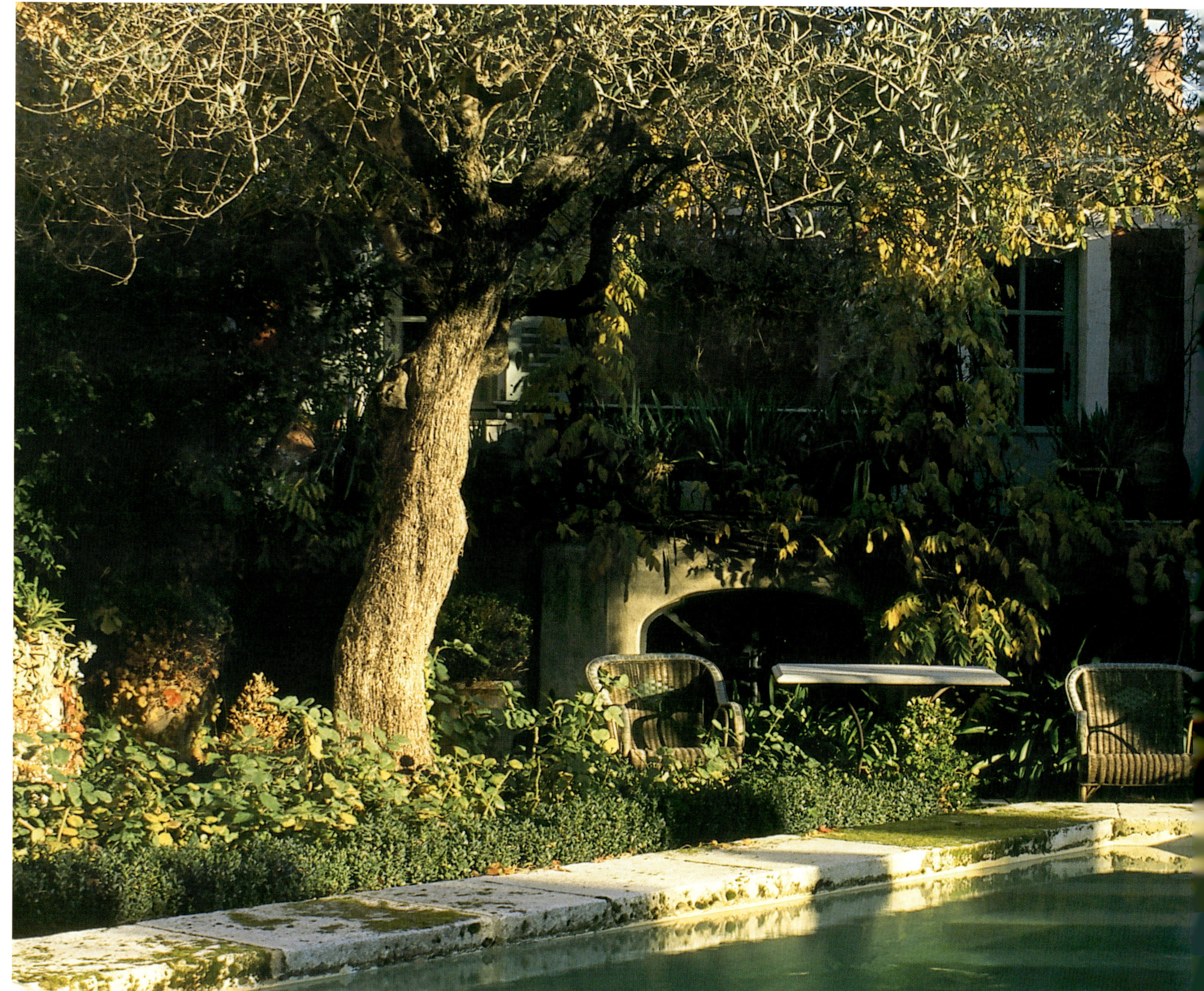

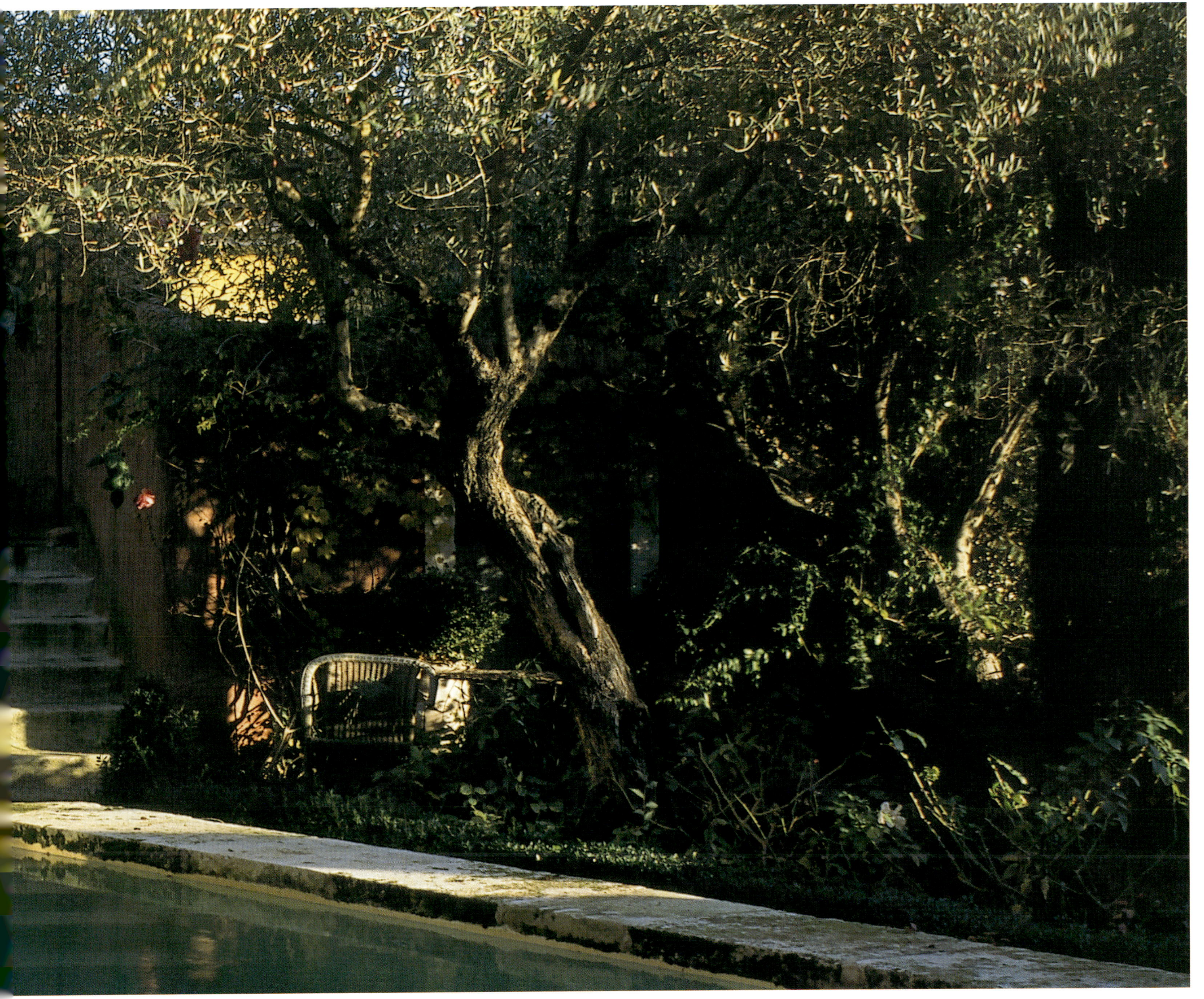

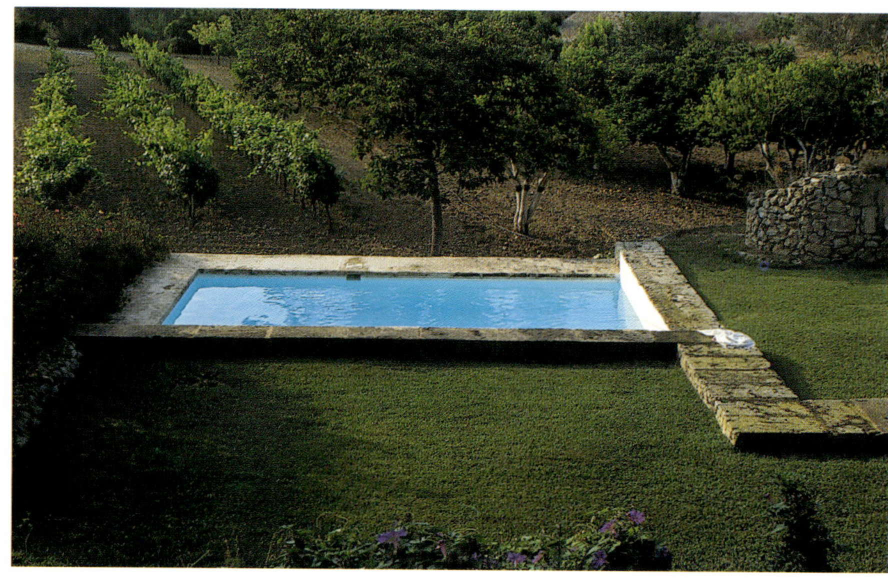

Recovering the Past

La Recuperación del Pasado | Vergangenheit neu erlebt | Reconquérir le passé

Sited between a small plot of cropland and an orchard of young fruit trees, is this swimming pool where the patina of time has left its mark. The original stones from the country home were used to divide up the main space into three areas: the swimming pool, the ancient watermill, and a sunbathing area on the upper level.

The old Z-shaped retaining wall becomes a path and shelters the pool, which was originally a reservoir that collected water to irrigate the field. On a second level, the tidy orchard still stretches out along with the remains of a small watermill, which is now recycled as a sculpture for contemplation.

Different elements from popular architectural tradition are used to design the space at different levels.

Entre una extensión de tierra de cultivo y un campo de árboles frutales se ubica esta piscina, enmarcada por una hilera de piedras en la que la pátina del tiempo ha imprimido su huella.

En este proyecto se han utilizado los elementos propios de la arquitectura popular para acondicionar el espacio en diferentes niveles. A este fin han servido las piedras originales de la construcción, que delimitan el espacio principal y lo dividen en tres partes: la piscina, un cuerpo que antaño desempeñó la función de noria y una zona donde tomar el sol. El antiguo muro de contención en forma de zeta cobija lo que originariamente fue una alberca destinada a la recogida del agua para el riego. En un segundo plano, se conservan los restos de una pequeña noria de piedra, actualmente convertida en una escultura, testigo mudo del pasado.

Zwischen Ackerland und einer Obstplantage liegt dieses Schwimmbecken, eingerahmt von einer Reihe von Steinen, auf denen die Zeit ihre Spuren hinterlassen hat. Bei diesem Projekt wurden volkstümlichen Architekturelemente verwendet, um den Raum auf verschiedenen Ebenen zu gestalten. Zu diesem Zweck bediente man sich der Originalsteine des Gebäudes, die den Bereich in drei Zonen unterteilen: das Schwimmbecken, die Überbleibsel eines uralten Wasserrads sowie eine Fläche für das Sonnenbad. Die alte Stützmauer in Z-Form umschloss einst die Zisterne, die das Wasser für die Bewässerung sammelte. Auf der zweiten Ebene erstreckt sich noch der alte Hain, und es finden sich die Ruinen eines steinernen Wasserrads aus Vorzeiten – heutzutage eine Skulptur, die als stummer Zeuge der Vergangenheit ihren Platz im Garten hat.

Cette piscine, située entre un terrain de culture et un champ d'arbres fruitiers, est encadrée par une rangée de pierres patinées par le temps. Ce projet a utilisé les éléments caractéristiques de l'architecture populaire dans l'arrangement de l'espace en différents niveaux. À cette fin, les pierres d'origine de la construction ont été réutilisées, délimitant l'espace principal et le divisant en trois parties : la piscine ; un élément qui remplissait autrefois la fonction de noria et un solarium. L'ancien mur de soutènement en forme de Z abrite ce qui était à l'origine un réservoir destiné à recueillir l'eau pour l'arrosage. Un petit verger ayant résisté au passage du temps s'étend en second plan et l'on trouve les restes d'une petite noria en pierre transformée en sculpture, témoin muet du passé.

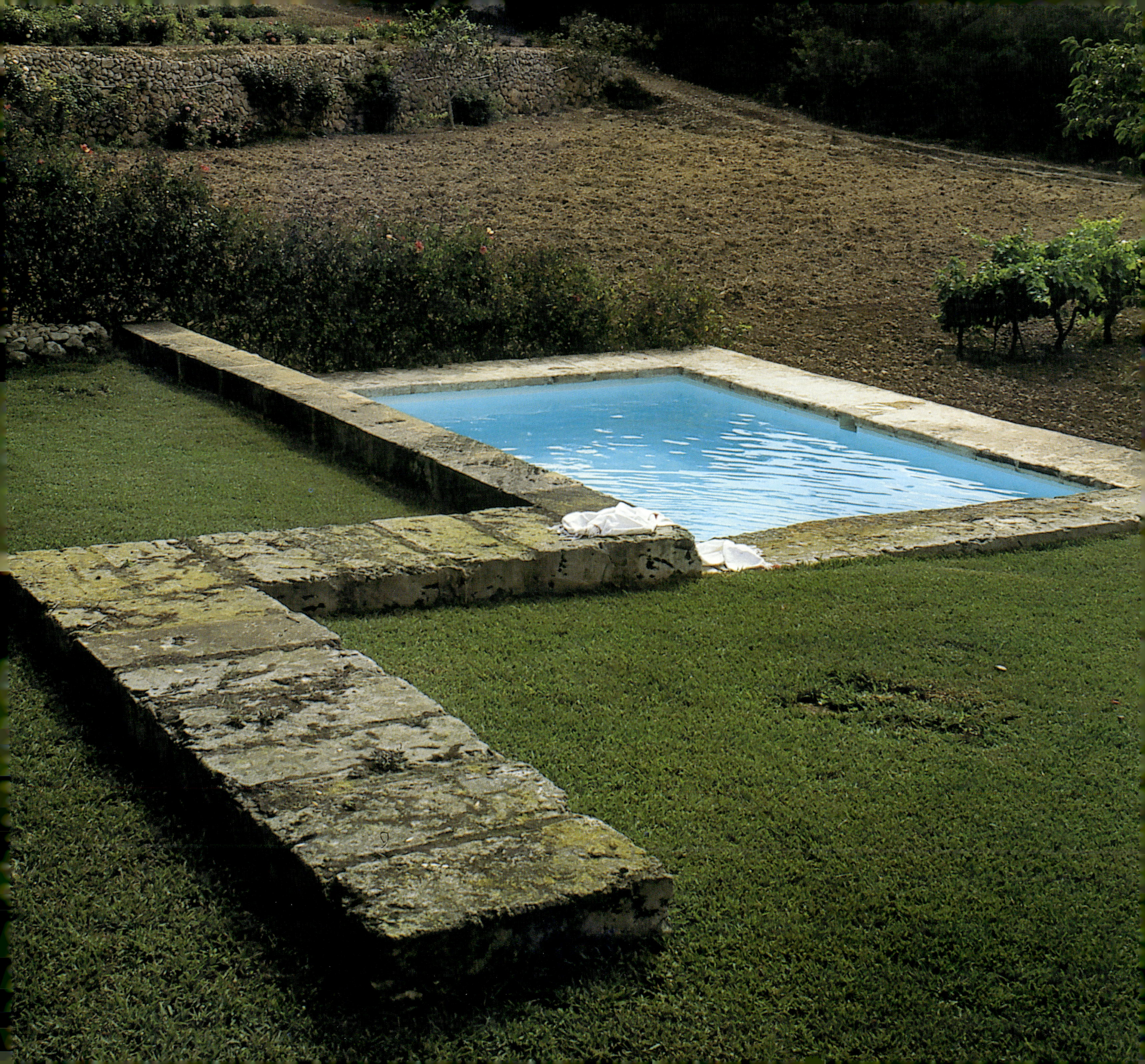

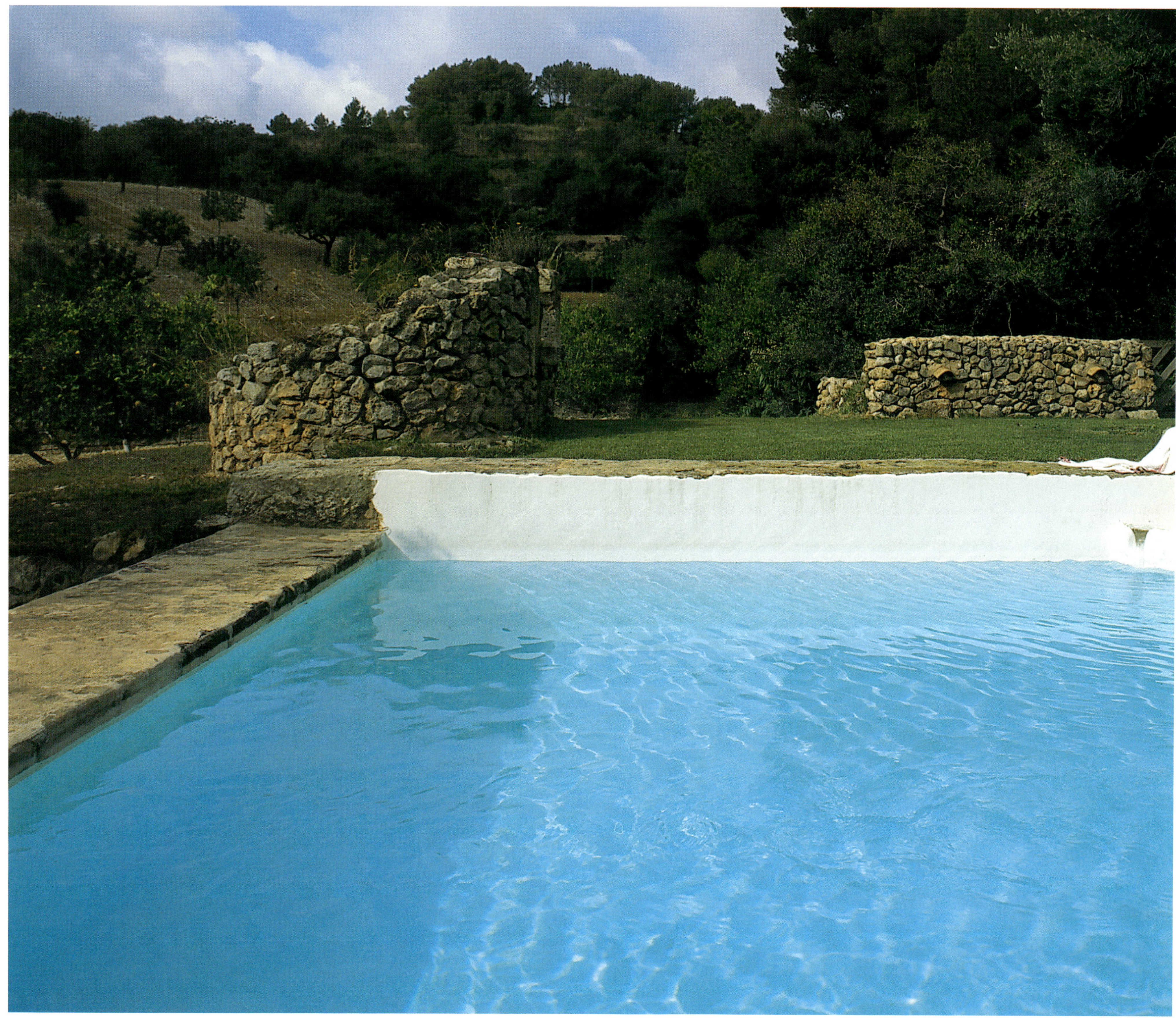

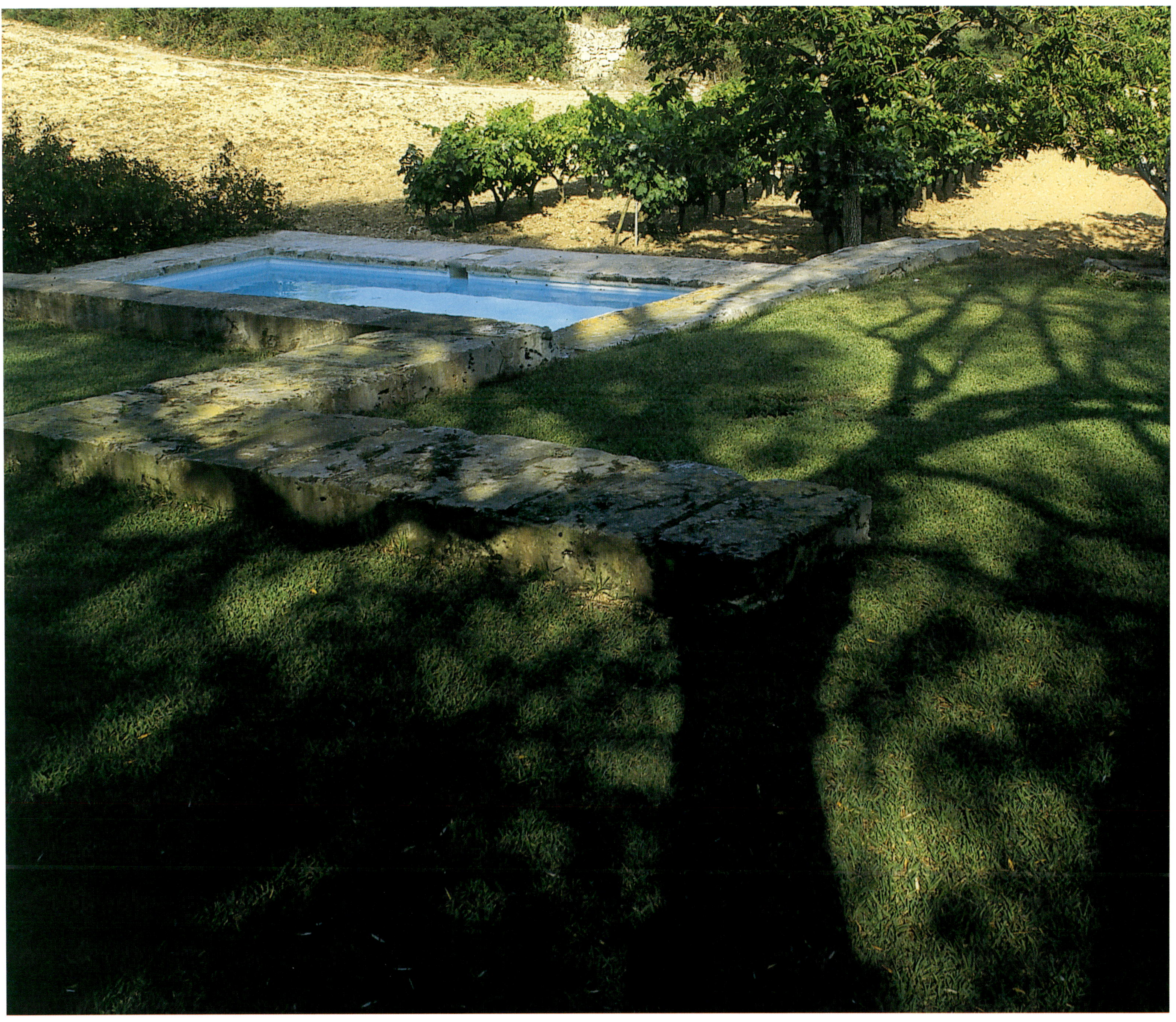

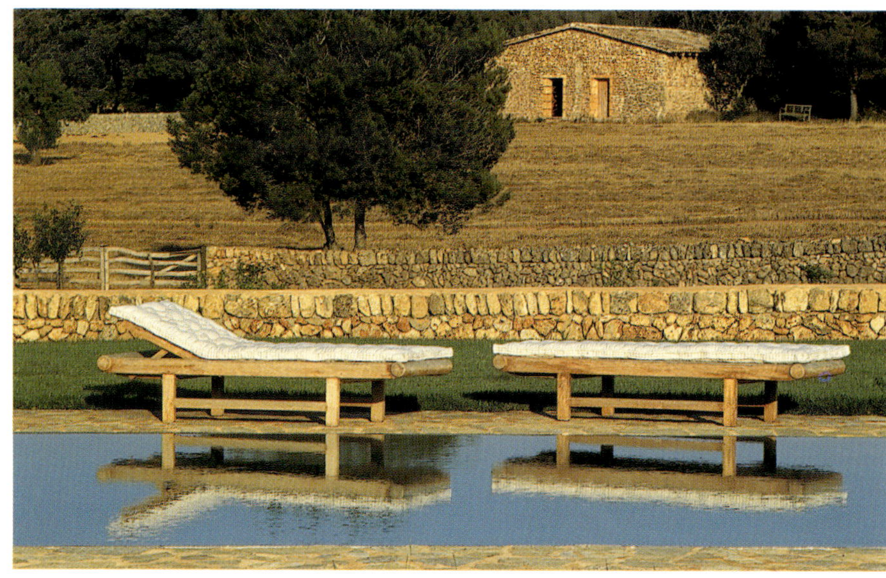

Color Contrasts

Contrastes de Color | Farbkontraste | Contrastes chromatiques

This small oasis emerges from the arid land that surrounds it. The geometric balance comes from the perfect relationship of the swimming pool, the semi-open porch, and the main building. A stone wall, perfectly restored, joins the two structures and defines the entire property, creating a dividing line between it and the setting, based on color and one sole texture; the roughness of the stone.
The intent was to bring out the play of contrasts resulting from the juxtaposition of the dry land and the lawn that surround the blue surface of the water. Stone and sand color become the chromatic base of the ensemble and purposely heighten the deep blue of the water and the green of the blanket of vegetation.

Como un refugio de paz y frescor emerge este oasis de entre la árida tierra que lo envuelve. El equilibrio geométrico nace de la relación de sus tres volúmenes: la piscina, rectilínea, el porche semiabierto y el edificio principal. Un muro de piedra de mediana altura, perfectamente restaurado, une los dos volúmenes arquitectónicos a la vez que rodea y delimita toda la finca creando una línea divisoria entre ésta y el entorno basada en el color y una sola textura, la rugosidad de la piedra. Se trataba aquí de potenciar el juego de contrastes que nace de la yuxtaposición de la tierra de secano con las praderas artificiales de hierba verde que rodean la superficie azulada del agua.
La piedra y el color arena se convierten en la base cromática del conjunto, y realzan a conciencia el intenso azul del agua y el verdor del manto vegetal.

Diese Oase ist umgeben von trockener Erde und wird damit ein Zufluchtsort der Stille und der Frische. Das geometrische Gleichgewicht basiert auf der Interkation der drei architektoischen Elemente von eckigem Schwimmbecken, der halboffenen Terrasse und dem Hauptgebäude. Eine mühselig restaurierte, mittelhohe Steinmauer verbindet die beiden architektonischen Ensemble und umgibt und begrenzt zugleich das gesamte Anwesen. Eine Trennlinie unerteilt das Anwesen von seiner Umgebung, basierend auf Farben und einer einheitlichen Oberflächenstruktur – der Rauheit des Gesteins. Anliegen war es, das Spiel der Kontraste zu verstärken, das aus dem Aufeinandertreffen des unbewässerten Landes mit dem grünen Kunstrasen, der die bläuliche Wasseroberfläche umgibt, besteht. Stein und Sand werden zur farblichen Grundlage des Ensembles und unterstreichen nachhaltig die Intensität des Blaus des Wassers und das Grün der Pflanzendecke.

Refuge de paix et de fraîcheur, cette oasis émerge de la terre aride qui l'entoure. L'équilibre géométrique naît de la relation de ses trois unités : la piscine, rectiligne, le porche semi-ouvert et le bâtiment principal. Un mur de pierre de hauteur moyenne, parfaitement restauré, unit les deux unités architectoniques, et entoure et délimite l'ensemble de la propriété en créant entre celle-ci et l'environnement une ligne de division basée sur la couleur et une texture unique : la rugosité de la pierre. L'idée était de renforcer le jeu de contrastes naissant de la juxtaposition des terrains non irrigués et des prairies artificielles d'herbe verte entourant l'étendue d'eau bleutée.La pierre et la couleur sable deviennent la base chromatique de l'ensemble et accentuent consciencieusement le bleu intense de l'eau et le vert de la végétation foisonnante.

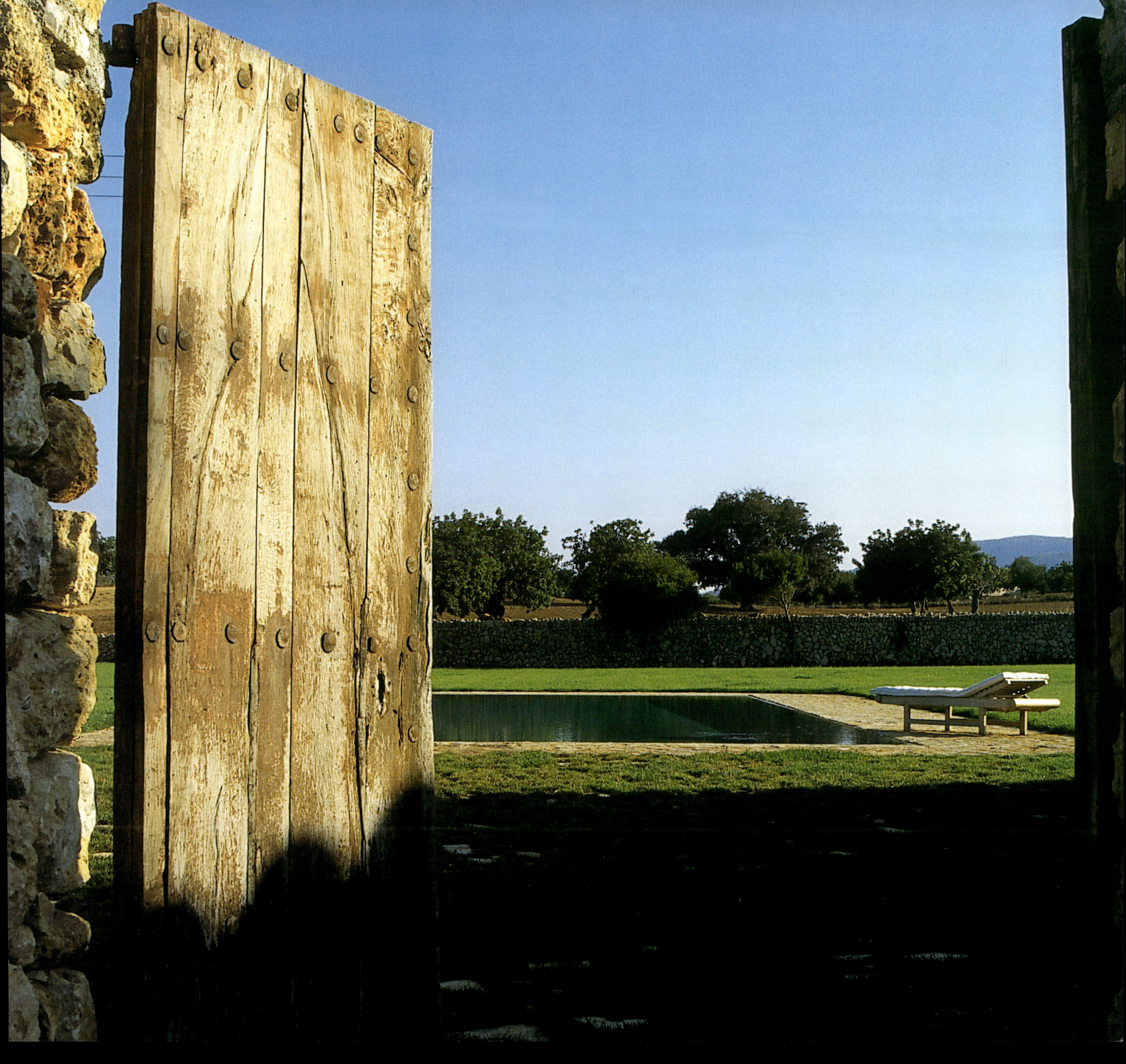

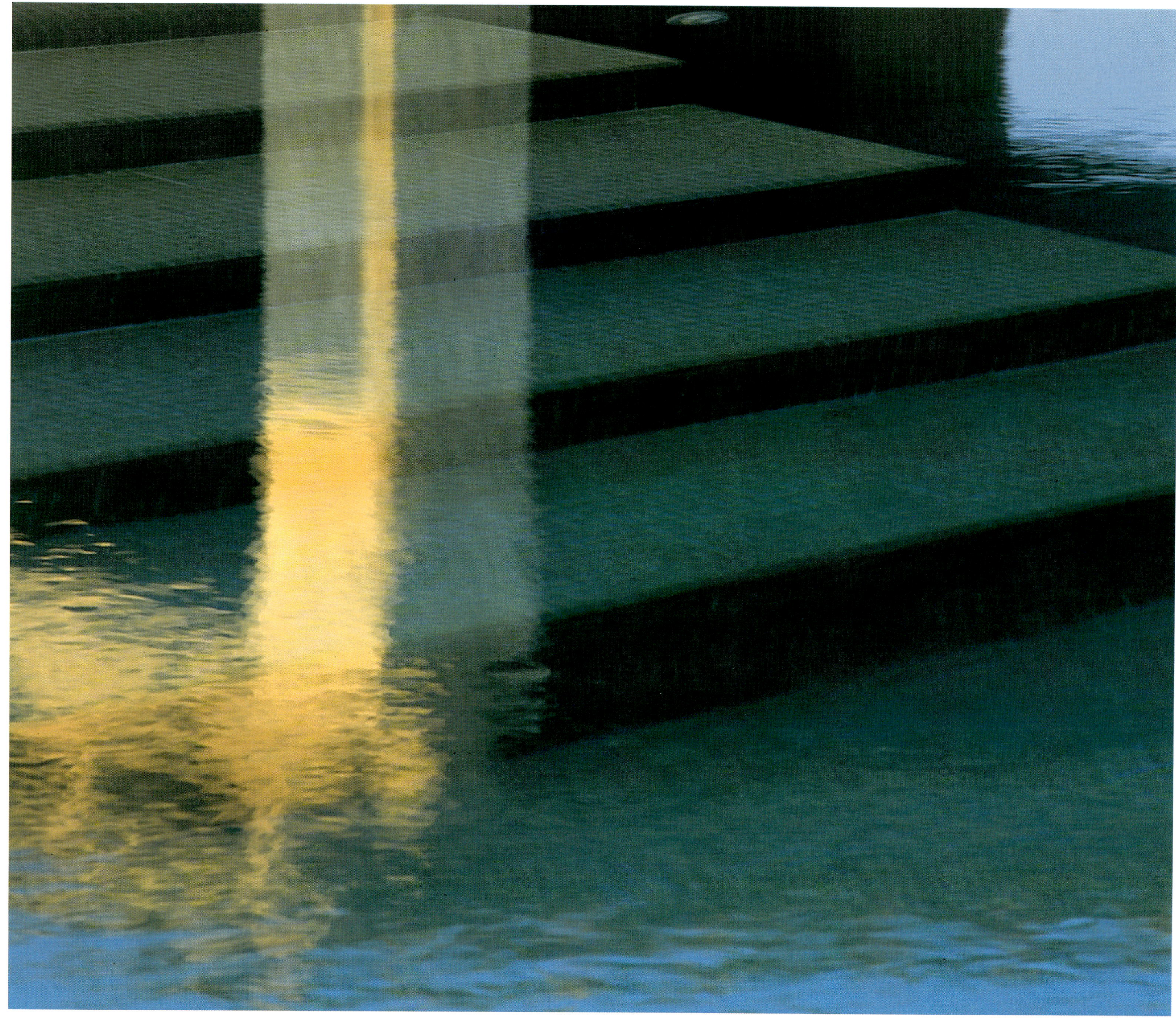

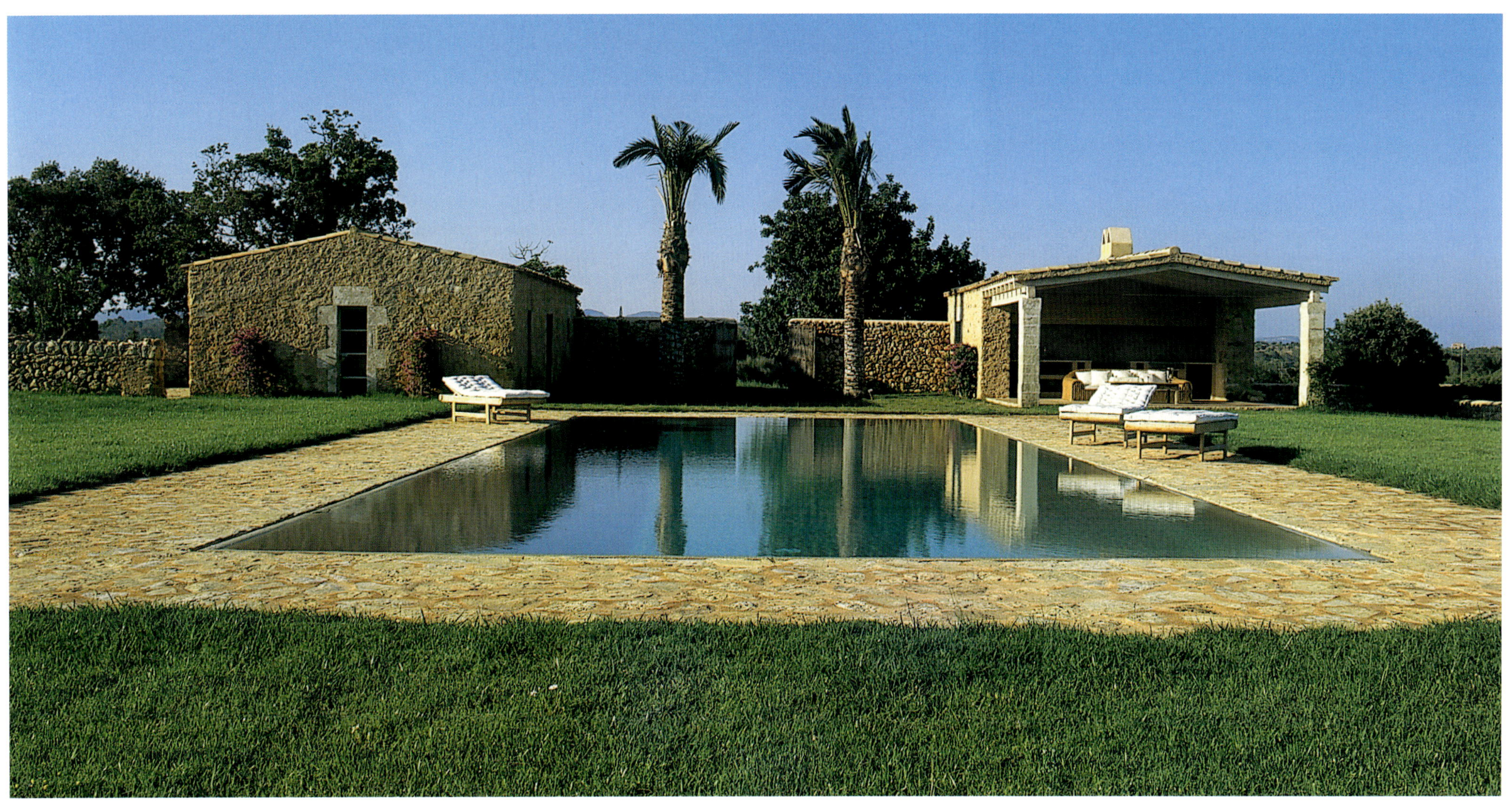

The porch, where the granary originally stood, opens up onto the pool, which is at the same level as the rest of the construction. The barbecue area can be seen next to the sofa.

El porche, donde se ubicaba originalmente el granero, se ha abierto a la piscina, que se desarrolla al mismo nivel que el resto de la construcción. Se puede apreciar, situada detrás del sofá, una zona destinada a la barbacoa.

Das Sommerhaus – einstmals die Scheune – öffnet sich zum Schwimmbecken hin, das mit den anderen Gebäuden auf einer Ebene liegt. Die Grillecke befindet sich hinter dem Sofabereich.

Le porche où autrefois se dressait la grange accueille la piscine, qui s'étale au même niveau que la construction. Derrière le canapé, on découvre un espace destiné au barbecue.

A Mirror Between the Earth and Sky

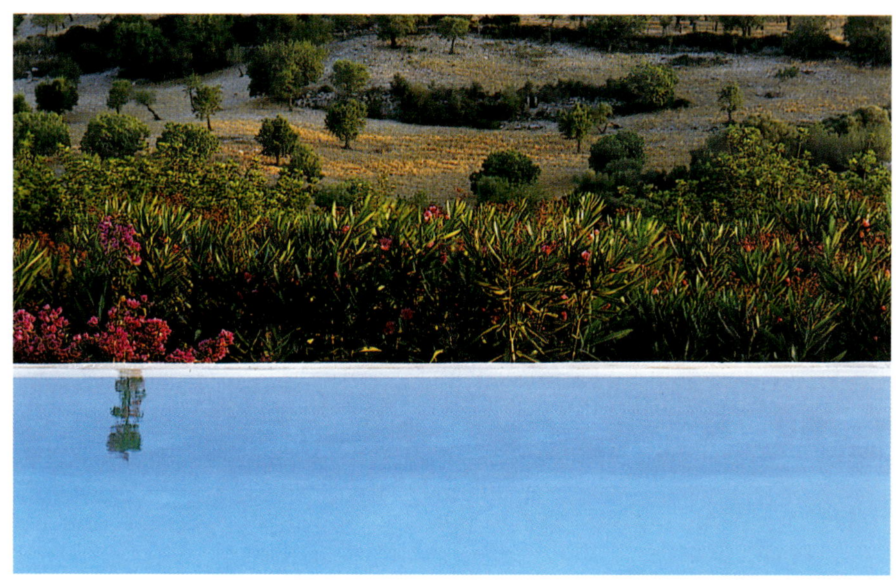

Un Espejo entre la Tierra y el Cielo | Ein Spiegel zwischen Himmel und Erde | Un miroir entre la terre et le ciel

The setting and the placement of this swimming pool were the determining factors in this project.
The irregularly-shaped swimming pool, dotted with small peninsulas of rock, resembles a calm natural lake. In one of the angles, one can see a tree trunk placed strategically for contemplation, in accordance with the tenets of Zen philosophy. In line with this approach the designers wanted to avoid overloading the space around the swimming pool, preferring to give a starring role to the natural surroundings. The edge of the pool is made of the same type of rock used for the small artificial peninsulas.

El emplazamiento y la magnífica orientación de esta piscina han sido dos factores determinantes en la elaboración de este proyecto.
La geometría irregular que presenta esta piscina, salpicada de pequeñas penínsulas de roca, emula la sensación de un apacible lago natural.
El tronco de un árbol retorcido que acusa el paso del tiempo obliga a la mirada a detenerse para contemplarlo, siguiendo las pautas de la filosofía zen. Esta doctrina ha marcado también la decisión de no sobrecargar el espacio que rodea la piscina y conceder el verdadero protagonismo al espléndido entorno natural que abraza todo el conjunto. Para delimitar el perímetro de la piscina se ha optado por aplicar el mismo tipo de roca utilizado en las pequeñas penínsulas artificiales.

Der Standort und die fantastische Ausrichtung dieses Schwimmbeckens waren die ausschlaggebenden Faktoren bei der Entwicklung dieses Projekts. Durch die unregelmäßige Geometrie des Schwimmbeckens mit seinen kleinen felsigen Halbinseln wird die Ausstrahlung eines ruhigen natürlichen Sees nachempfunden. Der durch den Lauf der Zeit gekrümmte Stamm eines Baumes fesselt den Blick des Betrachters und steht im Einklang mit den Idealen der Zen-Philosophie. Im Sinne dieser Philosophie wurde auch beschlossen, den Raum um das Schwimmbecken nicht zu überladen, und die zentrale Rolle dem wunderbaren, natürlichen Umfeld zu überlassen, welches das gesamte Ensemble einschließt. Zur Abgrenzung des Schwimmbeckens wurde deshalb dasselbe felsige Gestein gewählt, das für die künstlichen, kleinen Halbinseln verwendet wurde.

La situation et la magnifique orientation de cette piscine ont été des facteurs déterminants dans l'élaboration de ce projet.
La géométrie irrégulière de cette piscine, éclaboussée de petites péninsules de roche, reproduit la sensation que peut offrir un paisible lac naturel.
Le tronc d'un arbre tordu accusant le passage du temps invite l'œil à la contemplation, principe de la philosophie zen. Cette doctrine transparaît également dans la décision de ne pas surcharger l'espace qui entoure la piscine et de laisser le premier rôle au splendide environnement naturel qui accueille cet ensemble.
Pour délimiter le périmètre de la piscine, le même type de roche que celui qui compose les petites péninsules a été appliqué.

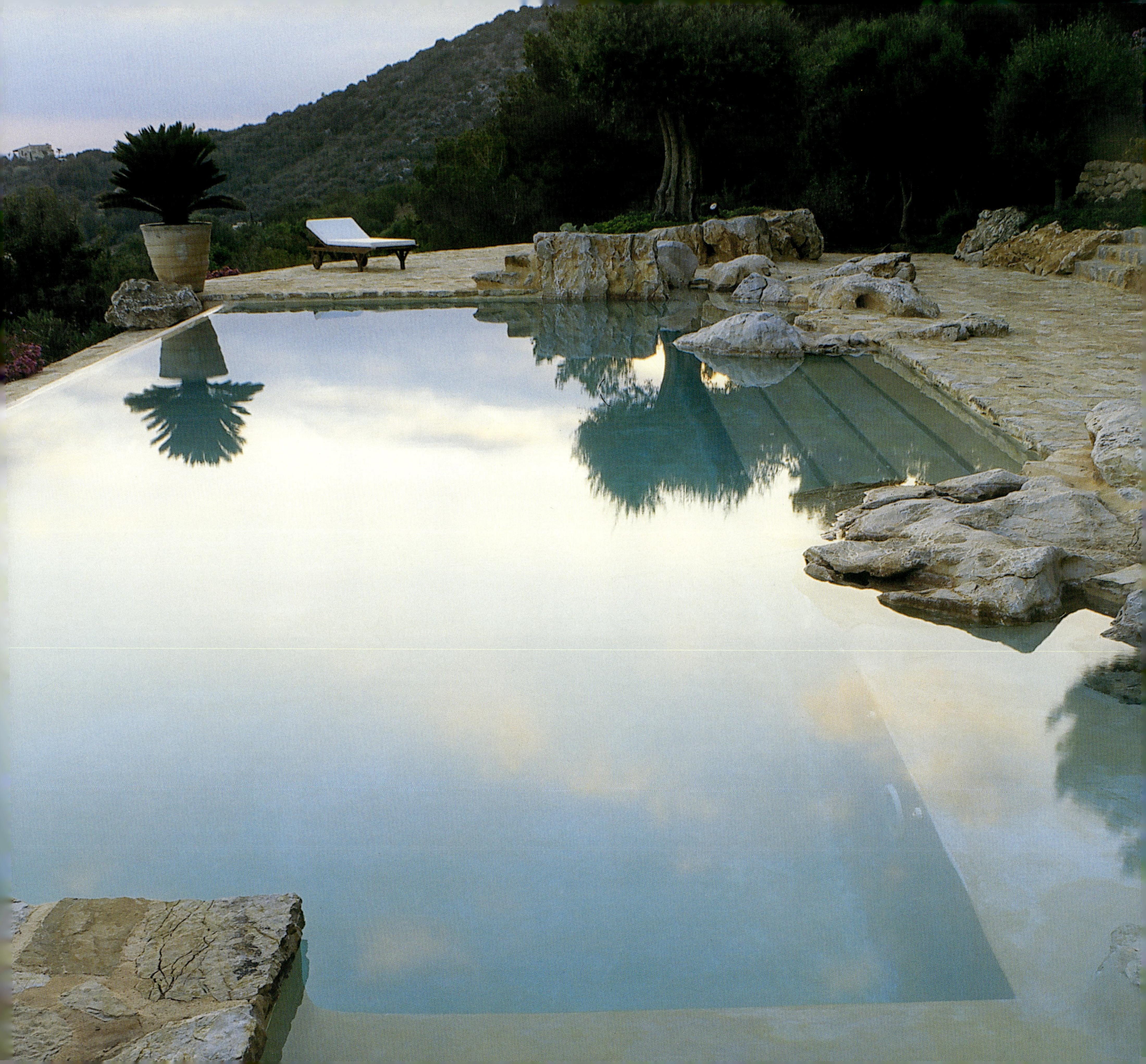

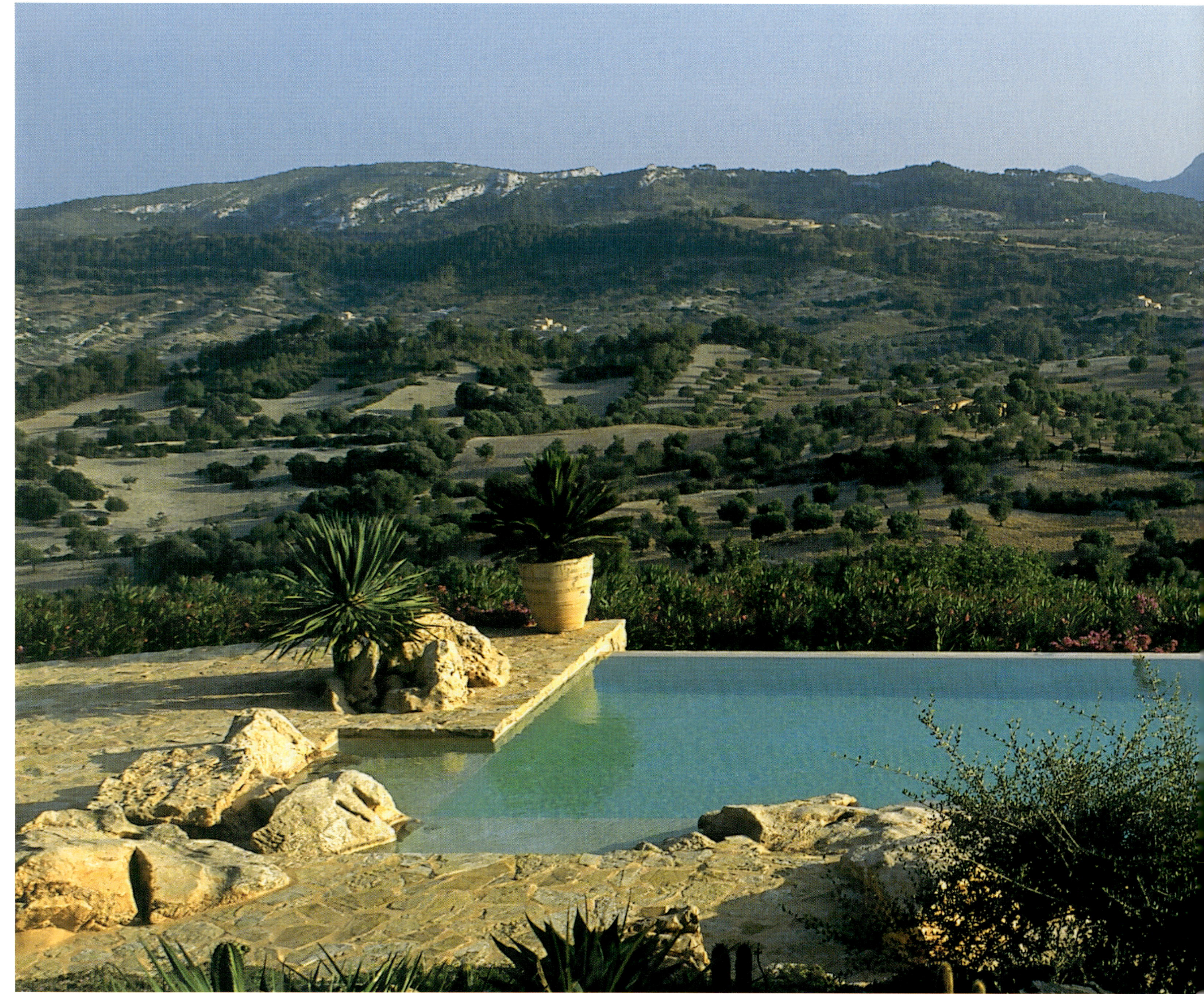

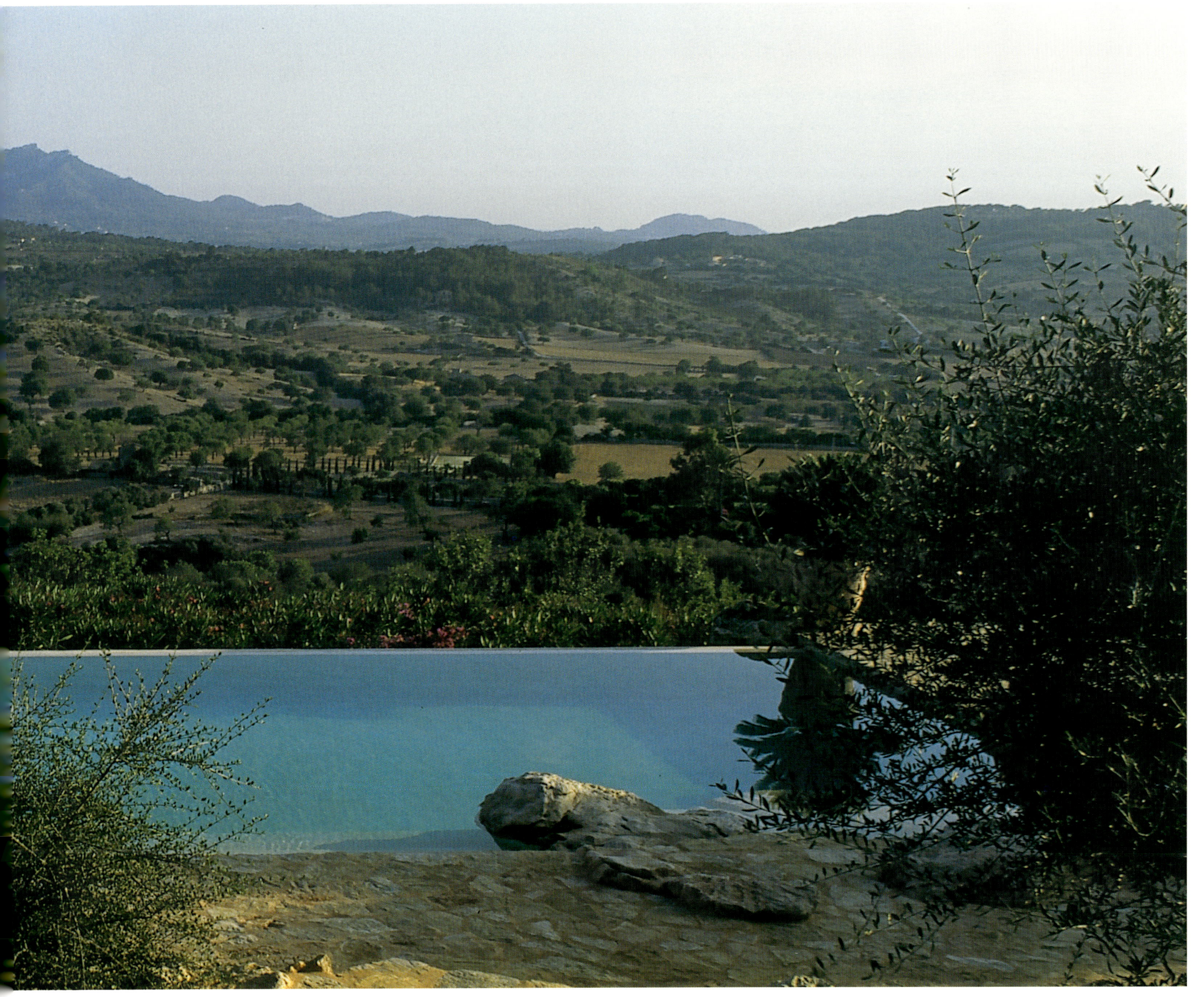

Traditional Inspiration

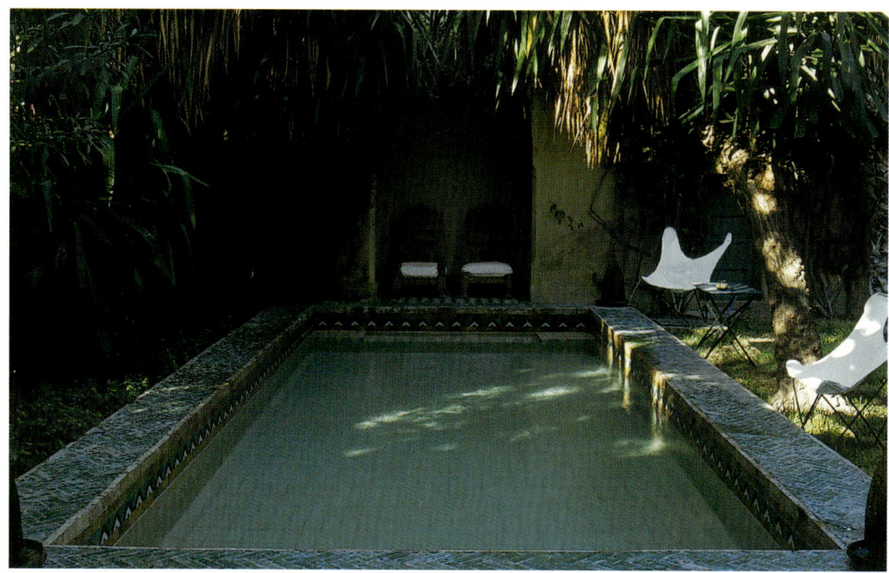

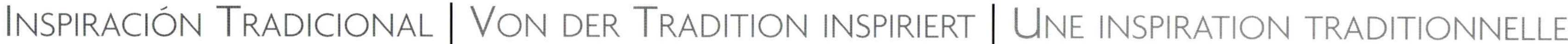

Inspiración Tradicional | Von der Tradition inspiriert | Une inspiration traditionnelle

A small pond in the intimacy of an interior Moroccan patio, this shallow pool is another example of the fine work still done with Moroccan mosaics. A bright turquoise finish that derives all of its splendor from the sun's reflection, crowns a bright border which extends around the entire interior perimeter of the pool. A soft salmon color covers the structure, creating a chromatic axis between the pool and the principal and side façades, which also boast Moroccan floor tiles and two wooden chairs. At a higher level, steps covered with mosaic tiles. Wrought iron and wood furnishings decorate a breakfast/dinner nook.

Estructurada como un pequeño estanque en la exótica intimidad de un patio interior marroquí, esta piscina de poca profundidad representa un ejemplo ilustrativo de cómo se trabaja todavía el mosaico en Marruecos. Un elaborado remate de color turquesa que adquiere todo su esplendor con los reflejos del sol corona una alegre cenefa que rodea todo el perímetro interior de la piscina. Un suave tono salmón reviste la estructura creando de este modo un eje cromático entre la piscina y las fachadas principal y lateral. En esta última se desarrolla un espacio pavimentado también con baldosas marroquíes. A un nivel superior y unida a la zona de agua mediante unos escalones tapizados con gresite del mismo tono que la piscina, se sitúa una pequeña terraza presidida por tres ventanas con forma de arco.

Dieses Becken erinnert an ein kleines, flaches Wasserbecken in der exotischen Intimität eines marokkanischen Innenhofs. Es ist ein anschauliches Beispiel dafür, wie Mosaikarbeiten noch heute in Marokko ausgeführt werden. Ein kunstvoll gearbeiteter Abschluss in Türkis, der unter den Strahlen der Sonne seine volle Pracht entfaltet, krönt eine heitere, über den gesamten Innenrand des Schwimmbeckens reichende Einfassung. Der zart lachsfarbene Ton des Ensembles stellt eine farbliche Achse zwischen dem Schwimmbecken sowie der Haupt- und Seitenfassade her. Letztere blickt auf einen Bereich, dessen Belag ebenfalls aus marokkanischen Fliesen besteht. Eine höher gelegene, kleine und von drei Bogenfenstern geprägte Terrasse ist mit dem Wasserbereich über Treppenstufen verbunden, die mit Glaskeramik im Farbton des Schwimmbeckens verkleidet sind.

Structurée comme un petit bassin dans l'intimité exotique d'une cour intérieure marocaine, cette piscine peu profonde illustre bien comment se travaille encore la mosaïque au Maroc.
Une finition élaborée de couleur turquoise, qui acquiert toute sa splendeur dans les reflets du soleil, couronne une bordure gaie qui entoure tout le périmètre intérieur de la piscine. Un ton saumon très doux revêt la structure, créant ainsi un axe chromatique entre la piscine, la façade principale et la façade latérale. Au pied de cette dernière, on trouve un espace pavé de carreaux marocains. Un peu plus haut se trouve, unie à la zone d'eau par quelques marches tapissées d'un Gresite du même ton que la piscine, une petite terrasse présidée par trois fenêtres en forme d'arc.

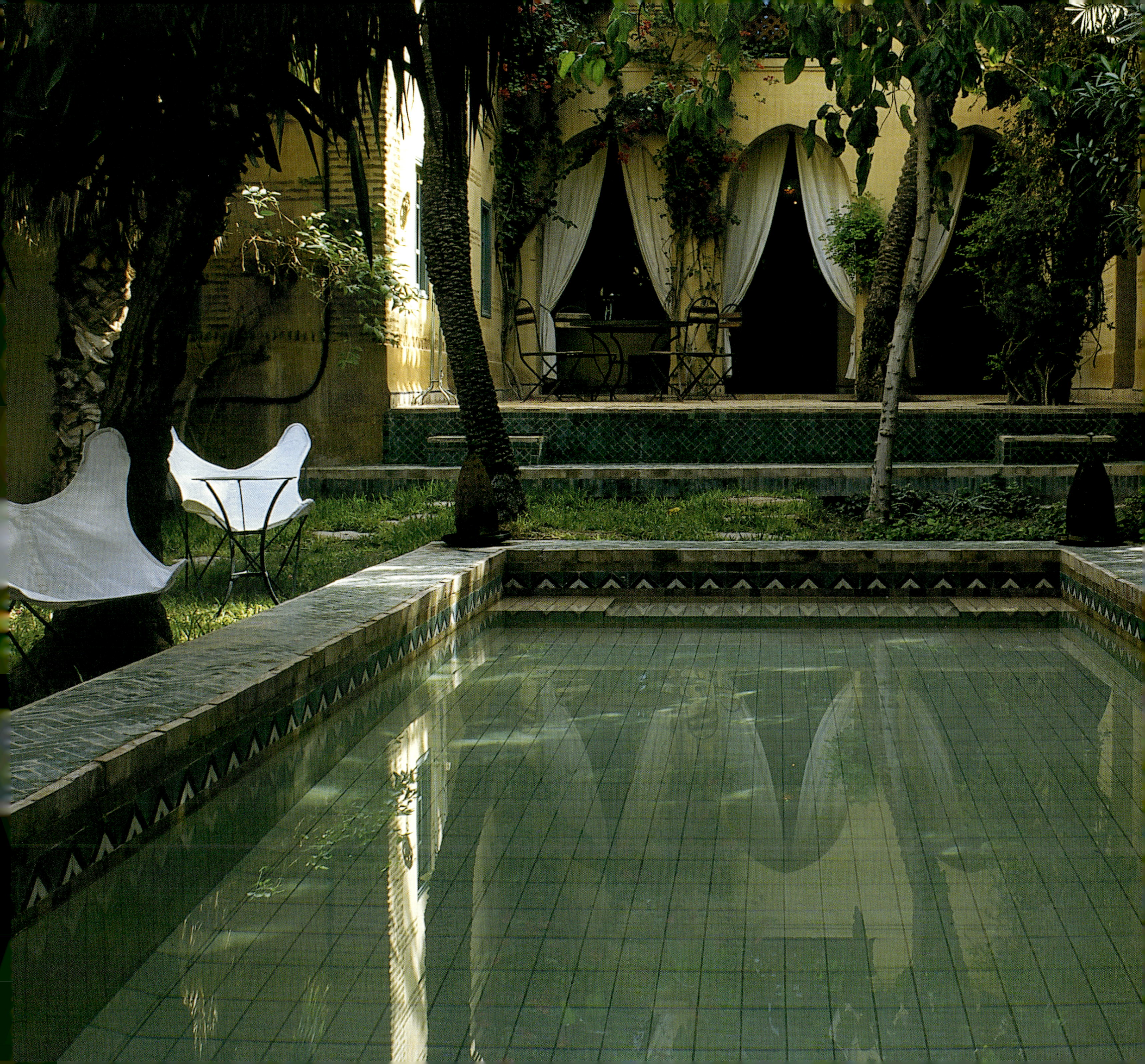

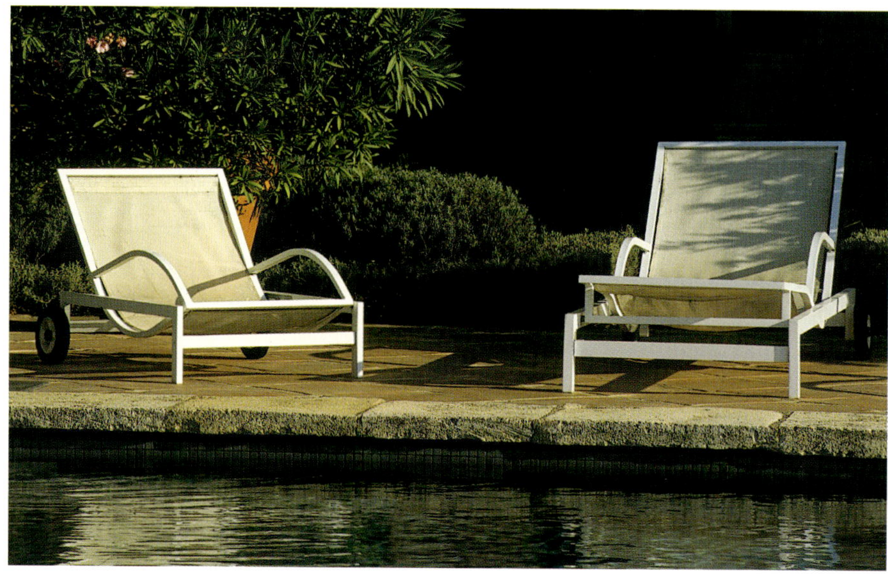

Classical Personality

Personalidad Clásica | Klassischer Charakter | Une personnalité classique

This pool's layout follows the model of the classical houses of French Provence, with two differentiated exterior spaces. Directly in front of the main rooms, this delicious water area is well-defined. Only the skilled hand of a fine gardener and the passage of time could achieve such elegance. On one level the pool is finished with a rustic crown of natural stone, and the inside is coated with blue mosaic tiles. Large slabs of unglazed, fired clay pave this recreational area.
The garden maintains a delicate symmetry of plant life. Boxwood hedges of different heights visually separate the various landscaped areas.

El planteamiento de esta piscina sigue las pautas de las clásicas casas de la Provenza francesa, que presentan dos espacios exteriores claramente diferenciados. Situada frente a la fachada de la casa, justo delante de las habitaciones principales de modo que facilita el acceso directo, se descubre esta deliciosa zona de agua. En un primer plano se sitúa la piscina con esa elegancia que sólo el paso del tiempo y la mano de un buen jardinero pueden conseguir. Formalmente, está rematada por una corona rústica de piedra natural y el vaso está revestido de gresite de color azul. Grandes losas de barro cocido sin barnizar pavimentan este espacio. El jardín, concebido como una prolongación natural de la vivienda, ofrece una delicada simetría vegetal a base de setos de boj de distintas alturas.

Die Anlage dieses Schwimmbeckens steht in der Tradition der typischen Häuser der Provence, die zwei klar differenzierte Außenbereiche aufweisen. Dieses herrliche Wasserbecken liegt den Haupträumen des Hauses genau gegenüber, wodurch man einen direkten Zugang hat. Das Schwimmbecken steht mit jener Eleganz im Vordergrund, die nur im Laufe der Zeit und dank der Arbeit eines guten Gärtners möglich geworden ist. Formal wird das Becken durch eine rustikale Einfassung aus Naturstein abgeschlossen, während die Verkleidung des Beckens aus blauer Glaskeramik besteht. Für den Belag in diesem Bereich wurden große, unlackierte Terrakottafliesen verwendet. Der als natürliche Verlängerung des Wohnhauses angelegte Garten weist eine wohl austarierte pflanzliche Symmetrie auf, die sich in mehreren Buchsbaumhecken unterschiedlicher Höhe manifestiert.

La conception de cette piscine s'inspire des caractéristiques des maisons de Provence classiques, qui présentent deux espaces extérieurs clairement différenciés. Face à la façade de la maison, juste devant les pièces principales afin de leur offrir un accès direct, on découvre cette délicieuse zone d'eau. Au premier plan figure la piscine, forte de cette élégance que seuls savent créer le passage du temps et la main d'un bon jardinier. Formellement, la finition consiste en une rustique couronne de pierre naturelle et le bassin est revêtu de Gresite bleu. De grandes dalles en glaise cuite non vernies pavent cet espace.
Le jardin, conçu comme une prolongation naturelle de l'habitation, offre une délicate symétrie végétale basée sur des haies de buis de hauteur différente.

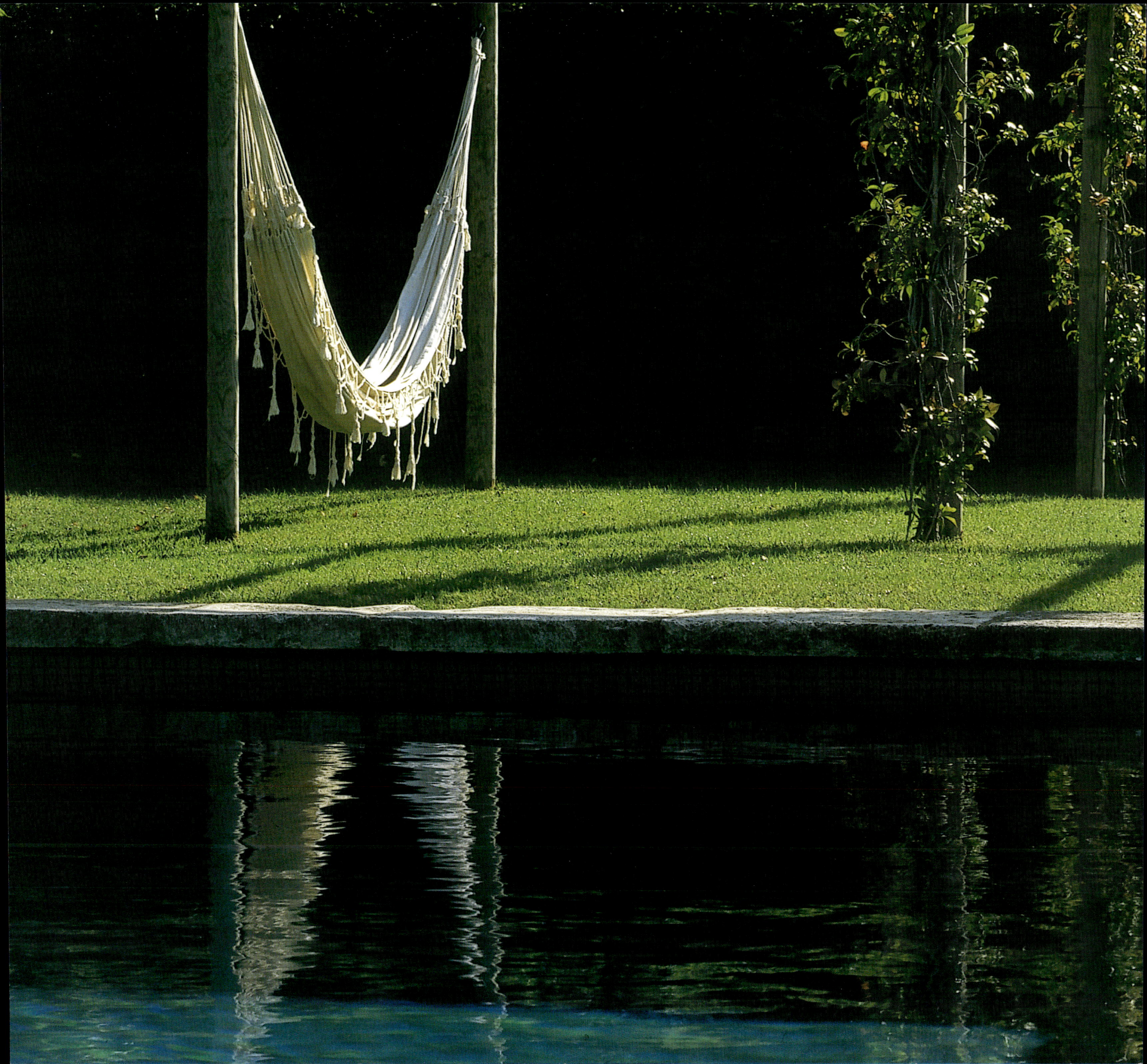

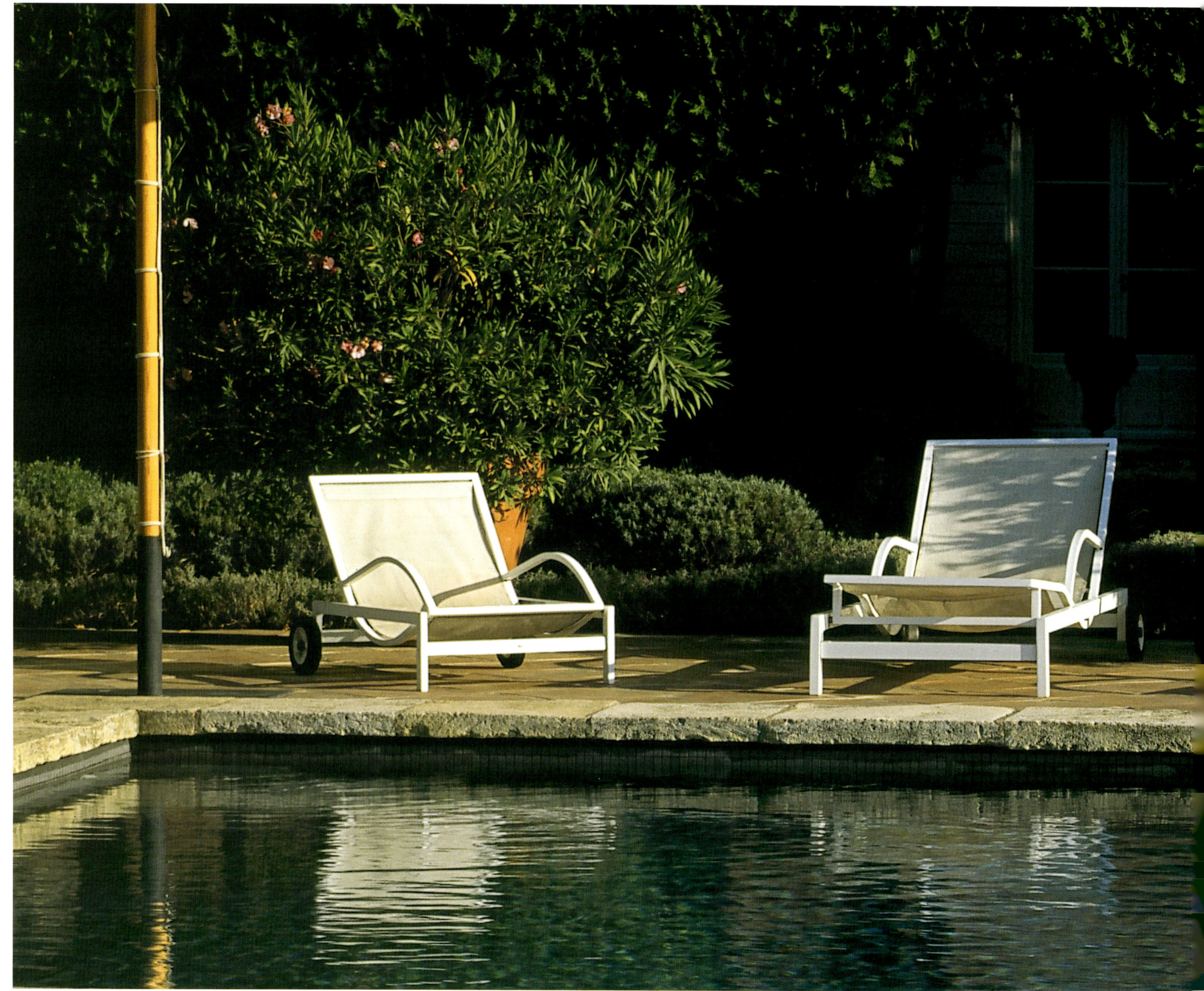

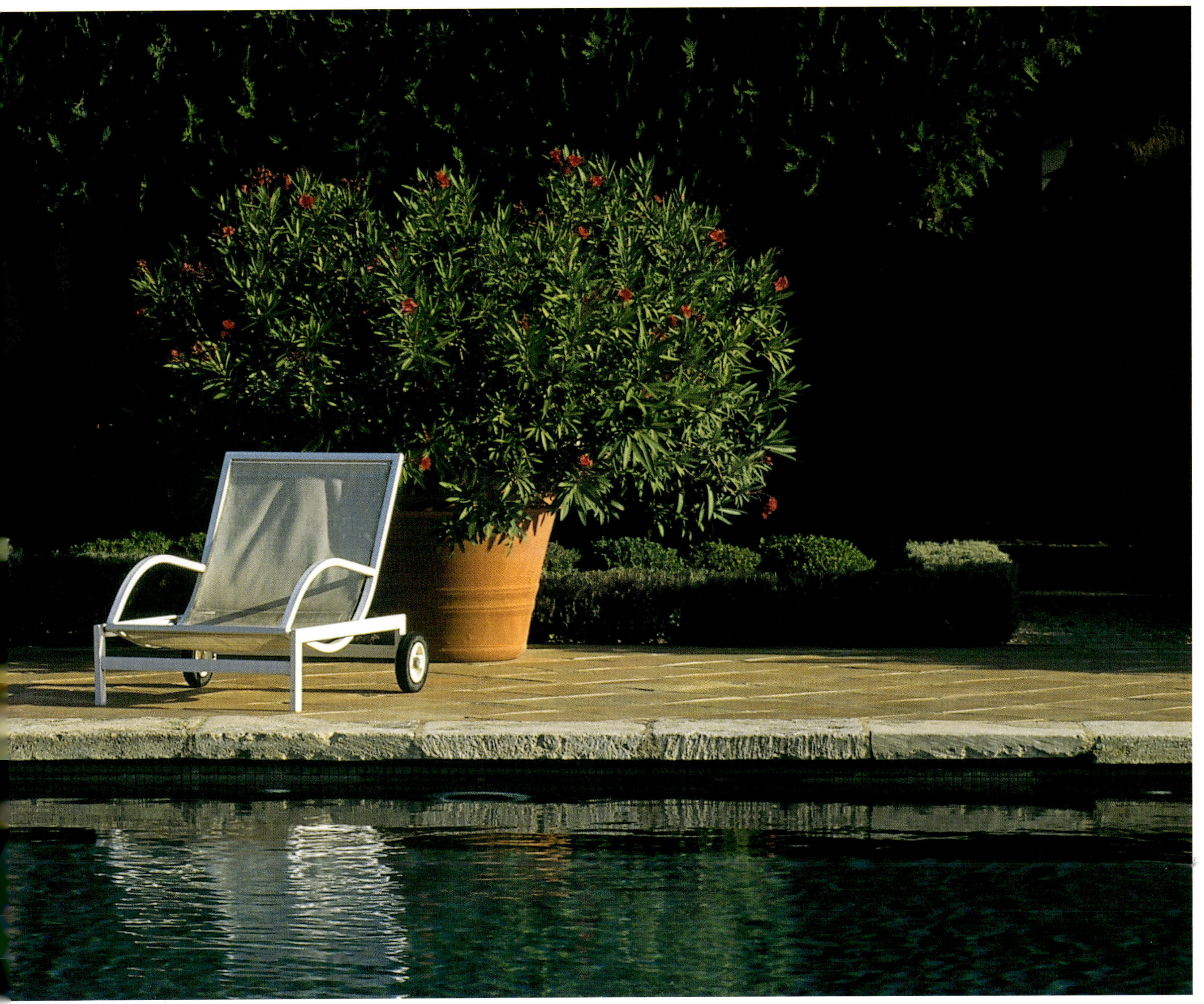

To Live in Paradise

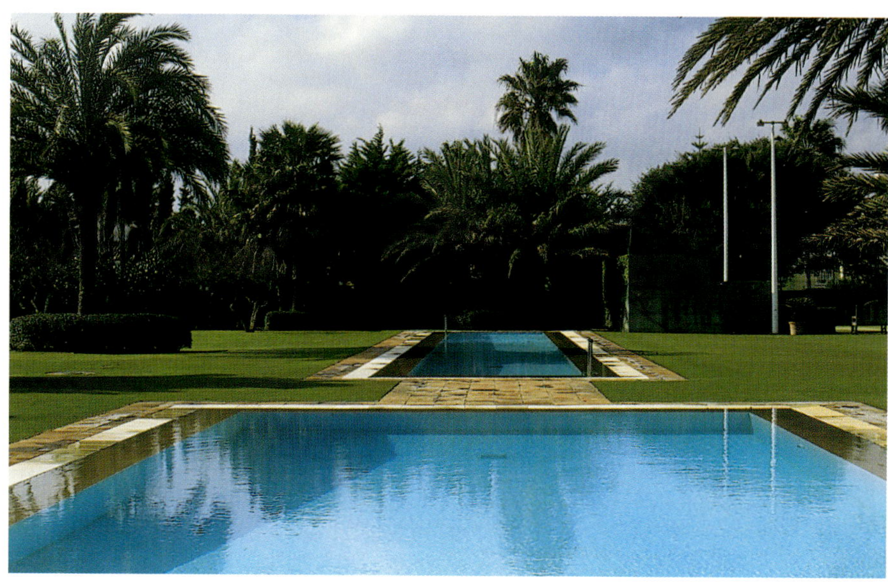

Vivir en el Paraiso | Leben im Paradies | Vivre au paradis

Drenched in the spectacular Mediterranean light of Cádiz, Spain, are these two geometric pools. The first, square and smaller, dates back to the 1960's, and was part of the original construction. As part of the restoration, the owners wanted to add another pool. The new pool was built to resemble the older one and the same design and materials were used. The interior and the bottom are painted white, which grants it a very evocative bluish tone that is an invitation to bathe.
The new pool, which is designed, above all, for swimming, is equipped with a ladder at both ends for easy access in and out.

Rodeadas de la maravillosa luz de Cádiz (España) se encuentran estas piscinas. Se trata de dos construcciones geométricas de dimensiones y formas ligeramente diferentes. La primera, cuadrada y más pequeña, es una piscina de los años sesenta ya existente en la construcción original. Iniciados los trabajos de reforma, los propietarios desearon añadir una piscina más. Se construyó a imagen de la preexistente, por lo que en ella se aplicaron las mismas técnicas y materiales constructivos.
Todo el interior, así como el fondo, se ha pintado de blanco para conseguir esa tonalidad azul tan sugerente que invita al baño.
La piscina nueva, al estar concebida principalmente para practicar la natación, cuenta con sendas escaleras de acceso en los extremos.

Das wundervolle Licht von Cádiz im Süden Spaniens umspielt diese Schwimmbecken. Es handelt sich dabei um zwei geometrische Körper mit leicht unterschiedlichen Dimensionen und Formen. Das erste, quadratisch und kleiner, ist ein bereits mit der ursprünglichen Anlage entstandenes Schwimmbecken aus den 1960er Jahren. Nach Beginn der Umbauarbeiten beschlossen die Eigentümer den Bau eines weiteren Schwimmbeckens. Es wurde nach dem Vorbild des bereits existierenden errichtet, weshalb dabei dieselbe Bautechnik und -materialien zur Anwendung kamen. Die gesamte Innenfläche wie auch der Grund wurden weiß gestrichen, um diesen suggestiven Blauton zu erzielen, der zum Baden einlädt. Das neue Schwimmbecken hat an beiden Enden eine Leiter.

C'est sous la merveilleuse lumière de Cadix (Espagne) que reposent ces piscines. Il s'agit de deux constructions géométriques de dimension et de forme légèrement différente. La première, carrée et plus petite, est une piscine des années 60, déjà présente dans la construction initiale. Au cours des travaux de rénovation, les propriétaires ont souhaité ajouter une autre piscine. Construite à l'image de la première, les mêmes techniques et les mêmes matériaux y ont été employés.
L'intérieur et le fond ont été peints en blanc afin d'obtenir cette tonalité bleue tellement fascinante, véritable invitation à la baignade.
La nouvelle piscine, conçue principalement pour la pratique de la natation, dispose d'un escalier d'accès à chaque extrémité.

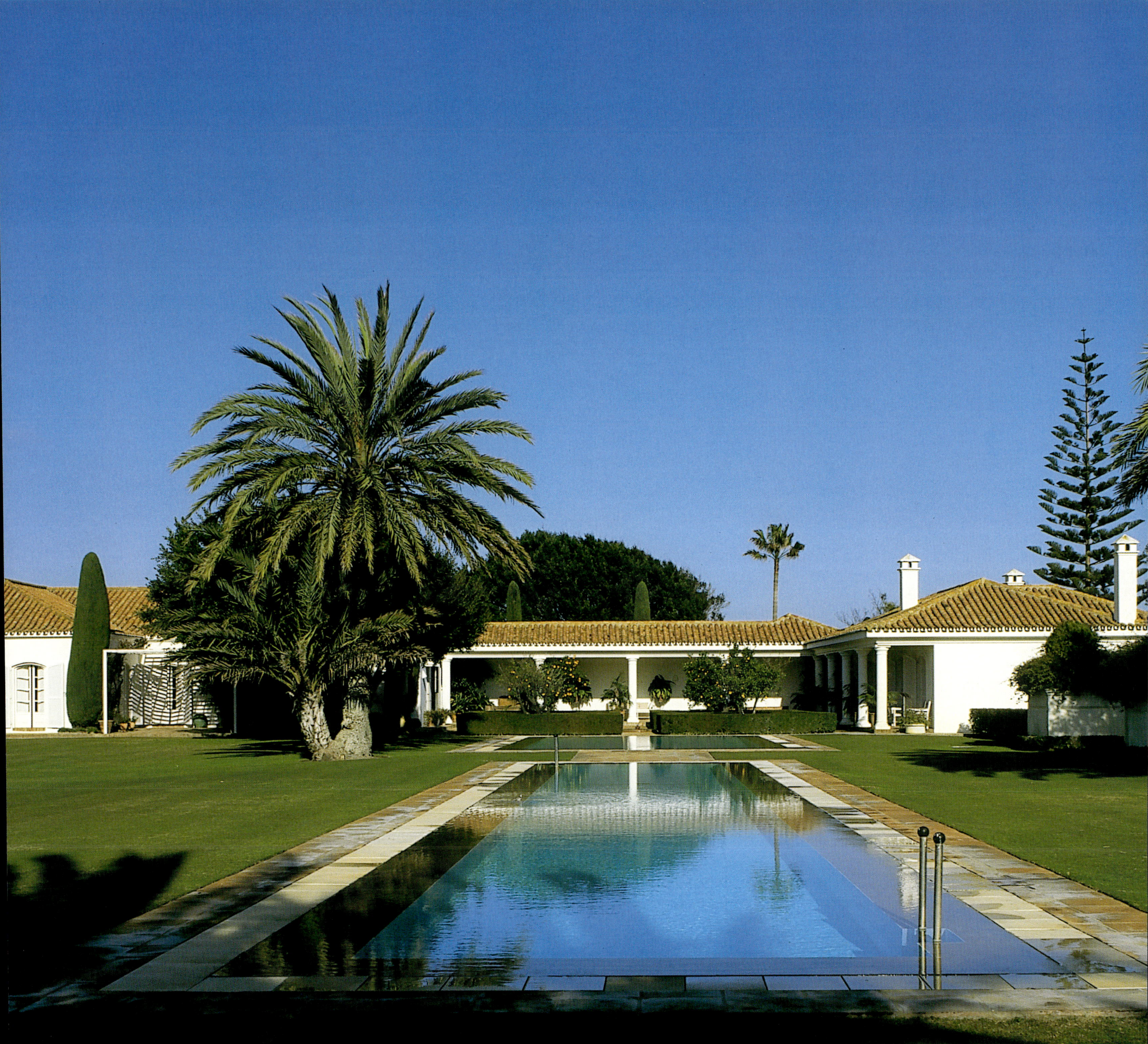

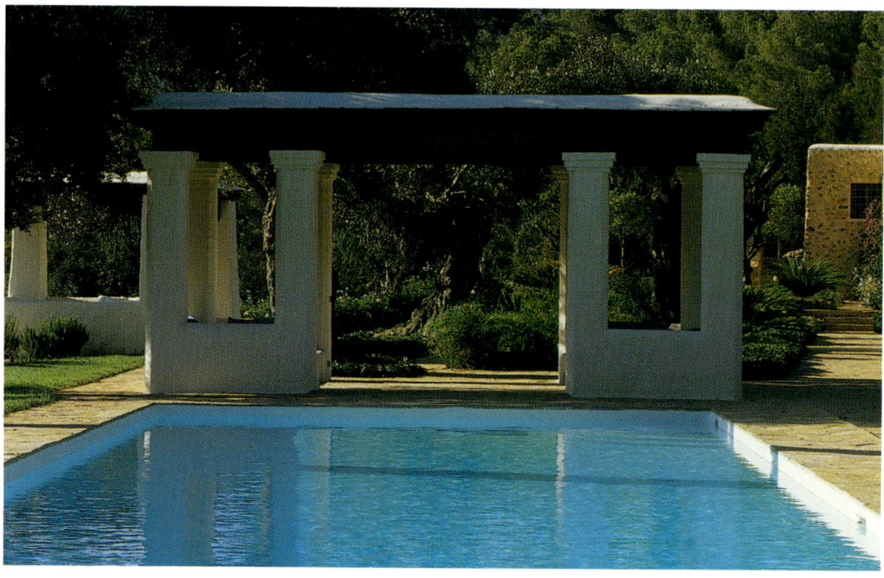

THE PATINA OF TIME

LA PÁTINA DEL TIEMPO | DIE PATINA DER ZEIT | LA PATINE DU TEMPS

The presence of many ponds, parterres and paved paths that lead unhurriedly to different areas of the garden, makes the pool a secondary element in this kaleidoscope of plant life.
Surrounding the pool area are several pavilions, whitewashed and coated with a layer of lime mortar. The body of the pool is a continuation of the materials and the tones of the setting. The surrounding area is organized around a low garden that includes papyrus, which grows in the ponds, and cycad, a very slow-growing Japanese species. This is combined with some ancient olive trees that preside over the entrance to the pool area.

La presencia de múltiples estanques y parterres, y de senderos pulcramente empedrados que nos conducen a las diferentes áreas del jardín convierten la piscina en un elemento secundario pero perfectamente integrado en este calidoscopio vegetal.
Bordeando el área de la piscina se han situado varios pabellones encalados y rematados con una capa de mortero de cal.
El vaso de la piscina marca la continuidad entre los materiales y la tonalidad del entorno.
El terreno, organizado a partir de una jardinería baja donde destacan el papiro, que crece en el agua de los estanques, y las cicas, una especie procedente de Japón, se combina con unos olivos antiquísimos que presiden la entrada del área de la piscina.

Die zahlreichen Wasserbecken und Blumenbeete und die säuberlich gepflasterten, in die verschiedenen Bereiche des Gartens führenden Pfade machen das Schwimmbecken zu einem sekundären, jedoch hervorragend in dieses pflanzliche Kaleidoskop integriertes Element.
Um den Beckenbereich herum wurden mehrere weiß getünchte, mit einer Kalkmörtelschicht verputzte Pavillons errichtet. Das Beckeninnere greift die Materialien und Farbtönen der Umgebung auf.
Das Gelände kombiniert eine durchgehend niedrige Bepflanzung – aus welcher der im Teich wachsende Papyrus und die japanischen Palmfarne besonders hervorstehen, ebenso wie einige uralte Olivenbäumen, die den Eingang zum Beckenbereich beherrschen.

La présence de multiples bassins, parterres et sentiers à l'empierrement soigné conduisant aux différentes parties du jardin relègue la piscine à un rôle secondaire, mais parfaitement intégré à ce kaléidoscope végétal.
En bordure de la zone de la piscine ont été construits plusieurs pavillons blanchis à la chaux, aux finitions en mortier.
Le bassin de la piscine établit une continuité entre les matériaux et la tonalité du cadre.
S'organisant autour d'un jardinage simple où se détache le papyrus qui pousse dans l'eau des bassins et les cycas, espèce provenant du Japon, le terrain compose également avec de très vieux oliviers qui président l'accès à la zone de la piscine.

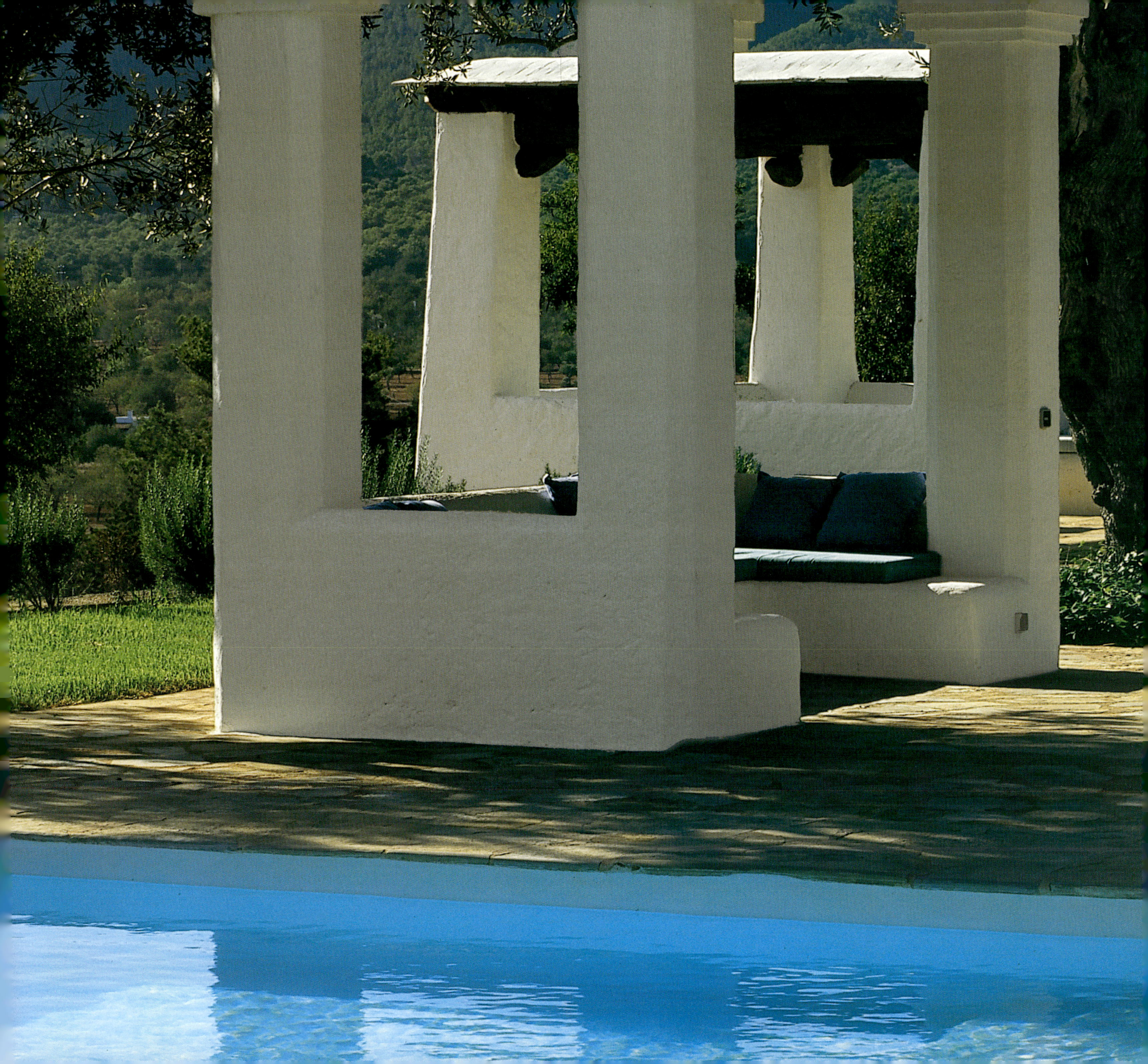

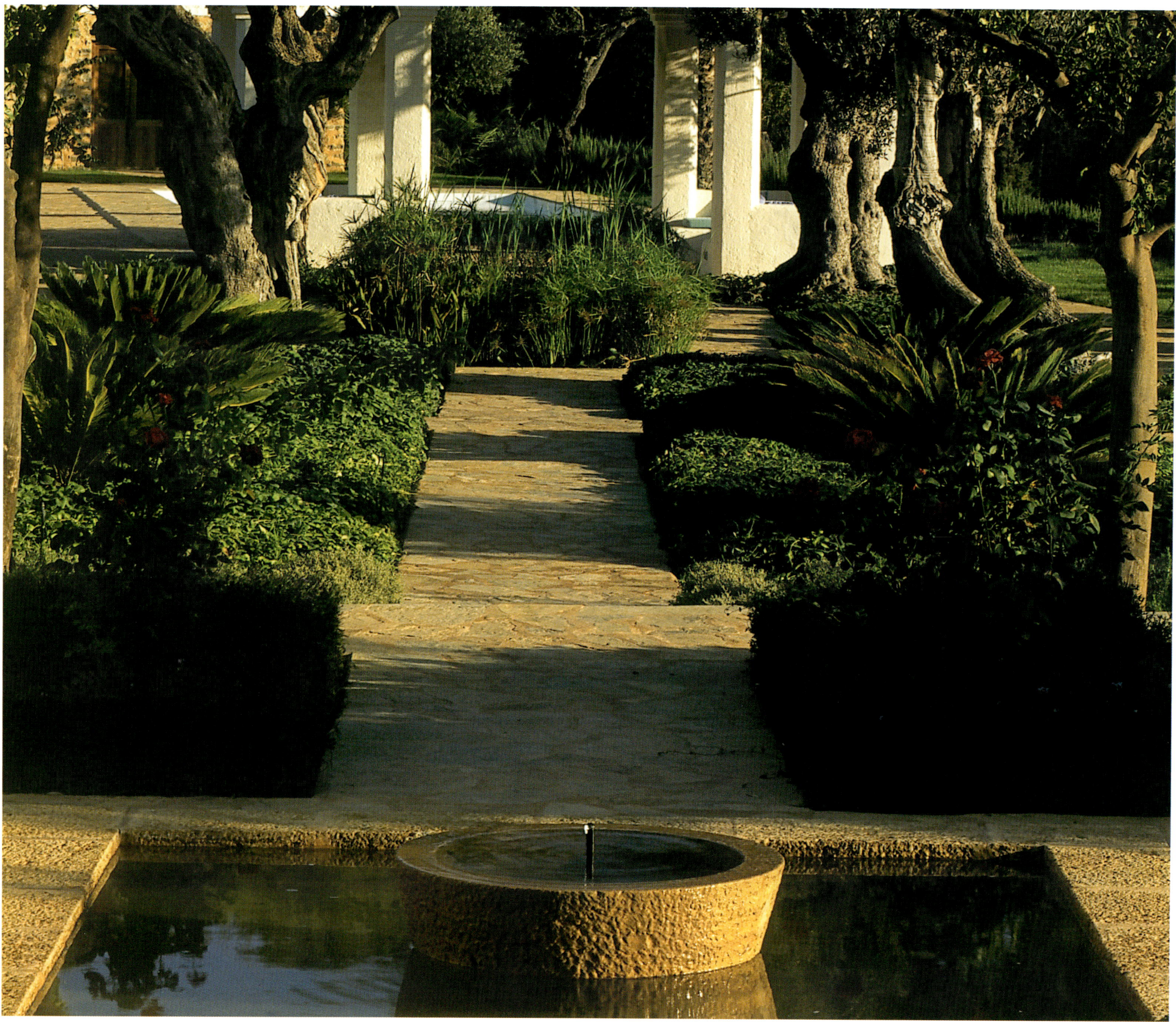

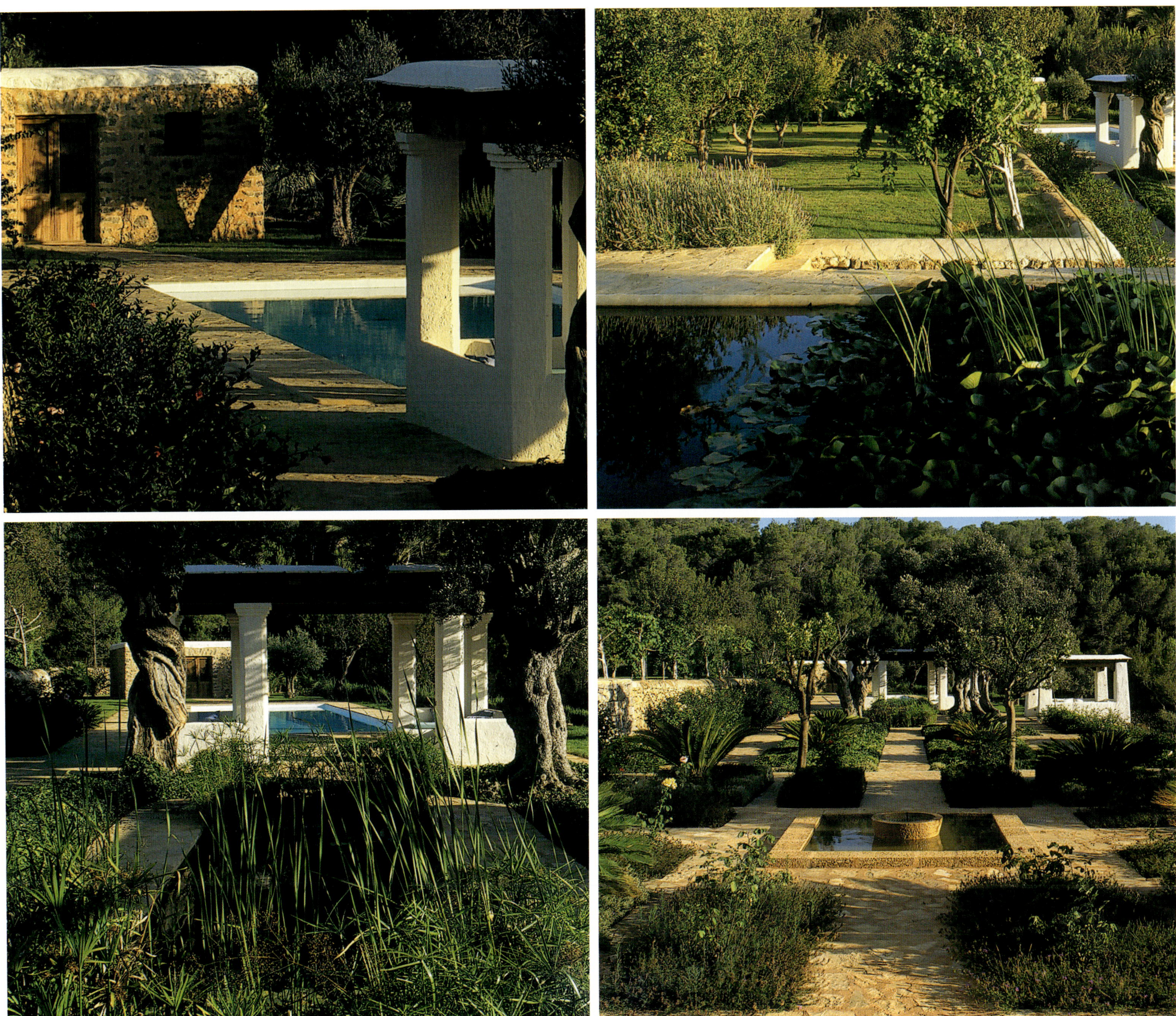

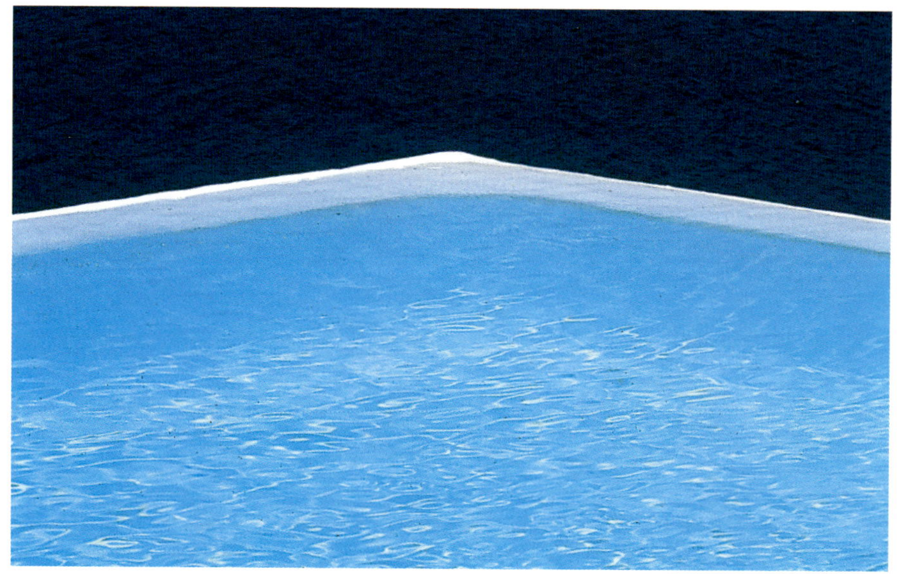

The Magic of a Setting

La Magia de un Entorno | Der Zauber einer Umgebung | La magie d'un décor

Through the use of carefully-placed gradients, a linear geometry that creates spectacular perspectives, and a palette based just on one color, blue, a magnificent composition has been achieved that extends visually to the depths of the sea and sky. The interior of the pool has been coated white, increasing the contrast of tones while creating a white geometric border, which is like an optical interlude between the deep blue of the sea and the crystalline tone of the pool water.
The simple lines of the two porches, combined with cement, which crowns the pool and covers its entire perimeter, and iron, which acts as the principal support of the exterior structure, are the key elements to the pool's integration with the surroundings.

Mediante unos estudiados desniveles, una geometría lineal que provoca espectaculares perspectivas y una paleta cromática basada en un único color, el azul, se ha desarrollado una magnífica composición que se prolonga visualmente en la profundidad del mar y del cielo.
Para destacar esta imagen se ha optado por revestir el vaso de la piscina de color blanco y así potenciar el contraste de tonos a la vez que se crea una franja geométrica blanca, como un interludio óptico entre el azul intenso del mar y la tonalidad cristalina del agua de la piscina. La sobriedad lineal de los dos porches junto a la utilización de materiales tan comunes como el cemento, que corona la piscina y cubre todo su perímetro, y el hierro, que actúa como soporte principal de la estructura exterior, se convierten en los elementos claves de su integración en el entorno.

Das wohl ausgeklügelte Gefälle, die lineare und spektakuläre Blickwinkel eröffnende Geometrie sowie die auf einem einzigen Grundton – Blau – aufbauende Farbpalette sind die Basis für eine herrliche Komposition, die sich optisch bis in die Tiefen von Himmel und Meer verlängert. Zur Betonung dieses Bilds wurde das Becken weiß ausgekleidet, um so den Kontrast zwischen den Farbtönen zu verstärken. Dadurch entsteht ein weißer geometrischer Streifen als optisches Element zwischen dem intensiven Blau des Meeres und dem kristallinen Farbton des Wassers des Beckens. Die lineare Nüchternheit der beiden Anbauten, die Verwendung solch alltäglicher Materialien wie Zement, der für die Einfassung des Schwimmbeckens verwendet wurde, oder Eisen, das den Hauptbestandteil der äußeren Struktur darstellt, werden zu Schlüsselelementen der Integration des Beckens in die Umgebung.

Faisant appel à de savantes dénivellations, à une géométrie linéaire créatrice de perspectives spectaculaires et à une palette chromatique basée sur une couleur unique - le bleu - une magnifique composition est née. La mer et le ciel lui offrent un prolongement visuel tout en profondeur. Pour que son image s'en détache, le bassin de la piscine a été revêtu d'une couleur blanche, renforçant ainsi le contraste des tons tout en créant une frise géométrique blanche, interlude optique entre le bleu intense de la mer et la tonalité cristalline de l'eau de la piscine. Sobriété linéaire des deux porches, utilisation de matériaux aussi communs que le ciment - qui couronne la piscine et en recouvre tout le périmètre - et le fer, support principal de la structure extérieure : tels sont les éléments clés de l'intégration de la piscine dans son environnement.

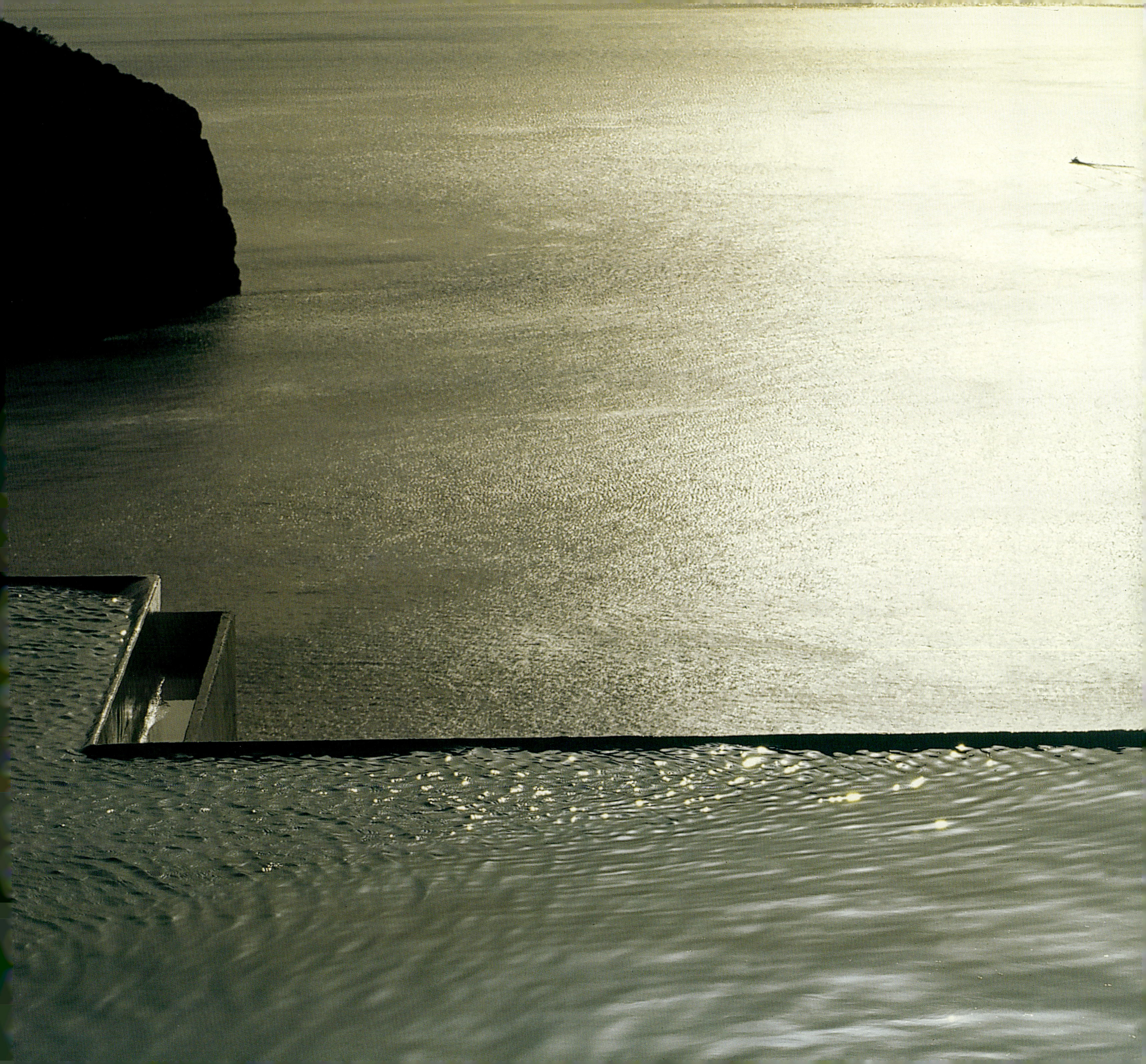

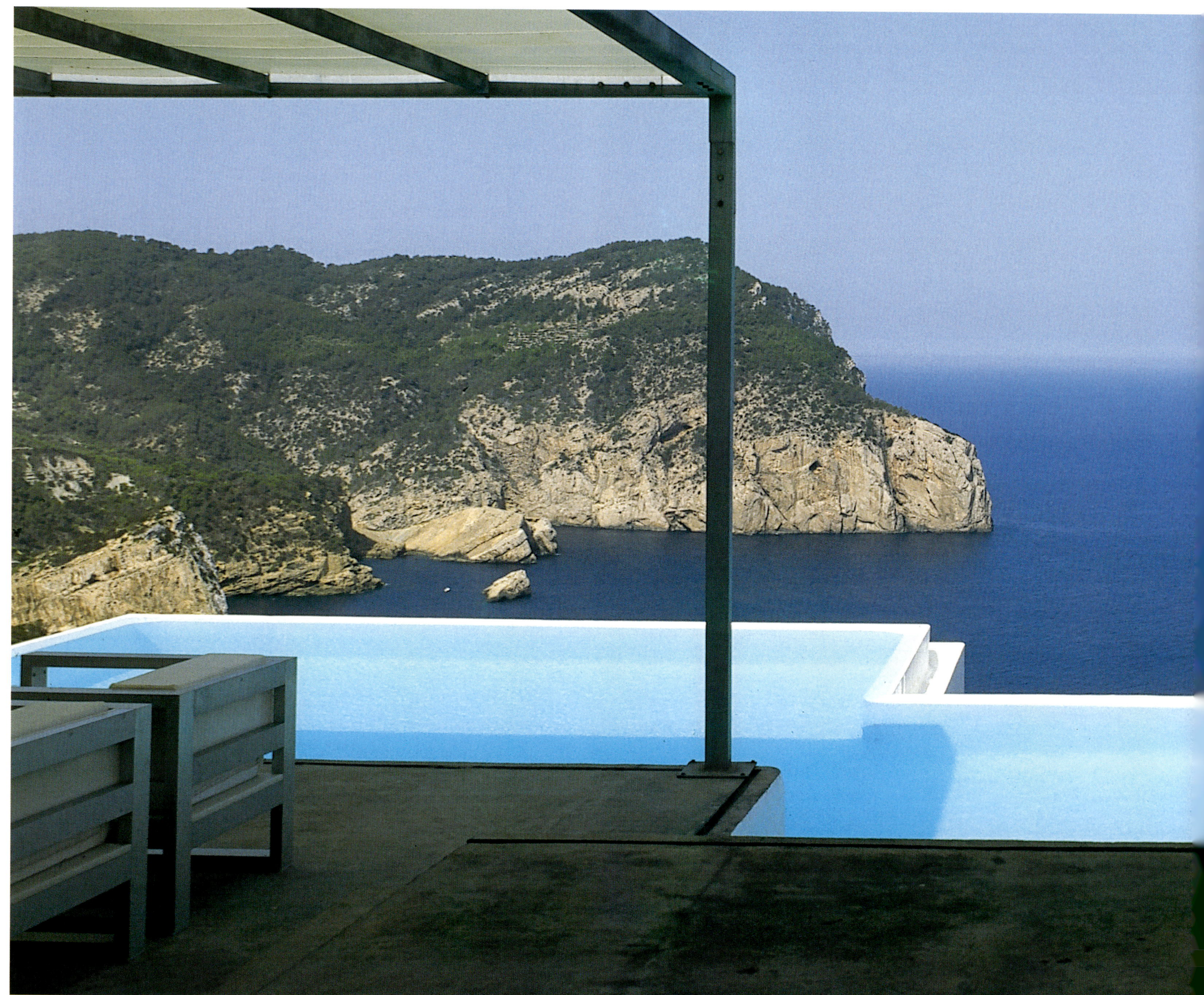

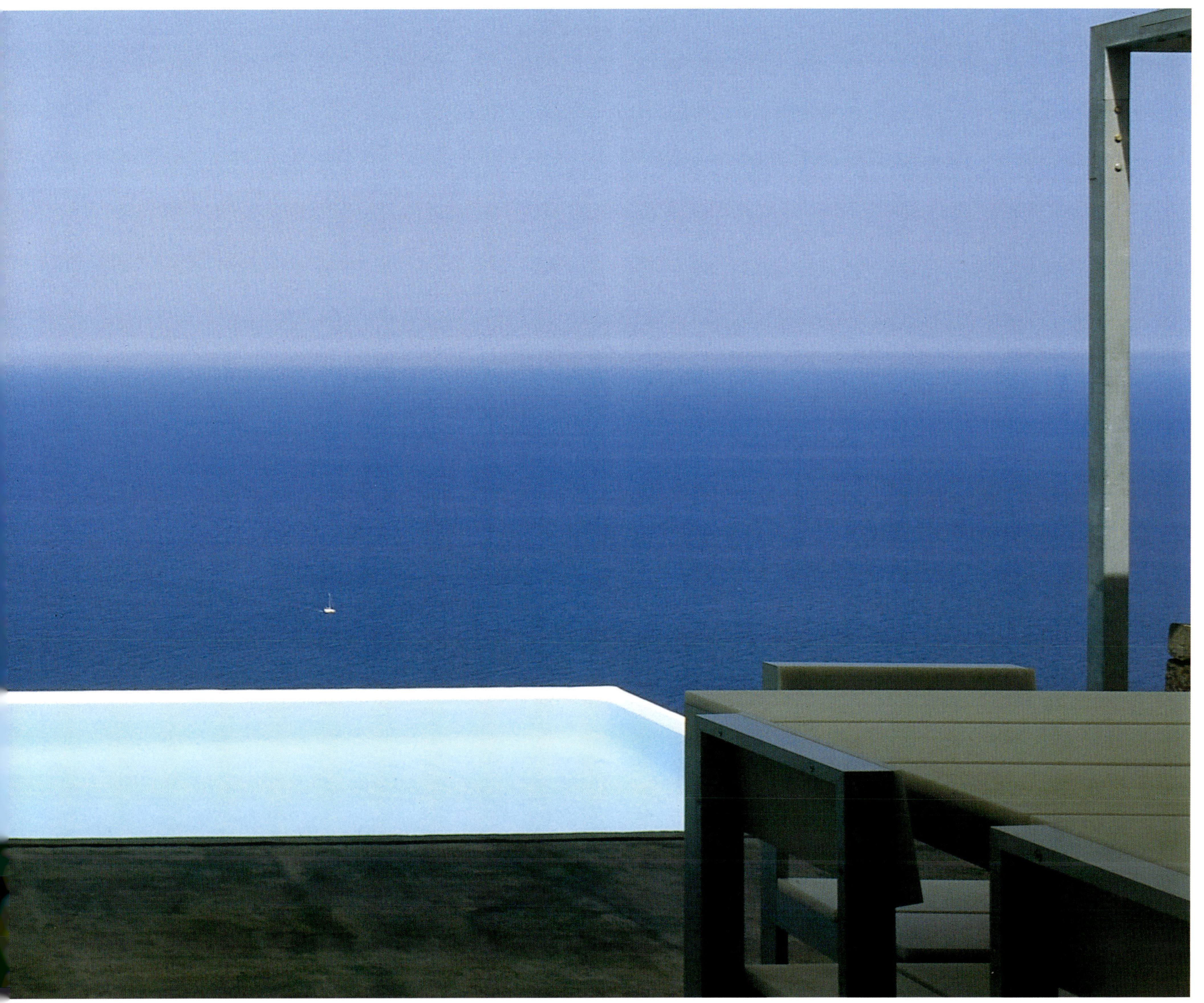

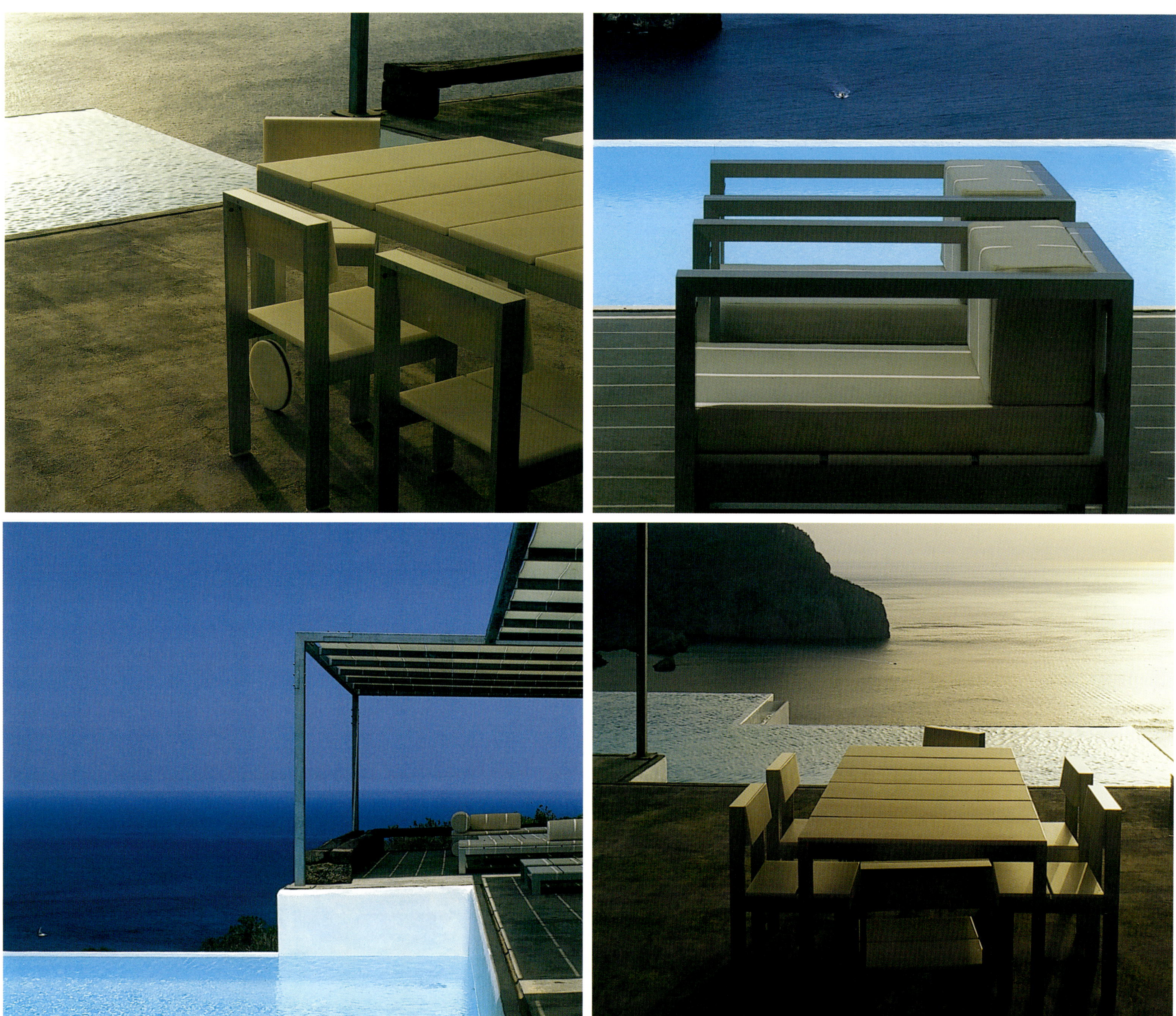

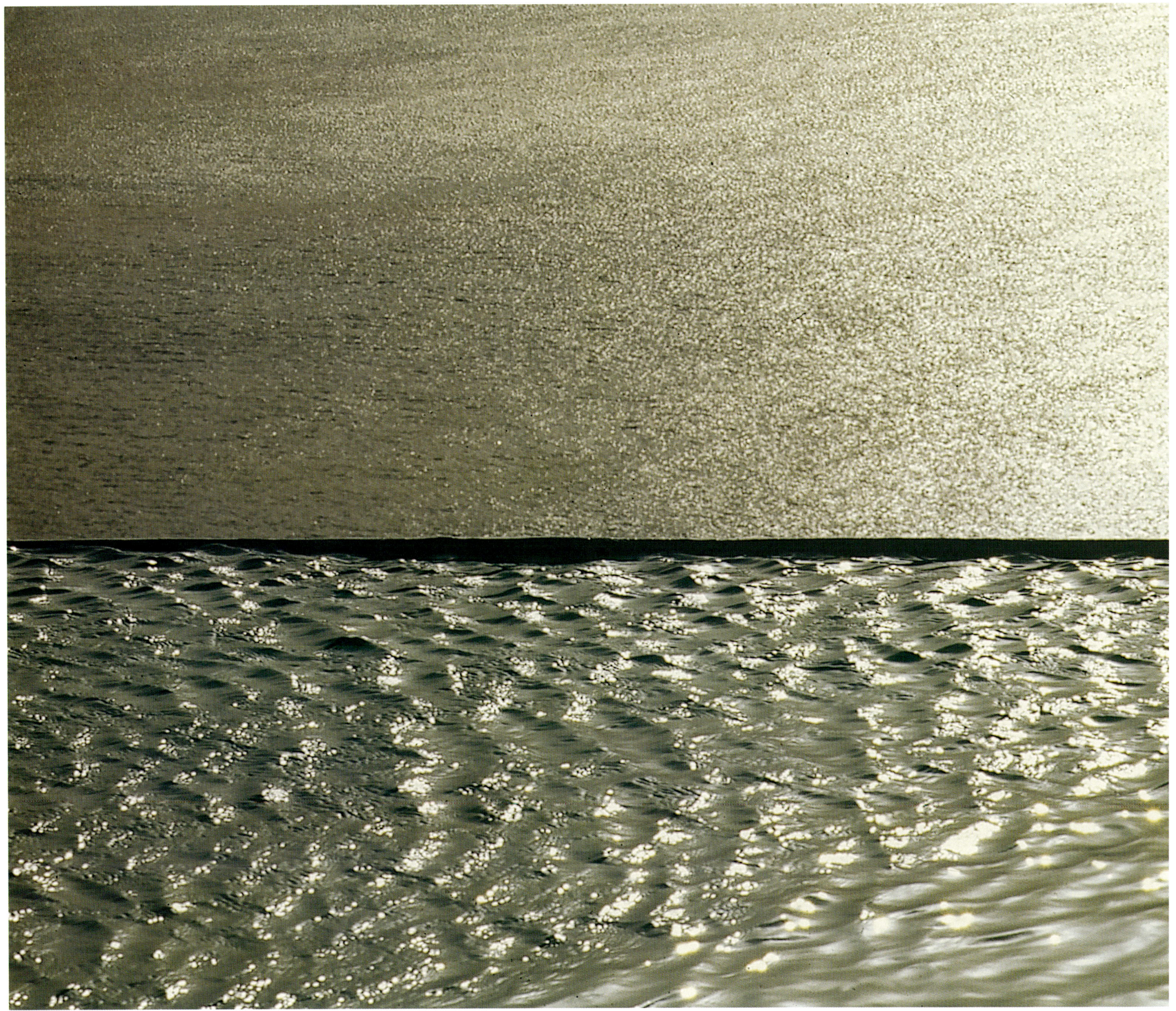

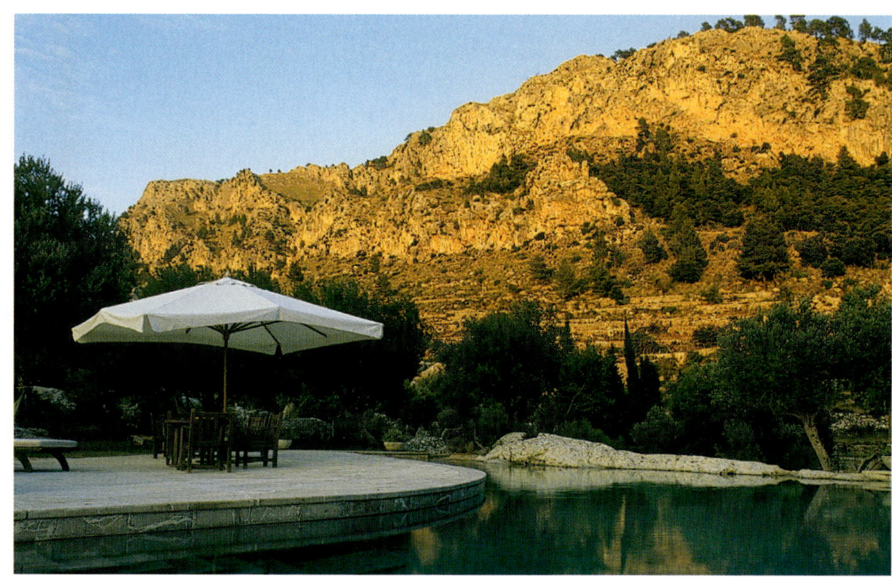

Unchanged Landscape

Sin alterar el paisaje | Unveränderte Landschaft | Un paysage préservé

Situated at the foot of a rocky mountain free of vegetation, the setting was the source of inspiration for the designers who approached the pool as if it were a natural pond. The perimeter consists of uneven broken lines and small pools and inlets where aquatic vegetation grows. Some rocks, native to the original terrain, break through the surface of the water. On one side a terrace juts into and over the pool and is the main recreational meeting place of the garden. The surrounding garden is adorned with a few pieces of modern sculpture and various restored traditional pieces such as a water trough.

Situada a los pies de una montaña rocosa y despejada de vegetación, sus diseñadores se dejaron llevar por un sentimiento de empatía hacia el entorno y la construyeron como si se tratara de una balsa natural. La superficie de agua no tiene un límite continuo sino que el perímetro se quiebra formando pequeños remansos de agua en los que crece la vegetación acuática. Algunas de estas rocas pertenecen al propio solar, de manera que emergen sobre la superficie desde la cota original del terreno.

En uno de los lados, se ha habilitado una península artificial que constituye el principal espacio de reunión del jardín. A su alrededor se han instalado algunas esculturas modernas y se han recuperado algunos elementos tradicionales, como una acequia de piedra.

Die Lage des Pool am Fuße eines vegetationslosen Bergfelsens diente den Architeken als Inspiration, weshalb sie es wie ein natürliches Wasserbecken gestalten. So hat Wasseroberfläche keine kontinuierliche Grenze. Vielmehr wird die Umrandung aufgebrochen und lässt das Wasser dadurch kleine, ruhige Stellen bilden, in denen Wasserpflanzen wachsen. Einige, vom Grundsück stammende Felsblöcke ragen aus der Wasseroberfläche heraus. Auf einer Seite wurde eine künstliche Halbinsel angelegt, die der wichtigste Ort des Zusammenkommens und der Erholung im Gartenbereich ist. Um sie herum wurden einige moderne Skulpturen aufgestellt, doch ebenso wurden verschiedene traditionelle Elemente integriert wie beispielsweise ein steinerner Wasserkanal.

Située au pied d'une montagne rocheuse dépouillée de toute végétation, ses concepteurs se sont laissés emporter par leur empathie envers l'environnement et l'ont construite comme s'il s'agissait d'une poche naturelle. L'étendue d'eau ne présente pas de limite continue. Le périmètre se brise, formant de petites nappes d'eau dormante où pousse la végétation aquatique. Les rochers qu'on y voit s'érigent directement sur le sol : ils émergent au-dessus de la surface à partir de la cote initiale du terrain.

Sur un côté, une péninsule artificielle a été créée, constituant le principal espace de réunion du jardin. Quelques sculptures modernes ont été installées autour et certains éléments d'origine ont été conservés, comme un canal d'irrigation en pierre.

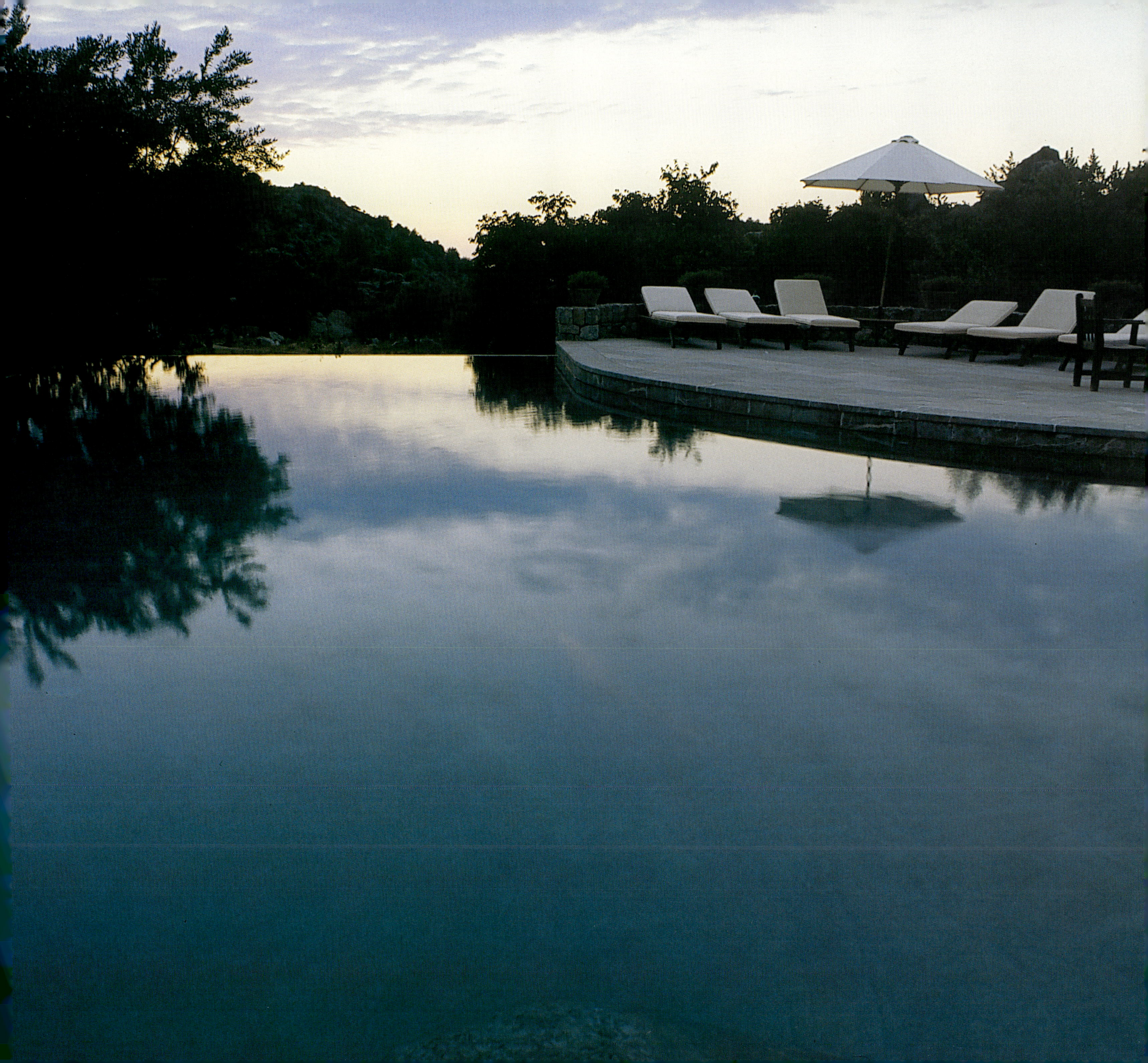

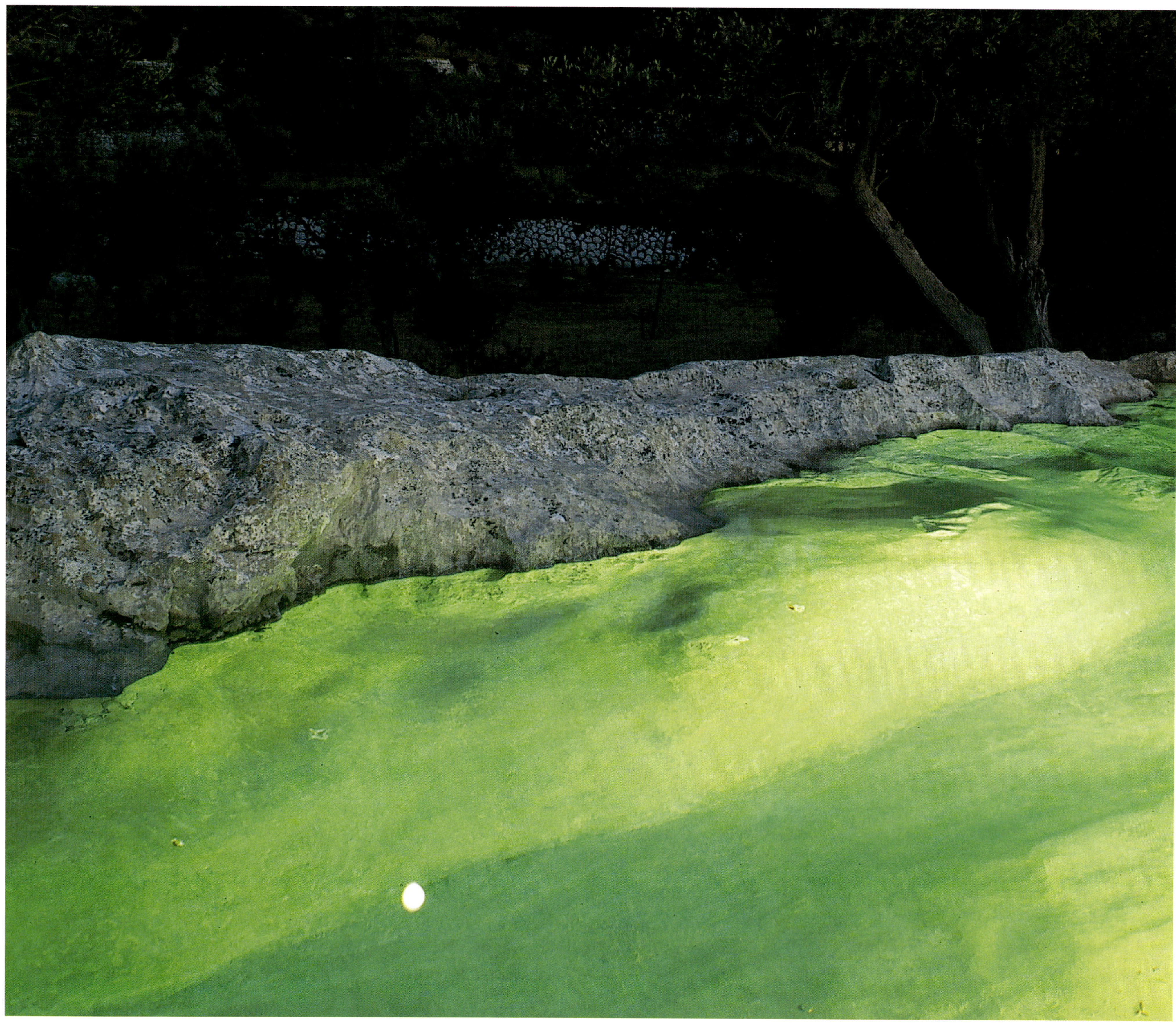

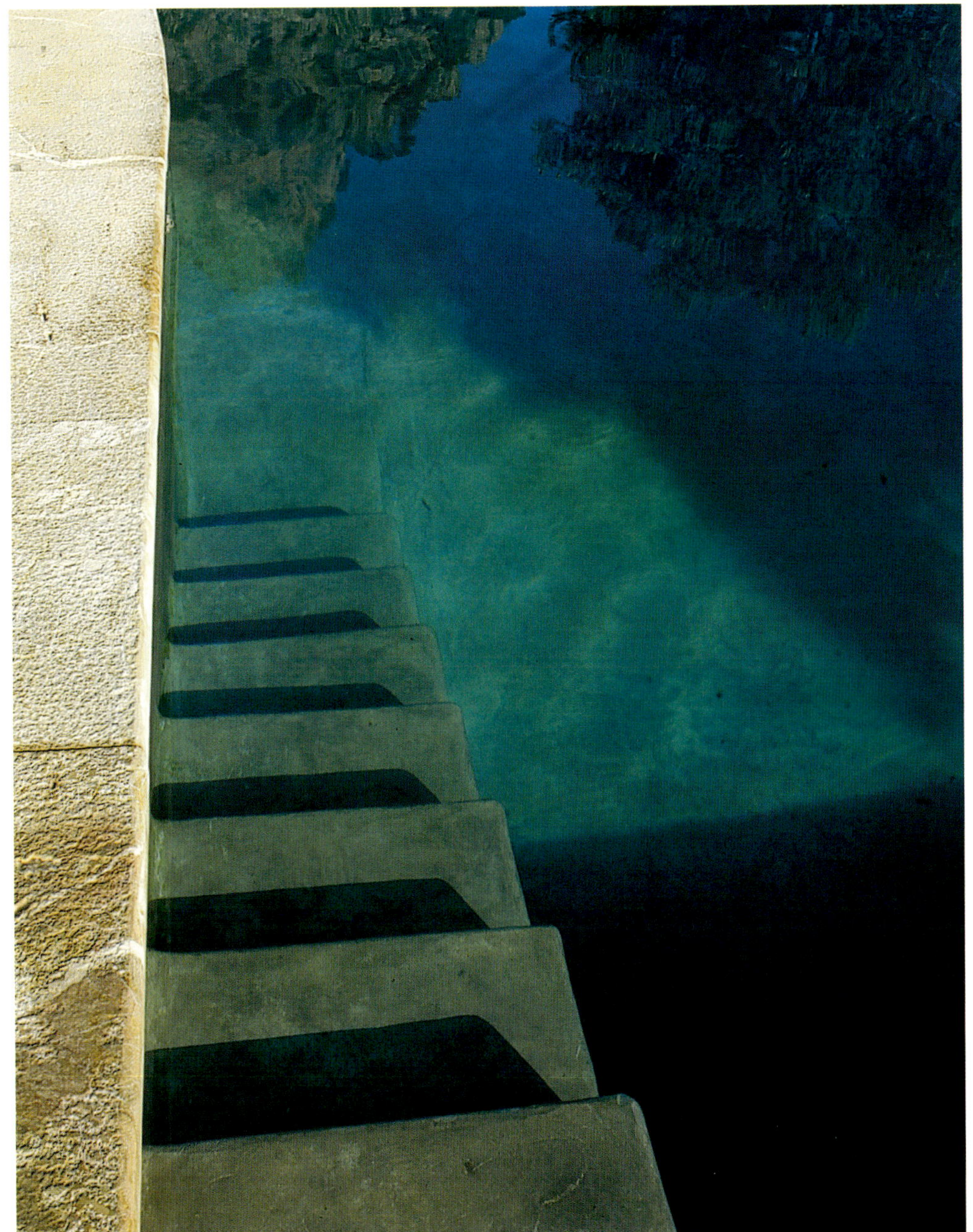

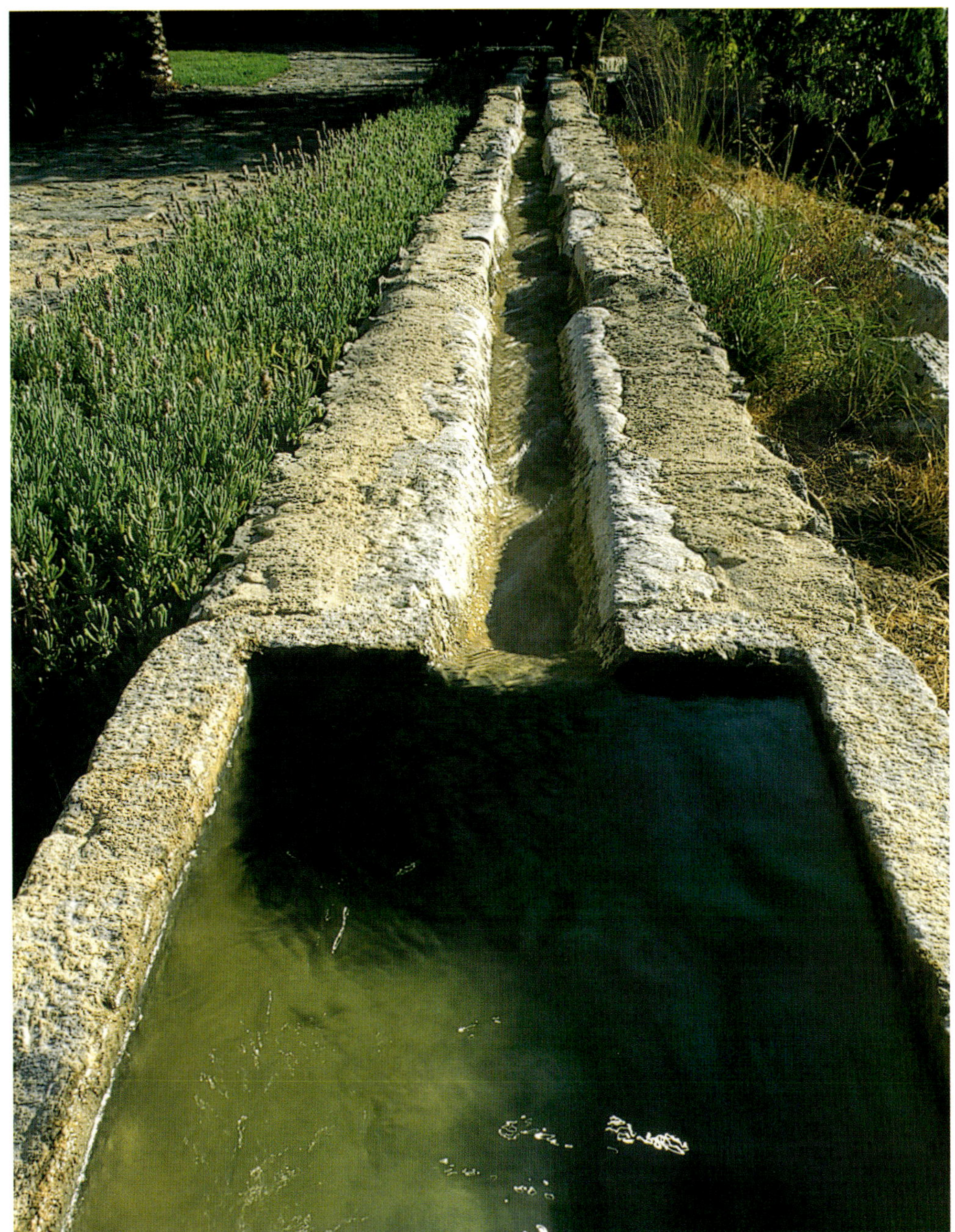

At sunset the water in the pool turns warm and enchanting, which leaves us spellbound as we descend into it, in the midst of the natural setting.

Al llegar el atardecer, el agua de la piscina adopta un color cálido e ineludiblemente encantador que hipnotiza a sumergirnos en sus profundidades, en medio de un entorno natural.

In der Dämmerung bekommt das Wasser des Pools eine warme und fesselnde Farbe, die uns dazu verleitet, in dieser natürlichen Umgebung in die Tiefen des Wasser hinein zu tauchen.

À la tombée du jour, l'eau de la piscine adopte une teinte chaude, véritable enchantement pour le baigneur qui s'immerge dans ses profondeurs, au milieu d'un cadre naturel.

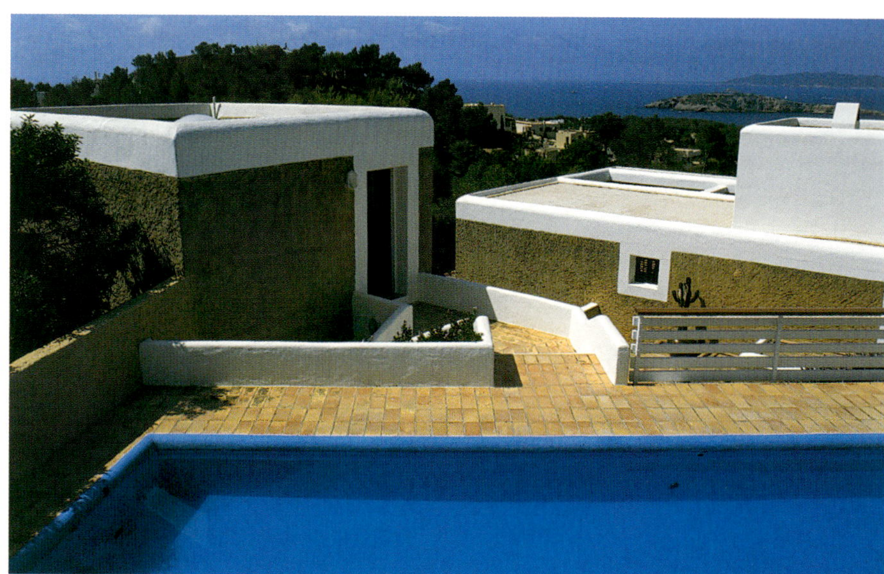

Original Blue

Azul Original | Original Blau | Bleu Originale

The starting point for the internationally recognized work of the Catalan Josep Lluís Sert (1902-1983) was his genuine respect for local tradition. A good example of this is the Can Pep Simó housing estate, popularly known as Punta Martinet, which Sert built in Ibiza from 1965 to 1968. In order to achieve an architecture that merges into its surroundings, he followed the contours of the terrain and did not build dividing walls to mark off the individual houses. The architect set aside one of the nine houses on the estate as his own summer home, and it boasts the only swimming pool in the complex, the result of the reconstruction of an old irrigation reservoir. The pool, situated at the top of a slope, successfully brings out the Mediterranean spirit of the house with its generous dose of blue paint.

Las obras internacionalmente reconocidas del catalán Josep Lluís Sert (1902-1983) tienen como punto de partida el auténtico respeto a los orígenes. Un buen ejemplo de ello es la urbanización Can Pep Simó, popularmente conocida como Punta Martinet, que Sert proyectó en Ibiza entre 1965 y 1968. Con la idea de realizar una arquitectura que se confundiera con el entorno, se respetaron los bancales y no se colocaron muros para separar las viviendas. El arquitecto destinó una de las nueve casas de la urbanización a su propia residencia de verano, y allí ubicó la única piscina del conjunto después de reconstruir una antigua alberca de regadío. La piscina, que se sitúa en el nivel más alto de la pendiente, consigue acentuar el espíritu mediterráneo de la vivienda gracias a la generosa dosis de pintura azul.

Ausgangspunkt für die international anerkannten Arbeiten des Katalanen Josep Lluís Sert (1902-1983) ist ein wahrer Respekt vor dem Ursprünglichen. Ein anschauliches Beispiel dafür ist die Siedlung Can Pep Simó – im Volksmund Punta Martinet genannt – die Sert zwischen 1965 und 1968 auf Ibiza entwarf. In der Absicht, Bau und Umgebung miteinander zu verschmelzen, blieben die Beete unberührt, während auf Mauern zur Abtrennung der einzelnen Wohnhäuser verzichtet wurde. Der Architekt entschied sich für eines der neun Häuser der Siedlung als sein eigenes Sommerdomizil und errichtete dort das einzige Schwimmbecken der Anlage, nachdem er eine alte, zur Bewässerung genutzte Zisterne rekonstruiert hatte. Das am höchsten Punkt des Abhangs gelegene Schwimmbecken akzentuiert den mediterranen Geist des Hauses dank eines großzügigen Umgangs mit der Farbe Blau.

L'œuvre internationalement reconnue du Catalan Josep Lluís Sert (1902-1983) s'appuie sur un authentique respect des origines. L'urbanisation Can Pep Simó, que Sert a conçue à Ibiza entre 1965 et 1968, plus connue sous le nom de Punta Martinet, en offre une bonne illustration. Dans l'idée de fondre cadre naturel et architecture, les terrasses naturelles ont été conservées et aucun mur ne sépare les habitations. L'architecte a fait de l'une des neuf maisons de l'urbanisation sa propre résidence d'été, et y a placé la seule piscine de l'ensemble, un ancien réservoir destiné à l'arrosage. La piscine, située tout en haut de la pente, vient renforcer l'esprit méditerranéen de l'habitation grâce à la peinture bleue.

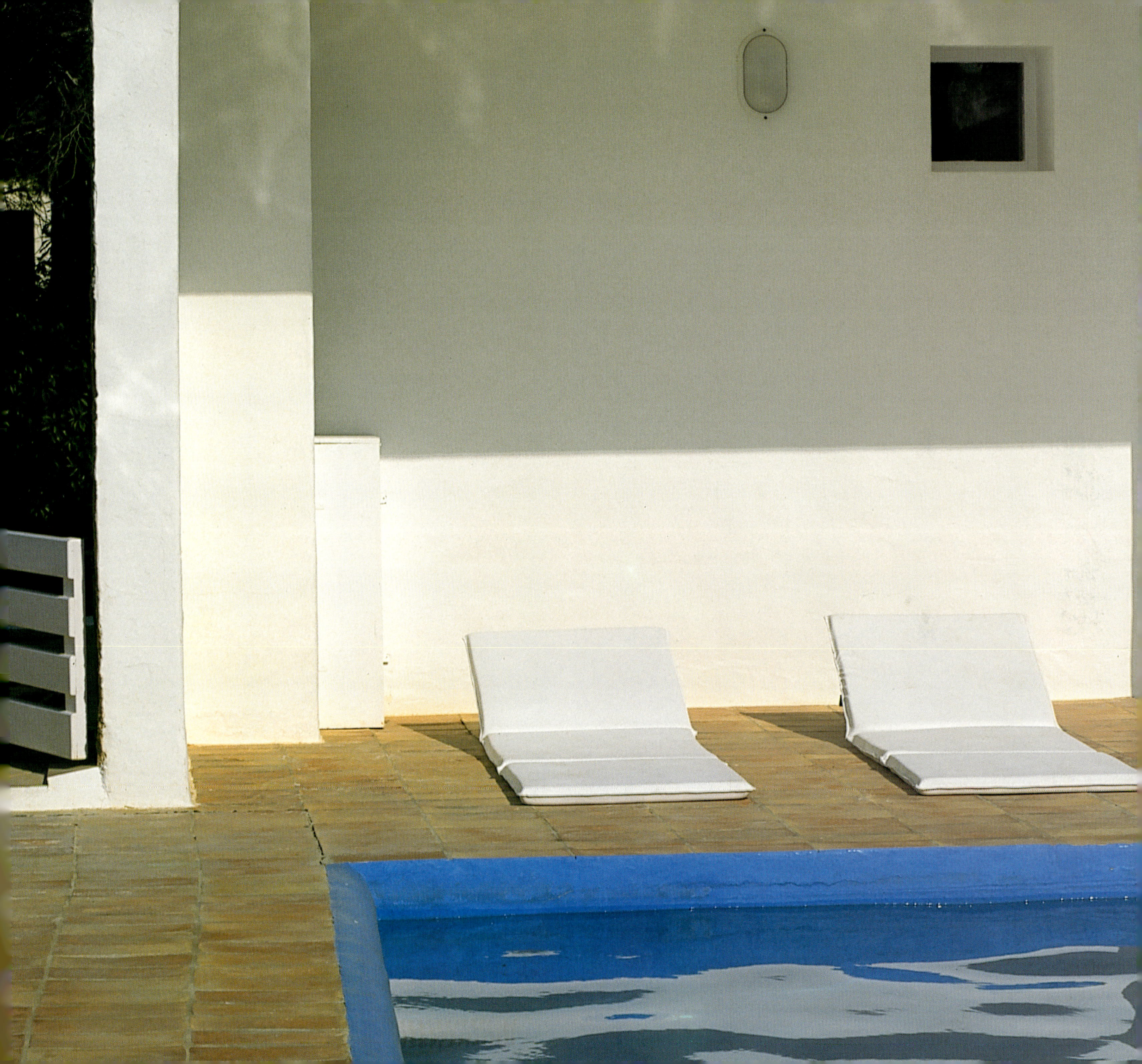

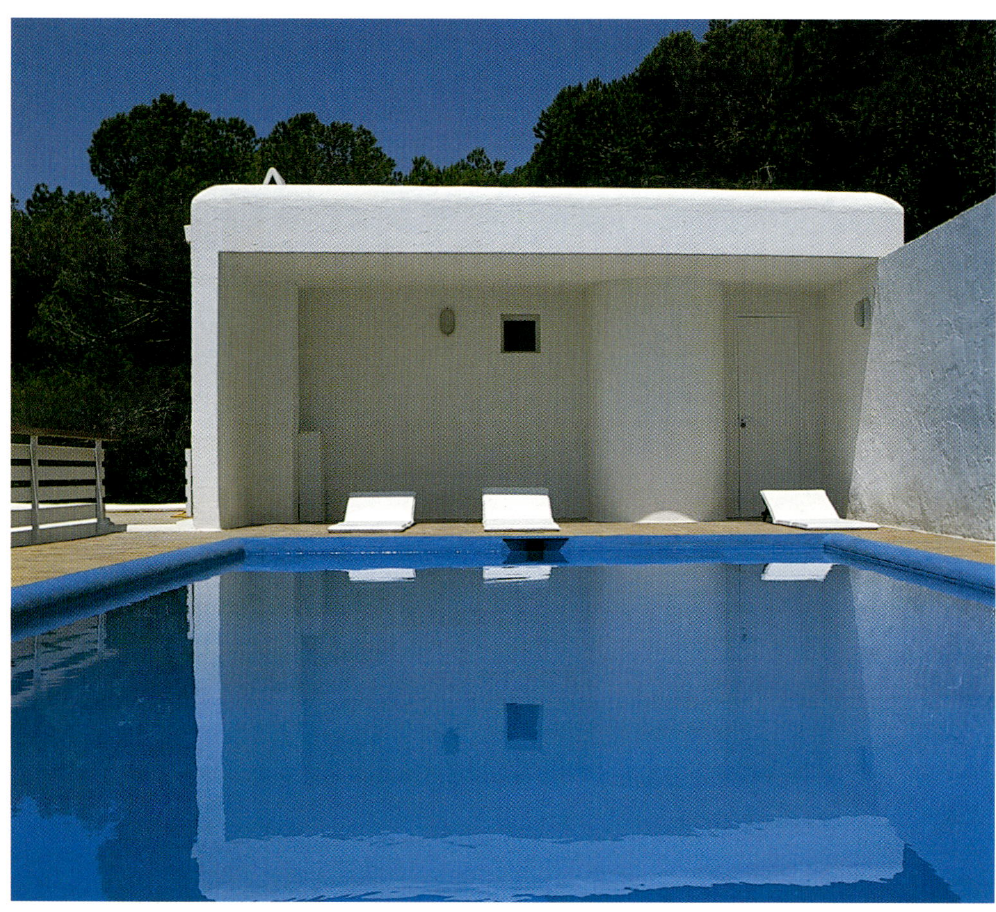

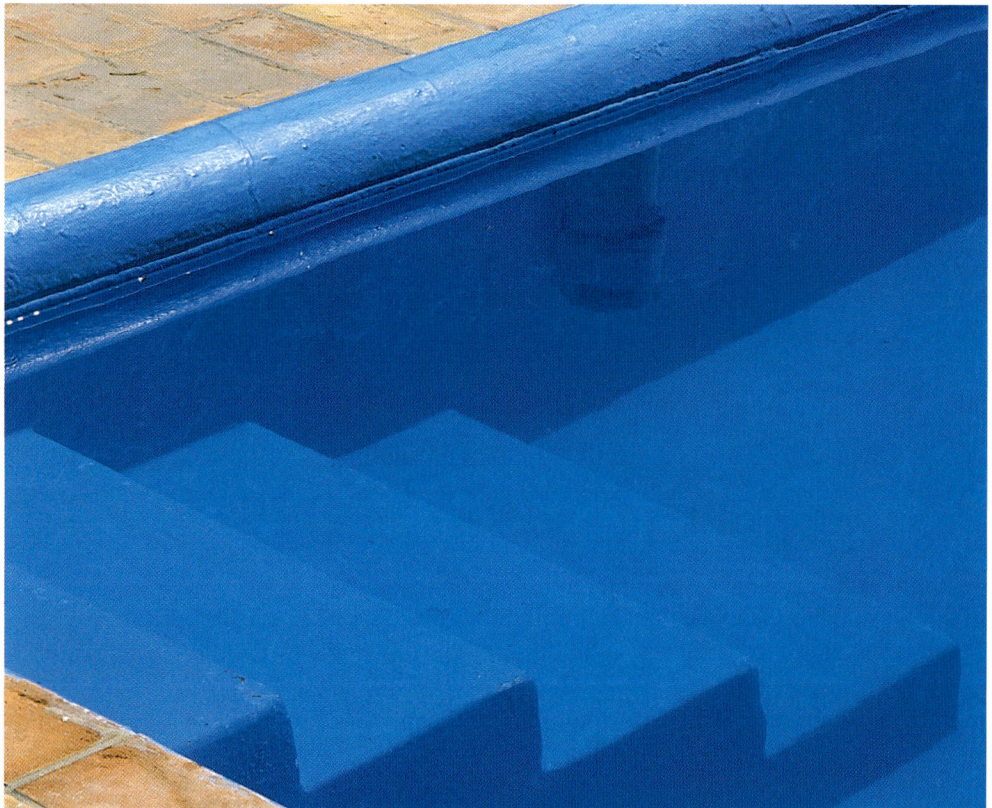

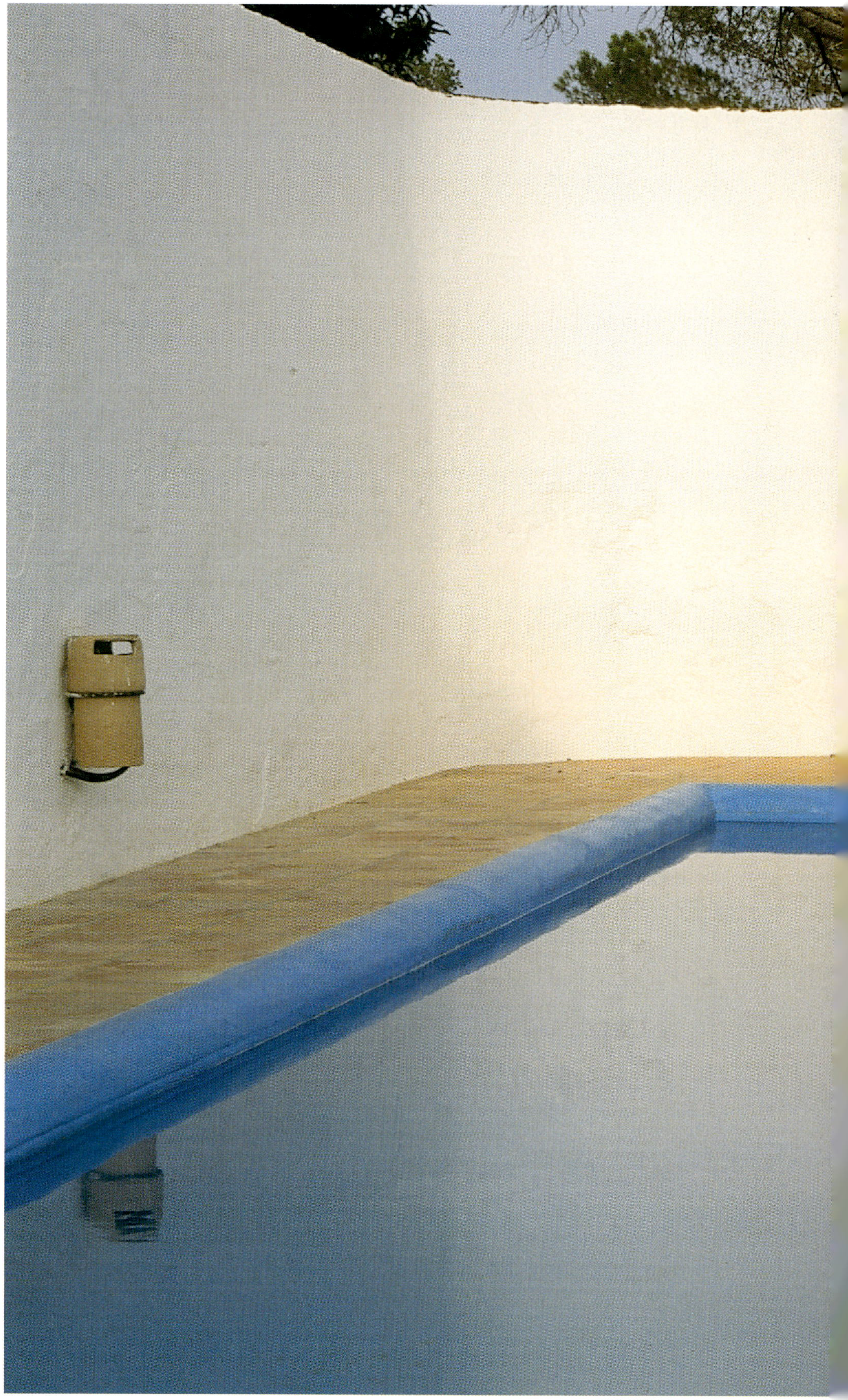

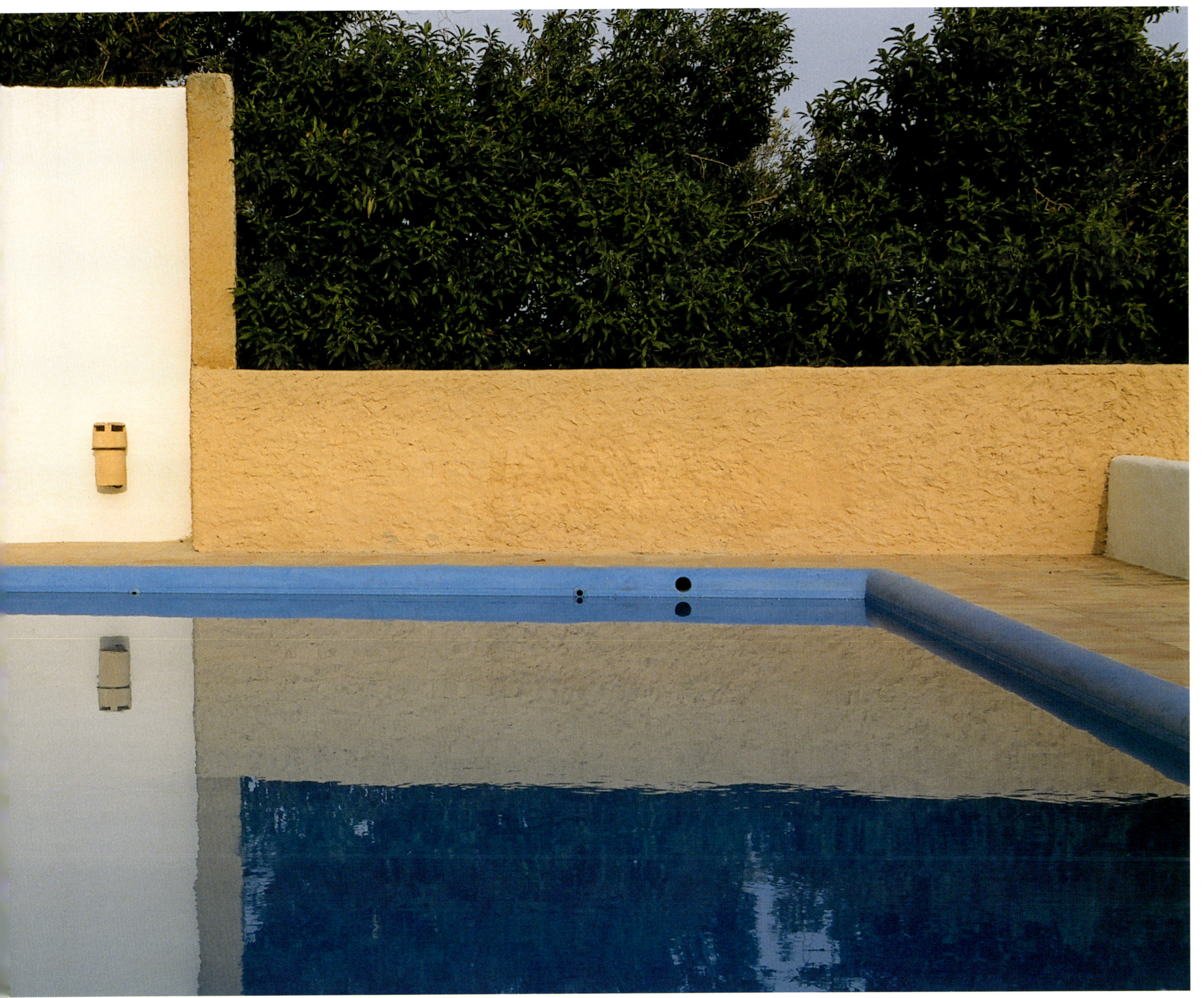

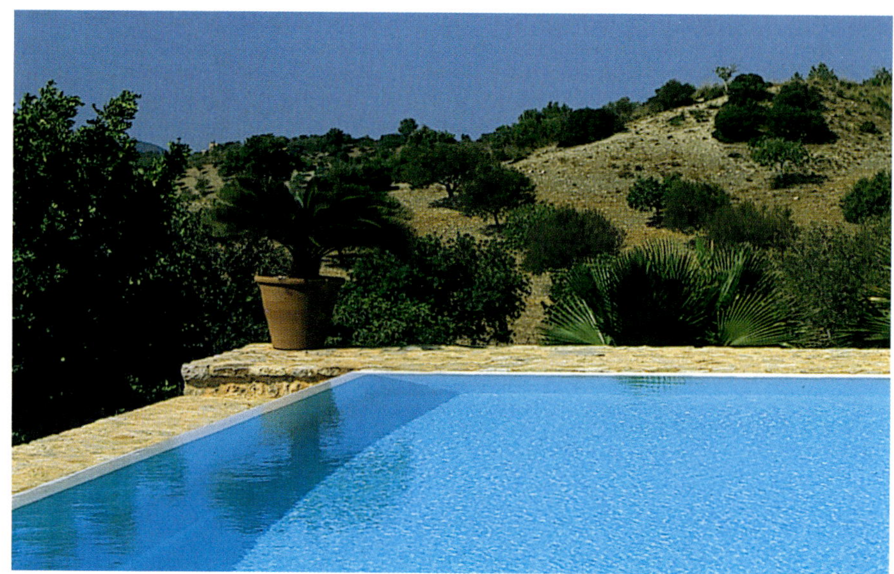

Blue Symmetry

Simetría en azul | Symmetrie in Blau | Une symétrie bleue

Thanks to the white lining of the pool, the water in the pool affords the appearance of a very light blue. With symmetry in mind, the design of the pool is simple, sober and precise and ornamentation is kept to a minimum. We are grateful for this as the setting is beautiful. Thus, the architecture does not attempt to compete with the landscape but rather, is the framework from where we may contemplate it.

The site for the pool was chosen for its magnificent views as one can contemplate the forests as they descend into the sea. Nonetheless, the swimming pool is not only simply a summer leisure element. It is a centerpiece and an important aesthetic element that creates ambience for the house all-year long.

El revestimiento es blanco, y el color resultante del agua es un azul muy claro. Esta es una piscina de líneas sencillas, sobrias, precisas. Se trabaja teniendo presente la simetría. La ornamentación se ha reducido al mínimo. Esta simplicidad se agradece cuando el entorno es, por sí mismo, bello. Así, la arquitectura no busca competir con el paisaje sino que sirve de marco desde el que se contempla.

El motivo por el que se decide construir la piscina en este punto tiene mucho que ver con la voluntad de disfrutar de unas vistas magníficas viendo cómo el paisaje del bosque desciende hacia la costa. El protagonismo que finalmente adquiere la piscina hace que no sólo sea un espacio para el ocio durante el verano, sino que se convierta en una referencia constante de todos los espacios de la casa a lo largo del año.

Die innere Beckenverkleidung ist ganz in Weiß gehalten, wodurch die Farbe des Wassers ein hellen Blauton hat. Der Pool zeichnet sich durch schlichte, nüchterne und präzise Linien aus – die Symmetrie ist ein wichtiges Element. Schmückende Elemente sind auf ein Minimum reduziert. Diese Schlichtheit wirkt besonders in der natürlich angenehmen Umgebung. Diese Ausgeglichenheit beruht darauf, dass sich die Architektur als Rahmen der Landschaft versteht. Der Grund für eben diese Standortwahl des Pools ergab sich aufgrund der herrlichen Aussicht, ein Blick, der vom Wald bis zur Küste reicht. Die zentrale Rolle, die dem Schwimmbecken letztendlich zukommt, führt dazu, dass es nicht nur ein Freizeitbereich im Sommer ist, sondern das ganze Jahr über den ständigen Bezugspunkt für sämtlicher Räume des Hauses darstellt.

Le revêtement blanc prête à l'eau une couleur bleue très claire. Cette piscine offre des lignes simples, sobres et précises. La symétrie a constitué la ligne directrice de ces travaux. L'ornementation se réduit au minimum. Cette simplicité est appréciable dans la mesure où l'environnement, à lui seul, est superbe. Ainsi, l'architecture n'entre pas en concurrence avec le paysage, mais constitue un cadre qui invite à le contempler. La décision de construire la piscine à cet endroit est étroitement liée à la volonté de savourer ces vues magnifiques, où le paysage boisé descend vers la côte Le rôle de la piscine dépasse finalement celui d'espace de loisir estival pour devenir la référence constante de l'ensemble des espaces de la maison tout au long de l'année.

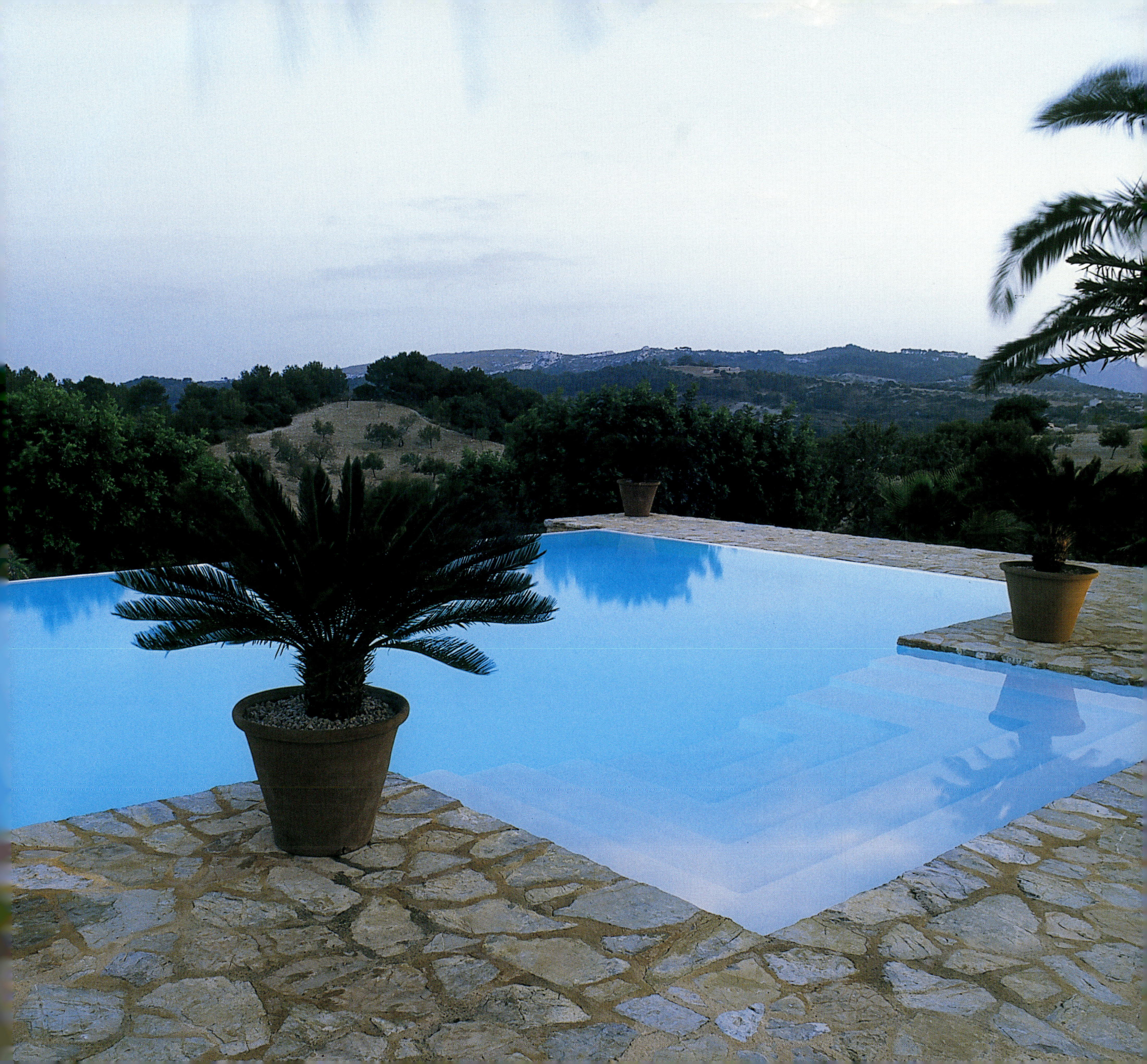

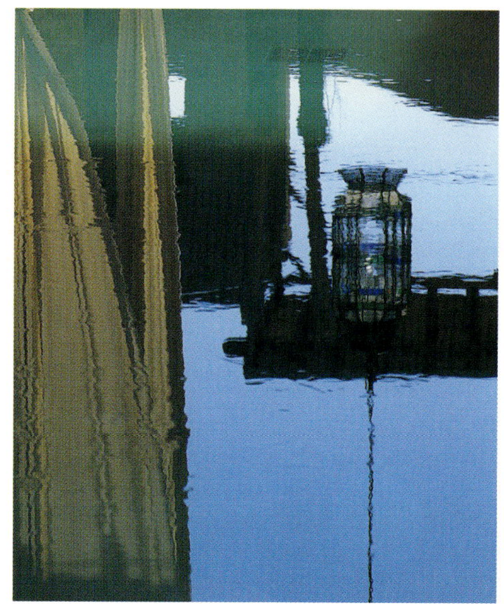

Captivating Calm

Remanso de paz | Ein Hort der Ruhe | Un havre de paix

In a charming village near Marrakech called Ouled Ben Rahmoune, this hotel offers the visitor the opportunity to become acquainted with traditional life in this area. The elegant and simple volumes afford an austere rural style consisting of open patios, colorful gardens, terraces and small domes that rise up. In the interior of the complex this magnificent pool emerges which is superbly integrated into the setting. Built with the same materials and techniques as those used for making the building, the pool sometimes seems to blend right in with the volumes of the façades. The entire edge and interior of the pool were constructed using a Moroccan technique known as "tadelack" (similar to dyed cement). In the interior of the pool beams of light are strategically placed which illuminate it and at nightfall create lovely images in the water.

Dieses Hotel in einem bezaubernden Dorf namens Ouled Ben Rahmoune in der Nähe von Marrakesch bietet dem Gast die Möglichkeit, das traditionelle Leben der Region kennen zu lernen. Die Gestaltung der Gebäude sind beredter Ausdruck der Eleganz und Schlichtheit eines nüchtern-ländlichen Stils mit offenen Höfen, farbenfrohen Gärten, Terrassen und kleinen Gewölben. Im Inneren der Anlage befindet sich dieses herrliche Schwimmbecken. Es wurde mit den Materialien, Farbtönen und Techniken errichtet, die bei den Gebäuden zur Anwendung kamen, sodass es mitunter scheint, als nutze das Schwimmbecken die Häuserfassaden als Tarnung. Der gesamte Rand wie auch das Becken wurden mit einer „tadelack" genannten marokkanischen Technik (farbigem Zement ähnlich) errichtet. Im Inneren wird durch strategisch verteilte Strahler bei Einbruch der Dunkelheit das Wasser erleuchtet, wodurch attraktives Gesamtbild entsteht.

En una encantadora aldea de nombre Ouled Ben Rahmoune, cerca de Marrakech, este hotel ofrece al huésped una manera de conocer la vida tradicional de la zona. Los volúmenes diseñados hacen alarde de la elegancia y simplicidad de un severo estilo rural entre patios abiertos, jardines coloristas, terrazas y pequeñas bóvedas que se alzan.
En el interior del recinto, emerge esta magnífica piscina que se integra perfectamente en el entorno. Se han empleado los mismos materiales, tonalidades y técnicas practicadas en la edificación, por lo que a veces parece que la piscina se mimetice con los volúmenes de las fachadas. Todo el borde, así como el vaso, se ha construido con una técnica marroquí denominada "tadelack" (similar al cemento tintado). En el interior, puntos de luz estratégicamente distribuidos consiguen que al anochecer el agua se ilumine creando atractivas imágenes.

Dans un charmant village situé près de Marrakech, Ouled Ben Rahmoune, cet hôtel propose à ses hôtes une manière de découvrir la vie traditionnelle de la région. Les unités créées arborent l'élégance, la simplicité et la sévérité du style rural à travers des cours ouvertes, des jardins coloristes, des terrasses et des petites voûtes. L' intérieur de l'enceinte abrite cette superbe piscine qui s'intègre parfaitement au décor. Les matériaux, les tonalités et les techniques employées sont les mêmes que celles qui caractérisent le bâtiment, aussi la piscine semble-t-elle parfois en reproduire les façades. Le bassin, ainsi que son rebord, a été construit selon une technique marocaine dénommée "tadelack" (similaire à la technique du ciment teint). À l'intérieur, des points de lumière stratégiquement distribués font qu'à la tombée de la nuit, l'eau s'illumine en produisant de fascinantes images.

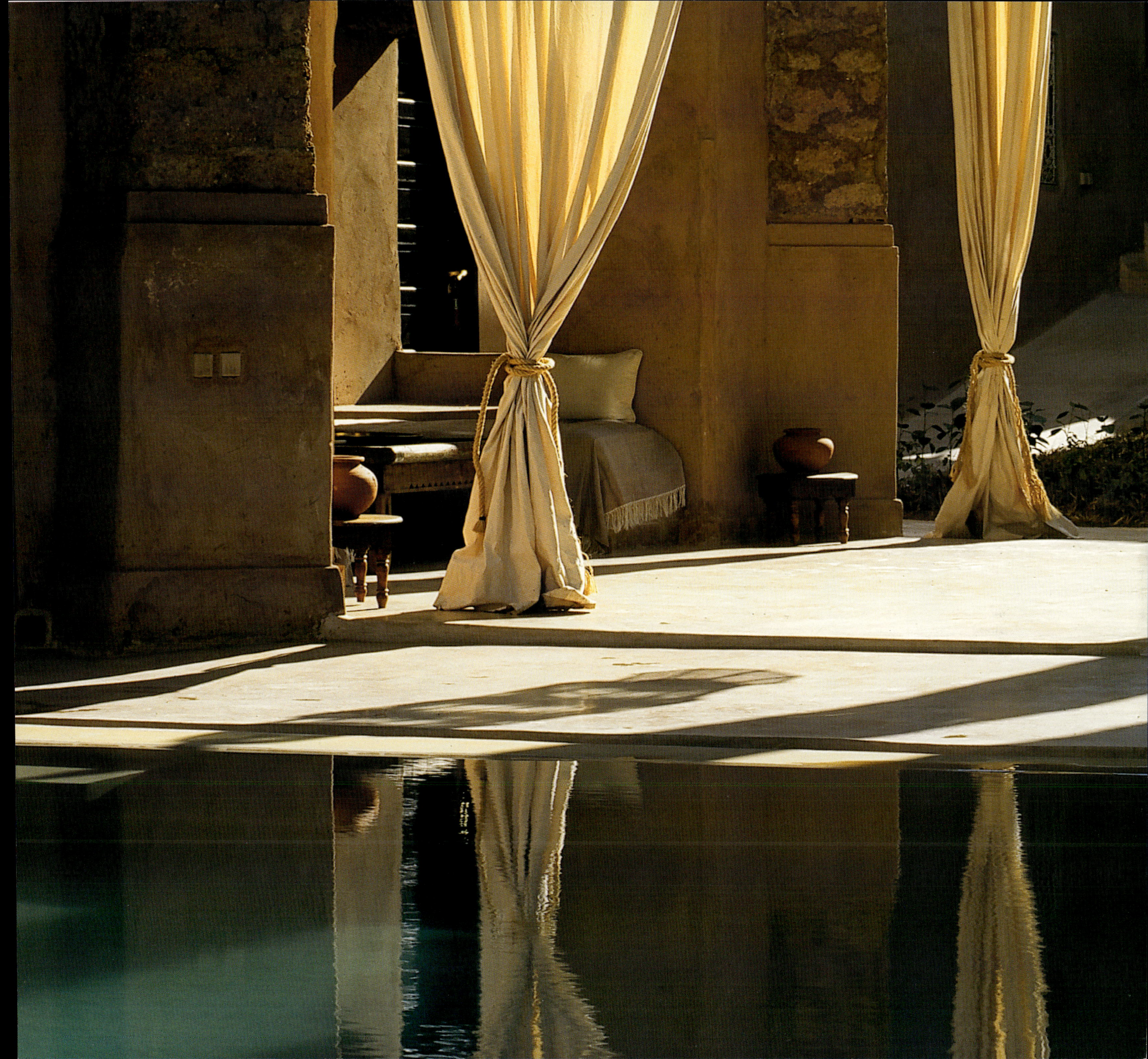

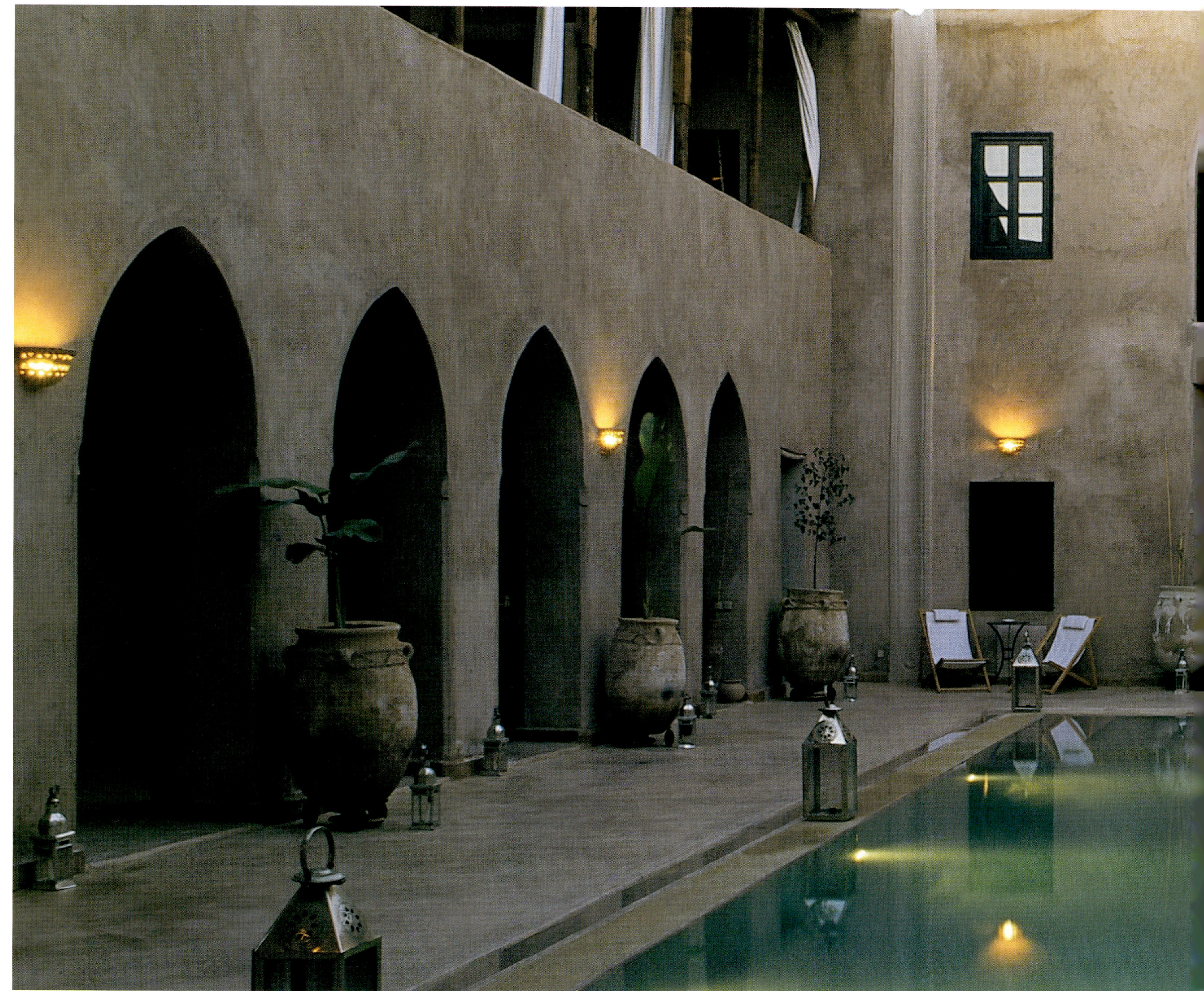

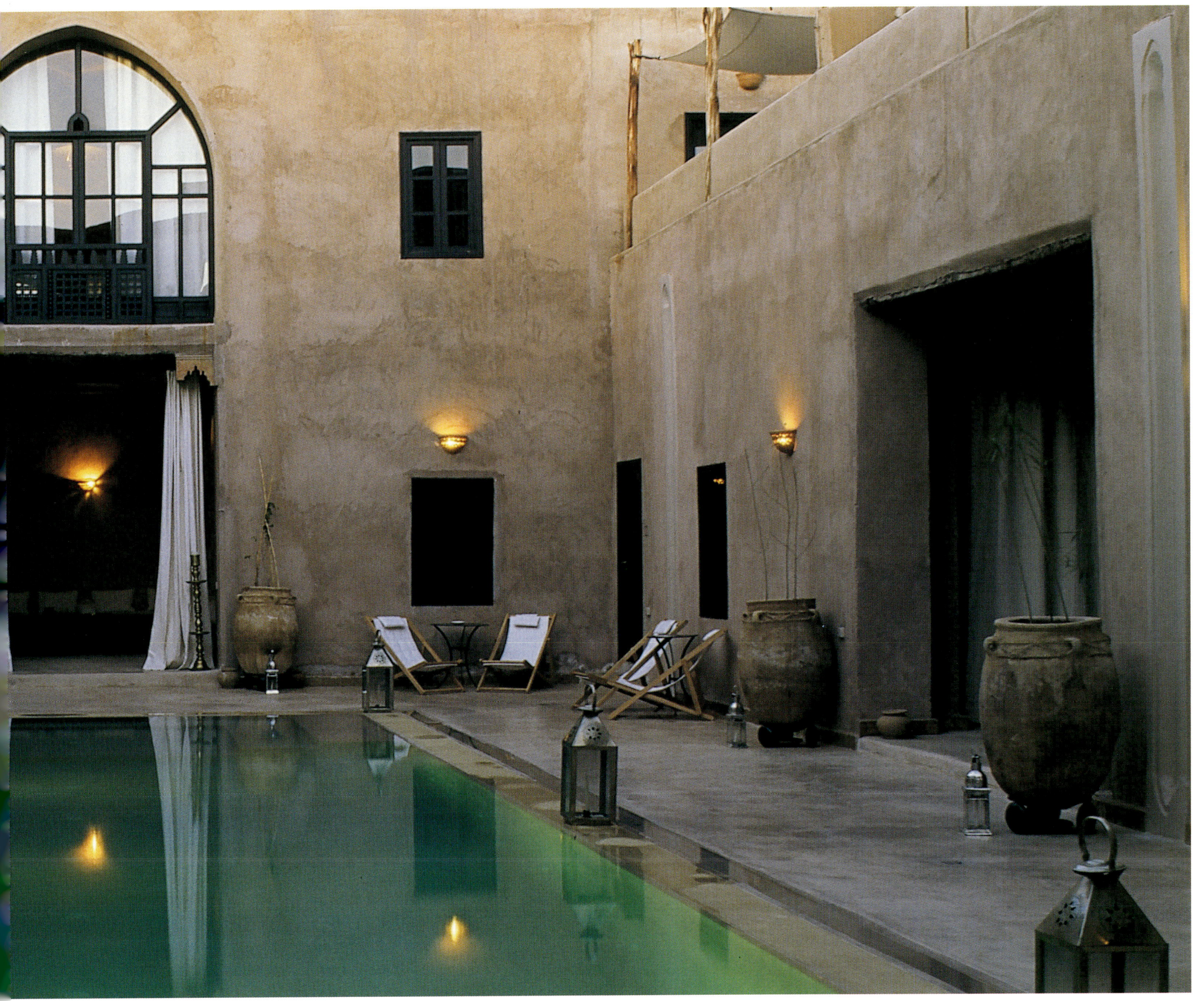

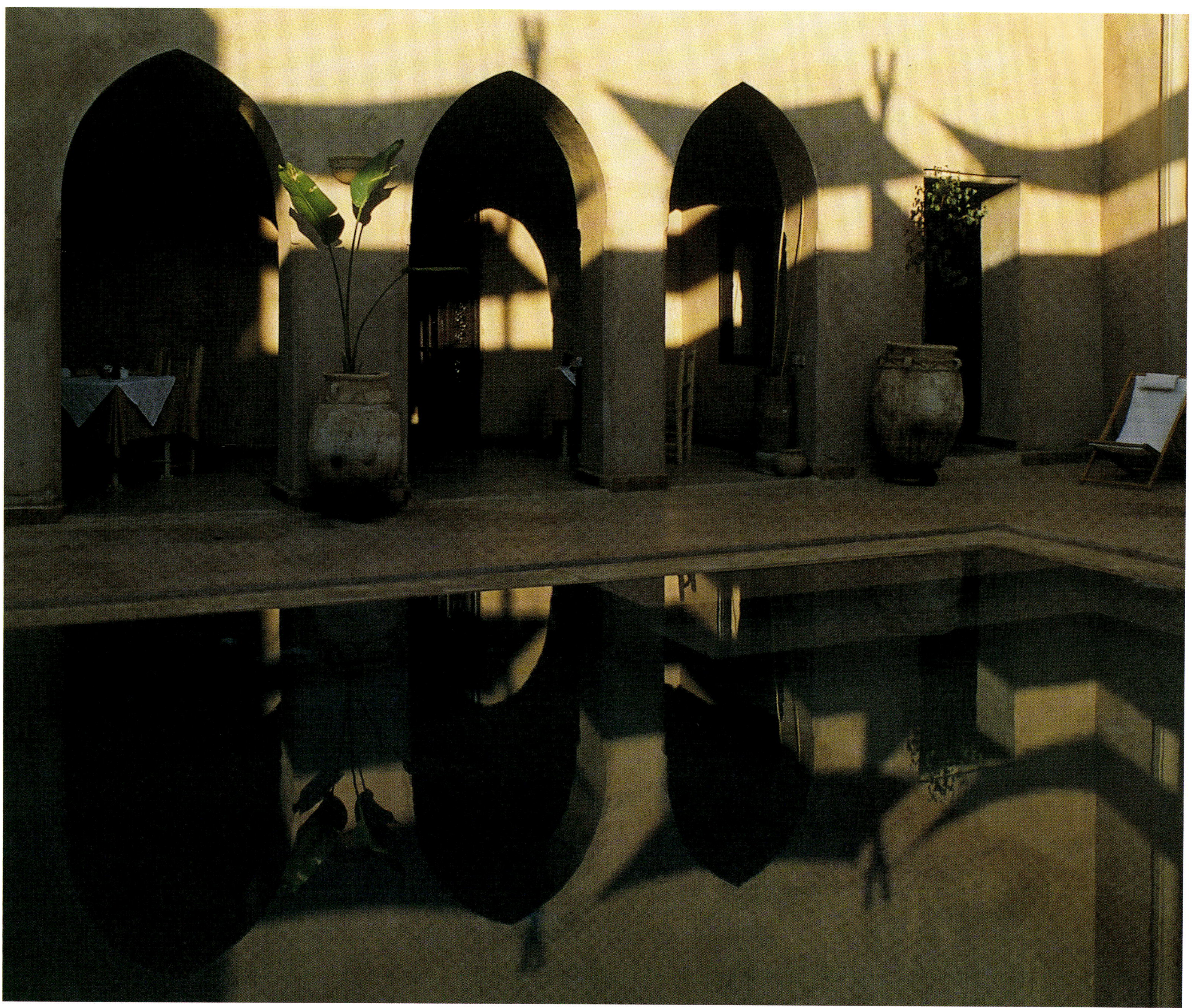

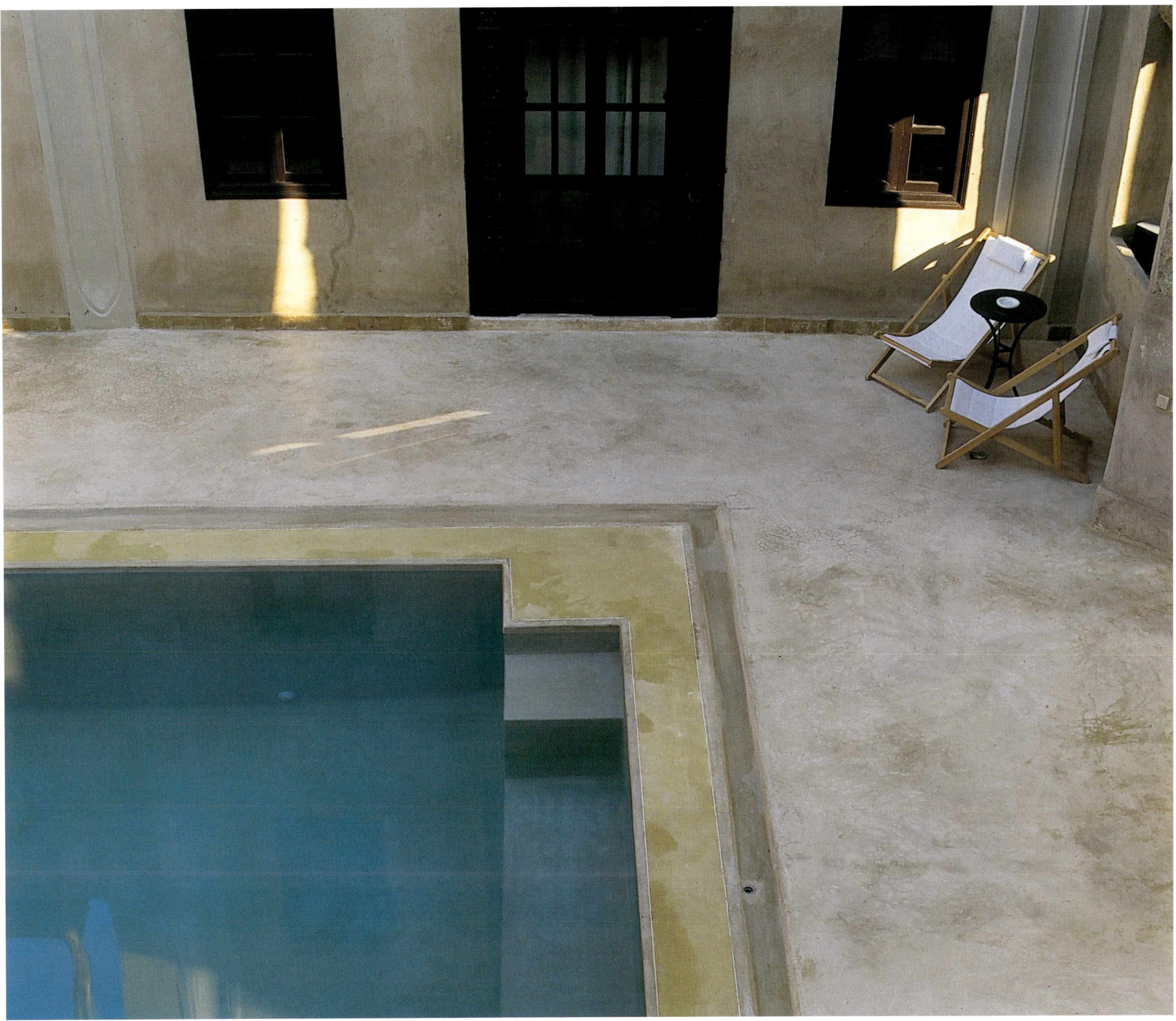

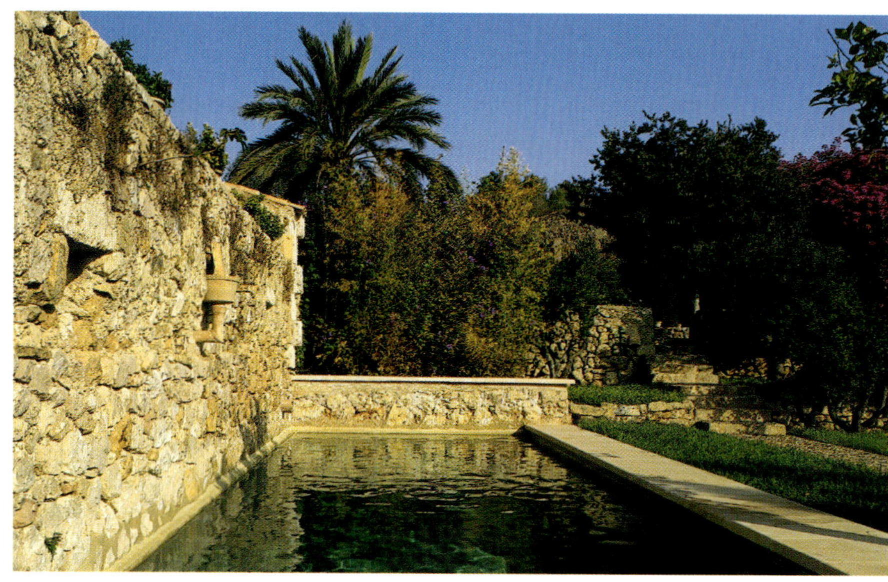

Between two Worlds

Entre dos Mundos | Zwischen zwei Welten | Entre deux mondes

This ancient reservoir, restored into a swimming pool, is sheltered by a 200-year-old wall. The pool's charm comes from the bewitching turquoise color if its water and the luminosity of an antique, ochre wall that functions as the project's starting point. So as to integrate the contours of the pool with the ensemble, a sandstone trim was chosen, whose sand color complements the rest of the materials. At one end, a small retaining wall, also covered with stones, becomes an informal diving board. Behind it, lush vegetation conceals a guesthouse. At one end of the pool we find the splendor of freely growing vegetation; at the other, the preciseness and simplicity of a monastic cloister

Esta antigua alberca, restaurada y convertida en una piscina, se cobija bajo un muro bicentenario. Su encanto lo constituyen el hechizante color turquesa de sus aguas y la luminosidad ocre de una pared muy antigua que funciona como punto a partir del cual se desarrolla la obra. Para integrar el perfil de la piscina en el conjunto, se ha optado por una corona de piedra marés cuyo color arena conjuga con el resto de los materiales. En uno de sus laterales, un pequeño muro de contención se convierte en un trampolín informal, detrás del cual florece una exhuberante vegetación que esconde una casa para invitados.
En los laterales de la piscina encontramos el esplendor de una vegetación que crece libremente, y por otro, la precisión y sobriedad de un claustro monacal.

Dieses restaurierte und in ein Schwimmbecken umgewandeltes, ehemaliges Wasserreservoir liegt im Schutz einer 200 Jahre alten Mauer. Sein Zauber beruht auf dem faszinierenden Türkiston des Wassers und dem leuchtenden Ocker der sehr alten Wand, die Ausgangspunkt für die Bauausführung war. Zur Integration des Schwimmbeckens in das Gesamtesemble wurde eine Einfassung aus Marès-Stein gewählt, dessen sandiger Farbton mit den übrigen Materialien harmoniert. Auf der einen Seiten wird eine kleine Stützmauer zum unorthodoxen Sprungbrett, hinter dem eine üppige Vegetation ein Gästehaus verbirgt. An den Flanken des Pools treffen die Pracht einer frei wachsenden Pflanzenwelt und die Präzision und Nüchternheit eines Klosters aufeinander.

Cet ancien réservoir, restauré et transformé en piscine, se tient au pied d'un mur bicentenaire. Son charme réside dans l'ensorcelante couleur turquoise de ses eaux et la luminosité ocre d'un très vieux mur, noyau de cette construction. Dans un souci d'intégrer le contour de la piscine à l'ensemble, sa couronne a été réalisée en pierre marés, dont la couleur sable se conjugue avec les autres matériaux. Sur l'un de ses côtés, un petit mur de soutènement joue le rôle d'un plongeoir informel. Derrière lui se développe une végétation exubérante où se cache une maison à la disposition des invités.
Un côté de la piscine offre la splendeur d'une végétation qui s'épanouit librement. Un autre côté se définit par la précision et la sobriété d'un cloître monacal.

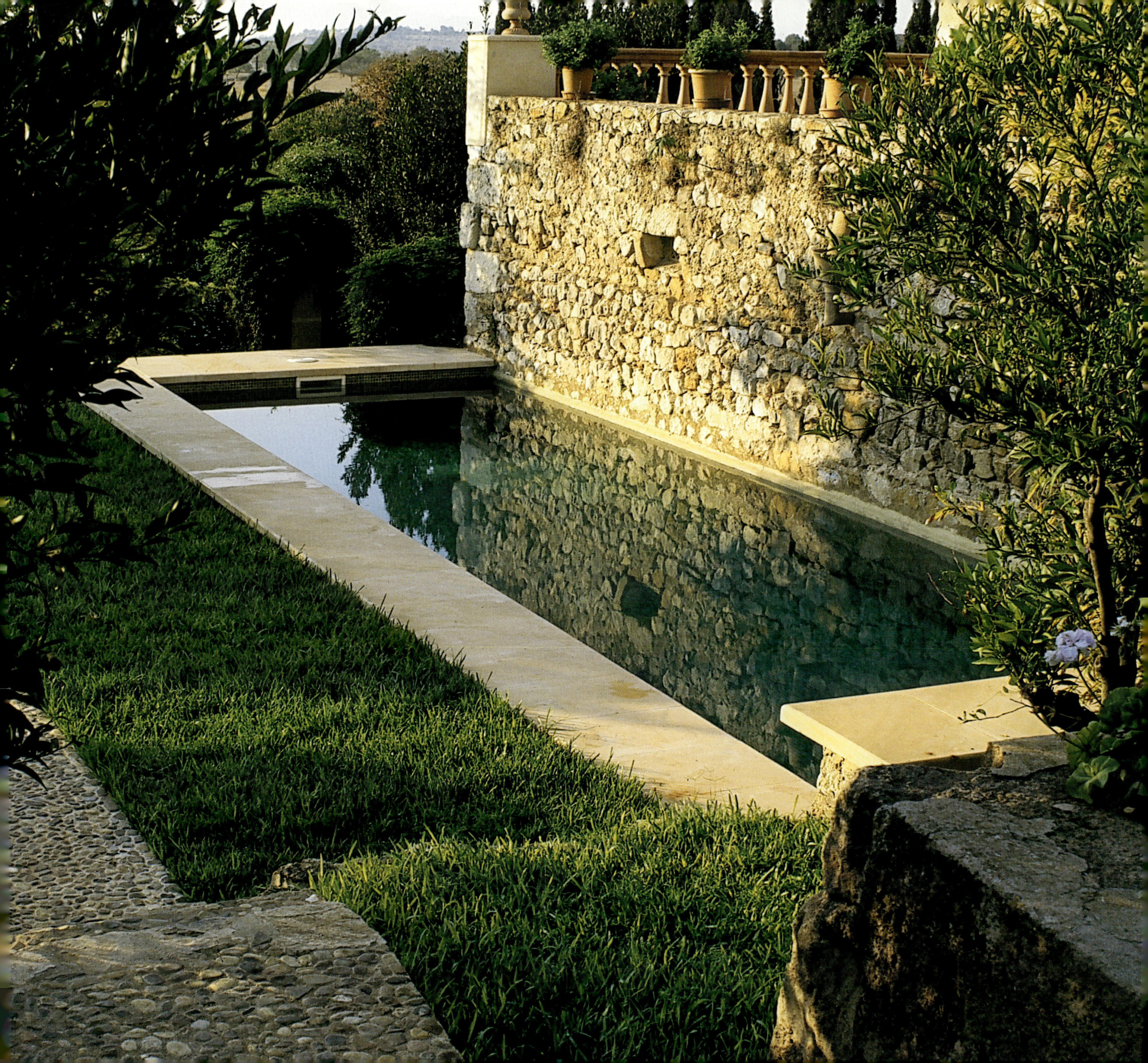

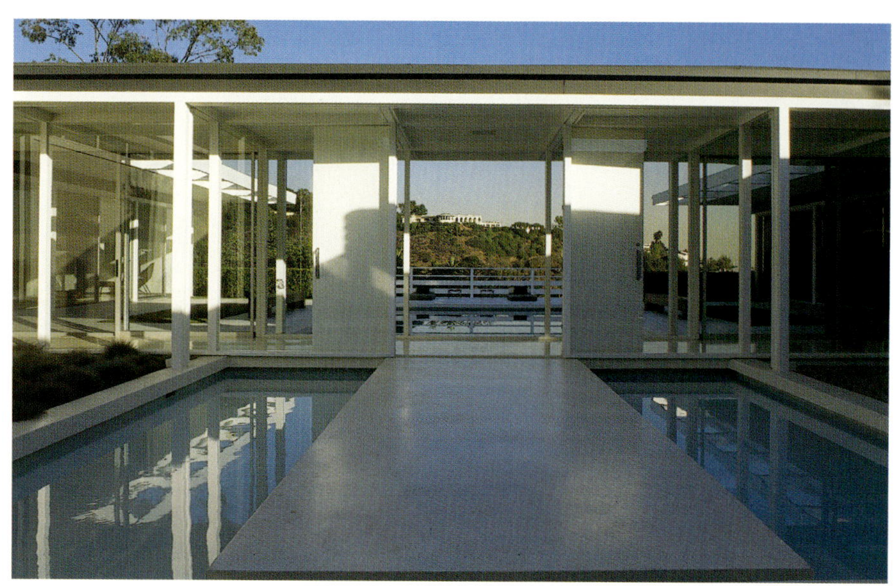

BETWEEN TWO WATERS

ENTRE DOS AGUAS | ZWISCHEN ZWEI WASSERELEMENTEN | ENTRE DEUX EAUX

The restoration of the building, originally constructed in the 1960's on a hill overlooking Los Angeles, included the placement of the house between two expanses of water, with a spectacular walkway at the entrance creating a striking first impression. The walkway leads up to the building and marks off the first receptacle of transparent water. Then a glass corridor delineates the common and private areas inside the house, which is built around an interior terrace. The pool's interior is made of white-stained concrete finished with small white tiles on the upper part. White terrazzo was used on the edges and around the rest of the terrace, which greatly increases the light. The furniture for the solarium zone is placed at the ends of the pool. One of the ends of the pool ends in a lookout point that affords vistas of the city and the hills of Beverly Hills.

Ausgangspunkt der Renovierung dieses Anwesens aus den 1960er Jahren, das auf einem Hügel über Los Angeles liegt, war, das Wohnhaus zwischen zwei Wasserelemente zu positionieren. Im Eingangsbereich – sozusagen das Aushängeschild – wurde ein spektakulärer Laufsteg angelegt. Er ist dem Haus vorgelagert und führt zum ersten transparenten Wasserbecken. Im Anschluss daran führt dieser gläserner Gang entlang der öffentlichen sowie persönlichen Bereiche des Hauses, die um die Innenterasse angelegt sind. Das Innere des Schwimmbeckens besteht aus weißem Zement, und an der oberen Hälfte führt ein Streifen aus weißer Glaskeramik entlang. An den Beckenrändern und um die gesamte Terrasse herum wurde zur Verstärkung des Lichts weißer Terrazzo verwendet. Das Mobiliar für die Sonnenterrassen wurde an den Beckenenden platziert. Den Abschluss des Schwimmbeckens bildet ein Aussichtspunkt mit Blick auf die Stadt und die Hügel von Beverly Hills.

La restauración de esta construcción, proyectada en los años 60 y situada en una colina que domina la ciudad de Los Ángeles, consistió en ubicar la vivienda entre dos aguas: en la entrada y como excelente carta de presentación, se proyectó una espectacular pasarela. Este elemento antecede a la construcción y separa un primer contenedor de agua transparente. A continuación, un pasillo de cristal ordena las zonas comunes y privadas de la residencia, que se han construido alrededor de la terraza interior. El interior de la piscina es de cemento tintado en blanco, con una franja de gresite blanco en la zona superior. En los bordes y alrededor de toda la terraza se utilizó terrazo de color blanco, que multiplica la luz. El mobiliario para la zona de solárium se ha colocado en los extremos de la piscina. La piscina termina en un mirador, con vistas a la ciudad y a las colinas de Beverly Hills.

C'est dans les années 60 qu'est né le projet de restaurer cette construction qui, de la colline où elle est située, domine la ville de Los Angeles. L'idée était de placer l'habitation entre deux eaux : à l'entrée, excellente carte de présentation, une passerelle spectaculaire a été conçue. Cet élément, qui a précédé la construction, isole un premier bassin d'eau transparente. Ensuite, un couloir de verre ordonne les zones communes et privées de la résidence, construites autour de la terrasse intérieure. L'intérieur de la piscine est en ciment teint en bleu et présente une bordure de Gresite blanc dans la partie supérieure. Sur les rebords et tout autour de la terrasse, l'utilisation de granito blanc multiplie la lumière. Le mobilier du solarium a été disposé aux extrémités de la piscine. Au bout de celle-ci, un mirador permet de contempler la ville et les collines de Beverly Hills.

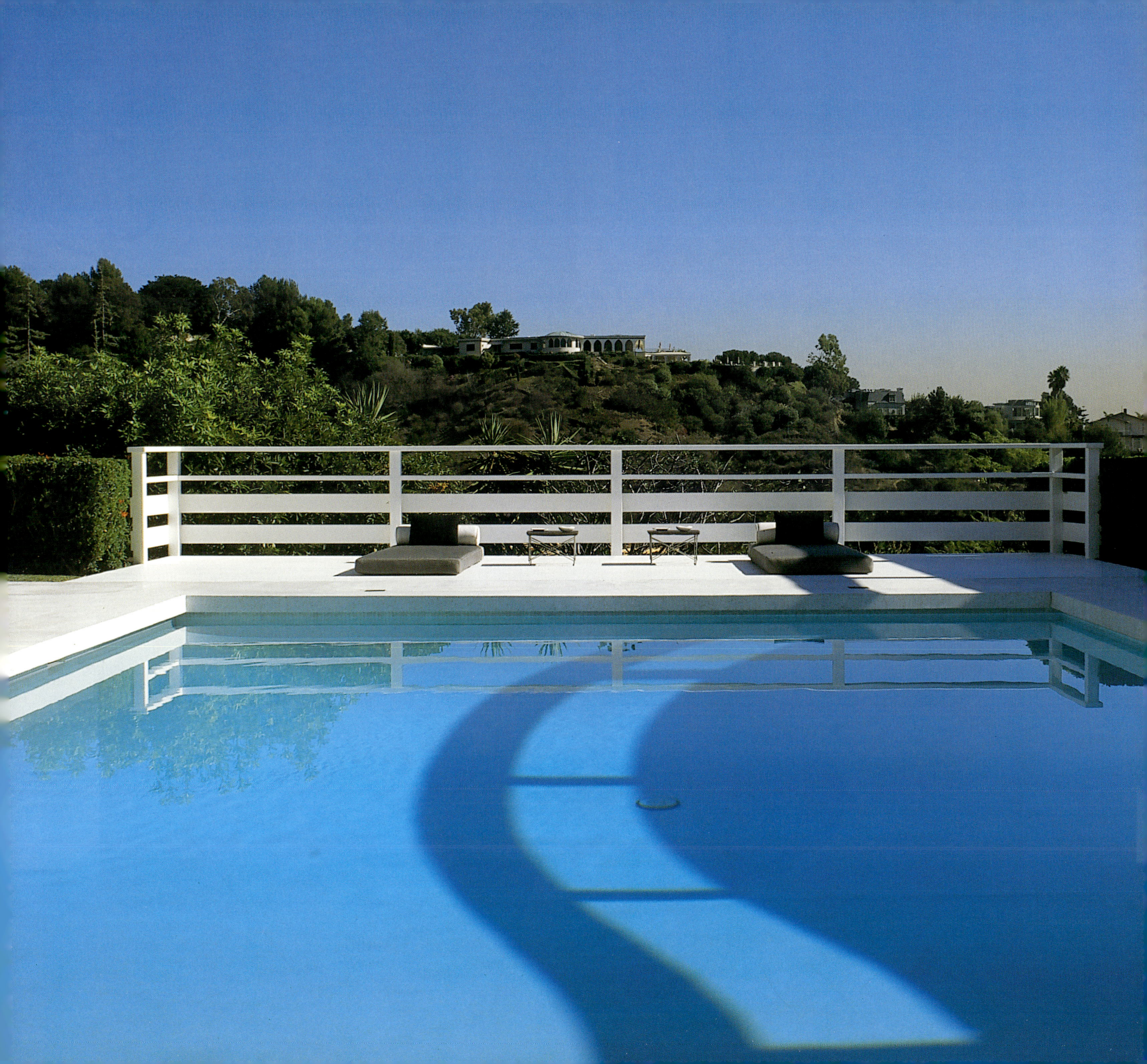

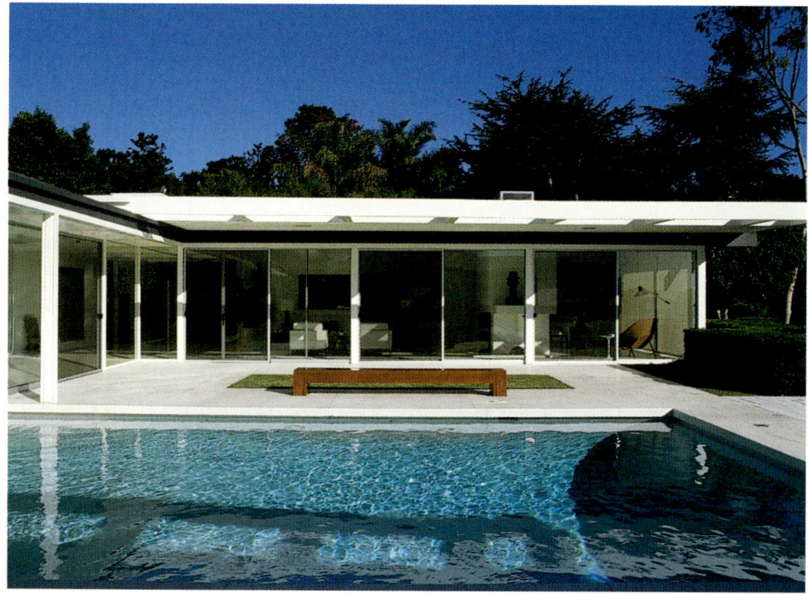

The furniture in the sunbathing area has been set at each end of the pool, although any part of the terrace can be used to enjoy the sun after a swim. The swimming pool leads to a belvedere with views of the city and the slopes of Beverly Hills.

Los muebles en el área para tomar el sol se han dispuesto al final de cada extremo de la piscina, aunque cualquier parte de la terraza puede ser utilizada para disfrutar del sol después de un baño. La piscina se encara hacia un mirador con vistas de la ciudad y las laderas de Beverly Hills.

Das Mobiliar für das Sonnendeck befindet sich am Beckenende, auch wenn die gesamte Terrasse für ein ausgibieges Sonnenbad zur Verfügung seht. Das Schwimmbecken grenzt an einen kleinen Aussichtspunkt, der einen herrlichen Blick auf die Stadt und die Hügel von Beverly Hills bietet.

Les meubles du solarium ont été disposés à chaque extrémité de la piscine, même si n'importe quelle partie de la terrasse se prête à une exposition au soleil après un bain. La piscine fait face à un mirador permettant de contempler la ville et les collines de Beverly Hills.

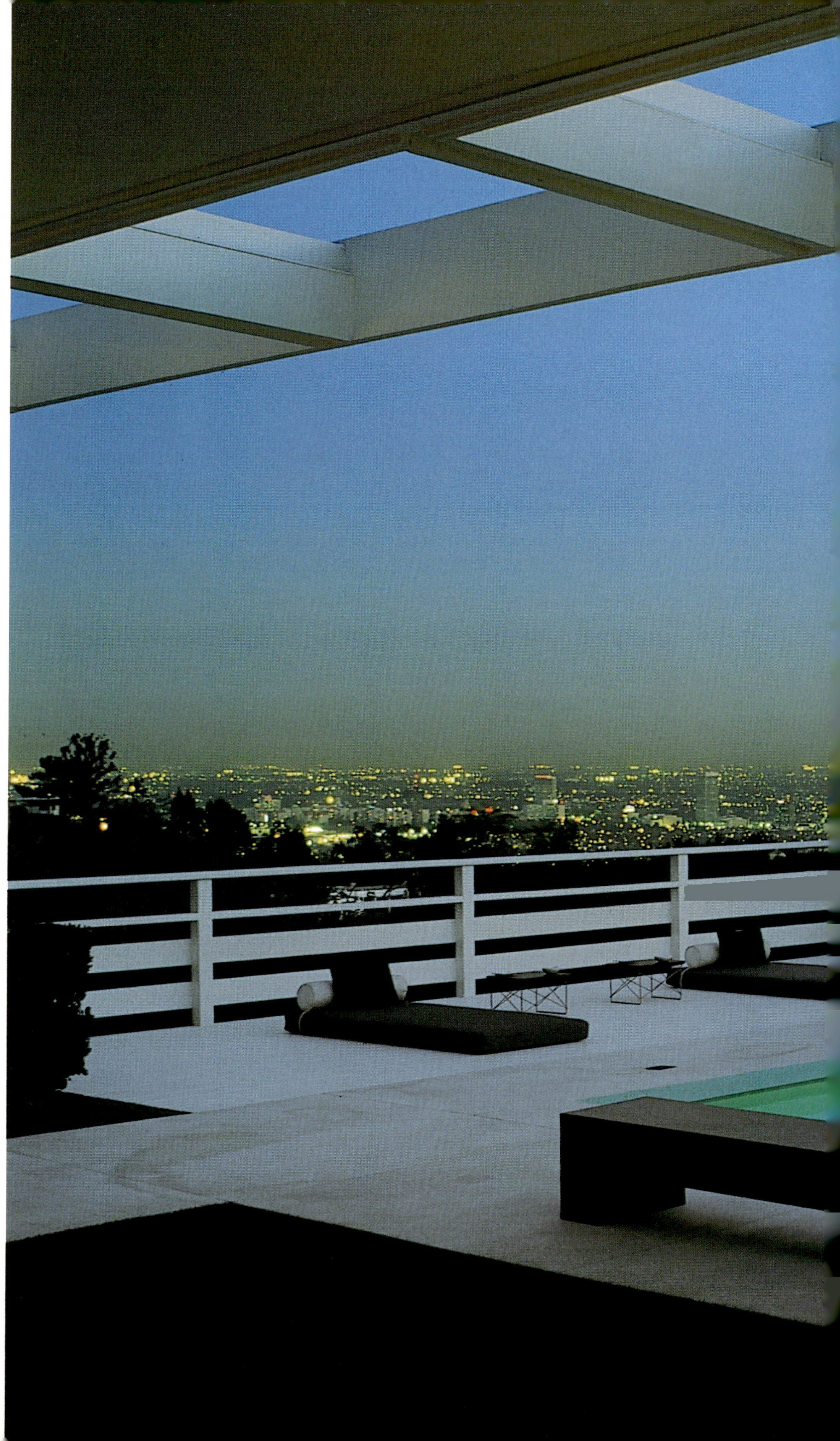

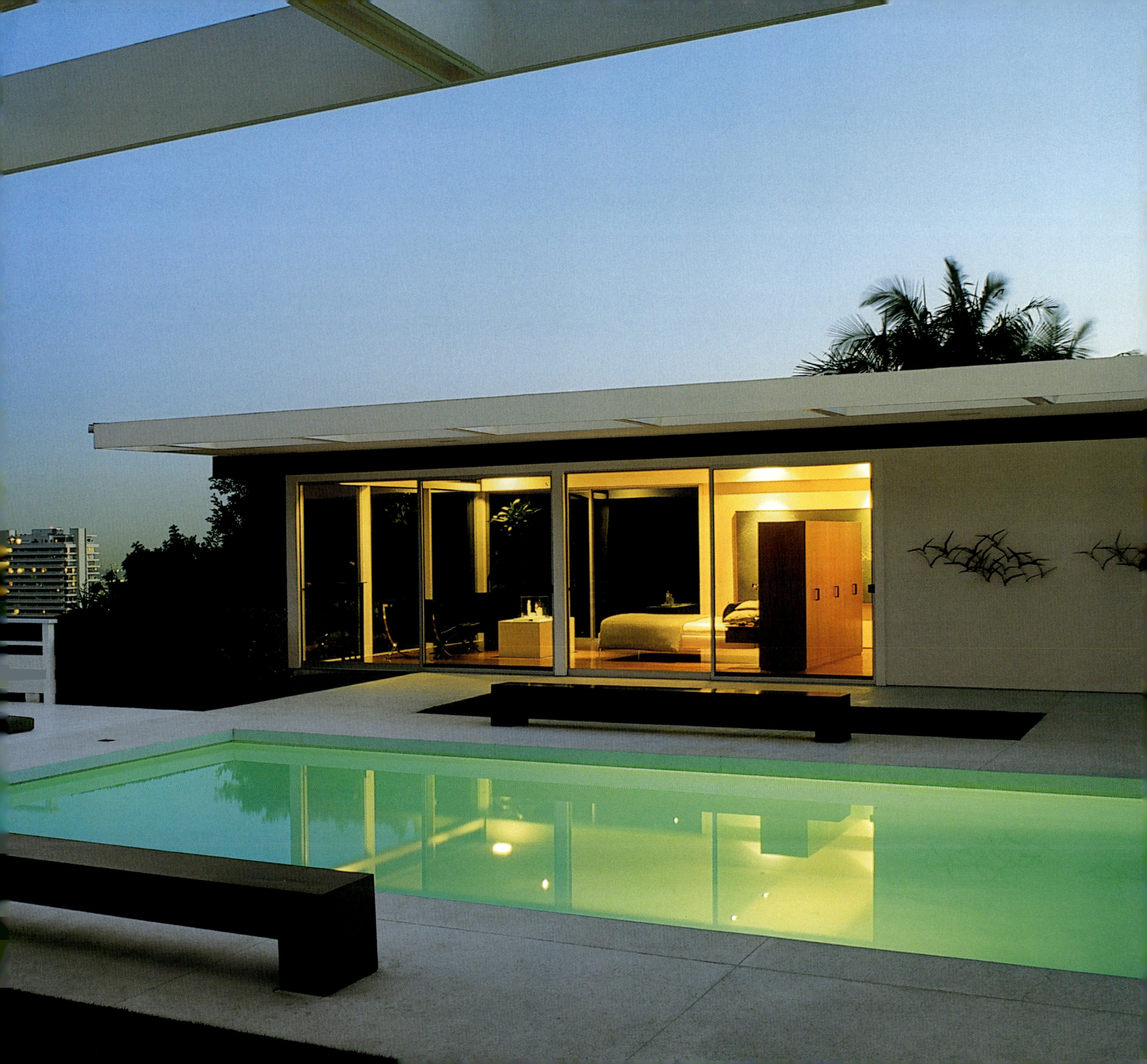

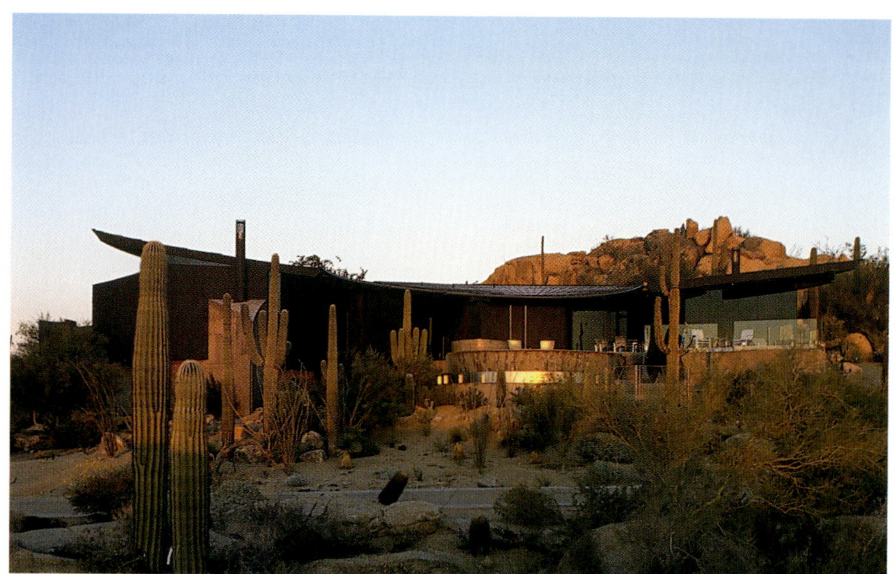

Circular Shapes

Formas circulares | Kreisformen | Formes circulaires

The cacti undoubtedly give away the location of this spectacular residential project, which incorporates a circular pool. The house is built on a slight slope, so it is divided into several levels to conform to the contours of the landscape. The bottom of the pool is made of concrete and rammed earth, while the interior sports white-stained concrete, complemented by the concrete slabs in the terrace area. The pool border is a stainless steel sheet with perforations that filter the water, performing an aesthetic function as well as a practical one. A high, sharply stylized staircase marks off the entrance to the pool; its steps echo the forms of the swimming pool and the distinctive rolling landscape.

Los cactus, sin duda, delatan la ubicación de este original proyecto residencial, que incorpora una piscina circular. Se trata de un terreno con una ligera pendiente dominado por grandes bloques de granito, por lo que la casa se ha construido a diferentes niveles, respetando la orografía del terreno. El contenedor se realizó con hormigón, cemento y tierra prensada para la base, cemento tintado de blanco para su interior y baldosas de cemento para la zona de terraza. El remate de la piscina es una plancha de acero inoxidable con pequeños agujeros por donde se filtra el agua a modo de rebosadero, que cumple una función estética a la vez que muy práctica. Marca la zona de entrada una escalera de líneas extremadamente estilizadas y de gran altura, con un peldaño que continua las formas de la piscina y la singular orografía del terreno.

Die Kakteen sind ein klares Indiz für den Standort dieses originellen Wohnprojekts, zu dem ein rundes Schwimmbecken gehört. Das Gelände weist ein leichtes Gefälle auf und wird von großen Granitblöcken beherrscht. Augrund des Gefälles erstreckt sich das Haus über mehrere Ebenen, um der natürlichen Bodengestaltung entgegen zu kommen. Beim Bau des Pools wurden Beton, Zement und gepresste Erde für den Untergrund, weißer Zement für das Beckeninnere und Zementfliesen für den Terrassenbereich verwendet. Den Rand des Schwimmbeckens bildet eine Edelstahlplatte mit kleinen Löchern, durch die das Wasser wie bei einem Überlauf gefiltert wird – nicht nur ein ästhetischer Aspekt, sondern auch praktische Funktionalität. Den Eingangsbereich prägt eine außergewöhnlich stilisierte und sehr hohe Treppe, deren Stufen die Formen des Schwimmbeckens und das einzigartige Oberflächenrelief des Geländes aufnehmen.

Les cactus ne laissent planer aucun doute sur l'emplacement de ce projet résidentiel original, qui inclut une piscine circulaire. Il s'agit d'un terrain légèrement en pente, dominé par de grands blocs de granit. La maison a donc été construite sur différents niveaux afin de respecter l'orographie du terrain. La base du bassin a été réalisée en béton, en ciment et en terre pressée ; l'intérieur, en ciment teint en blanc. Des dalles de ciment pavent la terrasse. Les finitions de la piscine consistent en une plaque d'acier inoxydable percée de petits trous permettant à l'eau de filtrer à la manière d'un déversoir, de fonction à la fois esthétique et pratique. L'entrée est valorisée par un grand escalier aux lignes extrêmement stylisées, très haut, dont les marches prolongent les formes de la piscine et la singulière orographie du terrain.

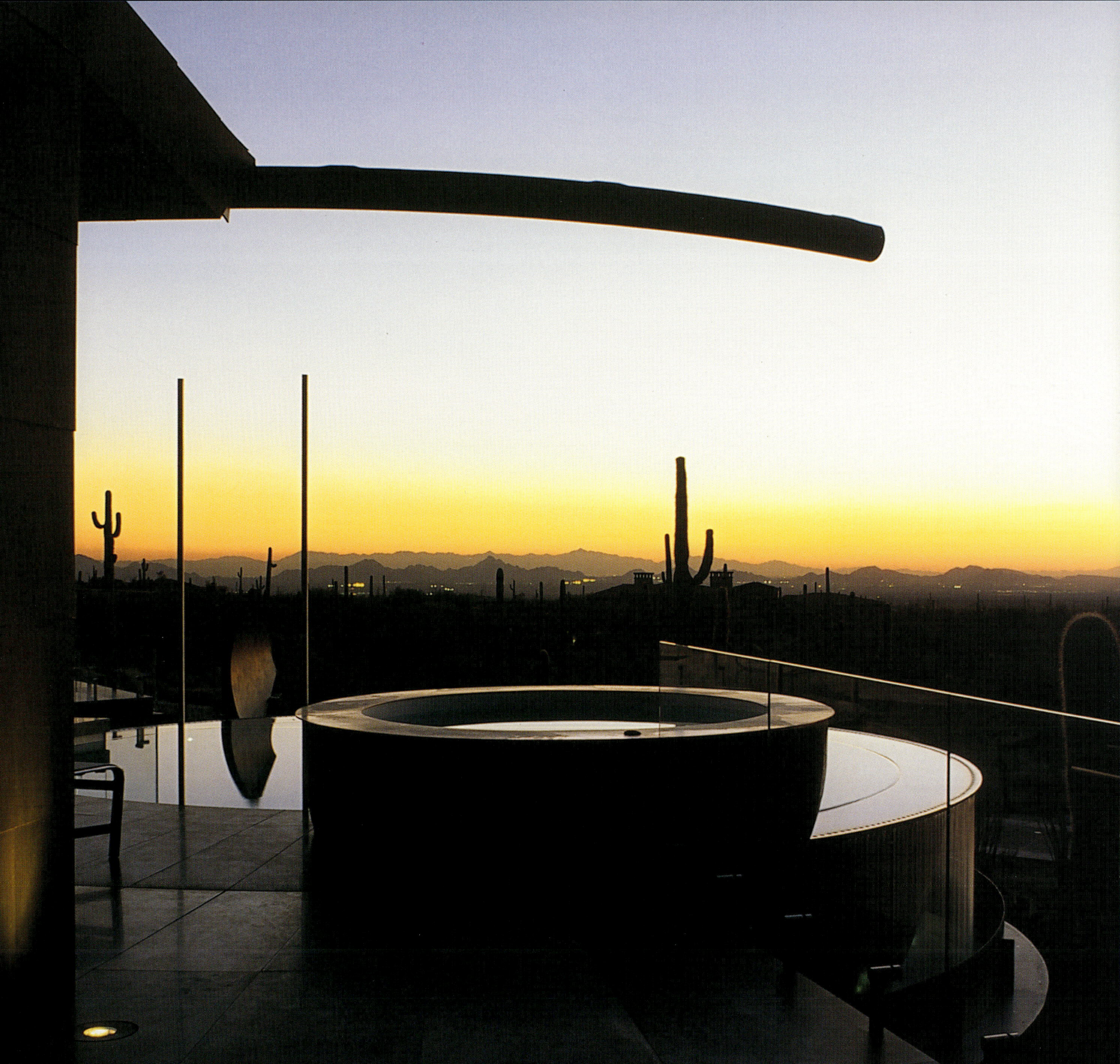

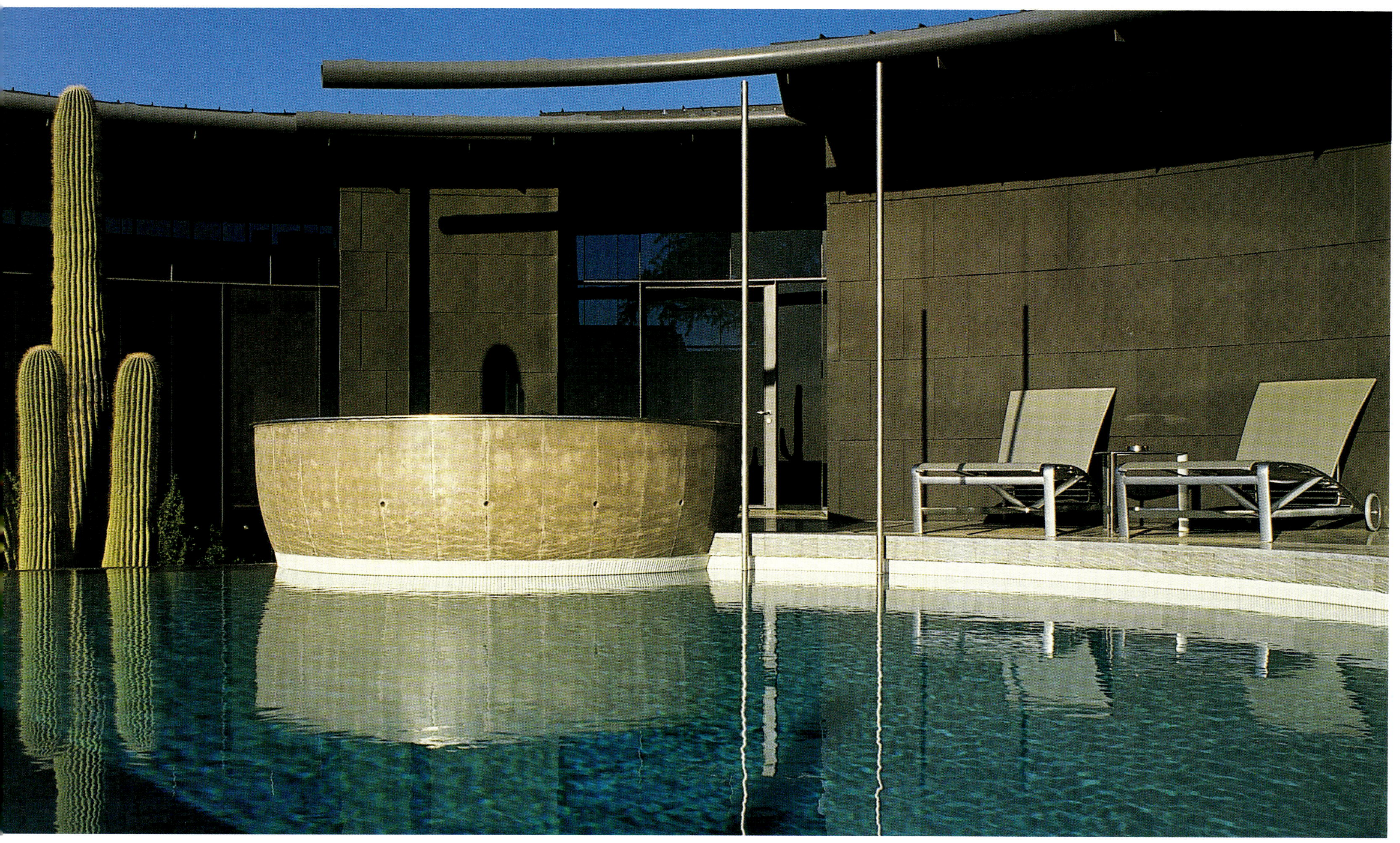

The circular jacuzzi also complements the larger pool.

El jacuzzi circular también complementa la piscina más grande.

Der runde Whirlpool ergänzt das größere Schwimmbecken.

La plus grande des piscines est également équipée d'un jacuzzi circulaire.

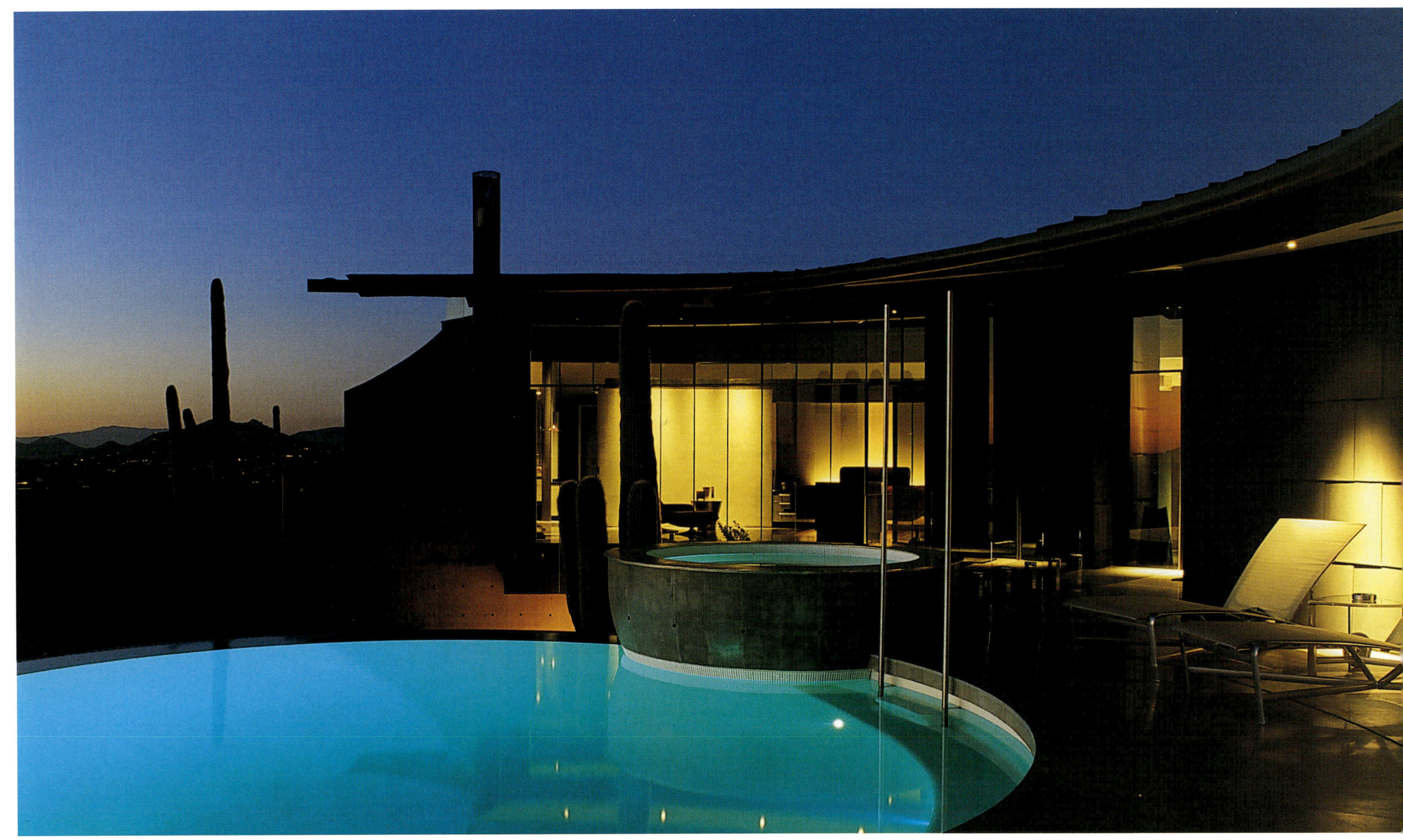

The sinuous circular forms of the pool are also extended to the sunbathing area

Las formas sinuosamente circulares de la piscina se extienden hasta la zona de tomar el sol.

Die kreisförmigen Konturen des Schwimmbeckens erstrecken sich bis zum Sonnendeck.

Les formes circulaires et sinueuses de la piscine s'étendent jusqu'au solarium.

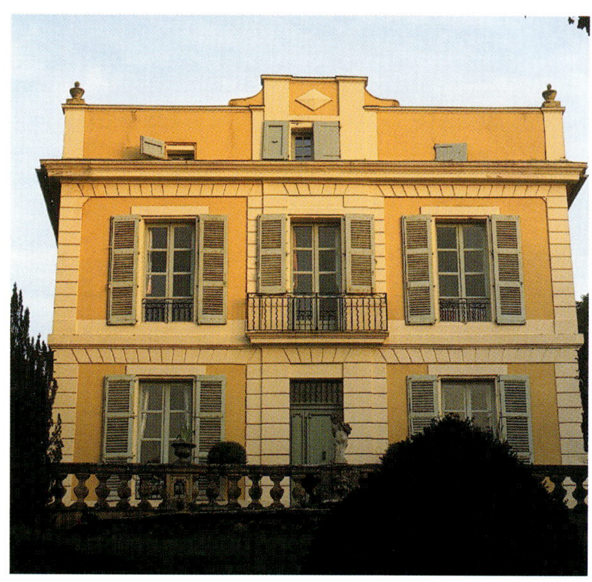

Classical Essence

Esencia clásica | Einfach klassisch | Essence classique

History relates that Pauline Bonaparte (1780-1825) –the Princess of Borghese, Duchess of Guastalla and Napoleon's sister- was a great beauty with very refined tastes. She commissioned this residence in Aix-en-Provence at the end of the eighteenth century as a rendezvous for her numerous lovers, and her personality and elegance are still pervasive –it is even called La Pauline in her honor. The house has now been restored without sacrificing the classical elegance characteristic of its time, and it is complemented by twenty acres of typical Provençal gardens. The present owners decided to take advantage of the hollow of an old pond, tucked into a steeply sloping area. The interior of the pool was finished with cement and local stone was used for the trim, which grants continuity to the classical style.

La historia atribuye a Pauline Bonaparte (1780-1825), hermana de Napoleón, una gran belleza física y un gusto excelente y refinado. La esencia de la personalidad de esta mujer, princesa de Borghese y duquesa de Guastalla, todavía permanece en esta residencia histórica que se hizo construir a finales del siglo XVIII para convertirla en lugar de encuentro con sus numerosos amantes. Situada en Aix-en-Provence, la finca, llamada La Pauline (en honor de su antigua propietaria), se ha restaurado conservando la esencia clásica de la época. La extensión ocupa ocho hectáreas de jardines de estilo provenzal francés.
Situada en una zona de fuerte pendiente, la piscina se construyó aprovechando el hueco de un antiguo estanque. El interior del contenedor se revistió de cemento y en los bordes se utilizó piedra de la región para dar continuidad al estilo clásico.

Pauline Bonaparte (1780-1825), einer Schwester Napoleons, ist berühmt für ihre große Schönheit sowie ihren exquisiten und erlesenen Geschmack. Die Persönlichkeit dieser Frau, der Fürstin Borghese und Herzogin von Guastalla, prägt noch heute die historische Residenz, die sie Ende des 18. Jahrhunderts erbauen ließ, um einen Ort für ihre Stelldicheins mit ihren zahlreichen Liebhabern zu haben. Das in Aix-en-Provence, Frankreich, gelegene Anwesen, das den Namen La Pauline (zu Ehren seiner ehemaligen Besitzerin) trägt, wurde unter Erhaltung der klassischen Grundzüge jener Epoche restauriert. Das Grundstück und seine Gärten erstreckt sich über acht Hektar und folgt dem provenzalischen Stil. Wo sich früher auf dem abfallenden Gelände der Teich befand, wurde das Schwimmbecken errichtet. Das Beckeninnere wurde mit Zement verkleidet und an den Rändern kamen Steine der Region zum Einsatz, womit man den klassischen Stil wahren wollte.

L'histoire attribue à Pauline Bonaparte (1780-1825), sœur de Napoléon, une grande beauté physique ainsi qu'un goût excellent et raffiné. L'essence de la personnalité de cette femme, qui fut princesse de Borghese et duchesse de Guastalla, subsiste dans cette résidence historique qu'elle se fit construire à la fin du 18e siècle pour y rencontrer ses nombreux amants. Situé à Aix-en-Provence, le domaine, baptisé La Pauline (en l'honneur de son ancienne propriétaire), a été restauré en conservant l'essence classique de l'époque. La propriété s'étend sur huit hectares de jardins de style provençal.
Située sur une forte pente, la piscine figure à la place d'un ancien bassin. Son intérieur a été revêtu de ciment et la pierre de la région qui revêt ses rebords s'inscrit dans la continuité du style classique.

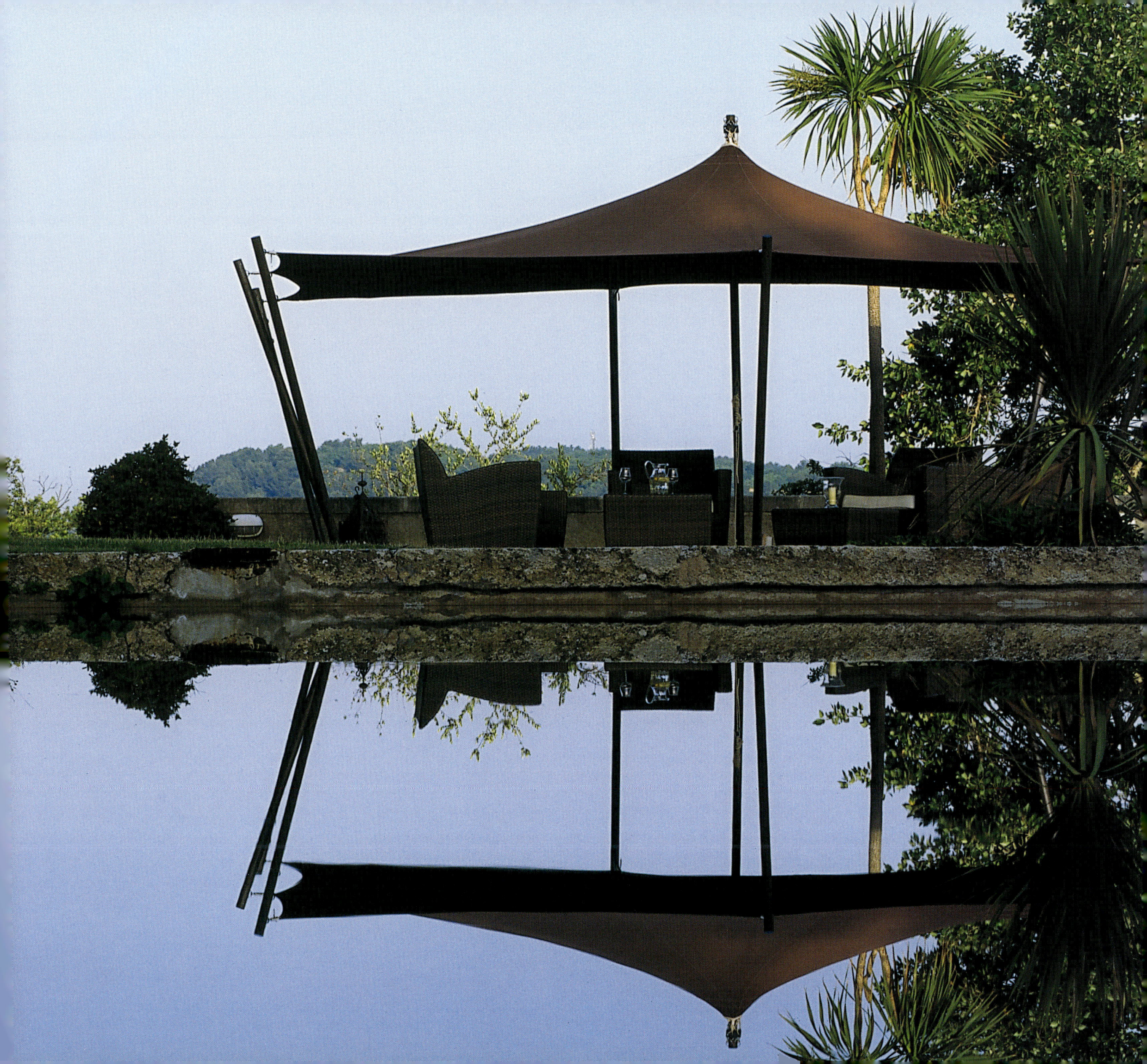

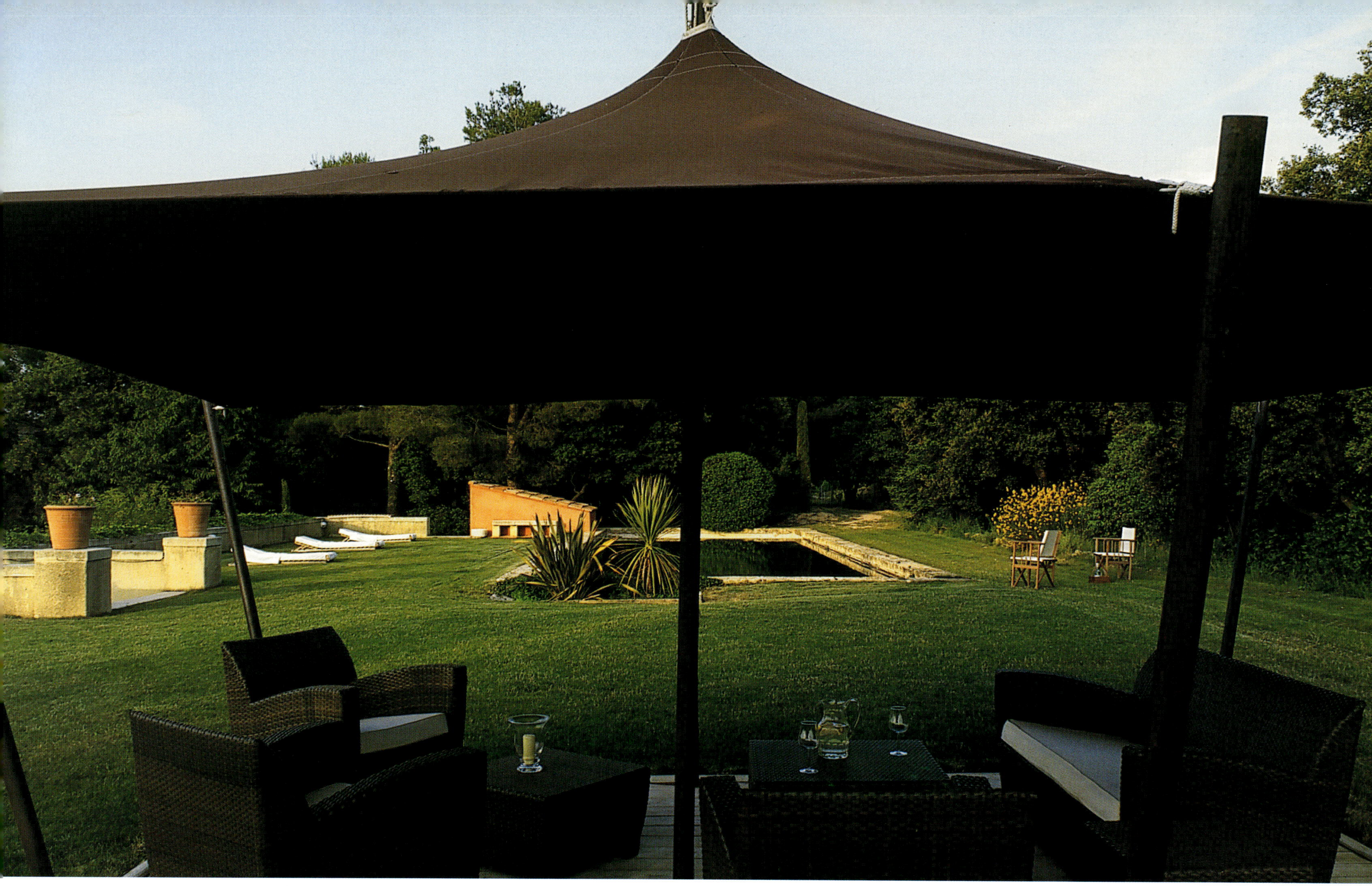

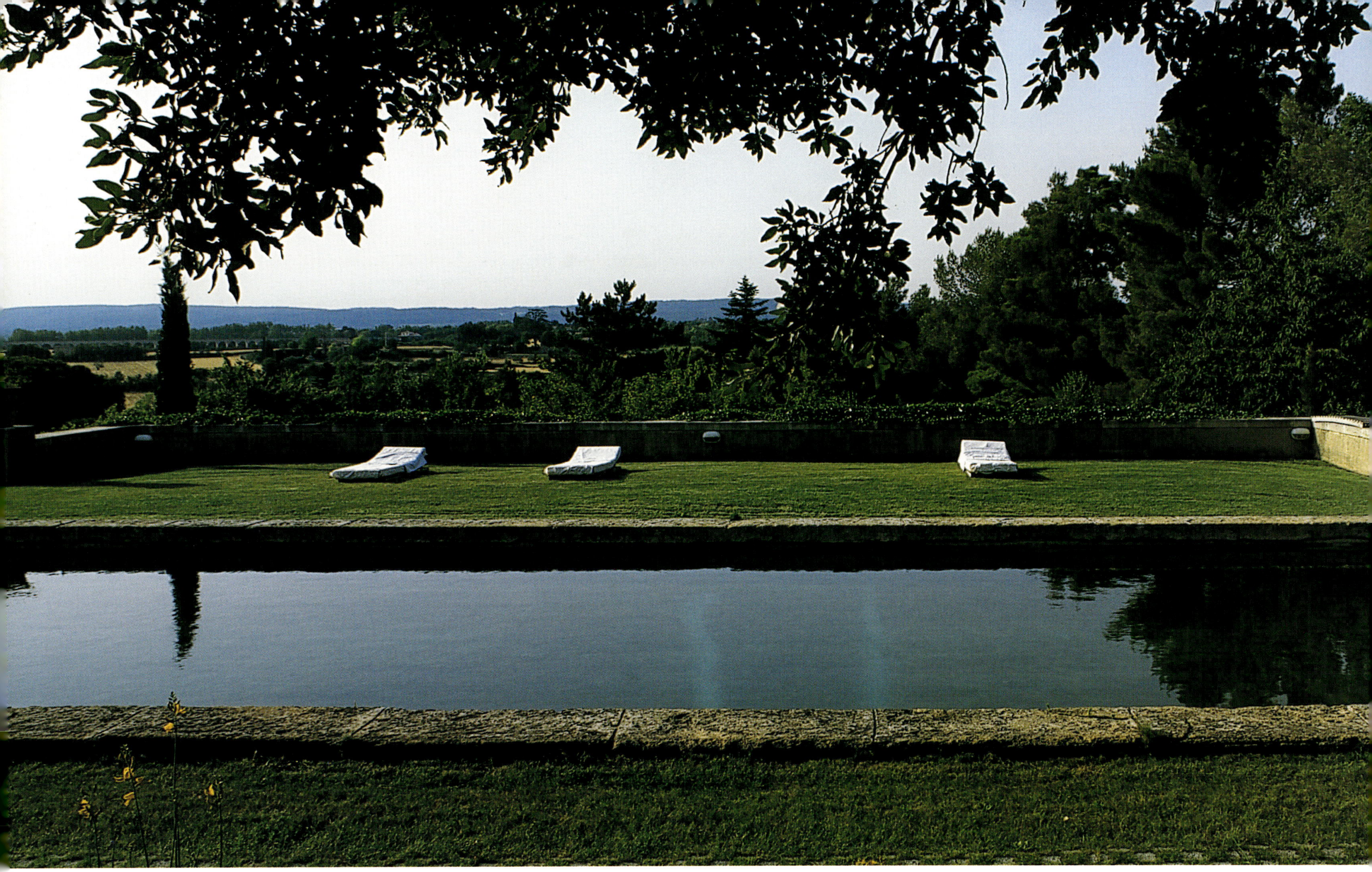

The pool is surrounded by vast expanses of typically Mediterranean vegetation.

La piscina reposa en una gran extensión repleta de vegetación mediterránea.

Das Schwimmbecken wird von üppiger mediterraner Vegetation umgeben.

La piscine repose dans un grand domaine recouvert par la végétation méditerranéenne.

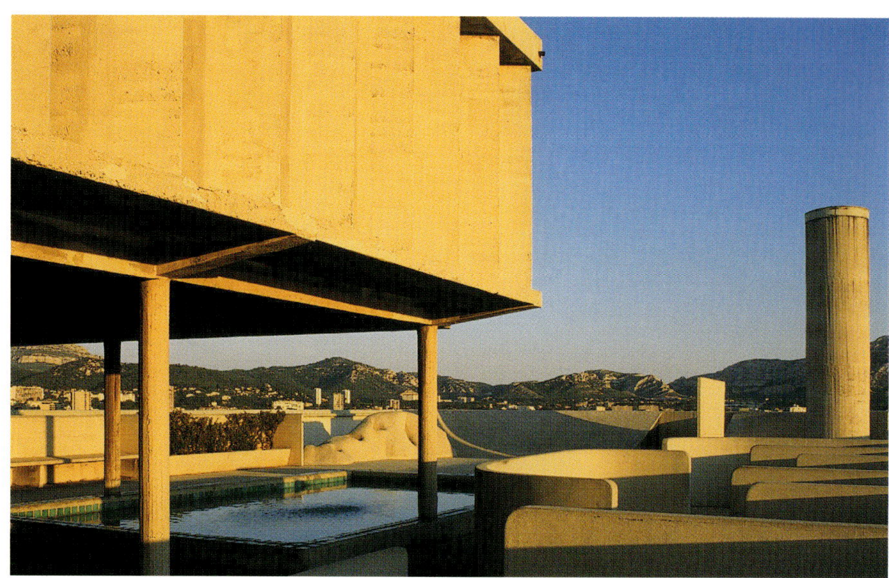

Vertical City

Ciudad vertical | Vertikale Stadt | Ville verticale

The Unité d'Habitation, built between 1945 and 1952 on the Boulevard Michelet in Marseille, is one of the crowning achievements of Le Corbusier's later architecture, far removed from the purist aesthetics of his work in the 1920's. This apartment block takes the form of a tall reinforced-concrete complex –in keeping with the architect's concept of a "vertical city"– and contains 337 apartments, along with shopping streets and spaces for leisure activities. The swimming pool lies on the building's terrace, which houses most of the communal facilities. The sculptural forms of the ventilation chimneys and the arrangement of the staircases convert the roof into an array of highly original abstract sculptures.

Ubicada en el bulevar Michelet de Marsella, la Unité d'Habitation, construida entre 1945 y 1952, representa una de las grandes obras de la arquitectura tardía de Le Corbusier, muy lejos de su estética purista de los años 20. El bloque de viviendas se proyectó como un alargado complejo de hormigón armado, en la estética de lo que él denominaba "ciudad en vertical", donde se encajaron 337 viviendas, así como calles comerciales y espacios de recreo. La piscina se construyó en la terraza del edificio, que albergaba gran parte de los servicios comunitarios. Las formas escultóricas de las chimeneas de ventilación o la disposición de las escaleras convirtieron la cubierta en un conjunto de esculturas abstractas y muy originales.

Die zwischen 1945 und 1952 errichtete Unité d'Habitation auf dem Boulevard Michelet von Marseille ist eines der großen Spätwerke von Le Corbusier, weit entfernt von seiner puristischen Ästhetik der 1920er Jahre. Der Wohnanlage wurde als lang gestreckter Komplex aus Stahlbeton in dem von ihm als „vertikale Stadt" bezeichneten Stil entworfen, und umfasste 337 Wohnungen und Einkaufsstraßen und Plätze für das Freizeitvergnügen. Das Schwimmbecken wurde auf der Dachterrasse errichtet, auf der ein Großteil der gemeinschaftlichen Einrichtungen untergebracht wurde. Die skulpturalen Lüftungsschächte sowie die Anordnung der Treppen machten das Dach zu einem Ensemble abstrakter und sehr origineller Skulpturen.

Située sur le boulevard Michelet de Marseille, l'Unité d'habitation, construite entre 1945 et 1952, représente une des grandes œuvres de l'architecture tardive de Le Corbusier, loin de son esthétique puriste des années 20. Le bloc d'appartements a été conçu comme un complexe allongé en béton armé, dans l'esthétique de ce qu'il désignait comme la "ville verticale". Ce bloc inclut 337 appartements, ainsi que des rues commerciales et des espaces de détente. La piscine a été construite sur la terrasse du bâtiment, laquelle abritait une grande partie des services communautaires. Le toit devient un ensemble de sculptures abstraites très originales avec les cheminées de ventilation et l'agencement des escaliers.

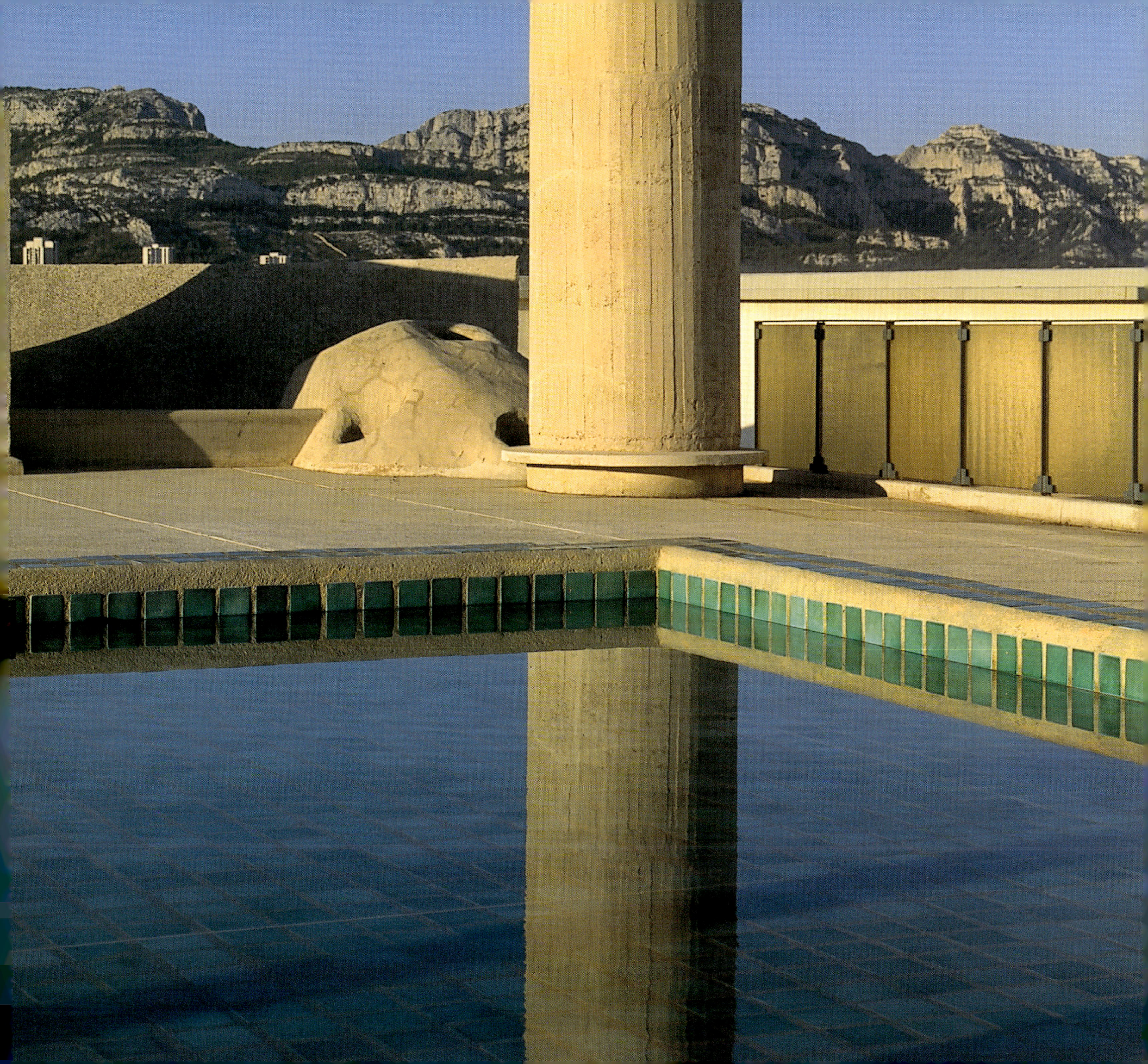

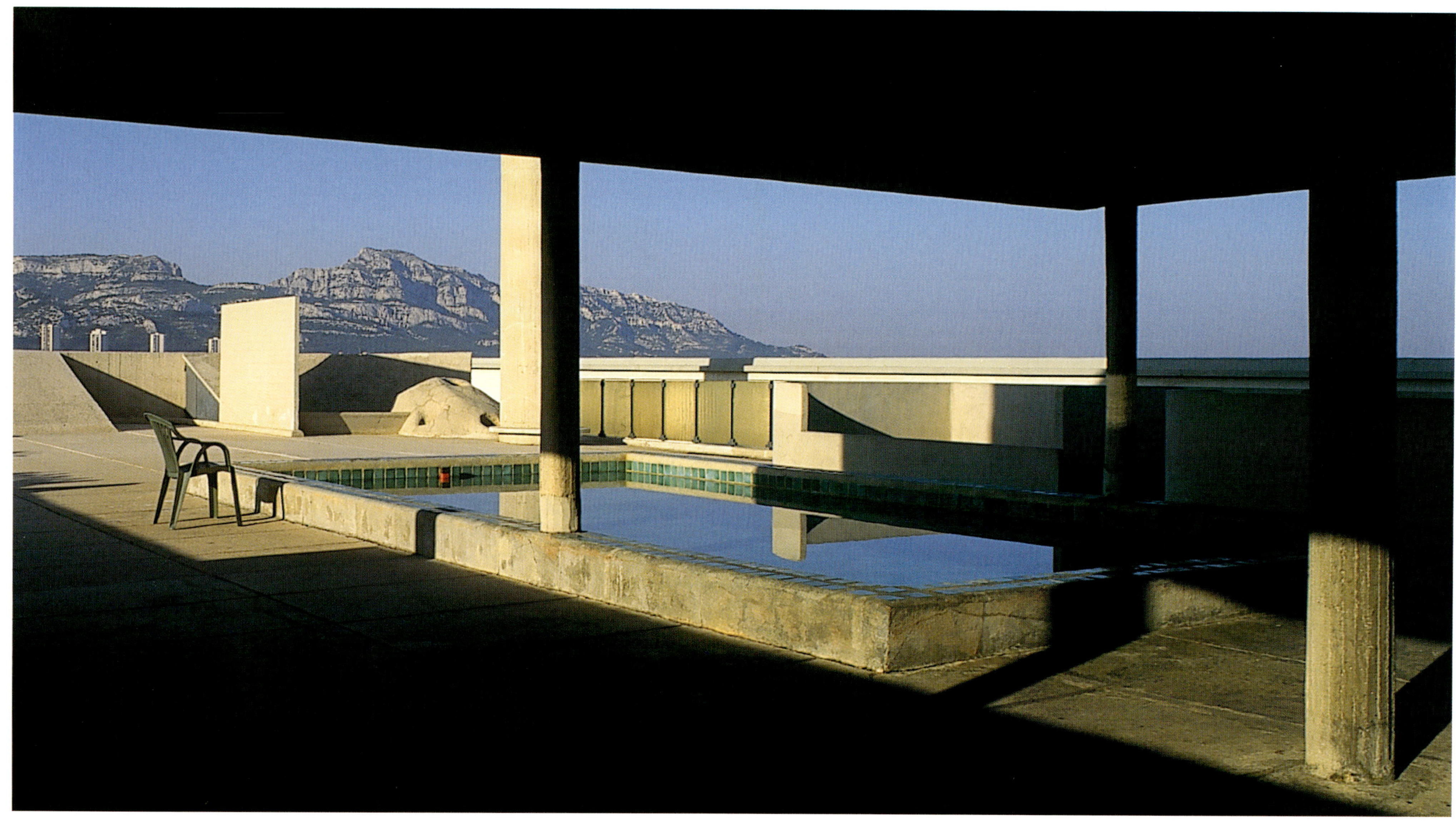

With fabulous vistas, the communal swimming pool occupies a large part of the terrace of La Unité. Le Corbusier used green tiles to soften the austerity of the concrete.

La piscina comunitaria ocupa gran parte de la terraza de la Unité, con grandes vistas. Le Corbusier utilizó losetas de color verde para suavizar la dureza del hormigón.

Der öffentliche Pool nimmt fast die ganze Dachterrasse der Unité ein, die einen spektakulären Blick bietet. Le Corbusier verwendete grüne Fliesen, um die Härte des Betons zu mildern.

La piscine communautaire occupe une grande partie de la terrasse de l'Unité et offre une vue dégagée. Le Corbusier a utilisé des carreaux de couleur verte pour adoucir la dureté du béton.

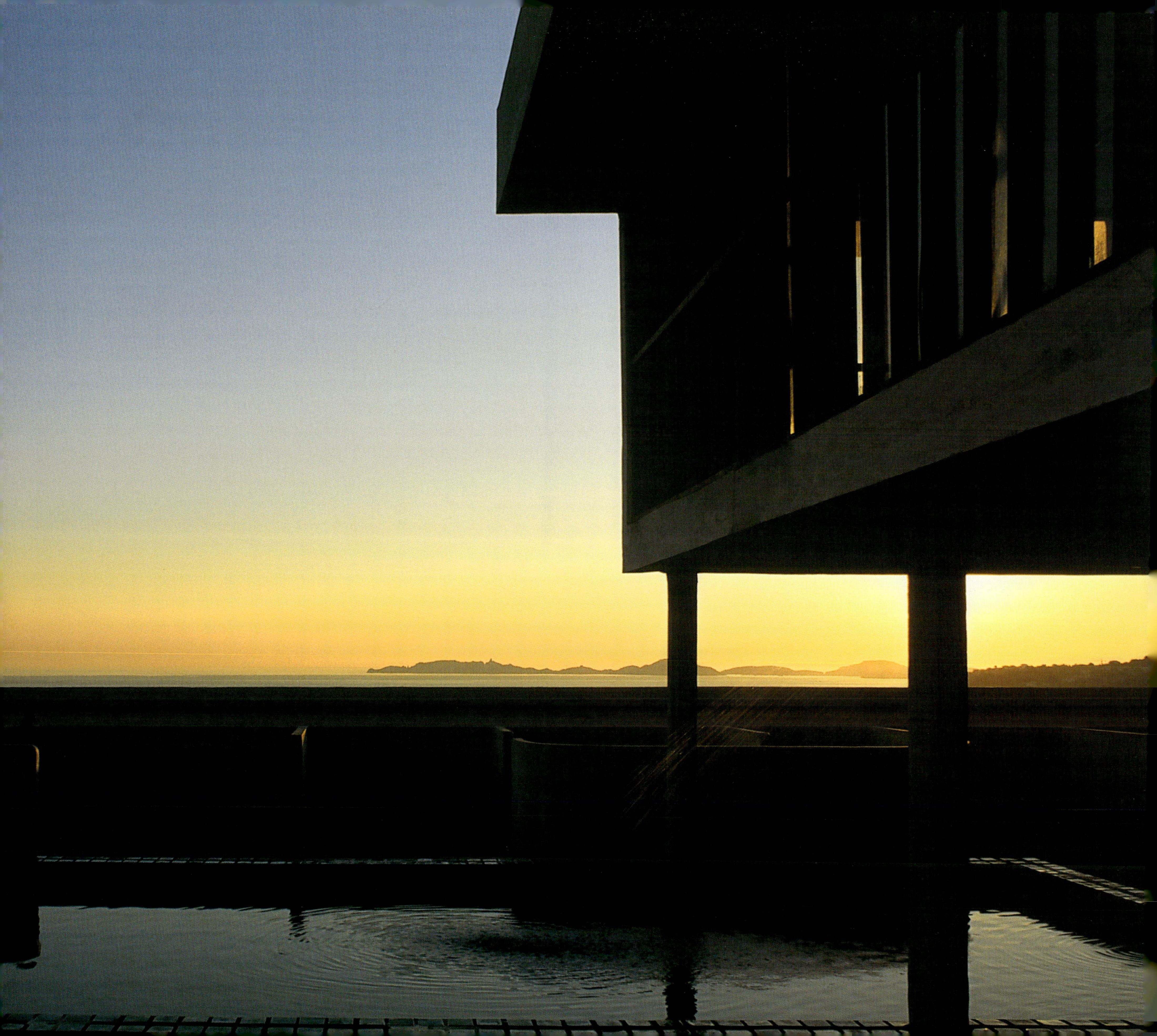

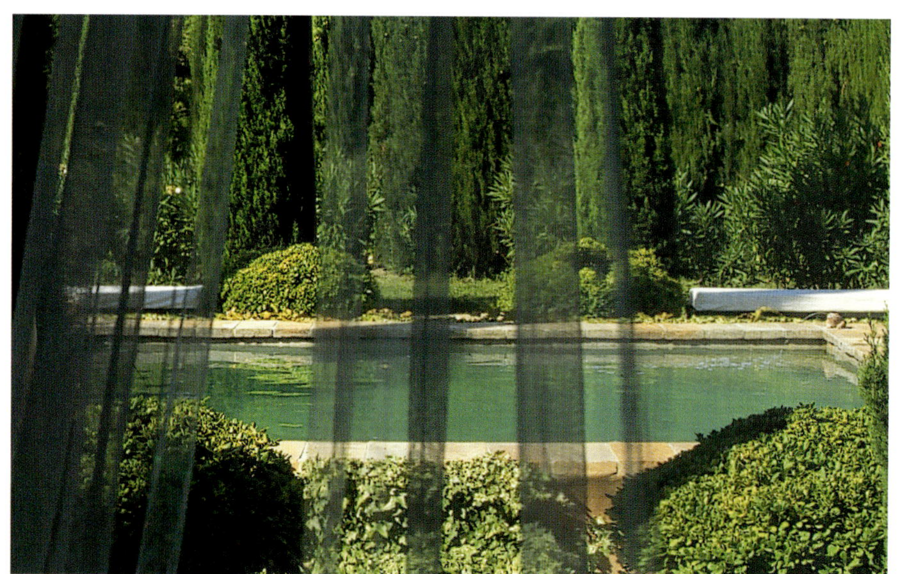

Water Path

Camino de agua | Wasserwege | Chemin d'eau

This splendid garden that generously surrounds the property, was designed to be a succession of chromatically differentiated individual spaces. At the same time they are united by an imaginary straight line, which on one side takes the form of a water path, and on the other side, consists of the green tone of the grass that covers the access to the rear gardens. This magnificent vanilla-colored restored house is the hub. From it four garden areas, with well-differentiated ambiences, extend out. Two conceptually distinct ponds were designed in. One is natural and attempts only to grant aesthetic beauty. The other has a dual purpose as it affords beauty and is also for leisure. The well-studied landscape is a framework that invites reflection while at the same time arouses secret creativity.

Este espléndido jardín, que rodea generosamente la propiedad, ha sido concebido como una sucesión de espacios individuales cromáticamente diferenciados pero unidos por una línea recta imaginaria que por un lado adquiere la forma de un camino de agua y por otro, la tonalidad verde de la hierba que tapiza el acceso a los jardines traseros. A partir de un único eje central constituido por la magnífica casa restaurada y pintada de color vainilla, se extienden cuatro espacios ajardinados con ambientes bien diferenciados, en los cuales se han diseñado dos estanques conceptualmente distintos: uno natural para la recreación visual y otro que desempeña una doble función, lúdica y estética. El estudiado marco paisajístico invita a la reflexión a la vez que suscita la secreta creatividad.

Dieser prachtvolle Garten, der das Anwesen umgibt, wurde als eine Abfolge von einzelnen Bereichen angelegt. Diese unterscheiden sich zwar farblich, werden jedoch wieder vereint durch eine imaginäre gerade Linie in Form eines Wasserwegs sowie durch den grünen Farbton des Rasens, der in den hinteren Garten führt. Ausgehend von der einzigen zentralen Achse, die das liebevoll restaurierte und vanillefarben gestrichene Haus bildet, gehen vier ganz unerschiedliche Gartenbereiche ab. Es wurden zwei in ihrer Konzeption völlig unterschiedliche Wasserbecken angelegt: ein natürliches als optischer Ruhepunkt und ein zweites mit einer doppelten, nämlich spielerischen und ästhetischen Funktion. Die sorgsam gestaltete Landschaft lädt zum Nachdenken ein und regt zugleich verborgene Kreativität an.

Ce splendide jardin qui entoure généreusement la propriété a été conçu comme une succession d'espaces individuels distincts sur le plan chromatique mais unis par une ligne droite imaginaire qui, d'un côté, prend la forme d'un chemin d'eau et de l'autre, la tonalité verte de l'herbe qui tapisse l'accès au jardins de la partie de derrière. A partir de l'axe central que constitue la splendide maison restaurée, peinte de couleur vanille, s'étendent quatre espaces de jardins aux cadres bien différents, dans lesquels ont été créés deux étangs de conception différente : l'un, naturel, relève de la recréation visuelle et l'autre remplit une double fonction, ludique et esthétique. Le cadre paysager, très étudié, invite à la réflexion et suscite secrètement la créativité.

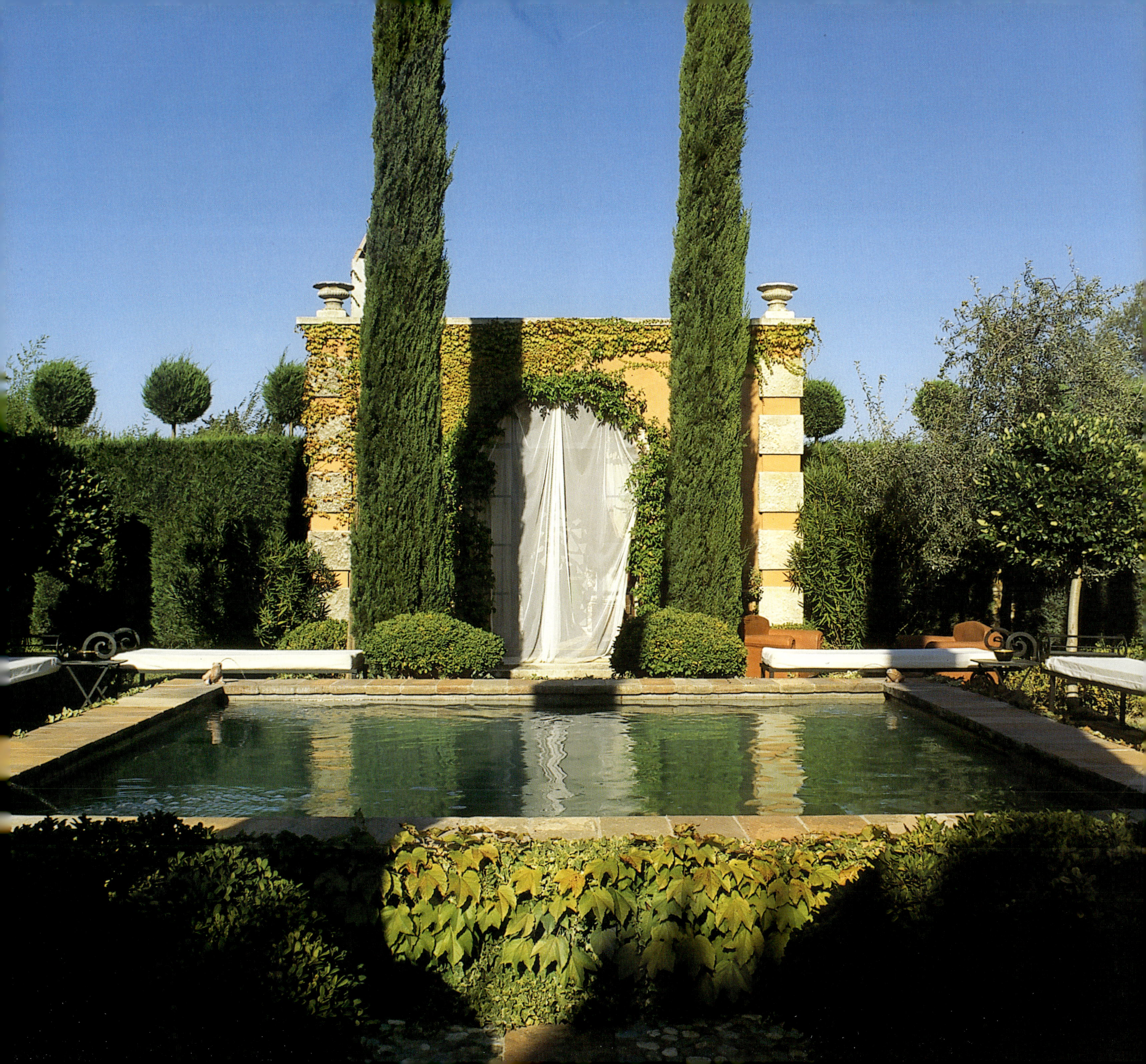

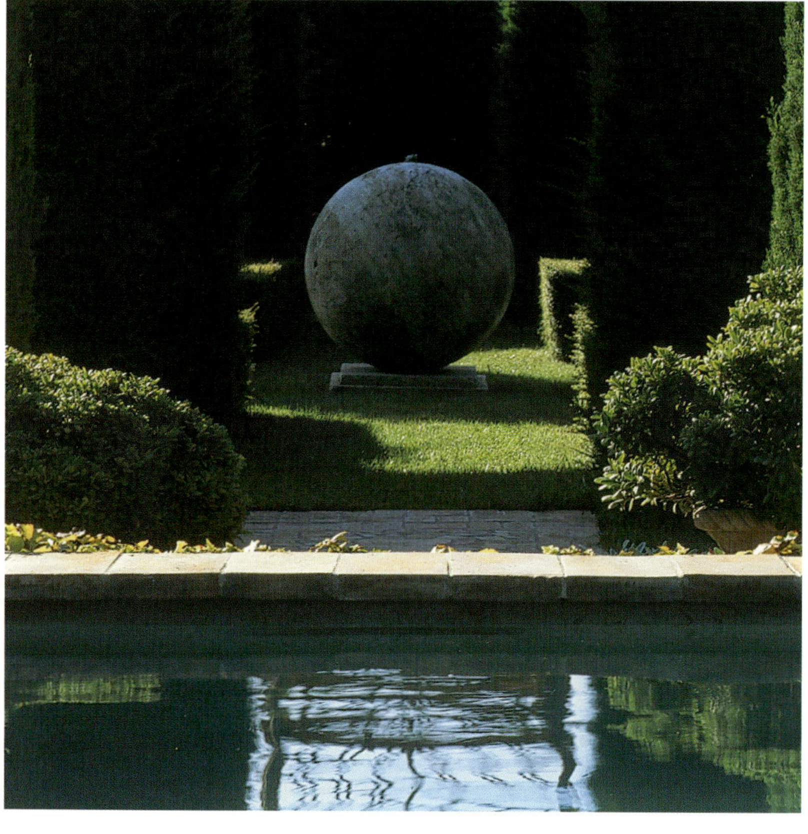

Although conceived as individual elements in a sequence, the spaces are united by a straight waterway edged by a long line of olive and cypress trees.

Aunque los espacios se han concebido como secuencias individuales, quedan unidos por un camino recto de agua bordeado por una larga hilera de olivos y cipreses.

Obwohl die Bereiche individuell konzipiert wurden, sind sie durch einen geraden Wasserweg verbunden, der von einer langen Reihe von Olivenbäumen und Zypressen gesäumt wird.

Même si les espaces ont été conçus comme des séquences individuelles, ils restent unis par un chemin d'eau rectiligne bordé d'une large haie d'oliviers et de cyprès.

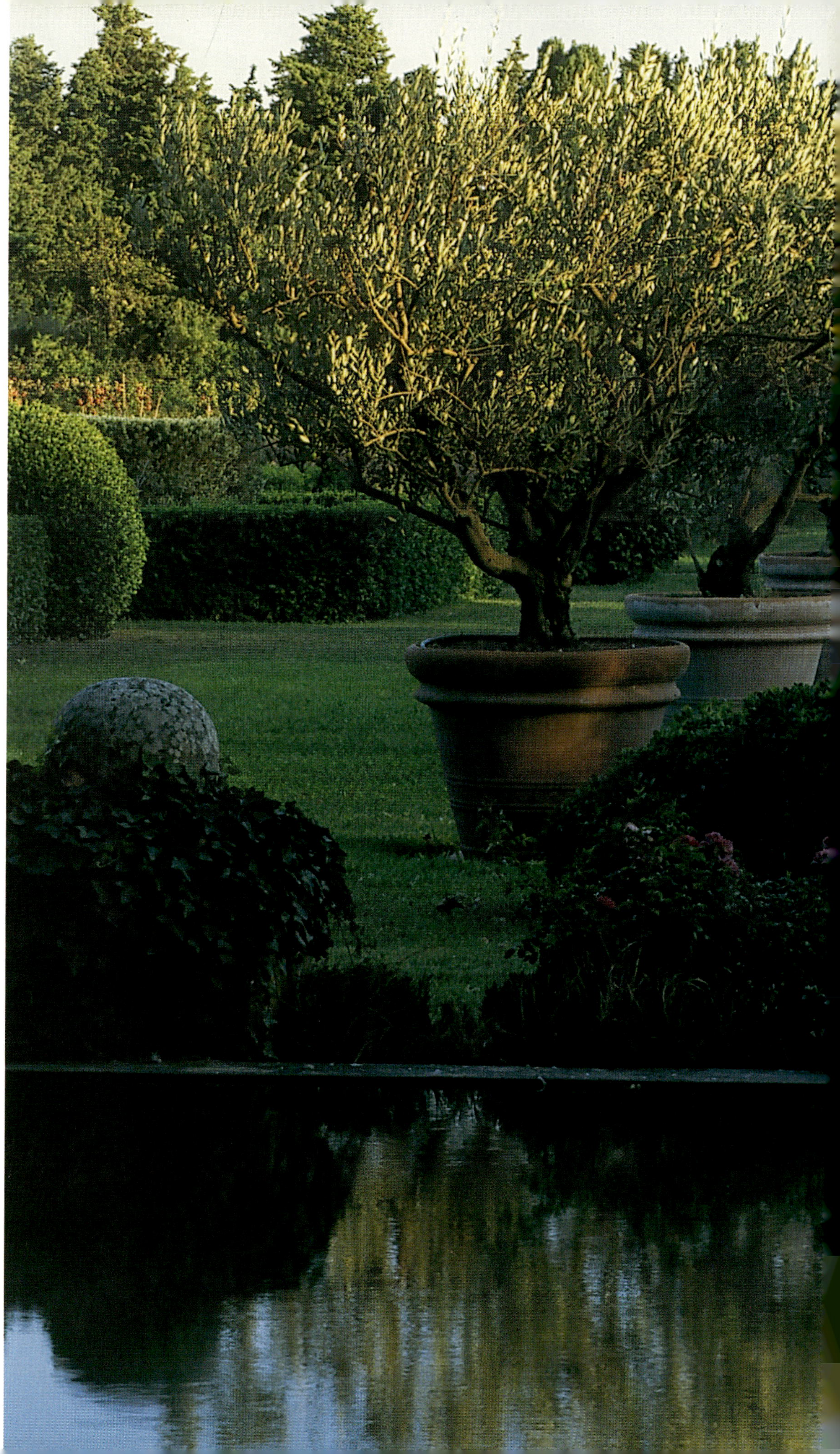

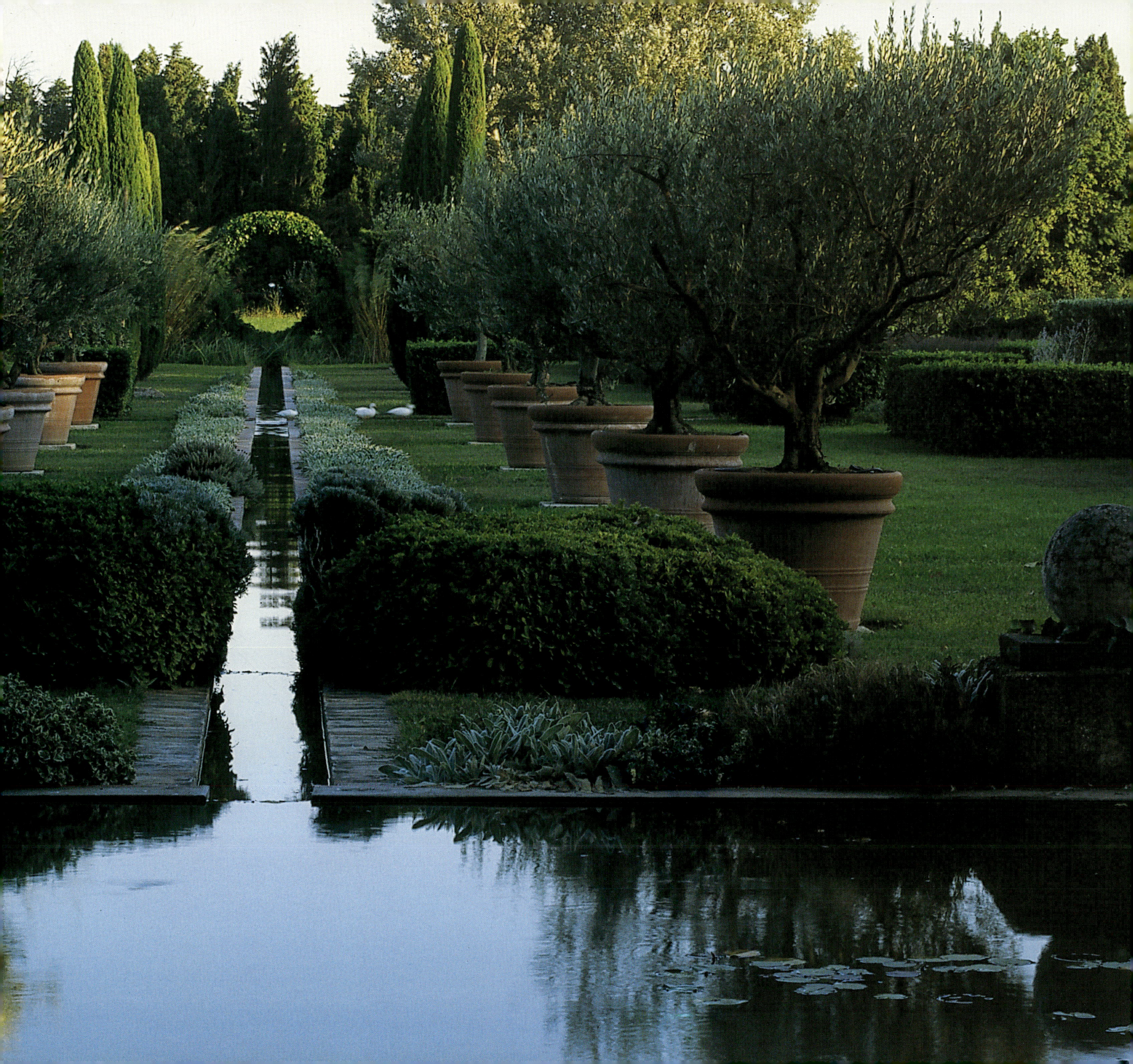

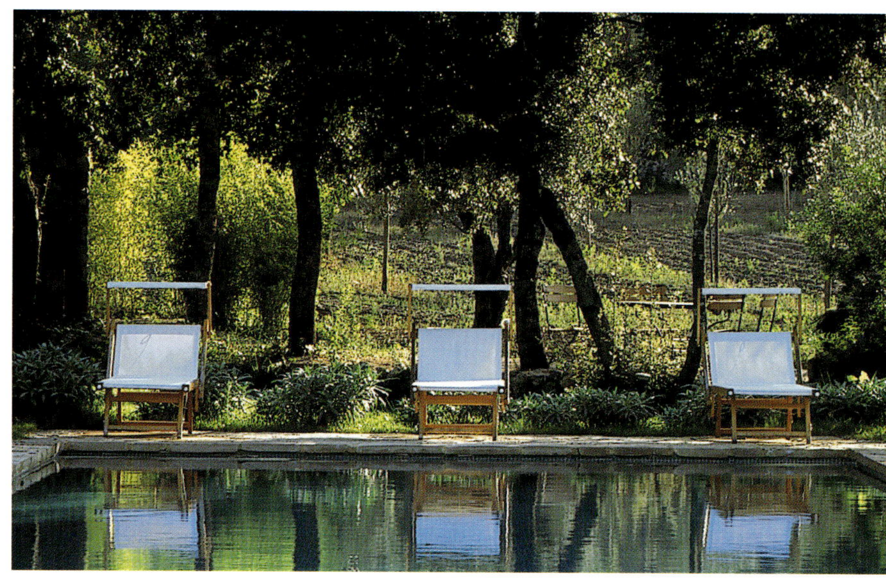

Mediterranean Refuge

Refugio mediterráneo | Mediterraner Zufluchtsort | Refuge méditerranéen

According to Greek mythology, Athena, the goddess of wisdom and crafts, gave a cutting from an olive tree to the city of Athens, and this gift allowed olives to be grown throughout the Mediterranean civilizations. This pool, with its pure Mediterranean style, is imbued with peacefulness and reverence for the past. Two olive trees rise up from the lawn, providing shelter for the pool area. The pool itself is lined with small bluish-gray tiles and its edges are clad in natural stone. A strip of pebbles at one end soak up the water, creating a fascinating contrast of materials, while at the other end, steps covered in the same bluish-gray small tiles span the entire breadth of the pool. Behind that, an authentic Arabian kaidal tent provides a shady refuge.

Cuenta la mitología griega que Atenea, diosa de la sabiduría y la artesanía, regaló un brote de olivo a la ciudad de Atenas, regalo que consagró el cultivo de las aceitunas en toda la civilización mediterránea. La pasión por los orígenes se llena de calma en este proyecto, de estética puramente mediterránea. Dos olivos descansan en el césped mientras resguardan la zona de la piscina, de gresite azul grisáceo y con los bordes revestidos de piedra natural. En uno de los márgenes del contenedor, una sucesión de cantos rodados recupera el agua, mientras logra un interesante contraste de materiales. En el otro extremo, los escalones ocupan toda la amplitud de la piscina. A continuación, una original tienda caidal árabe se convierte en cenador y zona de sombra.

Die griechische Mythologie berichtet, dass Athene, der Göttin der Weisheit und der Künste, der Stadt Athen einen Olivenbaum schenkte, wodurch der Grundstein für den Anbau von Oliven in den Kulturen des gesamten Mittelmeerraums gelegt wurde. Dieser typisch mediterrane Pool ist ein Symbol der Ruhe und gleichzeitig eine Refrenz an die Vergangenheit. Zwei Olivenbäume stehen auf dem Rasen und spenden dem Schwimmbecken, das mit blaugrauer Glaskeramik und mit natursteinverkleideten Rändern versehen wurde, willkommenen Schatten und Schutz. An einem Beckenrand wird das Wasser über eine Strecke aus grobem Kies aufgefangen, wodurch interessante Kontraste zwischen den einzelnen Materialien entstehen. Am anderen Ende nehmen die Stufen die gesamte Breite des Schwimmbeckens ein. Im Anschluss daran wird ein originelles, arabisches Zelt zur Gartenlaube und schattigem Ruheplatz.

Selon la mythologue grecque, Athéna, déesse de la sagesse et de l'artisanat, offrit un brin d'olivier à la ville d'Athènes, cadeau qui consacra la culture des olives dans toute la civilisation méditerranéenne. La passion des origines trouve un peu de calme dans ce projet à l'esthétique purement méditerranéenne. Deux oliviers qui se dressent sur le gazon gardent la zone de la piscine, en Gresite bleu grisâtre et aux bords revêtus de pierre naturelle. Sur l'un des bords du bassin, une chaîne de galets récupère l'eau, offrant un contraste de matériaux intéressant. De l'autre côté, les marches occupent toute la largeur de la piscine. Derrière, une tente caïdale arabe très originale fait office de tonnelle et de zone ombragée.

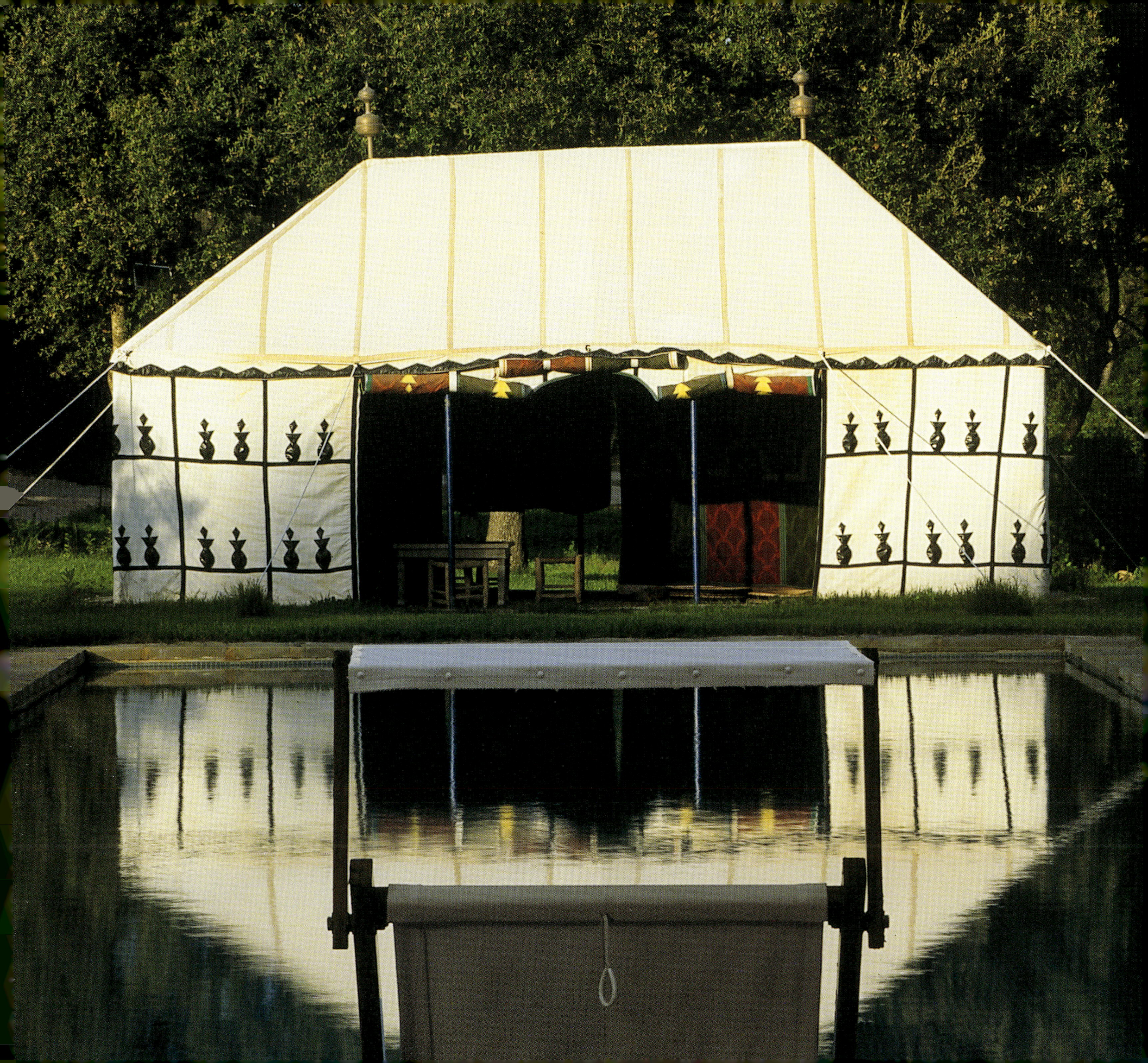

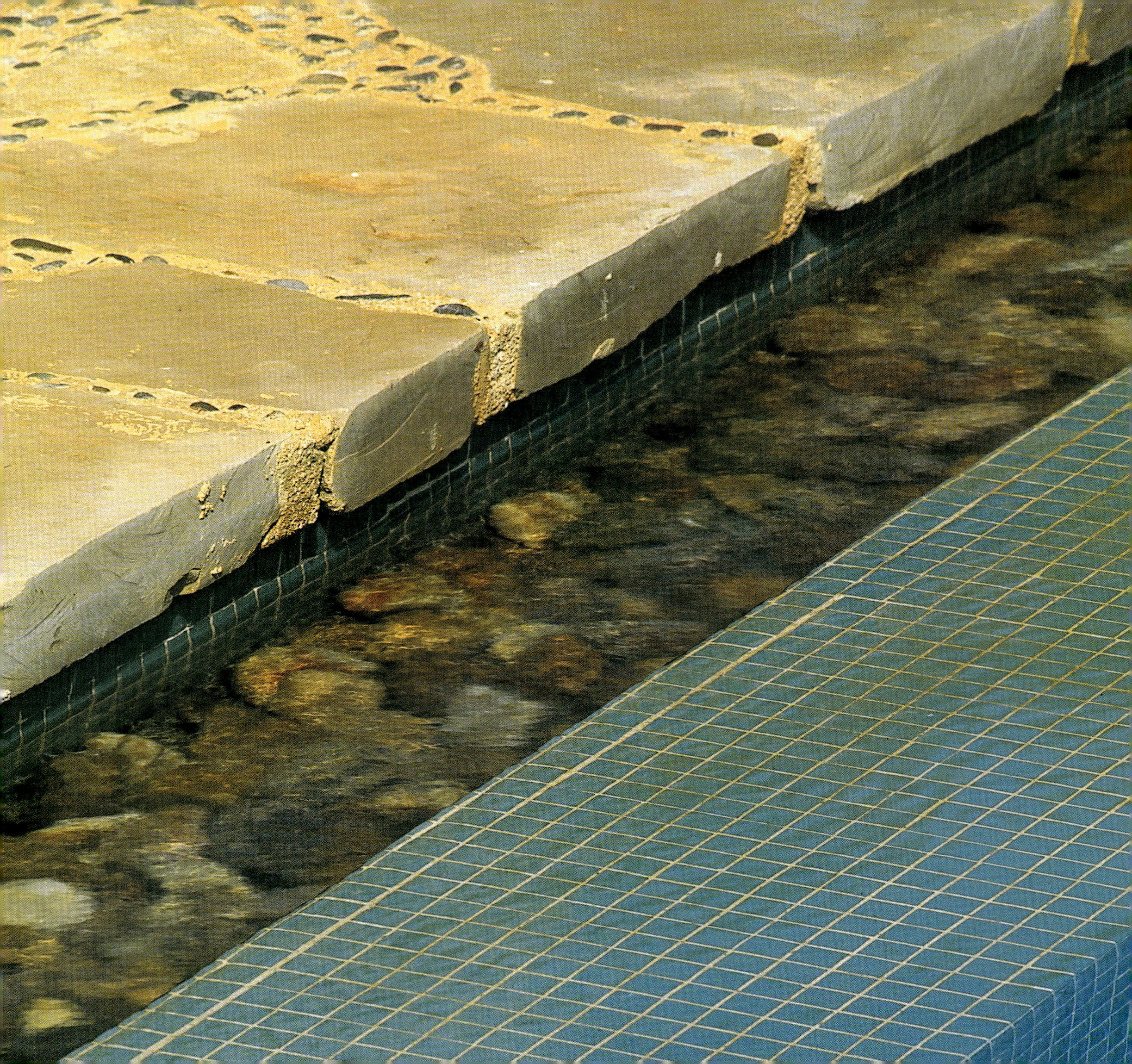

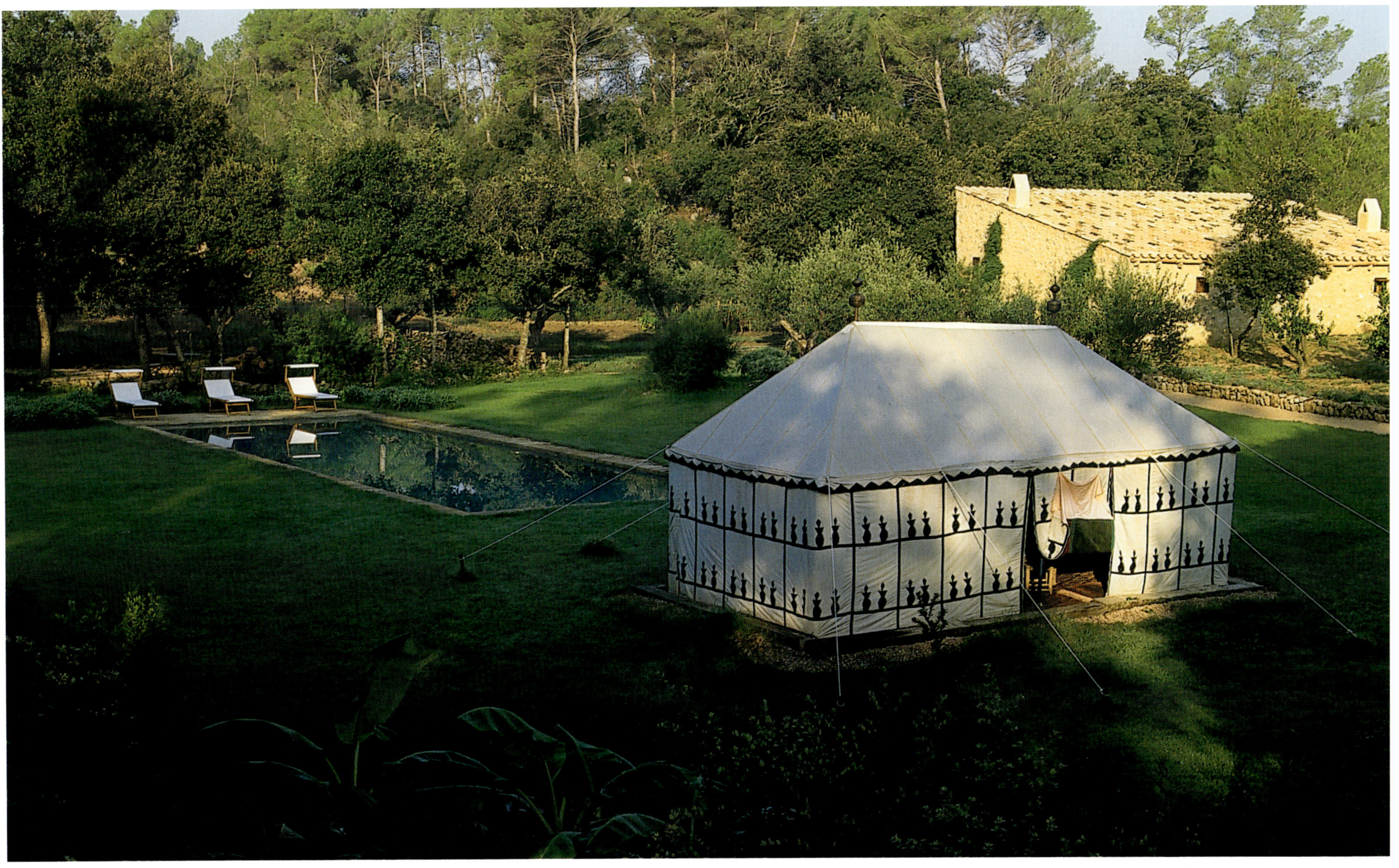

The small tiles on the steps contrast with the edge of the pool.
A arrangement of stones forms a water channel around the border.

Las escaleras de gresite contrastan con los márgenes de la piscina.
Una sucesión de cantos rodados forman un canal que la rodean.

Die Glaskeramikstufen stehen im Kontrast zur Umrandung des Schwimmbeckens.
Eine Strecke aus grobem Kies bildet einen Wasserkanal um den Pool herum.

Les escaliers de gresite contrastent avec les marges de la piscine.
Une chaîne de galets assure la distribution de l'eau au tour du bord.

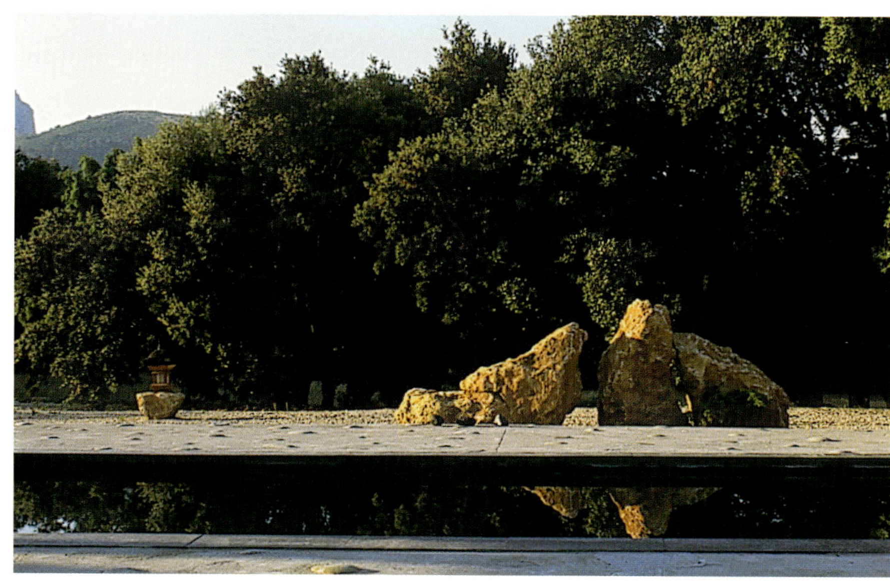

Perfect Symmetry

Simetría perfecta | Vollkommene Symmetrie | Symétrie parfaite

Located in Aix-en-Provence, water and nature come together in this project, inspired from thousand-year-old Asian traditions, to establish a great almost symmetrical space. The design called for a succession of ambiences laid out horizontally. The house is situated before the pool to be followed by a lotus and water lily pond. The structure is flanked by two Japanese-style arbours with bamboo canes that contrast with the pronounced horizontality of the forms. For the lining of the pool, the trim and the pond, a combination of sand, lime and marble powder mixed with dark natural pigments provide a matt bronze tone. The mixture contains mica particles, which is a mineral that sparkles. A treated wooden catwalk establishes a dividing line between the pool and the Zen garden.

Ganz in asiatischer Tradition steht dieses Projekt in Aix-en-Provence, wo sich Natur und Wasser vereinen zu einem fast symmetrischen, großen Raum. Die Anlage sieht eine horizontale Abfolge verschiedener Bereiche vor: Dem Haus schließt sich das Schwimmbecken an, und diesem wiederum ein Teich mit Lotos und Teichrosen. Das Gebäude wird von zwei Lauben im japanischen Stil flankiert, deren Bambusstäbe einen Kontrast zu der betonten Horizontalität der Formen bilden. Für den Bau des Beckens, des Beckenrands sowie des Teichs wurde eine Mischung aus Sand, Kalk und Marmorstaub verwendet, die in Verbindung mit natürlichen dunklen Farbstoffen einen matten, kohlschwarzen Ton annimmt. Das Gemisch enthält ebenso Partikel von Glimmer, einem funkelnden Mineral. Ein Laufsteg aus behandeltem Holz stellt eine Trennlinie zwischen dem Schwimmbecken und dem Garten im Zen-Stil dar.

Agua y naturaleza se aúnan en este proyecto, situado en Aix-en-Provence, para establecer un gran espacio casi simétrico, inspirado en la milenaria tradición asiática. La intervención establece una sucesión de ambientes en horizontal: la vivienda antecede a la piscina y, a continuación, a un estanque de lotos y nenúfares. La estructura está flanqueada por dos cenadores de estilo japonés, con cañas de bambú que contrastan con la acentuada horizontalidad de formas. Para la construcción del contenedor y el sobre de la piscina y el estanque se empleó una combinación de arena, cal y polvo de mármol que, mezclada con pigmentos naturales oscuros, consigue un tono atezado mate. La mixtura incorpora partículas de mica, mineral que irradia destellos de luz. Una pasarela de madera tratada establece una línea divisoria entre la piscina y el jardín zen.

L'eau et la nature s'allient dans ce projet situé à Aix-en-Provence, créant un vaste espace pratiquement symétrique inspiré de la tradition asiatique millénaire. L'intervention a consisté à établir horizontalement une suite d'espaces : l'habitation précède la piscine qui elle-même précède un bassin de lotus et de nénuphars. De chaque côté de la structure, la présence de deux tonnelles de style japonais et de cannes de bambou contraste avec l'horizontalité accentuée des formes. Le bassin et la partie supérieure de la piscine ont été construits avec un mélange de sable, de chaux et de poudre de marbre qui, mélangé à des pigments naturels sombres, leur donne un ton brun mat. Le mélange contient également des particules de mica, minéral qui irradie des éclairs de lumière. Une passerelle en bois établit une ligne de division entre la piscine et le jardin zen.

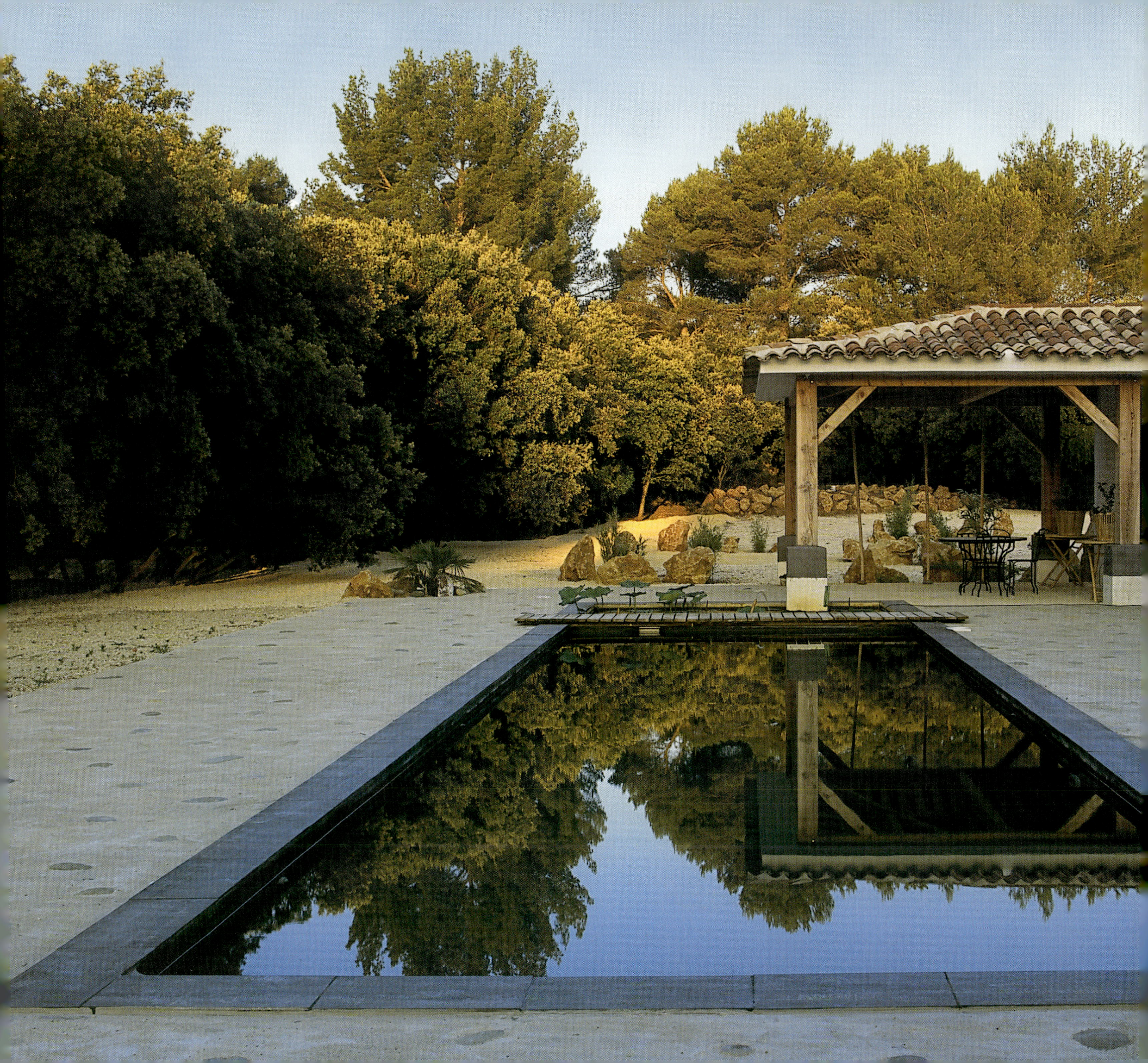

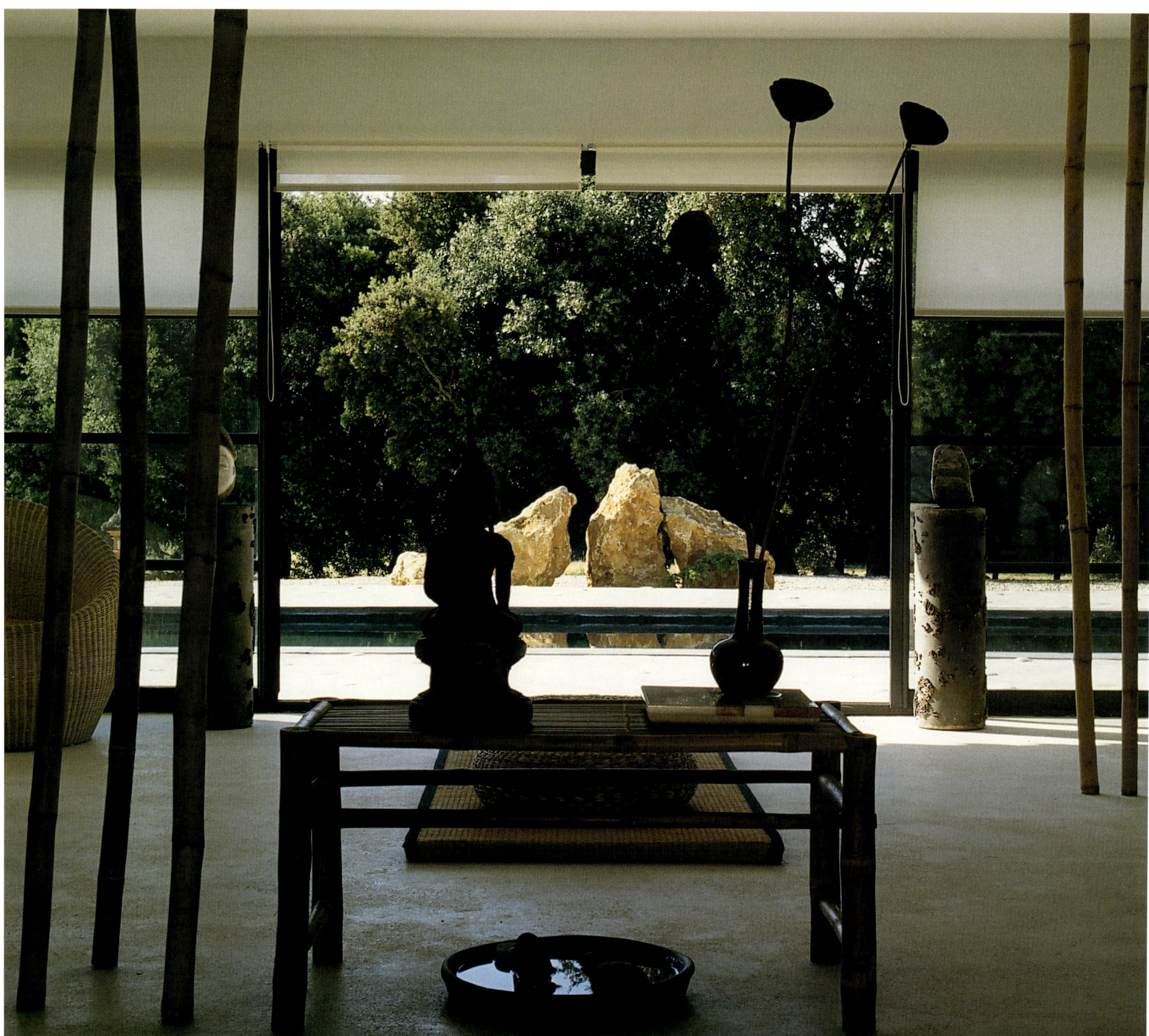

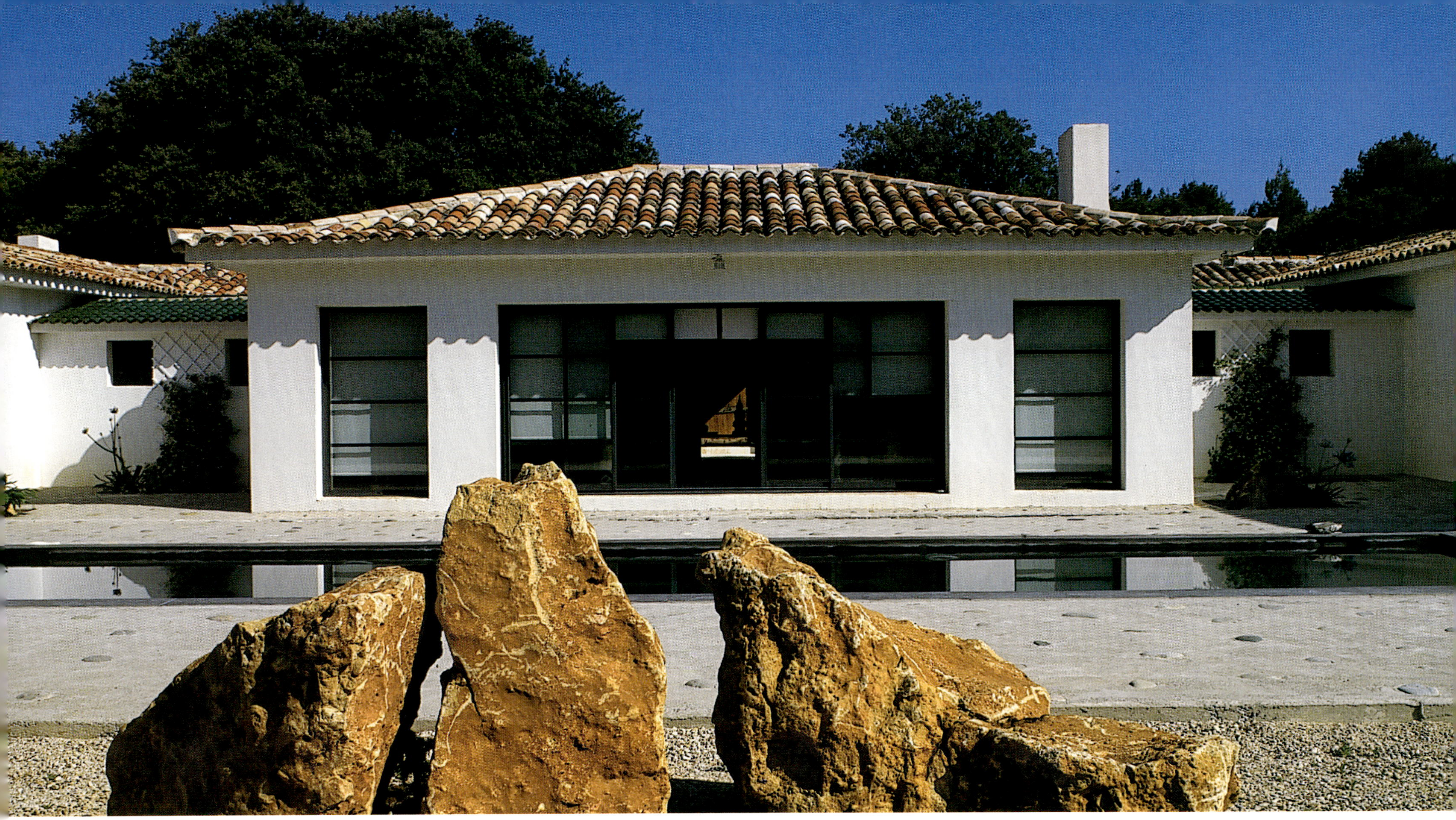

The pool is replenished by an original fountain that respects the spirit of the original period.

La piscina se llena a través de una antigua fuente que respeta el espíritu de la época original.

Das Schwimmbecken wird durch einen alten Springbrunnen gespeist, der dem Geist der damaligen Zeit entspricht.

La piscine se remplit au moyen d'une ancienne fontaine qui respecte l'esprit de son époque d'origine.

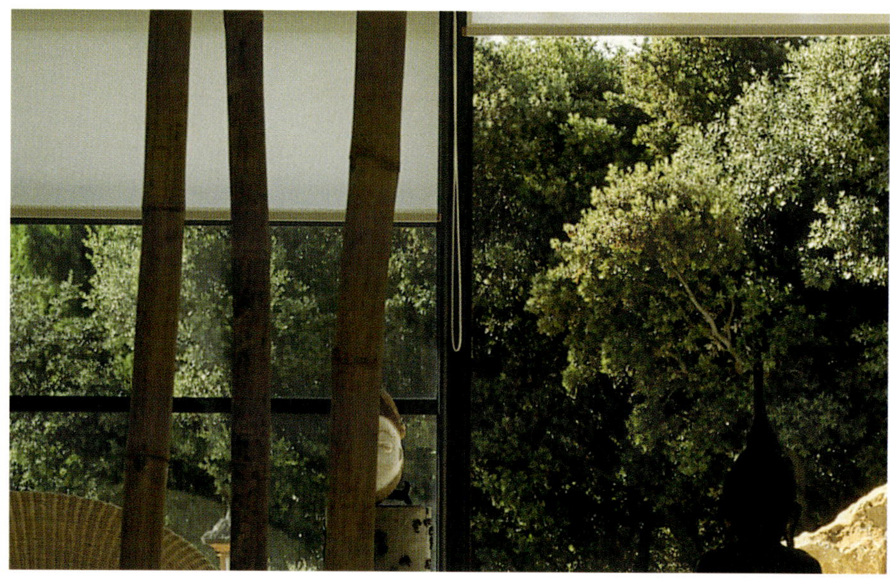

Continuous Perception

Percepción continua | Visuelle Kontinuität | Perception continue

The keys to the success of this project are the strict longitudinal geometry and pure minimalist lines of its forms. The home opens out onto the grounds by means of big, sliding glass doors, protected by iron structures, which unite the two spaces. The spacious terrace consists of a continuous teak platform that links the building to the pool, which is a strip of water that stretches towards the lush vegetation of pines and vineyards. For the receptacle of the pool a mixture of marble powder, cement, lime and light–colored natural pigments were used. It affords a striking appearance of blues and whites, which blends in with the horizon of the sea. It is an avant-garde style that allows the criteria of the maximum respect for nature, to come to the fore.

Los secretos de este proyecto son la estricta geometría longitudinal y la estética pura y minimalista de sus formas. La vivienda se comunica con el terreno exterior a través de grandes puertas correderas de cristal, protegidas por estructuras de hierro, que conectan ambos espacios. Una tarima de teca continua define la extensa terraza y hace de intermediario entre la construcción y la piscina, que se prolonga hacia la espesa vegetación de pinos y viñedos. Para el contenedor se utilizó una mezcla de polvo de mármol, cemento, cal y pigmentos naturales de tonalidades claras, produciendo un gran impacto de azules y blancos, que parecen confundirse con el horizonte del mar. El proyecto, de estilo vanguardista, refuerza el criterio de respetar al máximo el paisaje.

Das Geheimnis dieses Projekts liegt in seiner längslaufenden, strengen Geometrie sowie der Reinheit und dem Minimalismus seiner Formen. Die Verbindung der Wohnung mit Außenbereich wird über große Glasschiebetüren hergestellt, die durch Eisenkonstruktionen geschützt werden. Eine umlaufende Bank aus Teakholz charaktarisiert die weitläufige Terrasse und bildet den Übergang zwischen Haus und Schwimmbecken. Letzteres erstreckt sich bis zu der üppigen Vegetation der Pinien und Weinberge. Für den Pool wurde ein Gemisch aus Marmorstaub, Zement, Kalk und natürlichen Farbstoffen in hellen Tönen verwendet, wodurch äußerst effektvolle Blau- und Weißtöne entstehen, die mit dem Horizont des Meeres zu verschmelzen scheinen. Ein wichtiges Kriterium des Projekts im avantgardistischen Stil war es, so schonend wie möglich mit der Landschaft umzugehen.

Les secrets de ce projet : une géométrie longitudinale stricte et une esthétique pure et minimaliste des formes. L'habitation communique avec le terrain extérieur à travers de grandes portes coulissantes de verre, protégées par des structures de fer qui connectent les deux espaces. Une estrade ininterrompue en tek constitue le propre de cette vaste terrasse et sert d'intermédiaire entre la construction et la piscine, qui se prolonge vers l'épaisse végétation de pins et de vignes. Le bassin a été construit à partir d'un mélange de poudre de marbre, de ciment, de chaux et de pigments naturels aux tons clairs. Il en résulte un puissant impact de bleus et de blancs qui semblent se confondre avec l'horizon de la mer. Le projet, de style avant-gardiste, répond avec détermination à un critère de respect maximum du paysage.

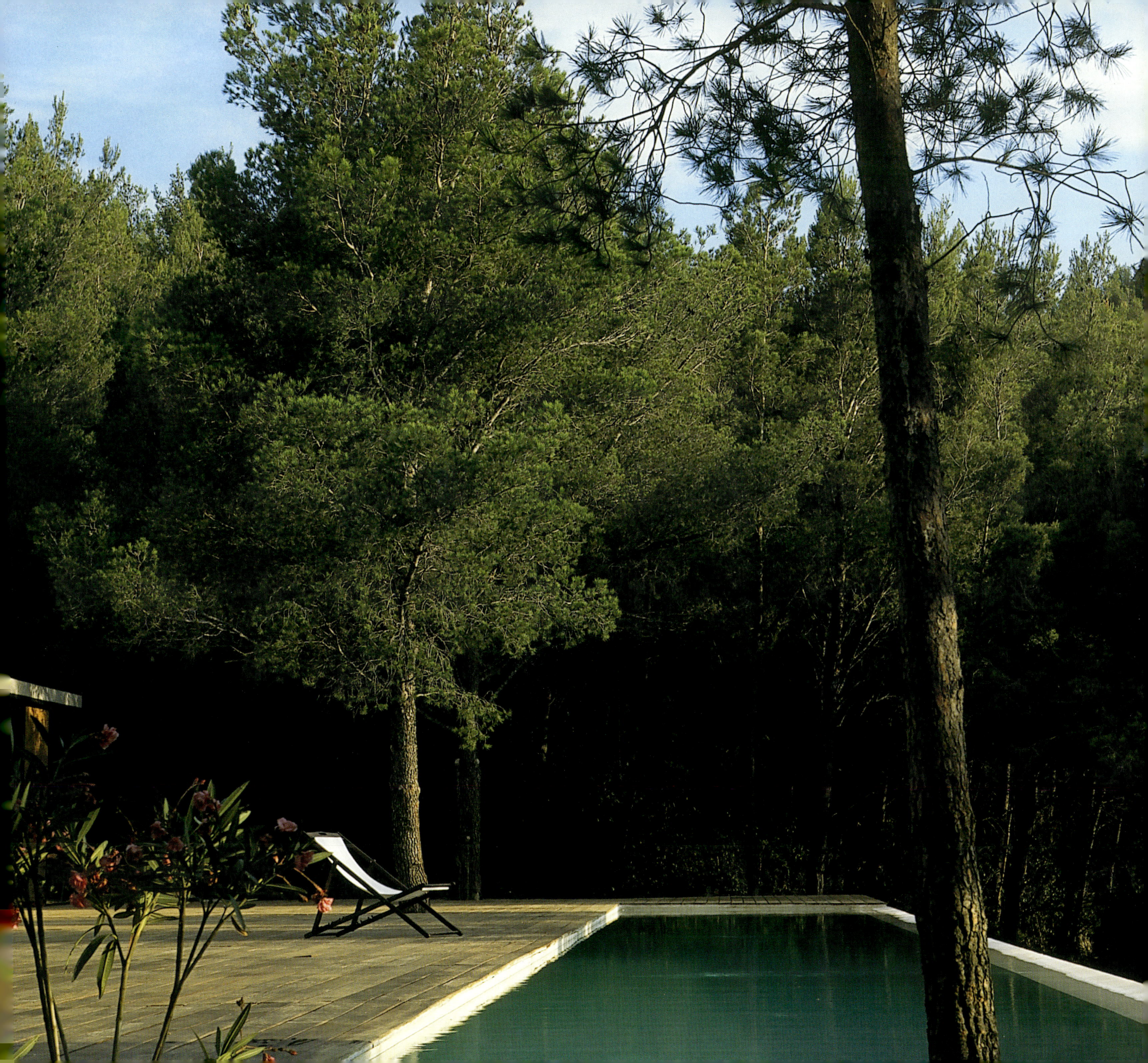

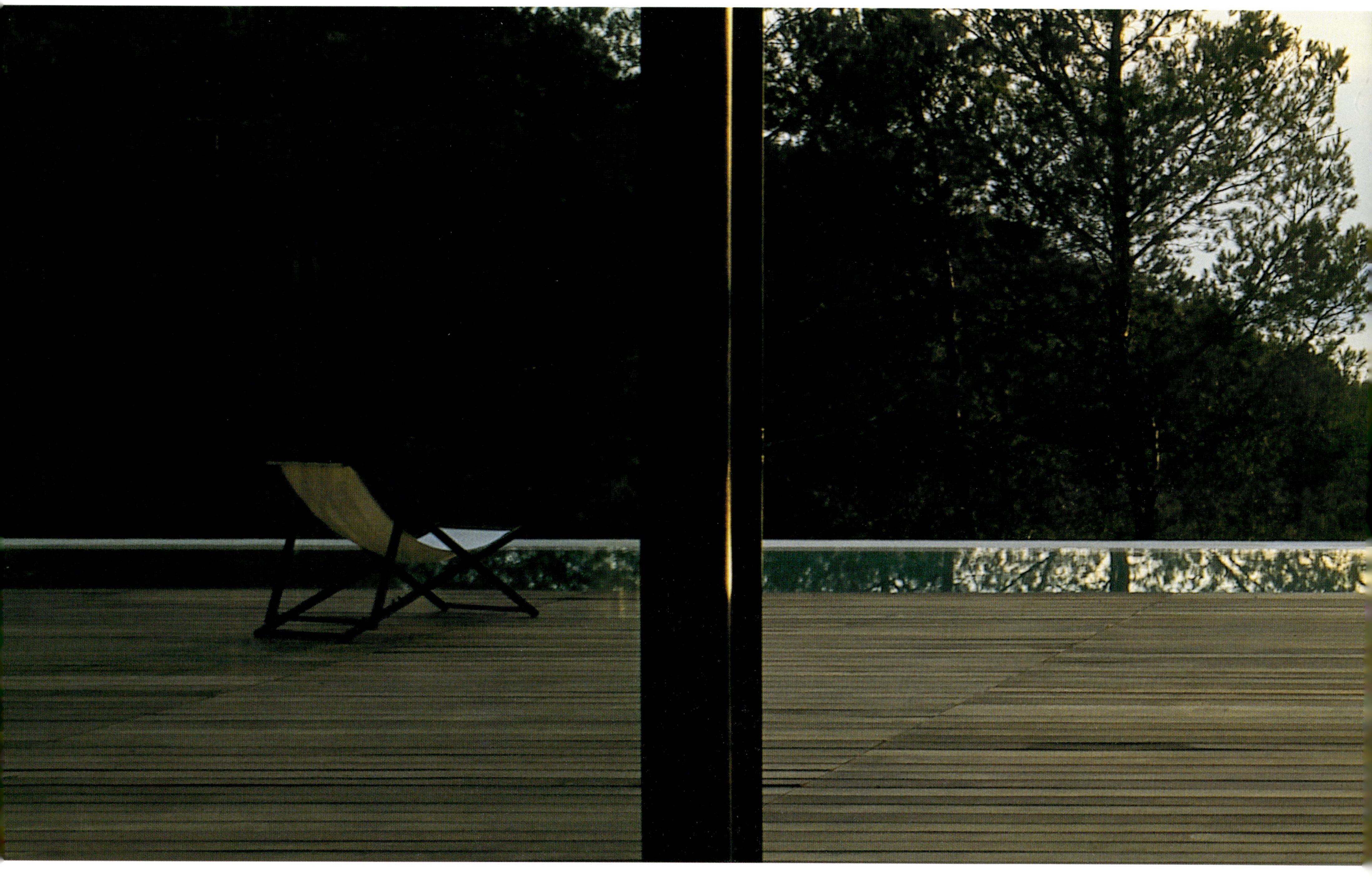

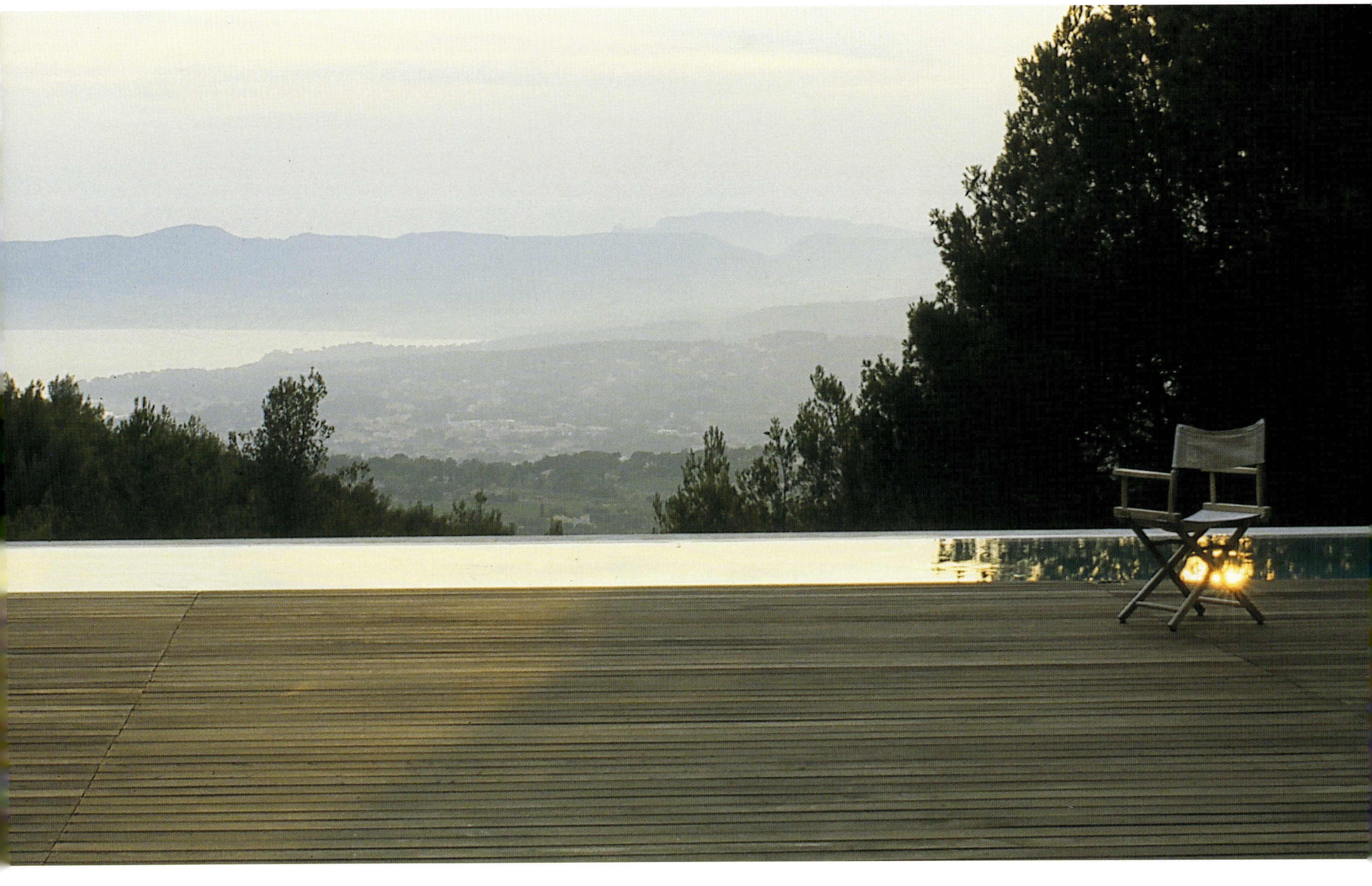

Lineality and continuity draw this idyllic space to the edge of the frame, which is the horizon, where a unique landscape unfolds before you at the foot of the waters of the pool.

Linealidad y continuidad empujan este espacio idílico al marco final del horizonte en el que se puede discernir un paisaje único supeditado a los pies del agua de la piscina.

Linearität und Kontinuität verbinden diesen idyllischen Ort mit dem Horizont, und eine einzigartige Landschaft erhebt sich vor dem Wasser des Schwimmbeckens.

Un anneau formé par un pavement de pierre naturelle entoure la piscine, qui ouvre sur une étendue de pelouse. La cascade est encadrée par deux constructions asymétriques : un banc et une gloriette.

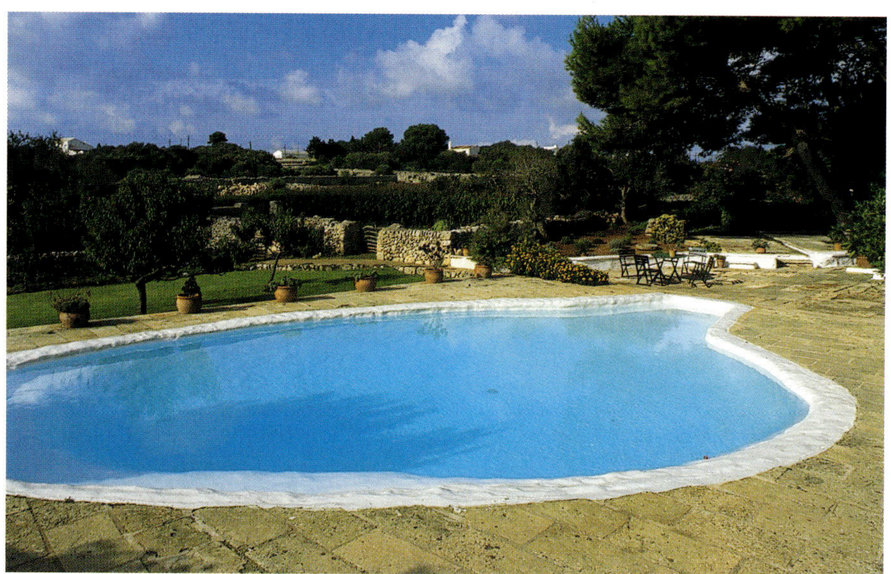

Balearic Charm

Encanto balear | Charme der Balearen | Le charme des baléares

In this traditional Menorcan-style estate with its walls stuccoed with white lime and others of stone, the swimming pool is a mixture of tradition and originality. Almost ovoid-shaped, the receptacle fits onto the contours of the terrain. At one end, the bottom rises up and almost becomes part of the edge of the pool. The most structured and geometrically laid out part is the area of the stairs. The coverings used are original and are perfectly combined with the traditional architecture of the house: marés sandstone, abundant in Menorca, and concrete covered with latex paint to assure that it is properly sealed. Near the stairs, an awning covered with climbing plants affords shelter to the arbour and the shade area.

En esta finca de típica concepción menorquina, con muros revocados de cal blanca y paredes de piedra seca, la piscina es una mezcla de tradición y originalidad. De forma casi ovoide, el vaso va adaptándose a la orografía del terreno: en uno de sus extremos, el suelo se alza y casi se confunde con el borde del contenedor. La parte más estructurada y ordenada geométricamente corresponde a la zona de las escaleras. Los revestimientos son empleados con originalidad y combinan a la perfección con la arquitectura popular de la casa: piedra marés –arenisca que abunda en Menorca– y hormigón recubierto de pintura plástica blanca para asegurar la estanqueidad. Cerca de las escaleras, un toldo recubierto de plantas trepadoras protege el cenador y la zona de sombra.

Das Schwimmbecken auf diesem typisch menorquinischen Anwesen mit seinen weiß gekalkten Mauern und Trockenmauern verbindet Tradition mit Originalität. Das nahezu ovale Becken passt sich an die Oberfläche des Geländes an: An einem Ende steigt der Boden an und verschmilzt fast mit dem Beckenrand. Der geometrisch strukturierteste und geordnetste Teil ist der Treppenbereich. Die Verkleidungen wurden fantasievoll eingesetzt und fügen sich hervorragend in die volkstümliche Architektur des Hauses ein: eine Kombination aus Marès-Stein, ein auf Menorca häufig vorkommender Natursandstein, und ein mit weißer Plastikfarbe überzogener Beton, der das Becken abdichtet. In der Nähe der Treppen schützt ein von Kletterpflanzen bewachsenes Sonnendach Laube und Schattenbereich.

Dans cette propriété de conception typiquement minorquine aux murs crépis à la chaux blanche et en pierre sèche à l'intérieur, la piscine mêle tradition et originalité. De forme quasiment ovoïde, le bassin s'adapte à l'orographie du terrain : à l'une de ses extrémités, le sol se dresse pour pratiquement se confondre avec le bord de la piscine. La partie la plus structurée et la plus ordonnée d'un point de vue géométrique est celle des escaliers. Les revêtements y sont employés avec originalité et s'harmonisent parfaitement avec l'architecture populaire de la maison : pierre marés – grès très répandu à Minorque – et béton recouvert de peinture plastique blanche pour garantir l'étanchéité. Près des escaliers, une bâche recouverte de plantes grimpantes protège la tonnelle et la zone ombragée.

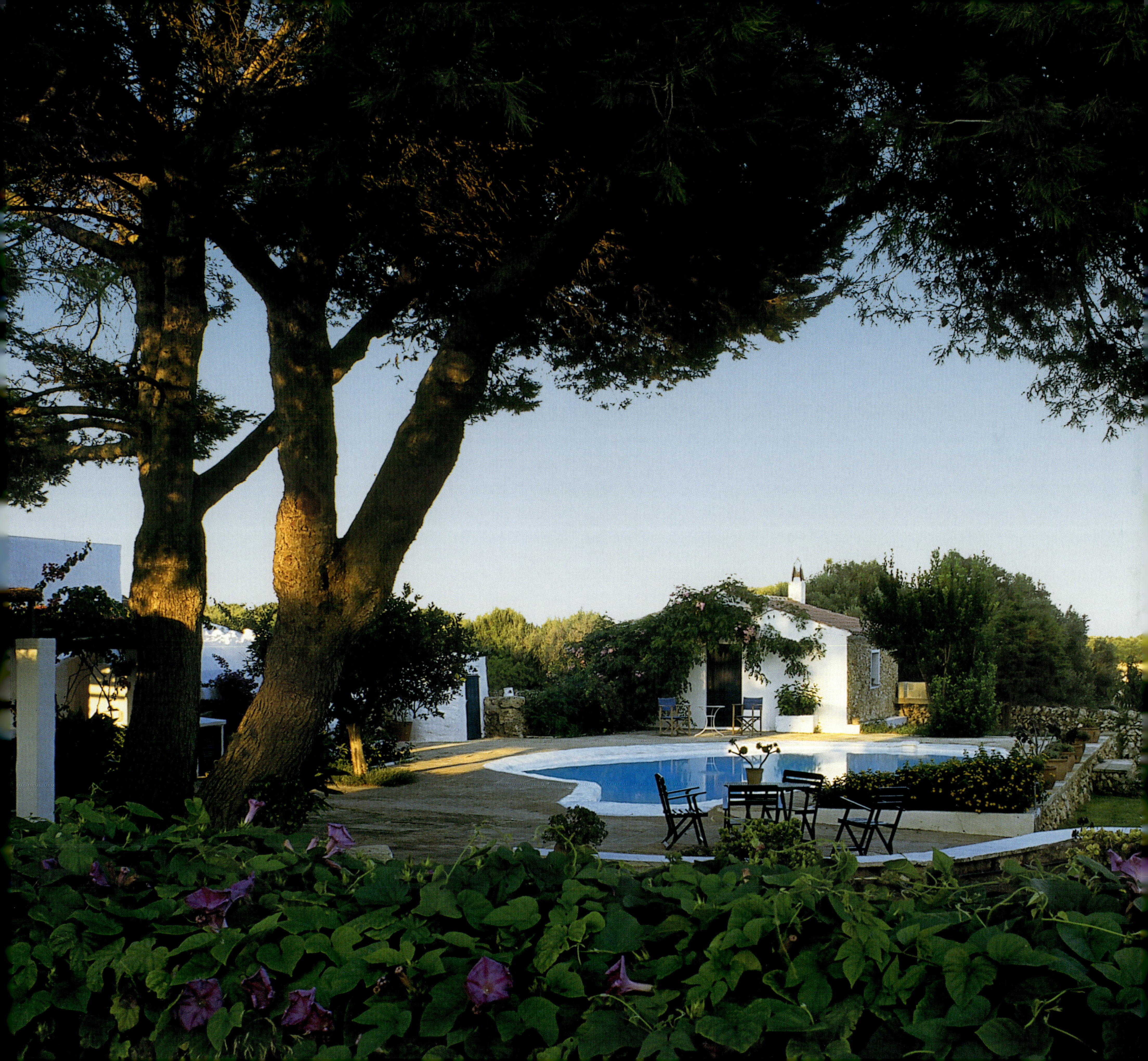

LINEAL ARCHITECTURE

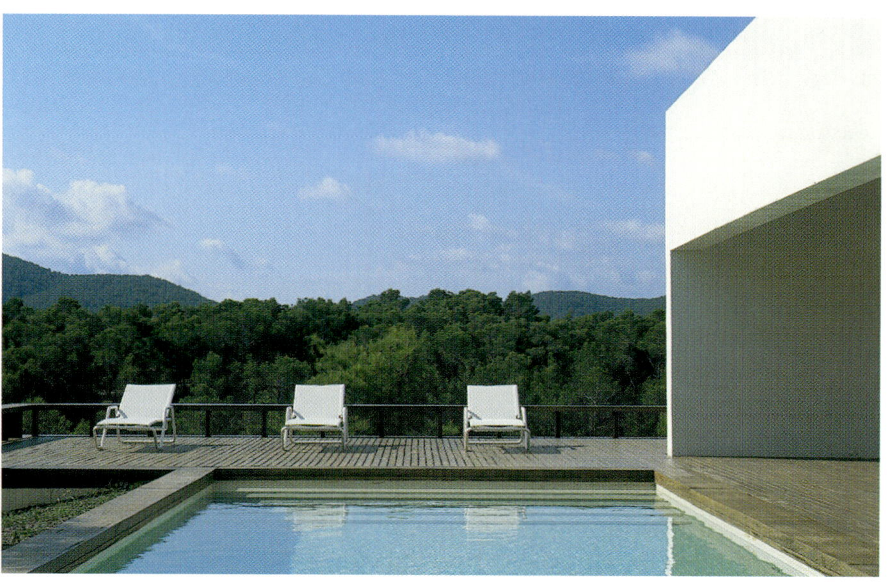

ARQUITECTURA LINEAL | LINEARE ARCHITEKTUR | ARCHITECTURE LINÉAIRE

This project in Ibiza is a tribute to the island's traditional architecture from a modern perspective. Cubes and rectangular white figures unfold before us in an orderly way. This interplay of geometric forms gives way to a spacious terrace with a platform made of tropical wood with a large structure in the center, which serves as a dining area and a shady arbour. Beyond this, at the rear of the property, lies a very large swimming pool of uniform depth. The pool is a concrete box clad with small white tiles that echo the exterior of the house. We are afforded access to the pool at one of the ends, specifically the area of the terrace for sunbathing.

Este proyecto, localizado en Ibiza, rinde homenaje a la arquitectura tradicional de la isla desde una perspectiva actual. Volúmenes en forma de cubos y figuras rectangulares en blanco van sucediéndose ordenadamente . El juego de formas geométricas de la vivienda da paso a una gran terraza revestida de una tarima de madera tropical. Los arquitectos proyectaron una gran estructura en la parte central de la terraza, articulada como cenador y zona de sombra. Una piscina llana, de grandes dimensiones, ocupa la parte posterior de la finca. El contenedor de la piscina es un rectángulo de hormigón recubierto con piezas medianas de gresite en blanco, a juego con el exterior de la vivienda. El acceso a la piscina se halla en uno de los extremos, concretamente en la zona de la terraza habilitada como zona de sol.

Dieses Projekt auf Ibiza ist eine moderne Reverenz an die traditionelle Architektur der Insel. Würfelähnliche Baukörper und rechteckige Formen in Weiß folgen in geordneter Weise aufeinander. Dem Wechselspiel geometrischer Formen des Hauses schließt sich eine mit einer Platte aus Tropenholz verkleidete große Terrasse an. Die Architekten entwarfen für die Mitte der Terrasse eine Konstruktion, die als Laube dient und Schatten offeriert. Ein weiläufiges und flaches Schwimmbecken nimmt den hinteren Teil des Anwesens ein. Das rechteckige Becken besteht aus Beton und ist mit mittelgroßen, weißen Fliesen aus Glaskeramik passend zum Äußeren des Hauses ausgekleidet. Vom Sonnendeck aus kann man das Schwimmbecken beosnders leicht erreichen.

Ce projet situé à Ibiza rend hommage à l'architecture traditionnelle de l'île à travers une perspective actuelle. Unités cubiques et figures rectangulaires blanches se succèdent de façon ordonnée. Le jeu de formes géométriques de l'habitation s'ouvre sur une grande terrasse surmontée d'une estrade en bois tropical. Les architectes ont placé une vaste structure dans la partie centrale de la terrasse, faisant office de tonnelle et de zone ombragée. Une piscine plane aux dimensions importantes occupe l'arrière de la propriété. Le bassin de la piscine est un rectangle de béton recouvert de pièces de Gresite blanc de taille moyenne, en harmonie avec l'extérieur de l'habitation. L'accès à la piscine se trouve à l'une des extrémités, concrètement, sur la terrasse organisée comme solarium.

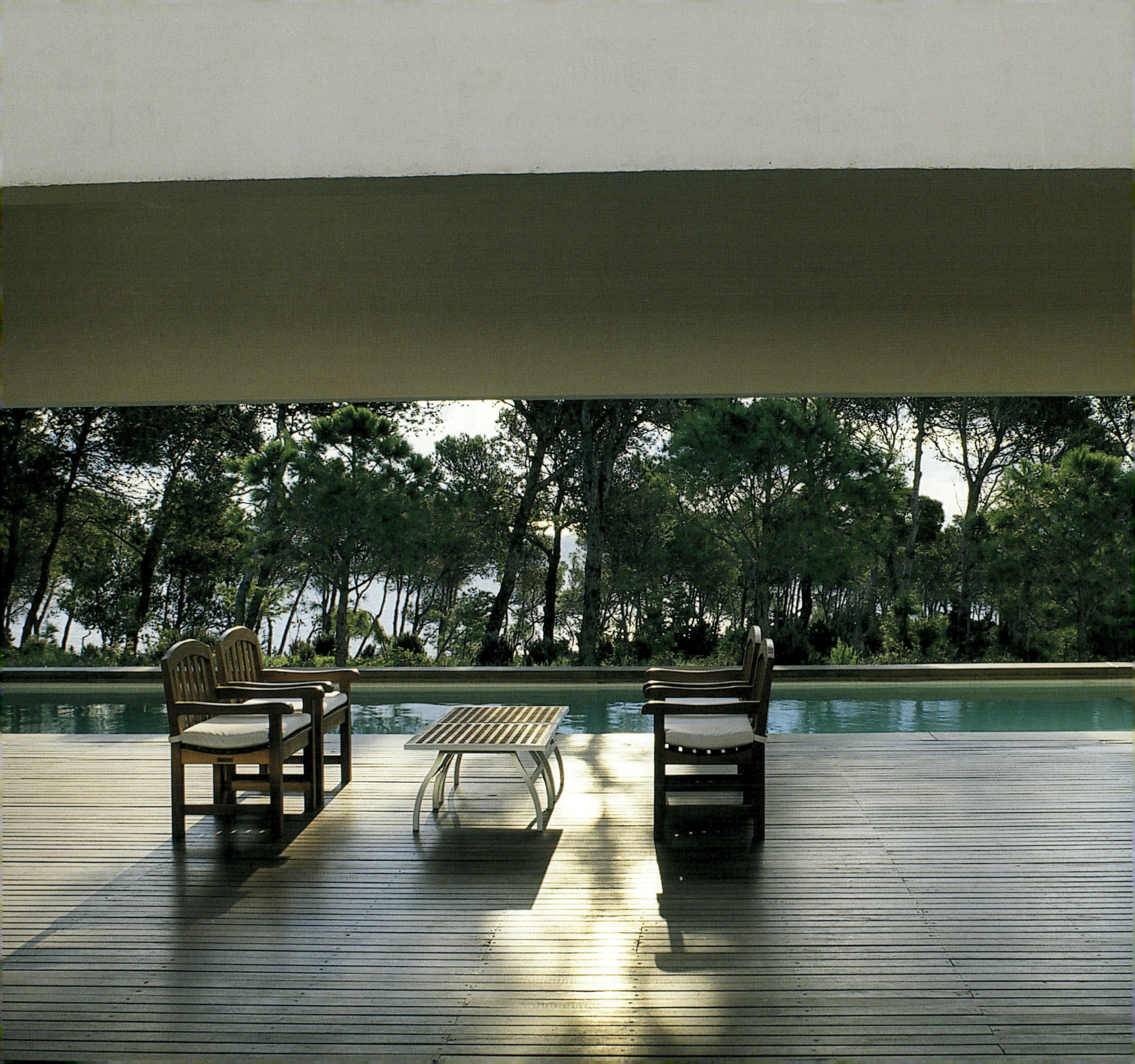

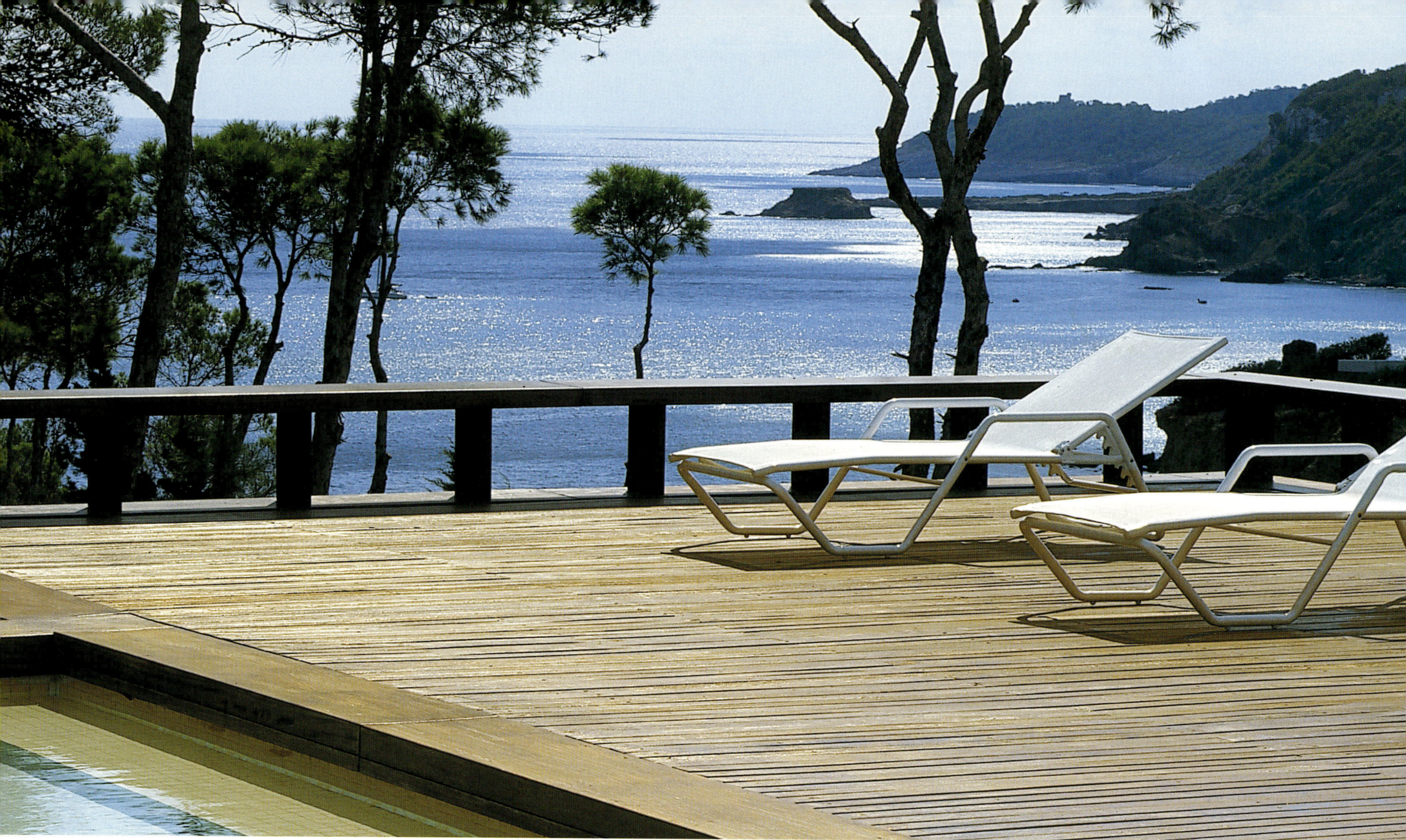

The large terrace is divided into clearly delineated sections. The sunbathing areas are located at each end of the pool.

La inmensa terraza distribuye de forma ordenada cada una de sus zonas. Los soláriums se colocan en los extremos de la piscina.

Die Aufteilung der Bereiche der riesigen Terrasse sind klar geordnet. Die Sonnenterrassen befinden sich jeweils am Ende des Schwimmbeckens.

L'immense terrasse distribue chacune des parties qui la composent de façon ordonnée. Les solariums se situent aux extrémités de la piscine.

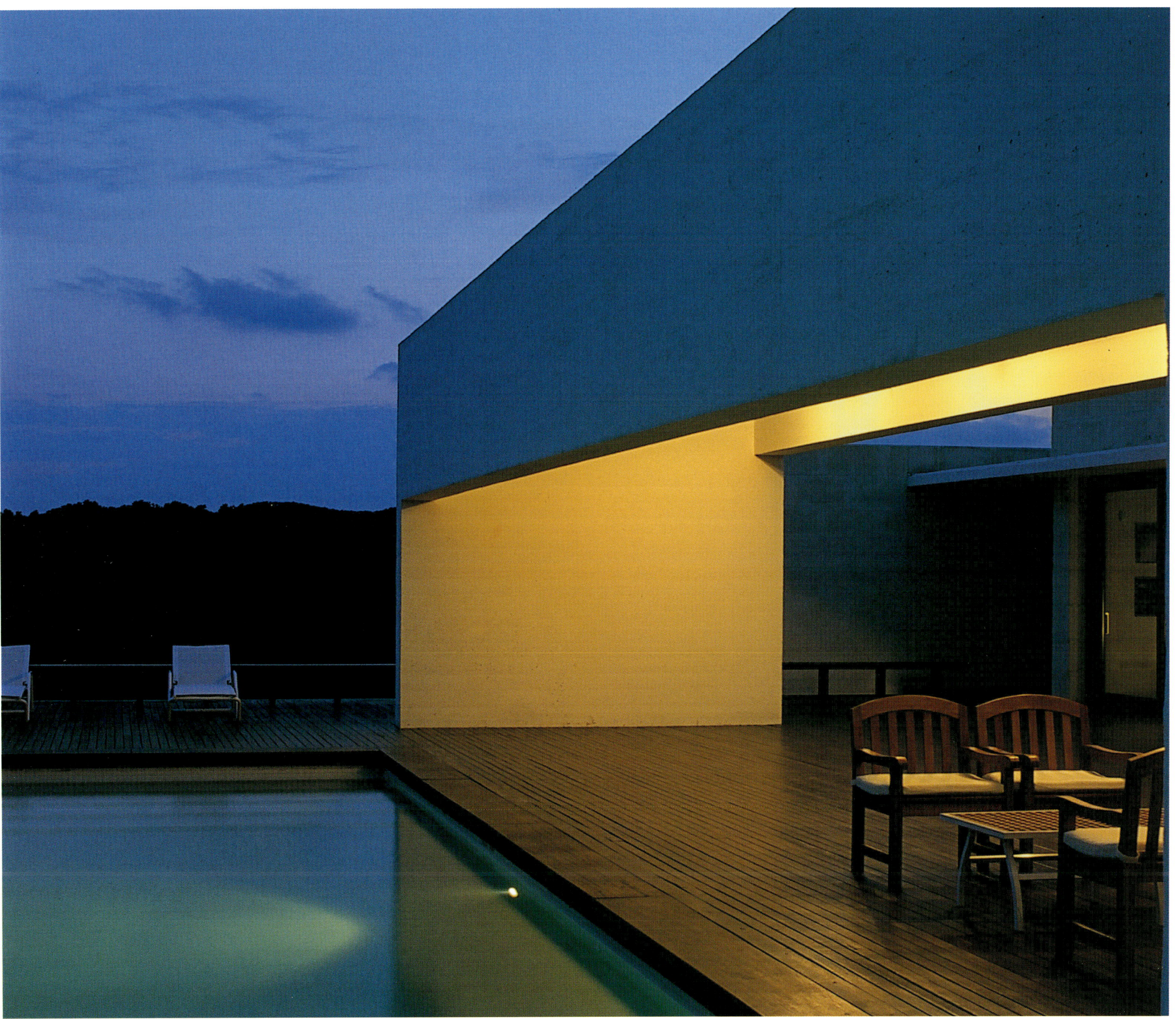

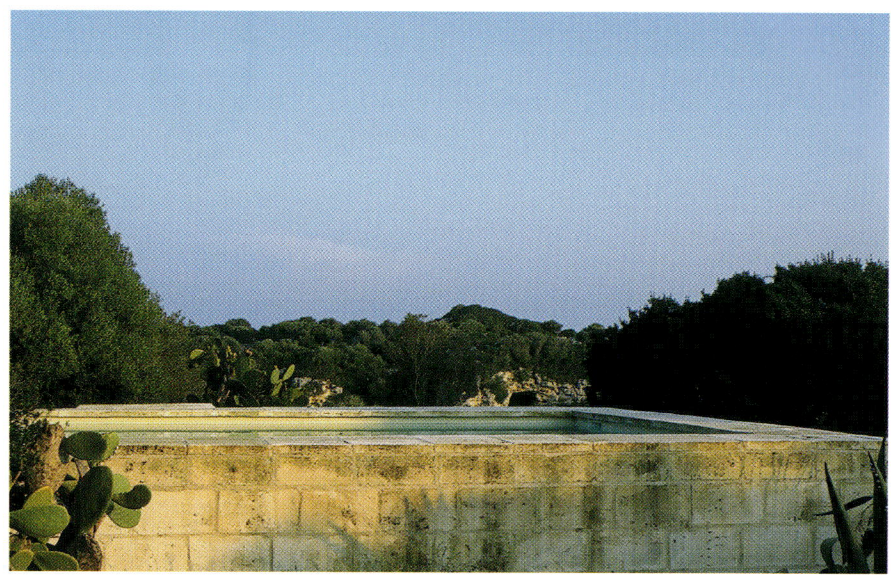

Natural Prolongation

Prolongación natural | Natürliche Verlängerung | Prolongation naturelle

In this almost untamed spot on the island of Menorca, the architect did not try to fight nature but opted for a more balanced approach, by challenging but also joining forces with it. The decision to integrate architectural forms into the natural landscape resulted in a pool that extends from the large oblique rock that marks the boundary of the property. The swimming pool is set at almost the same level as this rock and fits into it perfectly. Natural and new construction come together as the casing of the pool, made of the Menorcan marés sandstone, blends into the natural surroundings, while the interior, painted pale gray, recalls the typical local house fronts. On top of the rock there is a platform made of treated, water-resistant, non-slip pine. The rural estate has a garden of prickly pears that, combined with the native trees and bushes of the area, take you one step more along this journey into nature.

Dieses Projekt in einem noch nahezu wildem Gebiet auf der Insel Menorca sollte keinen Kontrapunkt gegen die Natur darstellen. Man setzte vielmehr auf eine Integration der Formen, im Zuge derer das Schwimmbecken als Verlängerung eines großen, quer liegenden Felsens entstand. Das Schwimmbecken befindet sich mit dem Fels fast auf einer Höhe und passt sich vollkommen an ihn an. Die Verbindung zwischen Natürlichem und neu Geschaffenem wurde durch einen rechteckigen, mit Marès-Steinen verkleideten Betonbau hergestellt. Im Inneren verwendete man Zement mit hellgrauem Anstrich in Anlehnung an die typische Verkleidungsart der Region. Der Felsgipfel wird von einer wasser- und rutschfesten Plattform aus mit einer mit Kupfernaphthenat behandelter Pinie gekrönt. Zu dem rustikalen Anwesen gehören Feigenkakteen, die gemeinsam mit den einheimischen Bäumen und Sträuchern der Gegend die Brücke zur Natur schlagenen.

En un espacio casi indómito, situado en la isla de Menorca, este proyecto rechazó luchar contra la naturaleza. La apuesta por la integración de las formas dio como resultado una piscina que se prolonga a partir de una gran roca transversal. La piscina se sitúa casi al mismo nivel de la piedra, a la que se adapta completamente. La unión de lo natural con la nueva construcción se consiguió gracias a una estructura rectangular de hormigón, que se recubrió con piedra de marés. En su interior, cemento pintado de color gris claro, que imita el revestimiento típico de la zona. En la cúspide de la roca se alza una plataforma de pino cuperizado –resistente al agua y antideslizante-. La finca rústica se acompaña de un jardín de chumberas que, junto con los árboles y los arbustos autóctonos de la zona, continúan el viaje hacia lo más natural.

Dans un espace quasiment sauvage de l'île de Minorque, ce projet a refusé de lutter contre la nature. Le pari pour l'intégration des formes a pour résultat une piscine qui se prolonge à partir d'une grande roche transversale. Elle se situe presque au niveau de la pierre, à laquelle elle s'adapte complètement. L'union de la nature et de la nouvelle construction a été réalisée sur la base d'une structure rectangulaire de béton, recouverte de pierre marés. Son intérieur est peint en gris clair, imitant le revêtement typique de la région. Au sommet de la roche se dresse une plate-forme de pin traité au naphténate de cuivre, résistant à l'eau et antidérapant. Cette propriété rustique s'accompagne d'un jardin de nopals qui, avec les arbres et arbustes autochtones, accompagnent ce voyage vers l'infiniment naturel.

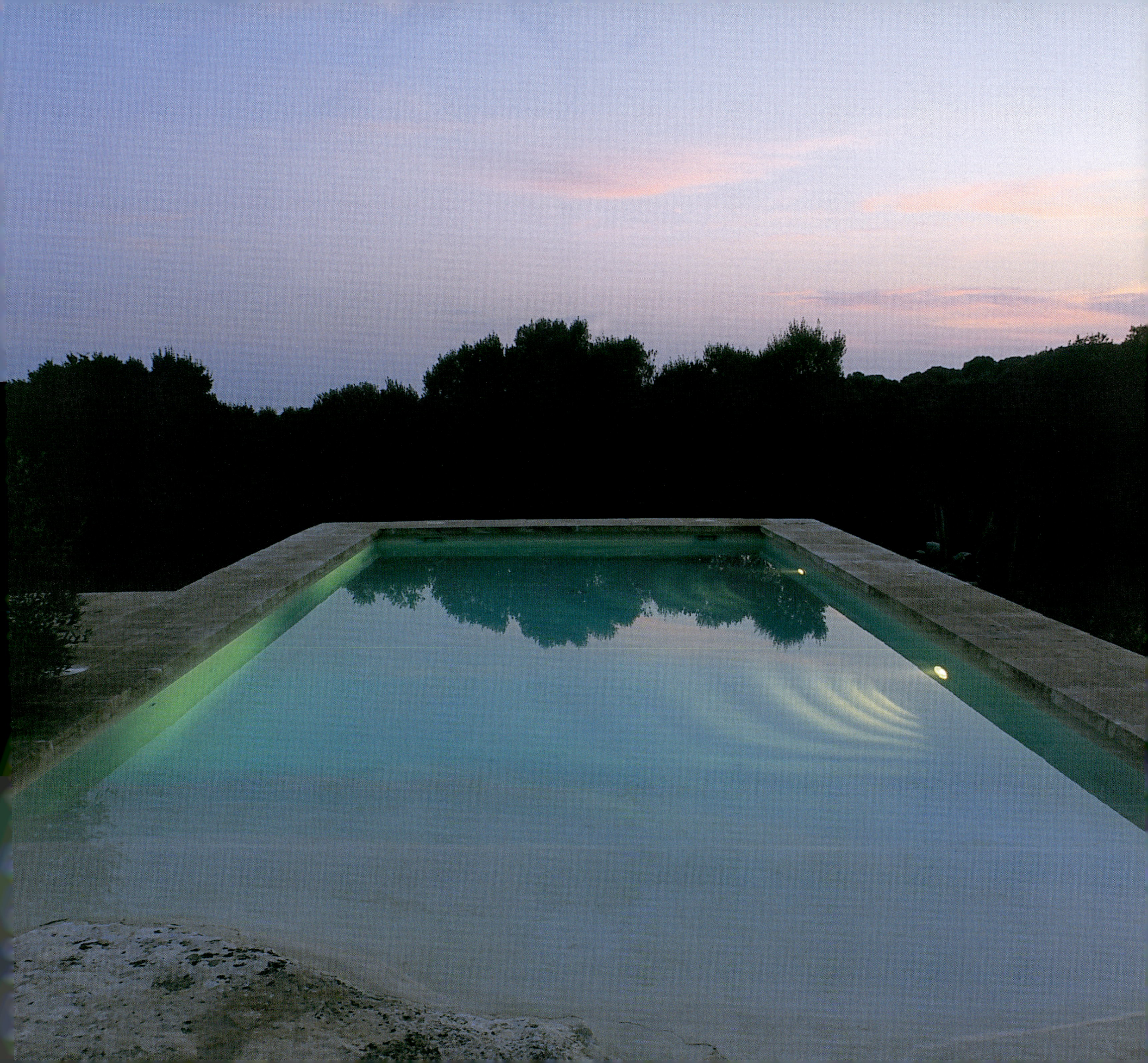

The estate is situated on a very uneven tract. The wave-shaped steps that lead into the pool, accentuate, even more, the sensation of the project blending in with nature, in its natural setting.

La finca se sitúa en una zona repleta de desniveles. Los peldaños que entran en la piscina, en forma de ondas, acentúan la intención de fundir el proyecto con la naturaleza.

Das Anwesen liegt in einem Gebiet mit großen Höhenunterschieden. Die wellenförmig in das Becken hinabführenden Stufen unterstreichen die Absicht, Architektur und Natur miteinander zu verschmelzen.

La propriété se situe dans une zone qui présente de nombreux dénivellements. Les marches permettant d'entrer dans la piscine, en forme de vagues, soulignent l'intention de fondre le projet dans la nature.

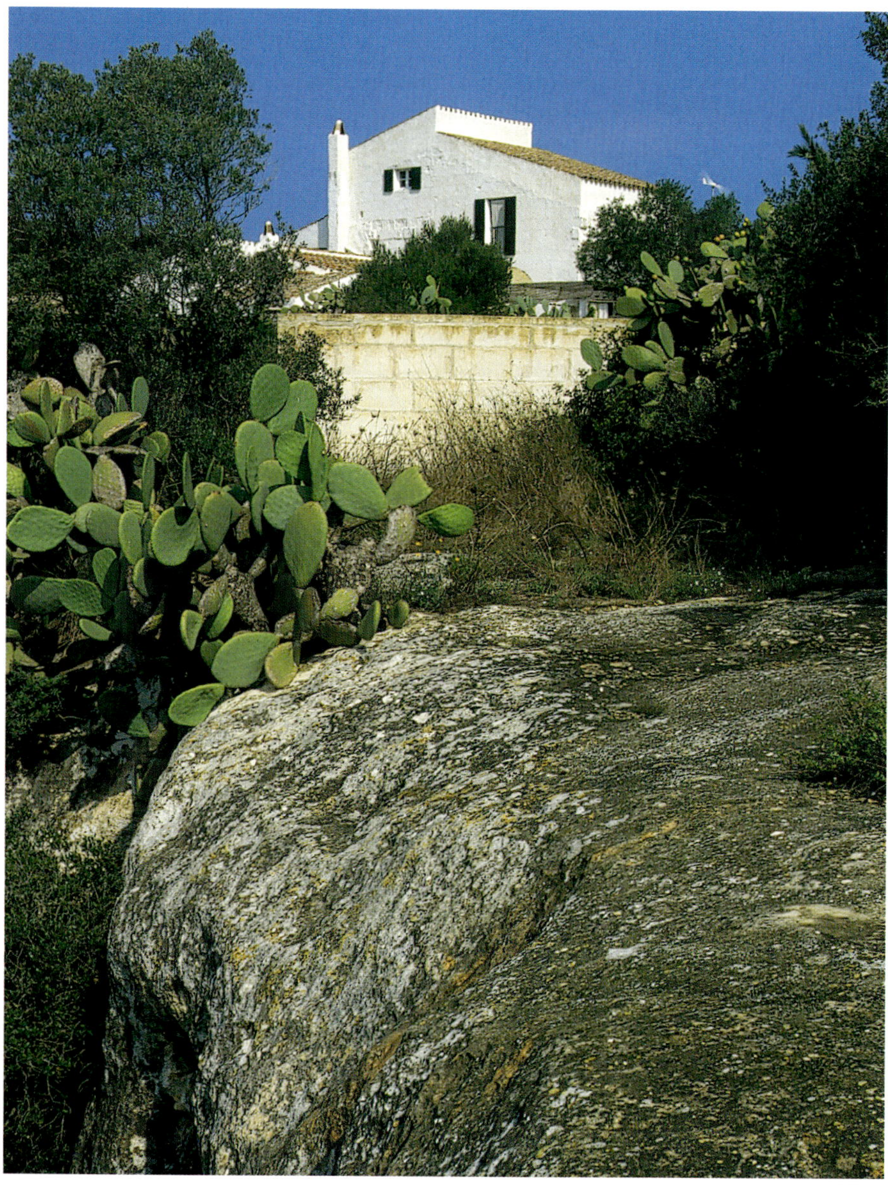

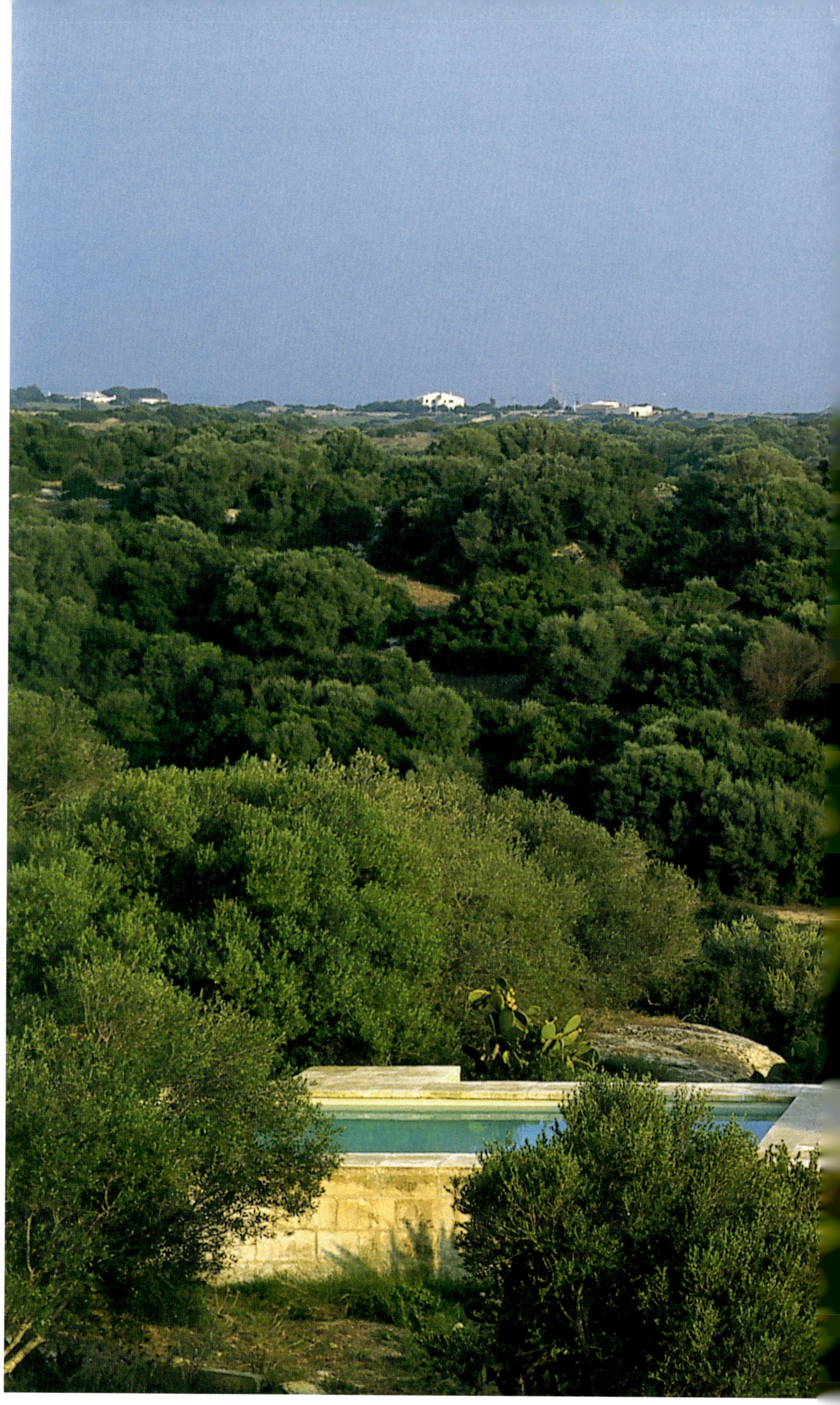

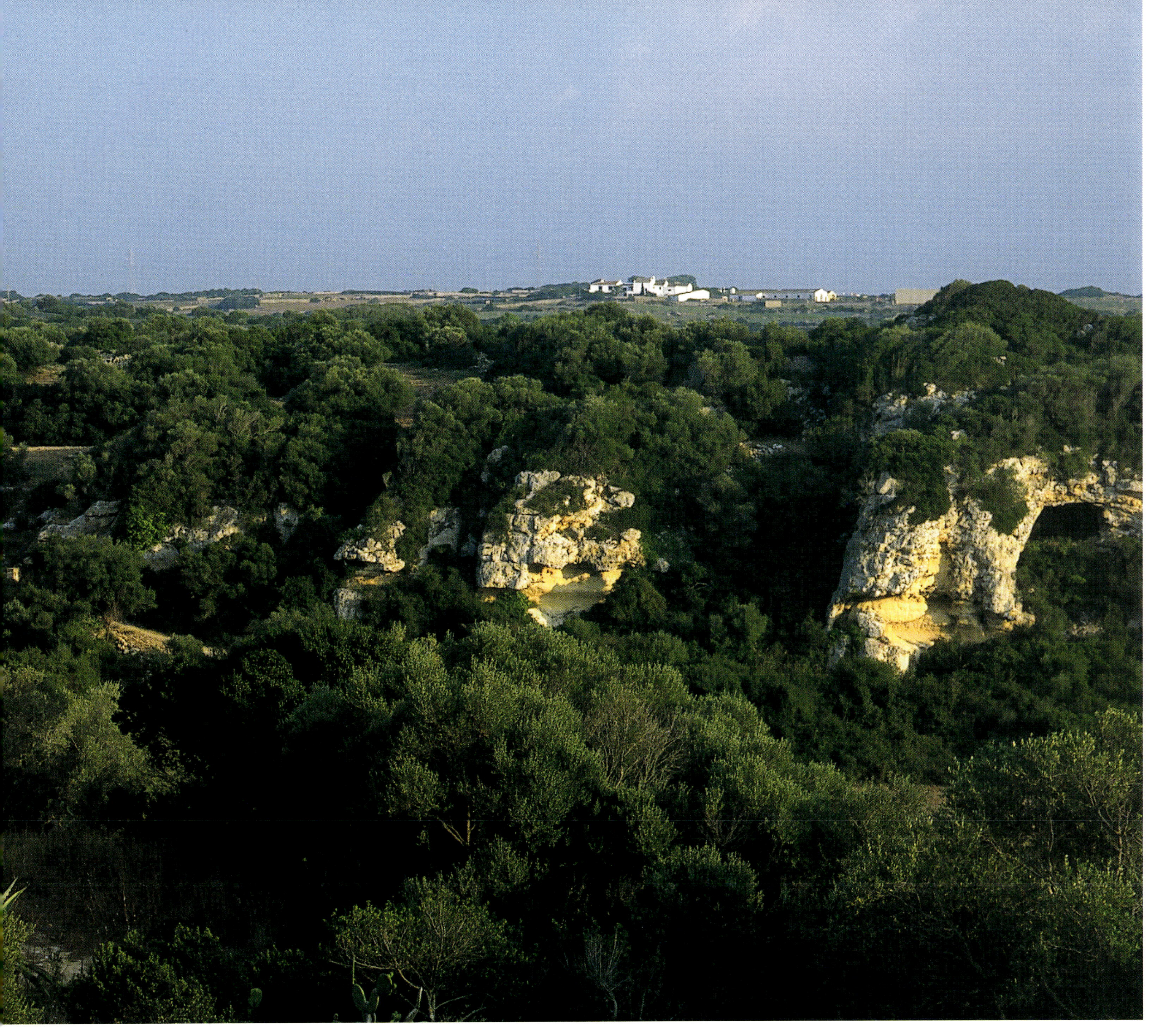

The authors wish to express their gratitude to the following people. Without their invaluable contribution, this book would not have been possible:

Los autores quisieran agradecer a las siguientes personas su colaboración y participación, sin su aportación este libro no hubiera sido posible:

Die Autoren möchten sich für die Mitarbeit bei folgenden Personen bedanken, ohne die dieses Buch nicht möglich gewesen wäre:

Les auteurs tiennent à remercier les personnes suivantes pour leur collaboration et leur participation, sans lesquelles ce livre n'aurait pas pu voir le jour :

In the Bay | En la bahía | In der Bucht | Dans la baie | Rolf Blackstad (architect)
No Limits | Sin límite | Grenzenlos | Sans limites | André Jacqmain (architect)
Constructing a Slope | La pendiente construida | Am Abhang gebaut | Construire sur une pente | Toni Obrador (designer)
Space and Proportion | Espacio y proporción | Raum und Proportion | Espace et proportion | Rolf Blackstad (architect)
Classical Atmosphere | Atmósfera clásica | Klassische Atmosphäre | Une atmosphère classique | B.B.&W Estudio de Arquitectura. Sergi Bastidas, Wolf Siegfried Wagner
Framing The Landscape | Paisaje enmascarado | Gerahmte Landschaft | Un paysage dissimulé | Joan Cardona (designer)
Red House | Una casa roja | Rotes Haus | Une maison rouge | Pablo Carvajal (architect), Fernando Caruncho (landscaping)
Between The Olives | A través de los olivos | Zwischen Olivenbäumen | Au milieu des oliviers | Lorenzo Marqués (architect)
The Privilege of a Secluded Hideaway | El privilegio de la intimidad | Das Privileg der Intimität | Le privilège de l'intimité | Wolf Siegfried Wagner (designer)
Sophisticated Geometry | Geometria Sofisticada | Ausgeklügelte Geometrie | Une géométrie sophistiquée | Valentín de Madariaga & Ernesto Merello (architects), Carme Brujó (decoration)
The Value of the Past | El Valor del Pasado | Wertvolle Vergangenheit | La valeur du passé | Charles Boccara (architect)
In the Heart of a Quarry | En el Corazón de una Cantera | Im Herzen eines Steinbruchs | Au cœur d'une carrière | Guillermo Maluenda (architect), Josep Armenter (coordination)
Chromatic Personality | Personalidad Cromática | Persönlichkeit in Farbe | Une personnalité chromatique | Àngels G. Giró & Luis Vidal (design)
Perfect Blend | Combinación perfecta | Perfect Blend | Alliance parfaite | Victor Esposito (design)
Bordering on the Theatrical | Al Borde de la Teatralidad | Am Rande des Theatralischen | À la limite de la théâtralité | Rudy Ricciotti (architect)
The Eternal Cycle of Water | El Ciclo Eterno del Agua | Der ewige Kreislauf des Wassers | Le cycle éternel de l'eau | B. B. & W. Estudio de Arquitectura. Sergi Bastidas, Wolf Siegfried Wagner.
The Reinterpretation of Water | La Reinterpretación del Agua | Wasser neu entdeckt | Réinterpréter l'eau | Charles Boccara (architect)
In the Garden of the Imaginary | En el Jardín de lo Imaginario | Im Garten der Fantasie | Dans le jardin de l'imaginaire | A.D.A. Maurice Savinel & Roland Le Bévillon.
Color Contrasts | Contrastes de Color | Farbkontraste | Contrastes chromatiques | B.B. & W. Estudio de Arquitectura. Sergi Bastidas, Wolf Siegfried Wagner.
A Mirror Between the Earth and Sky | Un Espejo entre la Tierra y el Cielo | Ein Spiegel zwischen Himmel und Erde | Un miroir entre la terre et le ciel | Wolf Siegfried Wagner (designer)

Traditional Inspiration | Inspiración Tradicional | Von der Tradition inspiriert | Une inspiration traditionnelle | Charles Boccara (architect)
Classical Personality | Bureau d'Etudes Bruno & Alexandre Lafourcade | Dominique Lafourcade (Landscape)
To Live in Paradise | Vivir en el Paraiso | Leben im Paradies | Vivre au paradis | Valentín de Madariaga & Ernesto Merello (architects)
The Patina of Time | La Pátina del Tiempo | Die Patina der Zeit | La patine du temps | Rolf Blackstad (architect)
The Magic of a Setting | La Magia de un Entorno | Der Zauber einer Umgebung | La magie d'un décor | Ramon Esteve (architect)
Unchanged Landscape | Sin alterar el paisaje | Unveränderte Landschaft | Un paysage préservé | Toni Obrador (designer)
Original Blue | Azul Original | Original Blau | Bleu Originale | Josep Lluis Sert (architect)
Blue Symmetry | Simetría en azul | Symmetrie in Blau | Une symétrie bleue | Wolf Siegfried Wagner (designer)
Captivating Calm | Remanso de paz | Hort der Ruhe | Un havre de paix | Charles Boccara (architect)
Between two Worlds | Entre dos Mundos | Zwischen zwei Welten | Entre deux mondes | Guillem Mas (engineer)
Between two waters | Entre dos aguas | Zwischen zwei Wasserelementen | Entre deux eaux | Marmol & Radziner (architects), Carole Katleman (interior design)
Circular Shapes | Formas circulares | Kreisformen | Formes circulaires | Jones Studio, Inc. (architect)
Classical Essence | Esencia clásica | Grundlegend klassisch | Essence classique | Ita & Regis Maquet
Vertical City | Ciudad vertical | Vertikale Stadt | Ville verticale | Le Corbusier (architect)
Water Path | Camino de agua | Wasserweg | Chemin d'eau | Bureau d'Etudes Bruno & Alexandre Lafourcade | Landscape | Dominique Lafourcade
Mediterranean Refuge | Refugio mediterráneo | Mediterraner Zufluchtsort | Refuge méditerranéen | B.B. Estudio de Arquitectura. Sergi Bastidas
Perfect Symmetry | Simetría perfecta | Vollkommene Symmetrie | Symétrie parfaite | Anne & Philippe Berthier
Continuous Perception | Percepción continua | Visuelle Kontinuität | Perception continue | Rudy Ricciotti (architect)
Balearic Charm | Encanto balear | Charme der Balearen | Le charme des baléares | Mariní Malagarriga.
Lineal Architecture | Arquitectura lineal | Lineare Architektur | architecture linéaire | Carlos Ferrater & Joan Guibernau (architects)
Natural Prolongation | Prolongación natural | Natürliche Verlängerung | prolongation naturelle | Javier Clarós (architect), Eduard Arruga (design), Pepote Comella (landscape architect)